SANCTIONS IN THE EU LEGAL ORDER

This open access book looks at the increasingly topical questionof sanctions in European Union law, and their recent roles in the Union's external relations and the area of EU criminal law.

Sanctions in EU law is a multifaceted topic as it is a cross-cutting area which engrains and influences very distinctive EU law policies and disciplines. This book adopts a very broad definition and approach to sanctions, examining the use of sanctions in distinctive internal EU policy fields and also within the external context. The collection covers EU economic sanctions, the sanctions regime on Russia, their role in criminal law, and how administrative sanctions work within the Union.

Sanctions in the EU Legal Order

Swedish Studies in European Law
Volume 23

Edited by
Jacob Öberg, Ester Herlin-Karnell
and Maria Bergström

•HART•
OXFORD • LONDON • NEW YORK • NEW DELHI • SYDNEY

HART PUBLISHING
Bloomsbury Publishing Plc
Kemp House, Chawley Park, Cumnor Hill, Oxford, OX2 9PH, UK
1385 Broadway, New York, NY 10018, USA
Bloomsbury Publishing Ireland Limited, 29 Earlsfort Terrace, Dublin 2, D02 AY28, Ireland

First published in Great Britain, 2026

1

A catalogue record for this book is available from the British Library.

Library of Congress Control Number: 2026944347

ISBN: HB: 978-1-50998-744-3
ePDF: 978-1-50998-746-7
ePub: 978-1-50998-745-0

Typeset by Amnet

Foreword

SANCTIONS LAW IS ONE of the fastest growing and most highly contested fields of EU law. Sanctions are situated at the heart of the enforcement of EU law and form key elements of now well-established fields of EU law, including EU criminal law and EU administrative law, while also having emerged as a kay component of the Union's Common Foreign and Security Policy. The present volume, which builds upon discussions taking place at a conference held in Lund in May 2024, brings together different threads of EU sanctions law. The book includes contributions on 'internal' sanctions law (focusing on a number of areas of EU general and economic criminal law) as well as on 'external' sanctions regimes (with a number of contributions addressing the evolution of the CFSP dimension of sanctions, including the emergence of sanctions regimes against Russia), as well as analysis of the interaction between the internal and external dimensions of sanctions law (focusing on the criminalisation of the violation of sanctions in EU law). A number of contributions provide political, theoretical and policy context, while the challenges posed by sanctions regimes to both EU institutional frameworks and to fundamental rights and the rule of law are highlighted. Presenting an ambitious multi-level, cross-disciplinary approach, the present volume presents a number of important insights on the content and evolution of EU sanctions law, insights which are enriched by the diversity of perspectives and analyses. The book is essential reading for all those interested in EU sanctions law and policy, but also to those with an interest in the institutional and constitutional evolution of a number of areas of EU law more broadly.

Valsamis Mitsilegas
Liverpool, 18 March 2026

Contents

PART III
CRIMINAL DIMENSION OF EU SANCTIONS

PART IV
ADMINISTRATIVE DIMENSION OF EU SANCTIONS

Contributors

Editors

Jacob Öberg is Professor of European Union Law and Deputy Head of Department (research) at the Department of Law of University of Southern Denmark and Guest Professor in EU law at Örebro University. His key research interests include EU constitutional law, EU criminal law and EU integration theories, and he has published extensively in journals such as *European Law Review*, *European Constitutional Law Review* and *European Law Journal*. His recent monograph titled *Normative Foundations of EU Criminal Justice: Limits, Powers and Justifications* was published in 2024 by Hart Publishing.

Ester Herlin-Karnell is Professor of EU Law at the Law Department within the Faculty of Law, Business, and Economics at the University of Gothenburg. Her research focuses on EU criminal law, EU constitutional law, comparative constitutional law and political theory, and the Area of Freedom, Security, and Justice Law.

Maria Bergström is Associate Professor of European Law at the Department of Law at Uppsala University. She holds a Doctor of Laws from the European University Institute in Florence and was a member of the Steering Group of the Swedish Network of European Legal Studies (SNELS) between 2012 and 2025. Her research and publications focus on the intersection between national law and EU law, particularly in constitutional law, administrative law, and criminal law and procedural law.

Authors

Bas Van Bockel is a climate and environmental lawyer in Amsterdam and visiting lecturer of environmental law at Anton de Kom University of Suriname.

Paul James Cardwell is Professor of Law and Vice Dean (Education) at Dickson Poon School of Law, King's College London. His research interest focuses on the governance of the EU and its external relations. He has published widely on institutional competences, the CFSP and sanctions policy. He also has interests in migration and how informality has come to the fore in this important, external-facing policy area. He is the editor of the *Journal of Common Market Studies*.

Celia Challet is Assistant Professor of Law at Université Catholique de Lille, European School of Political Science. Her research focuses on EU institutional law and EU external relations law. She has published on the sanctions adopted by the EU in the framework of the Common Foreign and Security Policy and their judicial review by the Court of Justice of the European Union. She is also an active member of the Multidisciplinary International Network on Sanctions (MINOS), a research and teaching network dedicated to the multidisciplinary study of international sanctions.

Louise Damkjær Christensen is Associate Professor at the University of Southern Denmark, Department of Law. Her primary research focuses on the regulation of payment services. Her book, *EU Payment Services: Regulation and Innovation* (2025) is published by Oxford University Press. She also researches crypto-assets and crypto payments, payment fraud, and anti-money laundering. Her work takes a law and economics approach, using economic theory and models to evaluate existing regulation. Louise's work is published in journals and edited works such as *European Business Law Review*, *Law* and *Financial Markets Review*.

Joana de Deus Pereira is Senior Research Fellow at RUSI Europe, Adjunct Professor at Sciences Po (Paris), and Visiting Fellow at the International Centre for Policing and Security, University of South Wales

Peter Van Elsuwege is Professor of EU law at Ghent University. His research focuses on the law of EU external relations and EU constitutional law. Specific attention is devoted to the legal aspects of EU enlargement, Common Foreign and Security Policy, and the EU's relations with neighbouring countries. He is the academic supervisor of the Multidisciplinary International Network on Sanctions (MINOS), a research and teaching network dedicated to the multidisciplinary study of international sanctions.

Francesca Finelli is Assistant Professor in Law, Luxembourg School of Business. Her research focuses on targeted sanctions, their design, enforcement, and judicial review, with a comparative perspective on EU, UK and US legal frameworks. Her PhD thesis analyses legal challenges in countering the phenomenon of sanctions evasion, also known as circumvention. She has published on targeted sanctions, EU external relations law and CFSP.

Rachel Frid is a Senior Lecturer of International Economic Law at Ono Academic College and Reichman University. She holds a PhD from the University of Amsterdam, and a postdoc from the University of Michigan, Ann Arbor, USA. Her recent research interests lie in trade and investment dispute resolution and EU external trade relations.

Lorenzo Grossio is a Postdoctoral Research Fellow and Adjunct Professor of EU Law at the Department of Law, University of Turin. His research interests focus on EU criminal law – concerning both its substantive dimension and judicial cooperation – as well as on EU Common Security and Defence and EU procedural law. Concerning sanctions in EU law, he authored a Hart Publishing monograph, *Proportionality of Criminal Offences and Penalties in EU Law*, focusing on the conceptualisation and application of the principle of proportionality of criminal offences and penalties.

Christian Kaunert is Professor of International Security at Dublin City University, Ireland. He is also Professor of Policing and Security, as well as Director of the International Centre for Policing and Security at the University of South Wales. In addition, he is Jean Monnet Chair, Director of the Jean Monnet Centre of Excellence and Director of the Jean Monnet Network on EU Counter-Terrorism.

Anton Moiseienko is an Associate Professor of Law at the Australian National University. His main areas of expertise are financial crime, including money laundering, terrorist financing and proliferation financing, and the legal and policy aspects of economic sanctions. He is the author of *Doing Business with Criminals* (Cambridge University Press, 2025) and *Corruption and Targeted Sanctions* (Brill, 2019), a co-editor of four volumes on transnational crime, and has published widely in leading law journals.

J Francien Rense is a Dutch White Collar Defence Lawyer, partner/shareholder within Greenberg Traurig LLP, Amsterdam. As a lawyer for over 25 years, she has assisted and advised corporations and corporate leaders on business integrity, compliance and enforcement-related issues initiated by the authorities or gatekeepers. She regularly teaches and publishes on topics in that field, including on the concept of corporate liability, how to interpret and approach that concept, and individuals' criminal liability in that respect.

Anna Södersten is a Senior Lecturer in Law at the Swedish Defence University. Her research interests include the EU's Common Foreign and Security Policy (CFSP) and Common Security and Defence Policy (CSDP), the rule of law, the EU's institutional framework, and treaty reform.

Dr Ermioni Xanthopoulou is a Senior Lecturer in Law at Brunel University of London, and her research interests include EU criminal and EU asylum law and fundamental rights.

Part I

General Issues on EU Sanctions

1

Introduction: Sanctions in the EU Legal Order

JACOB ÖBERG, ESTER HERLIN-KARNELL
AND MARIA BERGSTRÖM

1.1 THE LEGAL AND POLITICAL CONTEXT OF EU SANCTIONS

SANCTIONS IN EU law constitute a cross-cutting area that shapes and influences distinctive EU law policies and disciplines. While the imposition of sanctions is essentially about the effective enforcement of EU law, the question of sanctions has become in principle a self-standing legal area, particularly in the field of EU external relations law. Sanctions is traditionally divided between the 'external' dimension of the use of EU sanctions[1] and the EU internal dimension, which addresses the increasing use of administrative and criminal law sanctions for enforcing EU law against individuals and sanctions against EU Member States.[2] EU sanctions is clearly an important, dynamic and politically contested field of EU law and policy deserving serious scrutiny both in the literature on European studies and by EU policy-makers.

This book emerges from the intellectual discussions sparked by the conference 'in EU Law and Policy' held in Lund on 16–17 May 2024 at the Faculty of Law, kindly sponsored by the Swedish Network for European Legal Studies. Those conversations were focused, much like this volume, on the distinctive and specific meanings of sanctions within the EU legal order, both as a vehicle to conduct foreign policy and as a tool to promote and realise internal EU policies. The contributions to this volume have a very broad scope ranging from issues of EU external relations law to EU constitutional law, fundamental rights, EU criminal law, EU sanctions politics and EU financial law. Having said that there are at least three common themes emerging from this collection of chapters.

[1] Francesco Giumelli, Fabian Hoffmann and Anna Książczaková, 'The when, what, where and why of European Union sanctions' (2021) 30 *European Security* 1.

[2] Paulina Pospieszna, Michal Onderco and Reinout van der Veer, 'Comparing public attitudes towards internal and external EU sanctions: the role of populism, trust and Euroscepticism' (2024) 40 *East European Politics* 345; Adrienne Moor-van Vugt, 'Administrative sanctions in EU law' (2012) 5 *Review of European Administrative Law* 5.

First, many contributions in this volume touch upon the 'instrumental' use of sanctions. This theme seem to coincide with the ruling of the Court of Justice of the European Union (CJEU) in the seminal case *Greek Maize* where the Court proposed that sanctions to enforce EU rules must be 'effective, proportionate and dissuasive'.[3] On a theoretical note, sanctions are undoubtedly viewed in literature as secondary rules necessary to give force to more substantive rules and policies.[4] Whether sanctions are imposed in the external context or in the internal context (for sanctioning Member States) or for sanctioning individuals and firms breaching substantive EU rules, the overriding objective of sanctions is to ensure compliance with substantive EU policies. [5] In this way, the book considers EU sanctions – both in the internal and external sphere – as an essential vehicle to further the objectives and policies of the EU legislator.[6] Both external and internal sanctions have the same goals: they aim to (i) signal norm violations, and (ii) coerce and (iii) constrain a target into changing its behaviour.[7] It is an utilitarian vision of law designed, through the application of sanctions and costs for individuals, to reduce harmful activities or promote particular behaviour in order to secure other goals or benefits.[8]

A closely related theme to this is the effectiveness of EU sanctions. The effective employment of EU criminal[9] and administrative sanctions in EU policy fields such as migration law,[10] financial market law[11] and competition law[12] has been the long-standing object of both scholars of EU law and political science with a rich literature, focusing in particular on deterrence, and many contributions

[3] Case 68/88 *Commission v Greece* EU:C: 1989:339, para 24.

[4] Leo Kanowitz, 'The Place of Sanctions in Professor H.L.A. Hart's Concept of Law' (1966) 5 *Duquesne Law Review* 1; Eric Colvin, 'The Sociology of Secondary Rules' (1978) 28 *The University of Toronto Law Journal* 195; Anthony Kronman, 'Hart, Austin, and the Concept of a Legal System: The Primacy of Sanctions' (1974–75) 84 *Yale Law Journal* 581.

[5] See Jacob Öberg, *Limits to EU Powers; A Case Study of EU Regulatory Criminal Law* (Hart Publishing, 2017) ch 4 for the employment of criminal sanctions for enforcing EU policies; Madeleine de Cock Buning and Linda Senden, 'Introduction: EU Private Regulation and Enforcement – Mapping its Contextual, Conceptual, Constitutional and Citizens ' Dimensions' in Madeleine De Cock Buning and Linda Senden (eds), *Private Regulation and Enforcement in the EU: Finding the Right Balance from a Citizen's Perspective* (Hart Publishing, 2020).

[6] See Arts 83(2) and 215 TFEU, Art 29 TEU.

[7] Daniel S Nagin, 'Deterrence in the Twenty-First Century' (2013) 42 *Crime and Justice* 199; Roger Bowles, Michael G Faure and Nuno Garoupa, 'The Scope of Criminal Law and Criminal Sanctions: An Economic View and Policy Implications' (2008) 35 *Journal of Law and Society* 389; Heli Korkka-Knuts, Eelis Paukku and Jaako Markus, 'Reassessing Deterrence: The Effectiveness of Administrative Sanctions across three EU Regulatory Frameworks' (2025) 50 *European Law Review* 436.

[8] See Stephen Coutts, 'Supranational Public Wrongs: The Limitations and Possibilities of European Criminal Law and a European Community' (2017) 54 *Common Market Law Review* 771; Michael Moore, *Placing Blame: A Theory of Criminal Law* (Oxford University Press, 1997) 161–63.

[9] See Lorenzo Grossio, Stefano Montaldo and Valsamis Mitsilegas, *Proportionality of Criminal Penalties in EU Law* (Hart Publishing, 2025).

[10] Employers Sanctions Directive 2009/52/EC [2009] OJ L168/24 and Xanthopolou's chapter in this volume.

[11] Korkka-Knuts, Paukku and Markus (n 7) with further references to relevant literature.

[12] ibid with further references to relevant literature.

in this volume touch upon this perennial issue.[13] One contribution also considers central issues such as the overarching rationales for sanctions and how they should be designed to achieve effectively EU policies.[14] A further central issue for EU sanctions is to what extent the current decision-making framework is designed to make it possible for the EU to act swiftly and decisively when imposing sanctions and restrictive measures.[15]

The second major theme of the book is the politics and policy of EU sanctions. It is apparent that sanctions take a centre stage in the EU legal order, particularly within the current volatile geopolitical situation.[16] Sanctions in the external context are employed primarily to promote the EU's values outside its borders, including promoting democracy, to pressure other states to democratise, or to protect the rule of law or respect human rights.[17] External sanctions are punitive measures imposed by EU executive actors on non-Member States, which usually entail restrictions on the targets' economic and political linkages to the EU and its Member States. Within the Common Foreign and Security Policy (CFSP), the EU has imposed financial sanctions, freezing of assets, investment bans, flight bans, or embargoes on arms or other specific goods in non-member countries. Today, the EU is the only regional organisation that uses sanctions exclusively beyond its membership and against third countries.

Notable recent cases in point of EU external sanctions are those imposed on autocratic regimes, such as Belarus and Russia[18] many years before the Russian aggression against Ukraine beginning in 2014. Although CFSP objectives stress the need to 'preserve peace, prevent conflicts and strengthen international security', these concerns are only mentioned later, thus implying that rule of law concerns should be prioritised by the EU.[19] The Russian invasion of Ukraine

[13] See contributions by Damkjaer Christensen, Reinse and Van Bockel, and Finelli and Öberg in this volume. See more generally Vanessa Franssen and Chris Harding (eds), *Criminal and Quasi-criminal Enforcement Mechanisms in Europe: Origins, Concepts, Future* (Hart Publishing, 2022). Clara Portela, *European Union Sanctions and Foreign Policy: When and Why Do They Work?* (Routledge, 2012).

[14] ibid.

[15] See contributions by eg Södersten, Moiseienko, Van Elsuwege and Challet in this volume.

[16] Cardwell's contribution in this volume examines in depth the role of EU sanctions in EU foreign policy.

[17] Richard Youngs, 'Democracy Promotion as External Governance?' (2009) 16 *Journal of European Public Policy* 895; Francesco Giumelli, *Coercing, Constraining and Signalling: Explaining UN and EU Sanctions After the Cold War* (ECPR Press, 2011); Francesco Giumelli, 'How EU Sanctions Work: A New Narrative'(EU ISS Chaillot Paper No 129, 2013); Paulina Pospieszna and Clara Portela, 'Understanding EU Sanctioning Behavior' (2020) 1 *Przeglad Zachodni* 55; Clara Portela, 'The EU Human Rights Sanctions Regime: Unfinished Business.' (2021) 54 *Revista General De Derecho Europeo* 19; Elin Hellquist and Stefano Palestini, 'Regional Sanctions and the Struggle for Democracy: Introduction to the Special Issue' (2020) 42 *International Political Science Review* 437.

[18] Clara Portela, Paulina Pospieszna, Joanna Skrzypczyńska and Dawid Walentek, 'Consensus Against All Odds: Explaining the Persistence of EU Sanctions on Russia' (2021) 43 *Journal of European Integration* 683; Paul J Cardwell and Erica Moret, 'The EU, Sanctions and Regional Leadership' (2023) 32 *European Security* 1.

[19] Art 21(2) TEU.

highlights the fundamental societal implications of this contribution as EU sanctions have been used – as one of the primary foreign policy tools by the Union to intervene in the conflict.[20] Council Regulations adopted pursuant to Article 215 Treaty on the Functioning of the European Union (TFEU)[21] have put in place a series of Union restrictive measures against Russian and Belarusian individuals and companies, some of which date back to 2014.[22]

Nonetheless sanctions are also used as a policy tool employed by the EU to impose its values on their members.[23] The EU has powers to condemn individual Member States breaching the EU Treaties that usually can entail sanctions[24] or in more grave cases entail restrictions on the benefits of EU membership (such as cuts in funding or barring of voting rights).[25] Additionally, the EU can also theoretically use political conditionality[26] as a part of the accession process; such tools were considered as the most effective instruments in the EU's toolkit to promote Central and Eastern European (CEE) states that joined the EU in 2004 and 2007.[27] Yet, in recent years, democracy and rule of law were seriously curtailed in some CEE countries[28] and the EU has responded by introducing new internal sanctioning mechanisms in these areas, such as a rule of law conditionality mechanism[29] in the EU budget to complement the existing Article 7 procedure.[30]

[20] Moiseienko, and Kaunert and Deus Pereira examine this closely in their contributions to this volume.

[21] Art 215 TFEU enables the Council to adopt restrictive measures against natural or legal persons and groups, or non-state entities, or to adopt measures providing for the interruption or reduction, in part or completely, of economic and financial relations with one or more third countries, on the basis of a decision pursuant to Art 29 TEU.

[22] They include targeted individual measures (ie, asset freezes and restrictions on admissions (travel bans)), sectoral measures (ie arms embargoes), and economic/financial measures (eg import and export restrictions, restrictions on the provision of certain services, such as banking services). See for an overview, Council of the European Union, 'EU sanctions against Russia' explainer, www.consilium.europa.eu/en/policies/sanctions-against-russia.

[23] See also Södersten's chapter in this volume.

[24] See Arts 258–60 TFEU.

[25] See Art 7 TEU.

[26] Regulation (EU, Euratom) 2020/2092 of the European Parliament and of the Council of 16 December 2020 on a general regime of conditionality for the protection of the Union budget.

[27] Jon CW Pevehouse, 'Democracy with a Little Help from My Friends? Regional Organizations and the Consolidation of Democracy the Euphoria Third Wave of Democratization Began to Survival' (2002) 46 *American Journal of Political Science* 611; Frank Schimmelfennig and Ulrich Sedelmeier, *The Politics of European Union Enlargement: Theoretical Approaches*. (Routledge, 2005); Milada Anna Vachudova. 'Ethnopopulism and democratic backsliding in Central Europe' (2020) 36 *East European Politics* 318.

[28] Sophie Meunier and Milada Anna Vachudova, 'Liberal Intergovernmentalism, Illiberalism and the Potential Superpower of the European Union' (2018) 56 *Journal of Common Market Studies* 1631.

[29] Judgments in Cases C-156/21 *Hungary v Parliament and Council* EU:C:2022:97 and C-157/21 *Poland v Parliament and Council* EU:C:2022:98.

[30] Antonia Baraggia and Matteo Bonellli, 'Linking Money to Values: The New Rule of Law Conditionality Regulation and Its Constitutional Challenges' (2022) 23 *German Law Journal* 131; Michael Blauberger and Vera van Hüllen, 'Conditionality of EU Funds: an Instrument to Enforce EU Fundamental Values?' (2021) 43 *Journal of European Integration* 1.

The final important theme of sanctions is its relationship to fundamental rights and human rights and proportionality. Sanctions (and notably criminal sanctions) have significant and far-reaching implications for individuals subjected to sanctions.[31] In this manner the imposition of sanctions at EU level is a testament to the most intrusive exercise of public power by the EU legislator. This brings into play a number of questions of legitimacy, effectiveness and the overall policy rationale of sanctions.[32] The book seeks to also examine these issues critically and in-depth probing the extent to which sanctions is a normatively justified exercise of public power. The issues at stake have recently received particular prominence due to the inclusion of the European Charter of Fundamental Rights as key policy instrument guiding but also constraining the pursuit of EU sanctions policies. Recent substantial legislative and political developments in the field together with a stronger enforcement and fundamental rights dimension triggered by the Charter of Fundamental Rights, however, justifies taking a renewed perspective on EU sanctions. This is equally clear in the area of EU criminal law and EU migration law where recent case law on proportionality, sanctions and procedural safeguards highlights the increasingly complex and contested nature of sanctions as a tool for implementing EU policies.[33]

In light of all this, this book brings together leading scholars in EU law, international relations, trade policy and administrative law to reflect conjointly on this dynamic and changing area of EU law and politics. The book is also a testament to the cross-cutting and interdisciplinary notion of EU sanctions. It is impossible to obtain proper insights into the functioning of EU sanctions by looking at it from one single discipline or area of EU law and policy. The individual chapters to this volume seek to offer a collective significant contribution to this emerging field of EU law and policy, by offering both internal and external perspectives on EU sanctions and aiming to offer the first multidisciplinary examination of sanctions with perspectives ranging from EU law, international trade law, international relations, criminal law, migration law and political science. We envisage that political scientists can make sense of and provide insights into the political context and the driving forces of the pre- and post-Lisbon development of EU sanctions. Lawyers, in their turn, examine the extent to which lessons from political science may be employed to analyse and evaluate the effectiveness of and justifications for EU sanctions. We thus contend that a more contextualised view of the legal developments is indispensable for

[31] See Jacob Öberg, 'The Definition of Criminal Sanctions in the EU' (2013) 3 *European Criminal Law* Review 273.

[32] See eg Xanthopoulou's contribution to this volume.

[33] See chapters by Grossio, Finelli and Öberg in this volume.

an enhanced understanding of the institutional, legal and political dynamics of EU sanctions as a key element of European integration.[34]

1.2 OVERVIEW OF THE BOOK

Part one of the book examines some general issues on EU sanctions and the framework in which such sanctions are adopted.

Anna Södersten first evaluates the intersection of restrictive measures and rule of law sanctions within the EU, focusing on the implications of unanimity and potential treaty revisions. Her chapter begins by comparing these mechanisms, highlighting their shared objectives of promoting EU values but differing targets and content. She then discusses the procedures for treaty revisions, emphasising calls for amendments to allow qualified majority voting for both Article 7 sanctions and restrictive measures. Various alternatives for decision-making, such as abstentions, *passerelles*, and enhanced cooperation are examined, noting their applicability and limitations. The analysis concludes that while treaty revision appears necessary for effective enforcement of Article 7 sanctions, alternatives may enhance flexibility for restrictive measures.

Ester Herlin Karnell then explores the idea of a sanction in EU criminal law as a truly cross-policy phenomenon in EU law. The chapter first observes that EU sanctions play an important role in the EU's security strategies and external relations. The EU has currently adopted 19 packages of sanctions against Russia in response to the full-scale invasion of Ukraine in February 2022. While sanctions are not new in the history of the EU, the sanctions against Russia are unprecedented in their scale, due to the Russian war in Ukraine and the current security threat to Europe. This chapter examines the EU sanctions regime and its various aspects, with particular focus on the internal and external dimensions of the EU's sanctions policy. More specifically, the chapter focuses on the broader relationship between EU criminal law and security, as well as on the role of human rights justifications in sanction adoption. Additionally, the chapter emphasises the market-based rationale regarding human rights justifications for legislation.

Part two of the book focuses specifically on the external dimension of EU sanctions.

Paul James Cardwell examines the role of sanctions in the EU external relations probing on the maturity of EU Foreign policy. The Common Foreign and Security Policy (CFSP) has, since its difficult birth in the Treaty of Maastricht,

[34] Paul J Cardwell and Tamara Hervey, 'The Roles of Law in a New Intergovernmentalist European Union' in Chris J Bickerton, Dermot Hodson and Uwe Puetter (eds), *The New Intergovernmentalism: States and Supranational Actors in the Post-Maastricht Era* (Oxford University Press, 2015) 74; Christian Joerges, 'Taking the Law Seriously: On Political Science and the Role of Law in the Process of European Integration' (1996) 2 *European Law Journal* 105.

been dogged by accusations of lack of coherence, identity and – crucially – effectiveness. These criticisms were well founded, given that the EU's response to the break-up of Yugoslavia and the genocide in Rwanda in the 1990s fell far short of the ambitions for foreign policy coordination as laid down in the Treaty. Since Maastricht, there have been numerous attempts to forge an institutional path forward between making the EU both visible and effective in foreign policy and respecting the hesitancy for further integration of some of the Member States in this core area of state sovereignty. The ability of the EU to impose sanctions on third countries and individuals has, however, come to the fore in the past two decades. Sanctions have become a 'go-to' mechanism which, for the EU, has the dual advantage of being both a foreign policy instrument and reliant on the EU's status as a trade powerhouse. This chapter places sanctions in the context of the struggle for the EU to put in place a meaningful foreign policy. It argues that the legalisation of the CFSP has allowed the EU and its Member States to forge a path which allows for agreement and consensus whilst respecting differences. This is predicated, however, on the Member States continuing to have broadly the same views on those states and individuals on whom sanctions have been placed, and highlights the risk that sanctions – whilst held up as an example of successful cooperation – could very easily turn to the opposite example.

Peter Van Elsuwege and Celia Challet subsequently consider the unprecedented nature of the EU's sanctions against Russia. The EU's sanctions against Russia are deemed to be 'unprecedented' in both scale and character, raising questions about their specific nature and long-term institutional implications for the adoption of sanctions within the EU legal order. How do the EU sanctions against Russia differ from previous EU sanctions regimes, and to what extent does this affect the EU's sanctions policy in practice? Various dimensions can be identified to answer this question. First of all, there is an evolution towards broad designation criteria for the adoption of individual sanctions in combination with a wide range of sectoral sanctions. This evolution raises critical questions relating to the EU's compliance with fundamental rights, the principle of proportionality, and its own sanctions competence. Second, the unprecedented focus on ensuring sanctions effectiveness has led to new anti-circumvention mechanisms, which are also subject to questions of competence and proportionality. Third, the sanctions against Russia have triggered significant institutional innovations, most notably a substantial expansion of the European Commission's role since the start of Russia's full-scale war against Ukraine. In parallel, the EU has increasingly adopted complementary measures outside the CFSP, pointing to a gradual supranationalisation of EU sanctions policy. The combination of all these elements implies that the EU's sanctions against Russia may be regarded as a 'game-changer' in the EU's sanctions practice with long-term legal and institutional consequences. Sanctions are no longer merely a foreign policy instrument but increasingly permeate the entire EU legal order.

Anton Moiseienko subsequently examines frozen Russian state assets and reparations for Ukraine. Following Russia's full-scale invasion of Ukraine in February 2022, G7 economies and other like-minded nations froze US$300 billion in Russian foreign currency reserves. Since then, debates have been taking place as to whether, and how, these funds can be used to enforce Russia's obligation to pay reparations to Ukraine. This chapter explains the principal legal, economic and policy points of contention in these discussions. It also traces their evolution across three phases: the crystallisation of key disagreements in 2022–23; the utilisation of interest generated by frozen Russian state assets from 2024 onwards; and the EU's consideration of the proposed reparations loan in 2025. While the situation continues to develop at a rapid pace, this chapter will help the reader understand the main legal, policy and practical complexities involved.

Christian Kaunert and Joana De Deus Pereira examine the politics of EU sanctions against Russia within the context of the war against Ukraine (2014 and 2022 onwards). In February 2022, Vladimir Putin announced the beginning of a full-scale invasion of Ukraine, taking place across land, sea, and air. The EU significantly expanded its sanctions against Russia in response to the military aggression. This chapter asks how EU sanctions have been embedded in, and contributed to, an ontological securitisation process in which Ukraine and Europe are constructed as threatened reference objects in EU–Russia relations where Putin provoked a sense of disruption and insecurity through acts, images, and narratives derived from the masterful management of cognitive and normative maps, both of the Self (Russia) and the Other (EU), and of Russia as being ontologically stronger than Europe. Contrary to what happened throughout the Cold War, Russia is not interested in spreading the communist message across the continent or pursuing military control of the whole of Europe; the objective is now to reshape the continent's liberal and security order.

Rachel Frid analyses in her turn EU economic sanctions within the context of international trade law. The increase in recent years in the application and the harmful effects of unilateral economic sanctions has caused an increase in challenges to their legality brought by states targeted by sanctions. The growing use of economic sanctions is characterised by imposing sanctions for non-trade policy goals and invoking the national security exception in defence of violations of the World Trade Organization (WTO) obligations. This calls for a thorough consideration from the perspective of international trade law. In the EU, trade sanctions for non-economic purposes have enjoyed increasing application as a tool of the EU foreign policy. Therefore, the WTO consistency of the trade sanctions imposed by the EU on the Russian Federation is examined as a case study. It is argued that even if the EU trade sanctions would seem to satisfy the relevant WTO legal requirements, this would nonetheless call for the questioning of the harmful effects of economic sanctions, their doubtful effectiveness and the impact of using sanctions to achieve political objectives on the rule of international trade law.

In the part three of the book, criminal sanctions are explored within the context of EU law and EU politics.

Francesca Finelli and Jacob Öberg explore the normative justifications for enforcing EU restrictive measures through criminal law. The Union has today been conferred with an explicit competence to harmonise criminal laws and sanctions in Article 83(1) TFEU to 'establish minimum rules concerning the definition of criminal offences and sanctions in the areas of *particularly serious crime* with a *cross-border dimension* resulting from *the nature or impact of such offences* or from a *special need* to combat them on a common basis' (emphasis added). The provision has a predetermined list of offences – the 'Eurocrimes' – said to be satisfying those conditions. There is nonetheless a procedure for adding new crimes to the list according to which the Council unanimously adopts a decision identifying a certain offence as another area of crime meeting those criteria. This procedure was for the first time employed in respect of the Council decision to extend the list of Eurocrimes to the violation of EU restrictive measures and subsequent adoption of a Directive harmonising the Member States' criminal laws in respect of those criminal offences. The chapter seeks to critically examines the legal and normative justification for criminalising breaches of EU sanctions. It first looks at the fast-track criminalisation process pursuant to Article 83(1) TFEU, and the negotiation history of Directive (EU) 2024/1226. Subsequently, it examines the rationale behind this criminalisation process and illustrates the extent to which the introduction of a new Eurocrime is in line with the legal preconditions for exercising the competence in Article 83(1) TFEU. Finally, the chapter has some broader reflections on the impact and potential for this Directive being transposed into national laws and the future development in this field including the potential extension of the remit of the European Public Prosecutor's Office to deal with such offences.

Lorenzo Grossio revisits the principle of proportionality in the harmonisation of Member States' substantive criminal law. More specifically, the chapter assesses the proportionality constraints to both EU criminalisation choices underpinning harmonised offences and the approximation of the type and level of corresponding sanctions. To that aim, the analysis first delves into the relevant legislative practice to disclose how the EU legislature weights conflicting interests when shaping harmonising provisions on offences and penalties. In this context, the relevant *travaux préparatoires* witness an uneasy intersection between the EU concept of proportionality – whose matrix consists of the threefold suitability, necessity and proportionality *stricto sensu* assessment – and the criminal law one. When assessing the proportionality of EU harmonised offences and penalties, the threefold test is enriched with two further schemes, involving an assessment of the severity of supranational penalisation vis-a-vis, respectively, the attainment of a genuine dissuasive effect (prospective proportionality) and the seriousness of the wrongdoing (retrospective proportionality). Secondly, the chapter frames the CJEU's approach to the proportionality review of those harmonising provisions. In this regard, the chapter discusses the extent of the Court's scrutiny and the influence of prospective and retrospective proportionality, thus deepening the interaction between the EU and criminal law understandings of the principle in the context of supranational judicial review.

Francien Rense and Bas Van Bockel in their turn look at corporate criminal liability in the EU as a key concept for addressing when and how to attribute individuals' acts or omissions to corporations rather than considering actions of the legal entities on their own. They note first that standards for corporate liability in relation to criminal acts in the EU are divergent where some states do not recognise the concept whilst other states have developed nuanced and comprehensive criteria for establishing such liability. While explaining and referring to the flexible and neutral concept of corporate criminal liability under Dutch criminal law, the authors explain that such concept is playing out most effectively and fairly if: (i) it is able and tailored to identify and assess actions of the legal entities itself, not necessarily focussing on individuals' actions; and (ii) the concept is determining and establishing criminal liability of corporations. The paramount driver of proportionate, effective and dissuasive sanctioning when applied to legal entities, calls for consideration of the prevailing concept of corporate liability *ex crimine* under EU law. In addition, differences in various concepts throughout the whole of the EU hamper those sanctioning objectives and potentially carry negative implications for the protection of fundamental rights and the exercise of free movement rights by legal entities within the EU, as does the prevailing concept of corporate liability *ex crimine* under EU law. Therefore, this contribution aims to invite further reflection on the constituent conditions for and qualification of corporate liability *ex crimine* in the EU in the light of these various implications. The author argues that aspects of the flexible and neutral concept of corporate criminal liability under Dutch criminal law might be worth considering in that regard.

Ermioni Xanthopolou considers overcriminalisation and sanctioning in the field of EU immigration and migration law. The Facilitators Package has been the subject of intense academic and civil society debate. Key criticism contends that it has introduced an ambiguous scope leading to overcriminalisation in breach of fundamental rights and principles of EU law and international legal standards. While at the time of writing, a European Commission proposal for new legislation is being deliberated, the Court of Justice of the European Union (CJEU) has delivered its landmark ruling in the case of *Kinsa*, clarifying the interpretation of the Directive and setting a limit on excessive criminalisation at national level. The influential potential of *Kinsa* for shaping the reform of the law is undoubtable. Yet, reform is not without challenges, which range from EU constitutional constraints to institutional dynamics in a populist context. The chapter, after outlining the chronic pitfalls of the facilitation legal framework, evaluates the proposed changes, the potential of *Kinsa* and the broader challenges of EU constitutional law for decriminalisation. The chapter contends that, notwithstanding broader constitutional limitations in the absence of a clear legal basis for decriminalisation, the ruling has a clear decriminalisation message, in line with international and EU fundamental rights law.

Part four of the book looks critically at EU administrative sanctions. Louise Damkjaer Christensen examines the relationship between financial sanctions and the prevention of money laundering. She asks the basic question of why governments impose extensive regulatory frameworks and hefty financial sanctions upon financial institutions in the fight against money laundering. She notably examines why financial institutions are the target of anti-money laundering (AML) legislation. After defining what constitutes 'money laundering' and examining the sanctions in EU AML legislation, the financial institution's role in the money laundering process is interrogated. Money laundering is found to be an externality from financial service businesses, explaining why sanctions are needed to incentivise the financial institutions to internalise this externality. Comparing the costs related to governments drafting, adoption, and enforcement of AML legislation with the costs related to implementing and complying to AML legislation, it is argued that the Government is essentially outsourcing the costs of money laundering prevention to financial institutions.

1.3 CONCLUSION

EU sanctions continue to be a significant topic and have gained new momentum after Russia's full-scale invasion of Ukraine in 2022. The contributors to this book have been invited to explore various questions and aspects related to EU sanctions law. We would like to thank the Swedish Network for European Legal Studies for making this possible by generously sponsoring the conference at which most of the draft papers were initially discussed, and for including our book in the series on Swedish Studies in European Law.

2

Beyond Unanimity: Exploring Legal Pathways for a More Effective EU Sanctions Framework

ANNA SÖDERSTEN

2.1 INTRODUCTION

Since Russia's full-scale invasion of Ukraine in February 2022, the EU has adopted several packages of sanctions – referred to as restrictive measures – against Russia.[1] A wide range of restrictive measures has been applied under this regime, including asset freezes and travel bans on individuals and entities, export bans across various sectors, and measures targeting the Russian banking sector. This response to Russia reflects a broader trend: the EU is increasingly relying on restrictive measures as a tool to pursue its foreign policy objectives, aiming to induce a change in behaviour by a state, individual or entity.[2] Globally, more than 50 EU sanctions regimes are in place,[3] and a majority were implemented as geographically focused regimes aimed at a particular country or region.

The adoption of restrictive measures requires unanimous approval from all Member States. In recent years, however, this requirement has become increasingly difficult to achieve.[4] Most notably, Hungary has on several occasions

[1] Council Decision 2014/512/CFSP of 31 July 2014 concerning restrictive measures in view of Russia's actions destabilising the situation in Ukraine [2014] OJ L229/13.

[2] Paul James Cardwell and Erica Moret, 'The EU, sanctions and regional leadership' (2022) 32 *European Security* 1; Katharina Meissner and Chiara Graziani, 'The Transformation and Design of EU Restrictive Measures against Russia' (2023) 45 *Journal of European Integration* 377.

[3] Geographical sanctions regimes are presently enforced in over 40 states, affecting almost 5,000 individuals and entities. See the website of the European External Action Service: www.eeas.europa.eu/eeas/sanctions-what-types_en.

[4] See Clara Portela, Paulina Pospieszna, Joanna Skrzypczyńska and Dawid Walentek, 'Consensus Against All Odds: Explaining the Persistence of EU Sanctions on Russia' (2021) 43 *Journal of European Integration* 683, who argue that the EU has so far in fact effectively managed disparities among the Member States (at least until the full-scale Russian invasion of Ukraine).

exploited the unanimity requirement to threat to block new sanctions against Russia.[5] In a wider context, as pointed out in a European Parliament study, EU Member States invoked their veto rights at least 30 times between 2016 and 2022, blocking or significantly delaying the EU's ability to act on foreign and security policy issues, including sanctions.[6]

The restrictive measures are ultimately about enforcing EU values,[7] listed in articles 2 and 21 Treaty on European Union (TEU), including democracy, the rule of law, human rights and fundamental freedoms, human dignity, and respect for international law. when it comes to Hungary, the reluctance to adopt sanctions against russia appears to signal that it does not fully share these values. its threat to veto is just one aspect of a broader pattern of conduct that has become increasingly unacceptable to most eu member states. in order to try to reverse democratic backsliding in Hungary, the eu has applied several instruments, including the warning mechanism (article 7(1) TEU) and the conditionality mechanism.[8] as these instruments seem to be inefficient, some member states and commentators argue that article 7(2) TEU should be applied,[9] which could result in the suspension of Hungary's voting rights in the council. academic proposals have also been made to expel Hungary from the union,[10] although the EU Treaties do not contain an express expulsion mechanism, or even a mechanism to dissolve the union and re-establish it without Hungary as a member.[11] In addition, some scholars have argued for 'neutralising' Hungary's obstruction

[5] In a similar vein, see Mitchel O Orenstein and Daniel Kelemen, 'Trojan Horses in EU Foreign Policy' (2017) 55 *Journal of Common Market Studies* 87.

[6] Wessel and Szép explain that the reported number likely underrepresents the total instances of vetoes, as some may have occurred in informal settings. Ramses A Wessel and Viktor Szép, 'The implementation of Article 31 of the Treaty on European Union and the use of Qualified Majority Voting: Towards a more effective Common Foreign and Security Policy?' Study Requested by the AFCO committee (November 2022). For a list with examples of how some Member States have blocked CFSP decisions, see Nicole Koenig, 'Towards QMV in EU Foreign Policy: Different Paths at Multiple Speeds' Policy Brief, Hertie School, Jacques Delors Centre (14 October 2022).

[7] Case T-536/21, *Belaeronavigatsia* EU:T:2023:66, para 34. '[Restrictive] measures constitute targeted preventive measures, which are intended, in accordance with Article 21(2)(b) TEU, to consolidate and support democracy, the rule of law, human rights and the principles of international law.' Christophe Hillion, 'The EU External Action as Mandate to Uphold the Rule of Law Outside and Inside the Union' (2023) 29 *Colombia Journal of European Law* 228; Peter van Elsuwege, 'Upholding the rule of law in the Common Foreign and Security Policy: H vs. Council' (2017) 54 *Common Market Law Review* 841; and Charlotte Beaucillon, 'Restrictive Measures as Tools of EU Foreign and Security Policy: Promoting EU values, from Antiterrorism to Country Sanctions' in Stefano Montaldo, Francesco Costamagna and Alberto Miglio (eds), *EU Law Enforcement: The Evolution of Sanctioning Powers* (Routledge, 2021) 187.

[8] Anna Södersten and Edwin Hercock, 'The Rule of Law in the EU: Crisis and Solutions' (SIEPS, 2023) Report no 1op, Stockholm, April 2023.

[9] Luke Dimitrios Spieker, 'Tackling the Union's 'Orbán Problem' Now: Seizing Momentum, Reviving Article 7 TEU, Sharpening Conditionality' VerfBlog (10 April 2025).

[10] Michael Dougan and Christophe Hillion, 'The EU's duty to respect Hungarian sovereignty: An action plan' (2022) 59 *Common market law review* 181.

[11] Merijn Chamon and Tom Theuns, 'Resisting Membership Fatalism: Dissociation through enhanced cooperation or collective withdrawal' VerfBlog (11 October 2021).

of sanctions against Russia by claiming that its actions breach the duty of solidarity.[12]

Yet, the Russian aggression might not be the only threat, and Hungary is not necessarily the only problem: the respect for rule of law and democracy is in decline in several Member States.[13] Moreover, achieving unanimity might be even more difficult to reach in the future. Since the full-scale invasion of Ukraine, enlargement is on the top of the political agenda. Growing disparities between future Member States may hinder the efficiency of the EU's decision-making process, making unanimity difficult to achieve in the Council.[14]

This situation has sparked discussions about the need for Treaty reform and that the EU must adapt its decision-making processes to accommodate a more diverse and larger union.[15] A central question in the reform process is how to integrate the Common Foreign and Security Policy (CFSP) more effectively into the EU's legal framework, where qualified majority voting (QMV) is the norm.[16] A main focus of such a reform is the adoption of EU sanctions, which make up more than 70 per cent of all CFSP decisions.[17] Indeed, in the last few years, there have been persistent calls to amend the Treaties and to introduce QMV for the CFSP. However, Treaty amendments take a long time and are complicated, and some Member States are of the position that the process may entail risks and potentially harm the EU.[18] For instance, it could trigger extensive debate, as ratification in the Member States is usually required, which can cause distractions and foster division.

Given the ongoing war in Europe and the broader decline of democracy, preserving unity is more crucial than ever. It may therefore be preferable to seek solutions within the existing Treaty framework, especially considering the Union's proven ability to respond effectively to past crises. This chapter explores

[12] Armin von Bogdandy and Luke Dimitrios Spieker, 'Overcoming the Hungarian Veto: Advancing Europe's Geopolitical Agency' VerfBlog (13 June 2025). See further discussion on their proposal below.

[13] V-Democracy, '25 Years of Autocratization: Democracy Trumped?, Democracy Report 2025', available at www.v-dem.net/publications/democracy-reports.

[14] Jean-Claude Piris, *The Future of Europe: Towards a Two-Speed EU* (Cambridge University Press, 2012).

[15] See, for example, the 2023 report from the Working group on EU institutional reforms (a body appointed by the French and German Governments).

[16] See Paul J Cardwell 'The Legalisation of European Union Foreign Policy and the Use of Sanctions' (2015) 17 *Cambridge Yearbook of European Legal Studies* 287, who argues that the CFSP has become more 'legalized', with sanctions playing a central role. This shift puts emphasis on the EU's growing capacity in foreign policy and the importance of continued legal focus on the CFSP.

[17] Ramses A Wessel, Elias Anttila, Helena Obenheimer and Alexandru Ursu, 'The future of EU Foreign, Security and Defence Policy: Assessing legal options for improvement' (2020) 26 *European Law Journal* 371.

[18] This is why several Member States oppose treaty change. See 'Non-paper by Bulgaria, Croatia, the Czech Republic, Denmark, Estonia, Finland, Latvia, Lithuania, Malta, Poland, Romania, Slovenia, and Sweden on the outcome of and follow-up to the Conference on the Future of Europe' (9 May 2022).

whether the adoption of sanctions can be improved without resorting to formal treaty revision. It argues that several institutional and procedural alternatives could be considered, including shifting certain areas of decision-making from unanimity to QMV, or transitioning from special legislative procedures to the ordinary legislative procedure through so-called *passerelles*. Some Member States can also initiate enhanced cooperation in specific areas, enabling them to move forward even if unanimity is not achieved. Additionally, the Treaties provide mechanisms that allow Member States to abstain in various ways during Council votes, potentially eliminating blockage. Both the Commission and the European Parliament have suggested making use of these possibilities to facilitate the adoption of sanctions,[19] and this chapter examines the scope and feasibility of these mechanisms in adopting sanctions.

What this chapter does not address is the possibility of permanently freezing Russian assets, an issue that was discussed within the European Council at the time of writing (December 2025). The European Commission has put forward a proposal under which the extension of existing asset-freeze measures would be decided on the basis of QMV.[20] However, this would not alter the decision-making rules for the adoption of *new* sanctions, which would still require unanimity in the Council.

Following this introduction, section 2.2 outlines the EU's legal and institutional framework for adopting sanctions, highlighting main actors, the decision-making procedure, and the role of unanimity in the Council. This is followed by three sections that explore ways to enhance the effectiveness and flexibility of the sanctions adoption process, all without resorting to formal treaty change. Section 2.3 discusses the use of *passerelles*, and considers both their legal basis and political feasibility. Section 2.4 analyses the potential of enhanced cooperation for adopting sanctions when unanimity cannot be reached, assessing the legal requirements and practical implications of its use in this context. Section 2.5 discusses the possibility of expanding the use of abstentions by Member States from voting in the Council. It explores how abstentions can be employed to avoid blockage while preserving the unity and legitimacy of EU external action. Section 2.6 concludes by reflecting on strengths and limitations of these alternative approaches, and their potential in establishing a more effective EU sanctions policy in a shifting geopolitical setting.

[19] The Commission's presidents have also called for the introduction of QMV for sanctions at various occasions. See European Commission President von der Leyen's State of the Union Address 2020 and State of the Union Address 2022. See also, European Commission President Jean-Claude Juncker's State of the Union Address 2017.

[20] For an overview, see Peter Van Elsuwege, 'Walking a Tightrope: On the Legal Stakes of the EU's Proposed Reparations Loan for Ukraine' VerfBlog (8 December 2025) https://verfassungsblog.de/on-the-legal-stakes-of-the-eus-proposed-reparations-loan-for-ukraine.

2.2 LEGAL BASES AND PROCEDURE FOR ADOPTING EU SANCTIONS

This section outlines how EU sanctions are adopted, detailing actors involved, the legal bases used, and the requirement of unanimity within the Council. It also highlights the limitations of the existing framework for exploring alternative pathways in subsequent sections.

The EU's sanctions framework consists of three types of regimes:[21]

1. the implementation of UN sanctions into EU law;
2. mixed regimes, where the EU strengthens UN sanctions with additional measures; and
3. autonomous sanctions, imposed independently of the UN framework.

Most of the autonomous sanctions, which are the focus of this chapter, are state based – that is, they are limited to a geographical region, and bear the state name in their title.[22] However, in recent years, the EU has started to adopt horizontal sanctions regimes, which allow for the listing of individuals and entities responsible for activities that contravene a specific norm, everywhere in the world.[23]

Most of the autonomous sanctions are adopted in two steps: first by a Decision in the CFSP Council; and then by a Council Regulation. In the first step, Article 29 TEU provides the legal basis stipulating that 'the Council shall adopt decisions which shall define the approach of the Union to a particular matter of a geographical or thematic nature'. It also requires the Member States to align their national policies with the Union's position. Article 29 TEU is the most employed legal basis in the CFSP,[24] and the decisions adopted based on it are binding for the Member States.[25]

The process to adopt sanctions is regulated by Articles 30–31 TEU. The proposal for a CFSP decision is put forward by the High Representative of the Union for Foreign Affairs and Security Policy (HR) or any Member State (Article 30).[26] The proposed measures are discussed by preparatory bodies of the Council[27] and by the Committee of Permanent Representatives (Coreper II). The European External Action Service (EEAS) recommends appropriate measures,

[21] For this typology, see for example the Council's website on sanctions: www.consilium.europa.eu/en/policies/sanctions-different-types/#regimes.

[22] Clara Portela, 'The Spread of Horizontal Sanctions' CEPS Commentary (2019).

[23] See for example Council Decision (CFSP) 2020/1999 of 7 December 2020 concerning restrictive measures against serious human rights violations and abuses [2020] OJ L410I/13; and Council Regulation (EU) 2020/1998 of 7 December 2020 concerning restrictive measures against serious human rights violations and abuses [2020] OJ L410I/1.

[24] According to Wessel et al (n 17), 47% of all CFSP decisions are based on Art 29 TEU.

[25] Case C-72/15, *PJSC Rosneft Oil Company v Her Majesty's Treasury and Others* EU:C:2017:236.

[26] The proposal can also be put forward by the High Representative with the Commission's support.

[27] The Council working party responsible for the geographical region of the targeted country, the Working Party of Foreign Relations Counsellors (RELEX) and the Political and Security Committee.

identifying sanction targets and drafting the legal framework. The decision to adopt the sanctions is then taken by the Council, requiring unanimity (Article 30 TEU). Indeed, it is the European Council and the Council that are the main actors within the CFSP, and they shall act by unanimity, 'except where the Treaties provide otherwise' (Article 24 TEU). The European Parliament is not involved in this procedure, although it frequently takes position by adopting resolutions.[28]

If the Council Decision includes measures such as asset freezes or other economic and financial sanctions, these actions must be implemented through a Council regulation, under Article 215 of the Treaty on the Functioning of the European Union (TFEU).[29] If the Council Decision includes travel bans and arms embargoes, these are implemented by national legislation and not by an EU Regulation, because such sanctions belong to national competence rather than EU competence.[30] Accordingly, even in later stages, decisions are not made by QMV. However, as Wessel notes, as different forms of sanctions may be adopted on the basis of one single Decision, the distinction between arms embargoes and other types of sanctions is often blurred.[31]

Under Article 215, the High Representative and the European Commission submit a joint proposal for a Council regulation. The proposal is reviewed by the Working Party of Foreign Relations Counsellors (RELEX), and then forwarded to Coreper II and the Council, where it is adopted by QMV.[32] The Regulations, which are non-CFSP acts and adopted by QMV, specify the scope of the measures and provide how they are to be implemented. They are binding on all individuals and entities within the EU, including companies, public authorities, and organisations.[33]

The content of the two instruments – the CFSP decision and the Council Regulation – is nearly identical, including the annex listing the names of targeted

[28] See eg, European Parliament resolution of 29 February 2024 on the need for unwavering EU support for Ukraine, after two years of Russia's war of aggression against Ukraine (2024/2526(RSP)).

[29] Art 75 TFEU provides a legal basis for measures concerning capital movement and payments, such as the freezing funds, for the purpose of preventing and combatting terrorism. However, the Court has ruled that Art 75 does not apply to restrictive measures. Case C-130/10, *European Parliament v Council* EU:C:2012:472, paras 54–66 and 73–75.

[30] Arms embargoes are an exception because of the national security provision in Art 346 TFEU. As Wessel notes, violations of arms embargoes may lead to the adoption of Council Regulations to ensure compliance. Ramses A Wessel, 'Legal Competences of the European Union in International Arms Control' paper presented at Contemporary Challenges in the Field of Non-Proliferation/Arms Control Policy and EU Responses, Vienna (2020). See also Francesco Giumelli, Fabian Hoffmann and Anna Książczaková, 'The when, what, where and why of European Union sanctions' (2020) 30 *European Security* 1. However, lists of dual-use items are exempted, and are outlined in ad hoc regulations. Council Common Position 2008/944/CFSP of 8 December 2008 defining common rules governing control of exports of military technology and equipment [2008] OJ L335/99.

[31] Wessel (n 30).

[32] See the Council's website at www.consilium.europa.eu/en/policies/sanctions-adoption-review-procedure. See also F Giumelli, 'How EU sanctions work: a new narrative' EU Institute for Security Studies, Chaillot Papers (May 2013); and Giumelli, Hoffmann and Książczaková (n 30).

[33] Art 288 TFEU.

individuals. They are adopted simultaneously and enter into force on the day of adoption, ensuring that both legal acts take effect at the same time. Thus, sanctions are an issue dealt with by provisions in both the TEU and the TFEU, and therefore, unanimity and QMV are used in parallel. The Regulation is adopted under the TFEU and is a supranational instrument, which means that it is subject to judicial review by the Court of Justice of the European Union (CJEU). By contrast, the Court has only limited jurisdiction over the CFSP decision.

The sanctions imposed by Council decisions are usually valid for 12 months, whereas the related Council regulations remain in effect indefinitely. Prior to deciding on an extension, the Council conducts a review of these measures. Based on this assessment, the Council may amend, renew, or suspend them.[34]

The Member States are primarily responsible for implementing and enforcing EU sanctions. The European Commission monitors the implementation and ensures that the sanctions are enforced. It should also be mentioned that third states (in particular EU candidate states, members of the European Free Trade Association, European Economic Area countries, and Eastern Partnership members) are routinely encouraged to align with EU restrictive measures.[35]

As explained, to adopt sanctions, the EU is dependent on unanimity for the CFSP Council decision, making the process particularly vulnerable to political deadlock, as any Member State can block agreement. This requirement reflects the politically sensitive nature of the CFSP. When the policy area was developed under the Maastricht Treaty, it was kept outside the European Community framework and placed in the TEU to preserve Member State control. The CFSP was designed as an intergovernmental pillar and, despite the institutional changes introduced by the Lisbon Treaty, it has largely retained this character. Article 24(1) TEU defines it as being subject to 'specific rules and procedures', meaning no legislative procedures apply and the CJEU has limited jurisdiction.[36] The European Council and the Council are the main actors, acting mostly by unanimity, while the Parliament has only an informal role. Implementation lies with the High Representative and Member States, and not the Commission.

In cases where the threshold of unanimity cannot be attained, there are nonetheless several options in the current EU Treaties that should be taken into consideration. These mechanisms include the use of *passerelle* clauses, enhanced

[34] See references in n 32. The EU's use of sanctions is governed by the 'Basic Principles', which outline the overall framework (Basic Principles on the Use of Restrictive Measures, Council doc 10198/1/04, REV 1); the 'Guidelines', which emphasise a targeted approach, aiming to limit civilian impact while increasing pressure on specific actors (Guidelines on implementation and evaluation of restrictive measures in the framework of the CFSP, Council document 15579/03, last updated by doc 11205/12); and 'Best Practices', which ensures uniform implementation across Member States (Update of the EU Best Practices for the effective implementation of restrictive measures, Council doc 11623/24).

[35] Cardwell and Moret (n 2).

[36] However, the Court's role in the CFSP is evolving, see eg, Joined Cases C-29/22 P and C-44/22 P, *KS and KD v Council and Others* EU:C:2024:725; and Case C-351/22, *Neves 77 Solutions* EU:C:2024:723.

cooperation, and the abstention from voting in the Council. These options have yet to be fully utilised, and their potential application in the field of sanctions merits closer examination, in particular given the growing challenges in adopting measures against Russia.

2.3 PASSERELLES

The first possibility to be explored is the use of *passerelles*. Through a *passerelle* (or 'bridge'), the EU can lower decision-making thresholds set in the treaties, making it easier to adopt legislation.[37] Most *passerelles* were introduced by the Lisbon Treaty,[38] but only one has been used so far.[39] Both the European Parliament and the Commission have suggested applying *passerelles* to this area, including those sanctions implemented under the EU Global Human Rights Sanctions Regime and those related to Russia's war of aggression against Ukraine.[40] The possibility has also been discussed in the General Affairs Council, where EU affairs ministers have shown relative openness to its application.[41] While no decision has yet been made to actually apply the *passerelles*, the question remains as to how such a measure would function in practice.

Two main types of *passerelle* procedures are outlined Article 48(7) TEU, which also governs Treaty amendments. The first allows a transition to QMV in the Council in areas where the Treaties currently require unanimity. Such a transition can apply to all areas covered by the TFEU, and also to Title V TEU on

[37] For a detailed discussion, see Robert Böttner and Jan Grinc, *Bridging Clauses in European Constitutional Law: Legal Framework and Parliamentary Participation* (Springer, 2018) 20–24.

[38] See Jean-Claude Piris, *The Lisbon Treaty: A Legal and Political Analysis* (Cambridge University Press, 2010) 107.

[39] In 2004, the Council decided to transition from unanimity to QMV and the co-decision procedure for certain decisions related to visas, asylum, immigration, and the free movement of persons. Council Decision 2004/927/EC of 22 December 2004 providing for certain areas covered by Title IV of Part Three of the Treaty establishing the European Community to be governed by the procedure laid down in Article 251 of that Treaty [2024] OJ L396/45. Note also Art 83(1) TFEU, which allows for a special procedure whereby the Council may identify new areas of crime, so-called euro crimes, that is, particularly serious crime with a cross-border dimension (which is not a *passerelle*, but of a similar nature). In 2022, the Council decided to add restrictive measures to the list of 'euro crimes' (Council Decision (EU) 2022/2332 of 28 November 2022 on identifying the violation of Union restrictive measures as an area of crime that meets the criteria specified in Article 83(1) of the Treaty on the Functioning of the European Union [2022] OJ L308/18).

[40] See European Parliament resolution of 11 July 2023 on the implementation of the *passerelle* clauses in the EU Treaties (2022/2142(INI)) (since the Treaty of Lisbon came into force, the European Parliament has advocated for the activation of passerelle clauses in more than 40 resolutions); and Communication from the Commission to the European Council, the European Parliament and the Council, 'A stronger global actor: a more efficient decision-making for EU Common Foreign and Security Policy', COM/2018/647 final. See also European Commission President Jean-Claude Juncker in the speech 'State of the Union' (September 2017).

[41] Council of the EU, 'General Affairs Council, 20 September 2022' (2022), www.consilium.europa.eu/en/meetings/gac/2022/09/20. See also the overview of the debate in Wessel and Szép (n 6) 75ff.

the EU's external actions and CFSP. However, decisions with military or defence implications, as well as certain specific provisions,[42] are excluded. The second type of *passerelle* involves shifting from a special legislative procedure to the ordinary legislative procedure.[43] It only applies under the TFEU and cannot be used for CFSP decisions under the TEU. Thus, only the first type could be used for the adoption of sanctions. To allow for a transition to QMV, the European Council must adopt an authorisation decision, which requires unanimity, and the European Parliament must approve it. Further, national parliaments have a veto right,[44] meaning that the process is halted if one or more national parliaments oppose it. Thus, at the national level, an authorisation decision can be blocked by both the executive and legislative branches (ie, the government and the national parliament). As a result, the threshold for applying this procedure is very high. The Treaty text does not explicitly define the scope of the authorisation decision, but it delimits it to 'a specific area or in a specific case'. This means that QMV cannot be introduced across all policy areas at once, but only in one area at a time. Consequently, the European Council's authorising decision could, in principle, be applied to the area of sanctions ('a specific area'). Politically, however, it might be easier to delimit it to adopt an authorising decision for each sanction regime, for instance, against Russia ('a specific case'), than to make a shift for all sanctions.

If the European Council did adopt a decision authorising the use of QMV for future sanction measures (or for a specific sanction regime), each individual sanction package would still require two subsequent (QMV) decisions: one for the Council decision that establishes the sanctions, and another for the corresponding Council regulation that implements them. Thus, dual QMV approvals would be needed. However, this does not necessarily imply that the process of adopting two decisions would be time-consuming: in practice, the process could proceed quite rapidly. In addition to this general *passerelle* in Article 48(7) TEU, there are also specific ones for particular policy areas,[45] including a CFSP-specific *passerelle* in Article 31(3) TEU. This provision stipulates that the European Council may unanimously adopt a decision on which the Council shall act by QMV. The European Parliament has no role, and national parliaments do not have a veto. Thus, this specific *passerelle* is easier to apply than the general one in Article 48(7) as it contains fewer constitutional safeguards. Given the overlap between Article 48(7) and Article 31(3), several explanations have been suggested as to how the relationship between them should be construed: 1) that Article 31(3) would take precedence as *lex specialis* (according to the principle

[42] According to Art 353 TFEU, the following provisions are excluded: the third and fourth paragraphs of Art 311, the first paragraph of Art 312(2), Art 352, and Art 354.

[43] Art 294 TFEU.

[44] An initiative from the European Council to use the passerelle must be forwarded to the national parliaments, which have six months to raise objections. See Art 6 of Protocol 1.

[45] There are specific *passerelles* in Arts 81(3), 153(2), 192(2), 312(2) and 333 TFEU; and Art 31(3) TEU.

lex specialis derogat legi generali); 2) that Article 31(3) TEU should not be seen as autonomous but read in combination with Article 48(7) TEU, which involves national parliaments and the European Parliament in the procedure; and 3) that the difference between the two is due to a drafting mistake.[46] As Wessel and Szép argue, given the existence of a specific *passerelle* clause (Article 31(3)), Article 48(7) should perhaps be interpreted as excluding that particular CFSP situation, despite its reference to the CFSP.[47]

Besides the *passerelle* clauses, there are four other specific possibilities in Article 31(2) TEU to switch to QMV.[48] Most important in this context is the provision that makes a transition possible 'when adopting any decision implementing a decision defining a Union action or position'. According to Wessel et al,[49] approximately 30 per cent of all CFSP decisions rely on this provision, most often to amend existing sanctions regimes. Thus, it has been used to adopt decisions to implement previously adopted CFSP decisions on sanctions,[50] primarily for amendments to listings when the changes were *not considered sensitive* by the Council of the EU.[51] Thus, many of the decisions on sanctions are already taken by QMV.[52]

Moreover, Article 31(2) provides for an 'emergency break', stating that any Member State can object to a decision being taken by QMV 'for vital and stated reasons of national policy', a provision designed to preserve the distinct (intergovernmental) character of the CFSP and to safeguard Member States that wish to preserve their sovereignty in this area.[53] It also states that the High Representative must seek a solution in close consultation with the Member State concerned. If no agreement is reached, the Council may, by qualified majority, refer the issue to the European Council for a unanimous decision. This means that efforts must be made to find compromise, and exceptions to QMV should

[46] For these various positions, see eg, Wessel and Szép (n 6); Silvia Kotanidis, 'Passerelle clauses in the EU Treaties: Opportunities for more flexible supranational decision-making' (European Parliamentary Research Service, December 2020); and Robert Böttner, 'The Treaty amendment procedure and the relationship between Article 31(3) TEU and the general bridging clause of Article 48(7) TEU' (2016) 12 *European Constitutional Law Review* 499. See also Steve Peers, 'The Future of EU Treaty amendments' (2012) 31 *Yearbook of European Law* 17, 73 who argues that there is no *lex specialis* rule as when it comes to different Treaty amendment procedures.

[47] Wessel and Szép '(n 6) 78.

[48] ibid, 73.

[49] Wessel et al (n 17) 385.

[50] See eg Council Implementing Decision (CFSP) 2018/1086 of 30 July 2018 concerning restrictive measures in view of the situation in Libya OJ L194/150.

[51] European Parliament resolution of 11 July 2023 on the implementation of the passerelle clauses in the EU Treaties (2022/2142(INI)), para 14; Communication from the Commission to the European Council, the European Parliament and the Council, 'A stronger global actor: a more efficient decision-making for EU Common Foreign and Security Policy', COM/2018/647 final.

[52] For the adoption of sanctions, Art 31(5) could also be of importance, stating that 'for procedural questions, the Council shall act by a majority of its members'. As it does not define what a procedural question is, one could argue that this provision could also apply to the adoption of sanctions. Wessel et al (n 17) 385.

[53] Ramses A Wessel and Robert Böttner, 'Article 31' in Hermann-Josef Blanke and Stelio Mangiameli (eds), *The Treaty on European Union (TEU): A Commentary* (Springer, 2013).

be avoided. However, it seems that this provision has never been used, at least not expressly.[54] There is also a limitation to Article 31(2) provided by Article 31(4) TEU, namely, that it is not possible to switch to QMV when it comes to decisions with military or defence implications. The terms 'military and defence implications' are vague and not defined in the Treaties. Therefore, it is not clear whether this limitation encompasses sanctions, although one might argue that they do not have military and defence implications as they are often adopted to come to terms with human rights violations. It should also be pointed out that Article 31(4) TEU makes no mention of the Common Security and Defence Policy (CSDP). Interpreting the provision as covering all CSDP matters would suggest that even non-military actions, such as humanitarian assistance, would require unanimity, which is not supported by the wording or practice.[55] One could therefore conclude that the limitation in Article 31(4) should be interpreted strictly.[56]

While the use of QMV within the CFSP could enhance decision-making efficiency, some commentators argue that there are also disadvantages.[57] One concern is the potential reduction in the influence of smaller Member States who see the national veto as an insurance policy to protect national interests. Others argue that unanimity strengthens the legitimacy of the decision-making process, and that shifting to QMV could undermine this legitimacy. However, as one commentator suggests, greater involvement of the European Parliament and the CJEU in CFSP matters could help address such concerns.[58] Moreover, decisions made without unanimous support can also weaken the EU's cohesion and effectiveness on the international stage. In addition, the Union's ability to ensure compliance with CFSP decisions is limited, as legal tools such as infringement procedures do not apply in this policy area. Nevertheless, as previously argued, existing mechanisms within the Treaty framework can be utilised to streamline decision-making within CFSP and applied to the area of sanctions. In this context, the use of *passerelles* may represent the most viable option available.

[54] For a discussion on that the emergency brake in EU criminal policy could be seen as a 'quasi-veto', see Jacob Öberg, 'Exit, Voice and Consensus: A Legal and Political Analysis of the Emergency Brake in EU Criminal Policy' (2021) 46 *European Law Review* 506.

[55] Hermann-Josef Blanke and Stelio Mangiameli, *The Treaty on European Union (TEU): A Commentary* (Springer, 2013).

[56] Manuel Kellerbauer, Marcus Klamert and Jonathan Tomkin (eds), 'Article 31 TEU' in Manuel Kellerbauer, Marcus Klamert and Jonathan Tomkin (eds), *The EU Treaties and Charter of Fundamental Rights: A Commentary*, 2nd edn (2024; online edn, Oxford Law Pro).

[57] Cecilia Navarra, Lenka Jančová and Isabelle Ioannides, 'Qualified majority voting in EU common foreign and security policy: A cost of non-Europe report' (European Parliamentary Research Service, 2023); Wessel and Szép (n 6) 78–79; Annegret Bendiek, Ronja Kempin and Nicolai von Ondarza, 'Introduction Qualified Majority Voting and Flexible Integration for a More Effective CFSP? A Critical Examination of the EU's Options' SWP Comment No 25 (June 2018); Tania Lațici, 'Qualified majority voting in foreign and security policy: Pros and Cons' (European Parliamentary Research Service, January 2021); Melanie C Papadopoulos, 'Do the Decision-Making Mechanisms in the EU Undermine Member States' National Interest?: A Case Study of the Sanctions Regime' (2017) 31 *Emory International Law Review* 553.

[58] Papadopoulos (n 57).

2.4 ENHANCED COOPERATION

Another possibility worth exploring is the establishment of enhanced cooperation for restrictive measures. An enhanced cooperation can be established where not all Member States agree and when only some of them choose to cooperate in certain limited areas. It allows participating Member States to use the EU's institutions and exercise EU competences by 'applying the relevant provisions of the Treaties' (Article 20 TEU).[59] The purpose is to 'further the objectives of the Union, protect its interests and reinforce its integration process'. Only a few enhanced cooperations have been established, concerning divorce and legal separation, a unitary patent system, and the property regimes of international couples.[60] The European Public Prosecutor's Office[61] and the Permanent Structured Cooperation in defence (PESCO) were also established as enhanced cooperations, though based on specific treaty provisions rather than the general rules.[62] Enhanced cooperation can be established in all areas of cooperation, including the CFSP,[63] and may therefore also be used for the adoption of sanctions. Further, an enhanced cooperation must only be a 'last resort' and can only be established if the objectives pursued cannot be achieved 'within a reasonable period by the Union as a whole' (Article 20 TEU).[64] These criteria seem rather unproblematic when it comes to enhanced cooperation for the adoption of restrictive measures under a sanction regime.

It is also worth noting that there is a specific *passerelle* clause, which allows the Council to switch from unanimity to QMV, or from a special to the ordinary legislative procedure (Article 333 TFEU). This mechanism could be applied in cases where an enhanced cooperation on sanctions is established. Thus, once enhanced cooperation is established, decisions to adopt sanction packages among the participating states could be taken by QMV instead of unanimity.

[59] See also Arts 326–34 TFEU.

[60] Council Decision 2010/405 of 12 July 2010 authorising enhanced cooperation in the area of the law applicable to divorce and legal separation [2010] OJ L189/12; Council Decision 2011/167/EU of 10 March 2011 authorising enhanced cooperation in the area of the creation of unitary patent protection [2011] OJ L76/53; Council Decision (EU) 2016/954 of 9 June 2016 authorising enhanced cooperation in the area of jurisdiction, applicable law and the recognition and enforcement of decisions on the property regimes of international couples, covering both matters of matrimonial property regimes and the property consequences of registered partnerships [2016] OJ L159/16. The Council has also decided on enhanced cooperation for a financial transaction tax, but it has not yet been implemented.

[61] For discussion, see Jacob Öberg, 'The Pitfalls of Enhanced Cooperation: The case of the European public prosecutor' VerfBlog (30 November 2022), https://verfassungsblog.de/the-pitfalls-of-enhanced-cooperation.

[62] Art 86 TFEU for the European Public Prosecutor's Office, respectively Arts 42.6 and 46 TEU for PESCO.

[63] For an historical account, see Marise Cremona, 'Enhanced Cooperation and the Common Foreign and Security and Defence Policies of the EU' Working Paper, EUI LAW, 2009/21.

[64] Joined Cases C-274/11, *Spain v Council* and C-295/11, *Italy v Council* EU:C:2013:240, para 50. For a discussion on these requirements, see eg Alberto Miglio, 'Differentiated integration and the principle of loyalty' (2018) 14 *European Constitutional Law Review* 475.

Yet, several requirements may make the establishment of enhanced cooperation for the adoption of sanctions difficult.[65] An enhanced cooperation 'shall not undermine the internal market', must not create obstacles or discrimination in trade, nor lead to distortions of competition between Member States (Article 326 TFEU).[66] An enhanced cooperation on restrictive measures may not fulfil these requirements if the restrictive measures take the form of an embargo, targeting certain goods and technology for use in certain sectors, or if the restrictions prohibit trade in certain goods or services. The question is how to deal with products that have entered the internal market from Member States not participating in the enhanced cooperation. In the same vein, imposing travel bans – by denying specific individuals entry to the EU at external borders or accessing EU airports for certain flights – could conflict with the free movement of persons. Such cooperation may also conflict with free movement of capital if Member States have different regimes for freezing funds.

To address these issues, the question arises whether the participating Member States may be permitted to adopt protective measures justified under Article 36 TFEU on grounds of public policy. Furthermore, could the EU itself introduce discriminatory measures that restrict the free movement of sanctioned products within the internal market? As Heber illustrates, these issues are complex,[67] involving considerations on non-discrimination, distortion of competition, and internal legal coherence. One possible solution could be to frame enhanced cooperation on sanctions as a 'value-based cooperation', which, according to Heber, would generally provide justification: Indeed, as previously mentioned in this chapter, sanctions are ultimately about enforcing the EU values. Nevertheless, there is also an obligation to respect the competences, rights and obligations of non-participating Member States (Article 327 TFEU), which may restrict the scope for such legislation or restrict the possibility of justifying the adoption of protective measures. In addition, although acts adopted under enhanced cooperation bind only participating Member States, non-participating states must not hinder their implementation (Article 327 TFEU), which may limit their ability to act within areas covered by enhanced cooperation.

In this context, the duty of sincere (or loyal) cooperation under Article 4(3) TEU may play a role. It requires that Member States shall 'refrain from any measure which could jeopardise the attainment of the Union's objectives'. The question is how far-reaching the duties of respect and non-obstruction extend in

[65] For a discussion on those requirements, see Steve Peers, 'Enhanced cooperation: the Cinderella of differentiated integration' in Bruno de Witte, Andrea Ott and Ellen Vos (eds), *Between Flexibility and Disintegration: The Trajectory of Differentiation in EU law* (Edward Elgar Publishing, 2017) 86; and Wolfgang Wessels and Carsten Gerards, 'The implementation of enhanced cooperation in the EU' Study for the Policy Department for Citizens' Rights and Constitutional Affairs (European Parliament, October 2018).

[66] Caroline Heber, 'Enhanced Cooperation and its Impact on the European Internal Market: Art 326 of the TFEU' in *Enhanced Cooperation and European Tax Law* (Oxford University Press, 2021).

[67] ibid.

the context of enhanced cooperation generally,[68] and more specifically, in relation to enhanced cooperation on sanctions. Again, one limit is the obligation to respect the competences, rights and obligations of non-participating Member States (Article 327 TFEU). In order to initiate enhanced cooperation, at least nine Member States must participate, and it must remain open to all (Article 328 TFEU). This requirement ensures that enhanced cooperation remains a tool for the advancement of integration. For CFSP-related cooperation, Member States must submit a request to the Council, which forwards it to both the High Representative and the Commission for opinions on its consistency with the CFSP and other policies. Thereafter, the Council must authorise it by unanimity among the participating Member States (Article 329 TFEU).

Given that enhanced cooperation does not establish a 'common' element within the *common* foreign and security policy,[69] considerations by the High Representative and the Commission on the consistency seem paradoxical to make. Likewise, the requirement in Article 20 TEU that an enhanced cooperation shall protect the Union's 'interests' might be hard to square if some Member States strongly oppose sanctions against a particular state. Indeed, a downside of enhanced cooperation in the CFSP is that it risks fragmenting the Union, which would be in direct contrast to the objective of establishing a *common* foreign and security policy.[70] As Cremona points out, an active and credible EU foreign policy cannot easily incorporate differentiated integration, as its strength relies more on political influence than on legally binding agreements or coercion.[71] The EU needs to speak with one voice, and enhanced cooperation on restrictive measures might therefore pose a threat to the EU: It could result in fragmentation, varying levels of integration, and a weakening of unity within the EU.[72]

A few additional points should be considered. First, an enhanced cooperation for sanctions could complicate the application of national rules implementing Directive (EU) 2024/1226, which defines criminal offences and penalties for the violation and circumvention of EU restrictive measures[73] by establishing mini-

[68] On the duty of loyalty and enhanced cooperation, see Alberto Miglio 'Differentiated integration and the principle of loyalty' (2018) 14 *European Constitutional Law Review* 475.

[69] On the common nature of CFSDP, see Anneke Houdé and Ramses A Wessel, 'A Common Security and Defence Policy: Limits to Differentiated Integration in PESCO?' (2022) 7 *European Papers* 1325.

[70] On the risks for EU consistency, see Ramses A Wessel, 'Differentiation in EU Foreign, Security, and Defence Policy: Between Coherence and Flexibility' in Martin Trybus and Nigel White (eds), *European Security Law* (Oxford University Press, 2007) 225, 247.

[71] Cremona (n 63).

[72] See further Robert Böttner, *The Constitutional Framework for Enhanced Cooperation in EU Law* (Brill, 2021); Robert Böttner, 'The Instrument of Enhanced Cooperation: Pitfalls and Possibilities for Differentiated Integration' (2022) 7 *European Papers* 1145; Wolfgang Wessels and Carsten Gerards, 'The implementation of enhanced cooperation in the EU' Study for the Policy Department for Citizens' Rights and Constitutional Affairs (European Parliament, October 2018); Ivana Kiendl Krišto and Cecilia Isaksson, 'Implementation of the Treaty provisions concerning enhanced cooperation: European Implementation Assessment' (European Parliamentary Research Service, December 2018); and Cremona (n 63).

[73] Directive (EU) 2024/1226 of the European Parliament and of the Council of 24 April 2024 on the definition of criminal offences and penalties for the violation of Union restrictive measures

mum rules. Enhanced cooperation is binding only on participating Member States which could result in inconsistent application and enforcement across the Union, undermining its overall effectives. Second, the use of enhanced cooperation may also weaken the external credibility and persuasive power of EU sanctions. Third states might be less inclined to align with restrictive measures adopted under enhanced cooperation, especially when such alignment is perceived as politically sensitive. As explained by Cardwell and Moret, alignment with EU sanctions often reflects a country's position within the enlargement process,[74] where failure to align might be seen as a lack of commitment and could impact accession prospects. However, if the restrictive measures are adopted by an enhanced cooperation rather than a decision of the Union as a whole, the political cost of non-alignment may appear lower, which could reduce their effectiveness.

In sum, enhanced cooperation does not seem to easily lend itself to restrictive measures.[75] Nevertheless, it may be worth further exploration as it could represent the only viable solution to address differing preferences among Member States while still enabling progress in this area. As discussed, one requirement for establishing enhanced cooperation is that it be used as a 'last resort' and that the objectives cannot be achieved within a reasonable time. In situations such as the imposition of sanctions to help stop a war, time is of the essence and enhanced cooperation may indeed represent the last resort.

2.5 ABSTENTIONS

Yet another possibility worth exploring is encouraging Member States to abstain when unanimity is required. This would enable decisions to proceed while perhaps being less controversial than the previously discussed alternatives. According to a Commission Communication from 2018, the use of abstention

---

and amending Directive (EU) 2018/1673 [2024] OJ L2024/1226/1. For a discussion on the application of enhanced cooperation using criminal law as an example, see Ester Herlin-Karnell, 'Enhanced Cooperation and Conflicting Values: Are New Forms of Governance the Same as 'Good Governance'?' in Martin Trybus and Luca Rubini (eds), *After Lisbon: The Impact of the New Treaty on European Union and the Treaty on the Functioning of the European Union* (Edward Elgar, 2012).

[74] Cardwell and Moret (n 2).

[75] There are also enhanced cooperations outside the Treaty framework, established through intergovernmental agreements. These are typically adopted in areas where the EU lacks competence. The EU institutions are not used; instead, the participating Member States must establish separate cooperation structures, where decisions are generally made by unanimity. See further Bruno de Witte, 'Constitutional Challenges of the Enlargement: Is Further Enlargement Feasible without Constitutional Changes?' Requested by the AFCO committee (March 2019) 21. In the *Pringle* case, the CJEU found that the Member States had not violated the EU treaties by establishing the ESM Treaty: Case C-370/12, *Pringle v Ireland and Others* EU:C:2012:756. In another case, the Court held that EU law takes precedence in cases where Member States have concluded agreements among themselves, and that Member States cannot create intergovernmental agreements to circumvent their obligations under the EU treaties: Case C-284/16, *Achmea* EU:C:2018:158. Thus, it seems that this type does not lend itself to the adoption of sanctions.

has 'great potential' and the Commission 'encourages the Member States in the Council to exploit this potential in its full extent by applying the Treaties in letter and spirit'.[76] The use of constructive abstention has also been proposed as a solution by a group of EU Foreign Ministers in 2023.[77] The challenge lies in identifying mechanisms to encourage Member States to utilise it in practice. There are two main types of abstentions: a general form that applies to all policy areas; and a specific one limited to the CFSP ('constructive abstention'). The general form is outlined in Article 238(4) TFEU, which states that 'abstentions by members present in person or represented shall not prevent the adoption by the Council of acts which require unanimity'. This means that a Member State choosing to abstain is still bound by the decision adopted by the other Member States. Abstention allows the Member State to express its position without voting against a proposal, thereby sending a much less confrontational signal compared to a 'no' vote.[78] To block a decision, a Member State must actively use its veto; otherwise, it is considered to have given tacit consent. The reason thereto is that in practice, formal votes are rarely held when unanimity applies; decisions are typically made by consensus.[79]

The first time a Member State abstained occurred in October 2022, when Belgium refrained from voting on the EU's eighth sanctions package against Russia.[80] Belgium's abstention was due to concerns over the impact on its steel industry, but it chose not to oppose the sanctions to maintain European solidarity. The second type of abstention applies only within the CFSP and is provided for in Article 31(2) TEU. This form is sometimes referred to as 'constructive abstention', though the term is not explicitly used in the treaties.[81] A Member State may abstain by issuing a formal declaration, which exempts it from the obligation to apply the decision. This differs from the general form, where abstaining states remain bound by the decision, although the abstaining Member State must still acknowledge that the decision is binding on the EU as a whole. Article 31(2) also emphasises the principle of (mutual) solidarity, which requires the abstaining

[76] Communication from the Commission to the European Council, the European Parliament and the Council, 'A stronger global actor: a more efficient decision-making for EU Common Foreign and Security Policy', COM/2018/647 final.

[77] 'It's time for more majority decision-making in EU foreign policy' (Politico, 12 June 2023), www.politico.eu/article/eu-foreign-policy-ukraine-russia-war-its-time-for-more-majority-decision-making.

[78] Philippe van Gruisen and Christophe Crombez, 'National parliamentary control and voting in the Council of the European Union' (2019) 58 *European Journal of Political Research* 981.

[79] See for example Fiona Hayes-Renshaw, Wim van Aken and Helen Wallace, 'When and Why the EU Council of Ministers Votes Explicitly' (2006) 44 *Journal of Common Market Studies* 161.

[80] Virginie Malingre and Philippe Jacqué, 'The sting of Russia sanctions: European solidarity with Ukraine tested by a lingering war' *Le Monde* (14 October 2022), www.lemonde.fr/en/international/article/2022/10/14/the-sting-of-russia-sanctions-european-solidarity-with-ukraine-tested-by-a-lingering-war_6000371_4.html#.

[81] See M Eugenia Bartoloni, 'Simple Abstention and Constructive Abstention in the Context of International Economic Sanctions: Two Too Similar Sides of the Same Coin?' (2022) 7 *European Papers* 1121; Wessel and Szép (n 6); and Daniel Thym, 'A New Institutional Balance for European Foreign Policy?' (2002) 7 *European Foreign Affairs Review* 369.

Member State to refrain from any action that could contradict or obstruct the implementation of the decision. It also requires other Member States to respect the abstaining Member State's position. Article 31(2) further stipulates that if at least one-third of the Member States abstain and represent at least one-third of the EU population, the decision cannot be adopted.[82]

However, the difference between simple and constructive abstention may not be as significant as it initially appears. Due to the principle of solidarity referred to in Article 31(4) TEU, even when a Member State abstains from a decision, it remains bound not to prevent its effective implementation.[83] Consequently, under both forms of abstentions, Member State cannot completely disregard a sanctions regime. In this light, a simple abstention may be sufficient for a Member State to signal political dissent. It was first used by Cyprus in 2008 when the EU established its Rule of Law Mission in Kosovo,[84] and later by Ireland, Malta, and Austria in February 2022 regarding the EU's decision to supply weapons to Ukraine under the European Peace Facility.[85] While these countries were not bound by the EU's decision, they expressed willingness to support Ukraine in other ways. Hungary also exercised constructive abstention in 2022 when the Council decided to establish a training programme for Ukrainian forces.[86] These instances were rather unproblematic: in the context of economic contributions and assistance, constructive abstentions simply means that the abstaining Member State does not contribute.

When it comes to sanctions, however, constructive abstention becomes a bit more problematic. As Bartoloni points out, it allows a Member State to refrain from enforcing certain restrictive measures, such as import or export bans of specific goods.[87] Nevertheless, if a product subject to an import ban enters the territory of an abstaining Member State, it may later circulate freely within the EU under the internal market rules. As this could undermine the effectiveness of sanctions imposed by other Member States, the abstaining (and non-complying) Member State could be required to adopt all necessary measures to compensate for its lack of enforcement under the solidarity principle.[88] In addition, the other

[82] This mechanism resembles the definition of a qualified majority in EU treaties, as it requires both a certain number of Member States and a proportion of the EU population to block a decision, effectively creating a 'reverse qualified majority'.

[83] Bartoloni (n 81).

[84] Council Joint Action 2008/124/CFSP of 4 February 2008 on the European Union Rule of Law Mission in Kosovo, EULEX KOSOVO [2008] OJ L42/92.

[85] Council Decision (CFSP) 2022/338 of 28 February 2022 on an assistance measure under the European Peace Facility for the supply to the Ukrainian Armed Forces of military equipment, and platforms, designed to deliver lethal force [2022] OJ L60/1. See Summary Record, Extraordinary meetings of the Permanent Representatives Committee, 22, 24, 27, 28 February, 1, 3 and 4 March 2022, Brussels, 16 March 2022.

[86] Council Decision (CFSP) 2022/1968 of 17 October 2022 on a European Union Military Assistance Mission in support of Ukraine (EUMAM Ukraine) [2022] OJ L270/85. See also A Tidey, 'EU Countries Agree to Train Ukrainian Soldiers as Part of New Mission' Euronews (17 October 2022), www.euronews.com/my-europe/2022/10/17/eu-ministers-to-sign-off-on-military-training-mission-for-ukrainian-soldiers.

[87] Bartoloni (n 81).

[88] ibid.

Member States could be permitted to adopt protective measures that might be justified under Article 36 TFEU on public policy grounds, and the EU could impose discriminatory measures that restrict the free movement of sanctioned products within the internal market.

The question remains how the EU can encourage a Member State to abstain as there is no obligation to do so. As mentioned, abstentions are perceived as a less confrontational way than an express 'no vote', but still, those Member States opposing a decision might prefer to block it actively rather than passively step aside. One way forward might be to apply the principle of loyalty which requires that a Member State shall 'refrain from any measure which could jeopardise the attainment of the Union's objectives' (Article 4(3) TEU).[89] There is also the CFSP-specific duty of cooperation, which states that Member States 'shall refrain from any action which is contrary to the interests of the Union or likely to impair its effectiveness as a cohesive force in international relations' (Article 24(3) TEU).[90] These provisions are overlapping and obligatory in nature,[91] and they both provide a 'negative side' of the duty, which requires Member States to refrain from actions.[92] As Elsuwege explains, the Court's case law establishes that the duty of cooperation entails concrete obligations for the Member States.[93] These obligations are especially strong when Member States' actions within international organisations or agreements directly affect the EU, or where Union and national competences are closely linked. The primary aim is to preserve the EU's unity in international representation, which supports the objectives of its external actions under Article 21 TEU. Ultimately, the duty of loyalty serves to protect the Union's interests, not those of individual Member States. It can, for example, be perceived as a 'duty to remain silent' implying that the Member States are restricted in expressing their own position when this could jeopardise the unity of the EU's representation.[94] However, it seems too stretched to assume that the duty of cooperation extends so far as to include a duty to abstain from voting 'no' in the Council when adopting sanctions; this is simply not where the principle operates.

[89] On the principle of loyalty, see Marcus Klamert, *The Principle of Loyalty in EU Law* (Oxford University Press, 2014).

[90] Peter van Elsuwege, 'The Duty of Sincere Cooperation and its Implications for Autonomous Member State Action in the Field of External Relations' in Marton Varju (ed), *Between Compliance and Particularism* (Springer, 2019). See also Marise Cremona, 'Defending the Community interest: The duties of cooperation and compliance' in Marise Cremona and Bruno de Witte (eds), *EU Foreign Relations Law: Constitutional Fundamentals* (Hart Publishing, 2008).

[91] Christophe Hillion and Ramses Wessel, 'Restraining external competences of the Member States under CFSP' in Marise Cremona and Bruno de Witte (eds), *EU Foreign Relations Law: Constitutional Fundamentals* (Hart Publishing, 2008).

[92] AG Mengozzi Opinion of 29 January 2015, *Commission v Council* C-28/12, EU:C:2015:43, para 63.

[93] van Elsuwege (n 90).

[94] Andrés Delgado Casteleiro and Joris Larik, 'The duty to remain silent: Limitless loyalty in EU external relations?' (2011) 36 *European Law Review* 524.

In this context, in a bold interpretative approach, von Bogdandy and Spieker suggest that in exceptional cases where the very existence of the Union is at stake, the obstruction by a Member State to vote 'no' to sanctions can constitute a breach of the principle of solidarity enshrined in Article 2 TEU. In their view, this could justify a shifting to QMV. The unanimity requirement in Article 31(1) could be interpreted in light of Article 2 TEU which would function as an 'unwritten passerelle clause'. They explain that Hungary's threat to veto sanctions against Russia constitutes a threat to the EU's constitutional core and propose that the obstruction can be 'neutralized'[95] by the Council Presidency noting that the obstructing vote is irrelevant, allowing the decision to be adopted under Article 238(4) TFEU as if it were a simple abstention. While this line of reasoning is compelling, it seems uncertain under what exact conditions such an approach would apply. In addition, as some scholars point out, it could set a dangerous precedence given that the EU values are vaguely defined.[96]

Finally, in this context, another mechanism that can yield a similar outcome to abstentions is the use of derogations. A notable example is found in the sixth sanctions package against Russia, adopted in June 2022, where the Commission granted Bulgaria a special derogation allowing it to continue importing and refining Russian oil until the end of 2024.[97] Indeed, the oil embargo was a particularly contentious issue as it concerned the impact on the economies of the Member States.[98] The derogation, however, was subject to strict conditions: it prohibited the transfer or transport of the oil to other Member States or to third countries (as well as its sale to purchasers in other Member States or third countries). In this way, the EU restricted the circulation of the oil and related products within the internal market. As Wessel and Szép explain,[99] while exemptions in EU sanctions risk fragmenting the Union, they enable the adoption of measures that might otherwise be unachievable. They offer a means of resolving deadlocks, enabling the EU to preserve unity while addressing the diverse interests of its Member States. Similarly, as de Witte argues, diversification is not necessarily a flaw of the EU system.[100] Rather, it allows the Union to accommodate diverse national interests, enabling both wider membership and deeper integration to progress simultaneously.

[95] von Bogdandy and Spieker (n 12).

[96] For a critique, see Martijn van den Brink and Mark Dawson, 'The European Union's Fantastical Constitution: A Response to von Bogdandy and Spieker' VerfBlog (27 June 2025).

[97] Council Decision (CFSP) 2022/884 of 3 June 2022 amending Decision 2014/512/CFSP concerning restrictive measures in view of Russia's actions destabilising the situation in Ukraine [2022] OJ L153/128. Exemptions or longer transition periods were also given to Slovakia, Czech Republic, Hungary, and Croatia.

[98] In the sixth package of sanctions adopted in June 2022, which included a partial embargo on Russian oil, Ben Cahill, 'European Union Imposes Partial Ban on Russian Oil', Critical Questions, Center for Strategic and International Studies (June 2022).

[99] Wessel and Szép (n 6) 82.

[100] Bruno de Witte, 'Variable Geometry and Differentiation as Structural Features of the EU Legal Order' in Bruno de Witte, Andrea Ott and Ellen Vos (eds), *Between flexibility and disintegration: The trajectory of differentiation in EU law* (Edward Elgar Publishing, 2017).

2.6 CONCLUSIONS

This chapter has examined how the decision-making procedure for restrictive measures can be improved. Although treaty changes are often seen as the solution, existing Treaties already offer mechanisms to enhance decision-making efficiency. This chapter examined various options, including *passerelle* clauses, enhanced cooperation, and abstention from voting in the Council. When it comes to *passerelle* clauses, both the general and the specific one could facilitate a shift from unanimity to qualified majority. The European Council could, in principle, adopt a single decision to authorise QMV for future sanctions. Given the undefined scope of such an authorising decision, it might be politically easier to restrict it to specific sanction regimes, such as those against Russia. The hurdle is of course how to reach unanimity in the European Council. If the general passerelle clause in Article 48(7) is to be applied, then the national parliaments also have a veto, and the European Parliament must approve.

The specific clause in Article 31(3) TEU is easier to apply due to fewer procedural hurdles. When it comes to enhanced cooperation for the adoption of sanctions, there are significant legal obstacles that make its implementation challenging. In addition, such cooperation could result in fragmentation, varying levels of integration, and a weakening of unity within the EU. Furthermore, enhanced cooperation for the adoption of sanctions raises concerns about the integrity of the internal market, as products banned under sanctions could circulate freely if a Member State fails to enforce them. To mitigate this risk, it might be necessary to implement discriminatory measures under Article 36 TFEU, justified by public policy considerations. Yet, flexible integration (which is the case of enhanced cooperation) may send a mixed message, potentially undermining the credibility and strength of EU external action. Nevertheless, enhanced cooperation might be the only viable solution to reconcile differing preferences among Member States.

By abstaining from voting in the Council, Member States can allow the EU to progress on an issue even without full unanimity. When it comes to 'constructive abstention', abstaining states are not bound to implement the decision, but must refrain from policies that contradict the EU's stance. Yet, those opposed to a decision often prefer to block it actively rather than step aside passively. The difficult question is how to incentivise abstention over obstruction. This approach might also risk undermining the integrity of the internal market if sanctioned goods move freely.

To conclude, previous experiences show that the process in finding a solution will not be an easy one. In the Joint Proposal presented in 2020 for the adoption of the horizontal sanctions regime to address human and fundamental rights,[101] the Commission and the High Representative introduced a novel proce-

[101] Joint Proposal for a Council Regulation concerning restrictive measures against serious human rights violations and abuses, JOIN/2020/20 final/2. Francesca Finelli, 'A New EU Sanctions Regime Against Human Rights Violations' (2020) 5 *European Papers* 1569.

dural element, including travel bans in the EU Regulation rather than solely in the CFSP decision. This would grant the Commission the authority to oversee the implementation of travel bans. In the final version, however, the traditional approach was maintained, keeping travel bans under Member State control.[102] As Eckes points out, this episode illustrates how Member States resist further centralisation of powers.[103]

However, assessing the advantages and disadvantages of each option remains valuable, and as explained, a more in-depth analysis of their respective dimensions is still needed. Ultimately, the challenge lies in reconciling efficiency in terms of achieving the EU's foreign policy objectives with the need to preserve unity among Member States. Yet, in light of the ongoing war in Europe and the erosion of democratic norms, there is growing public pressure on the Union to respond decisively. In this context, it becomes imperative to explore and make full use of the legal mechanisms embedded in EU law.[104] While there are limits of the EU legal framework, much can still be achieved within the existing one.

[102] See Council Decision (CFSP) 2020/1999 and Council Regulation (EU) 2020/1998 (n 23).

[103] Christina Eckes, 'EU Global Human Rights Sanctions Regime: is the Genie out of the Bottle?' (2021) 30 *Journal of Contemporary European Studies* 255.

[104] Armin von Bogdandy and Luke Dimitrios Spieker, Overcoming Objections to Overcome the Hungarian Veto: A Rejoinder to Dawson and van der Brink, VerfBlog (31 August 2025).

3

EU Sanctions: Some Reflections on Security, Criminalisation, Human Rights Justifications and Market Concerns

ESTER HERLIN-KARNELL*

3.1 INTRODUCTION

EU sanctions play an important role in the EU's security strategies and external relations. This chapter examines the EU sanctions regime and its various aspects, with particular focus on the internal and external dimensions of the EU's sanctions policy. More specifically, the chapter focuses on the broader relationship between EU criminal law and security, as well as on the role of human rights justifications in sanction adoption. Additionally, the chapter emphasises the market-based rationale regarding human rights justifications for legislation.

The role of sanctions in EU law is multifaceted. As Anton Moishenko has recently explained, targeted sanctions, such as asset freezes and travel bans, are no longer just tools of foreign policy.[1] Instead, sanctions are now used by governments in 'response to crime, such as corruption, human rights abuse, cybercrime, drug trafficking, and transnational organized crime writ large'.[2] While there has been extensive debate over the definition of a sanction, it is important to understand that sanctions used as tools of external relations – though intended to influence policies – often have a punitive aspect as well. Criminal law has its own

* Thanks to Jacob Öberg for helpful comments on the chapter. I would also like to thank EU Horizon (HRjust *Project 101094346 – WP 3*) for kindly sponsoring the research (all views and expressions are mine and not necessarily those of the funding body).

[1] Anton Moiseienko, 'Crime and Sanctions: Beyond Sanctions as a Foreign Policy Tool' (2024) *German Law Journal* 17.

[2] ibid.

set of legal safeguards, of course. The discussion about what exactly constitutes a sanction has persisted for some time.[3] This question is especially relevant to the classification of sanctions and the use of administrative sanctions, where strict liability is common. Previously, this meant that the EU and Member States did not always provide adequate judicial protection, and landmark cases on the right to judicial review are central in this area.[4] Indeed, high-profile cases like the *Kadi I* and *II* judgments show that there is a right to judicial review in Europe, even for assets frozen within the framework of non-penal sanctions. In *European Parliament v Council*, the Court emphasised that when selecting legal bases, it is not just the European Parliament's role or increased democratic input that matters.[5] The Court did not clarify which key factors rank equally, but it is reasonable to conclude that choosing the appropriate sanctions – and thus the legal basis – was just as crucial at the political level as enforcement effectiveness or how a sanction is defined.

The chapter is structured as follows. First, the EU legal framework for sanctions will be briefly addressed, along with some of the main reasons for adopting sanctions, including justifications for human rights when imposing sanctions is accounted for. In this context, the EU's criminalisation of violations of EU restrictive measures will be discussed. Third, the chapter briefly discusses Kantian theory in the context of the justification of sanctions before moving on to analyse sanctions related to financial crime. In doing so, the chapter addresses sanctions as an example of market-oriented trends and highlights the EU's broad policy mission, which balances dignity- and human rights-focused perspectives with internal market policies and goals. The complex legal structure of the internal market and its strong focus on market confidence are important when exploring the relationship with criminal law, which falls within the EU policy domain of the Area of Freedom, Security, and Justice (AFSJ). The chapter aims to argue that both approaches – the human rights and values-based EU law, and the market-oriented law – help explain much of the current thinking in the EU's sanction regime.

3.2 EU SANCTIONS LEGAL FRAMEWORK AND POLICY RATIONALES

The EU sanctioning regime is a core component of the EU's Common Foreign and Security Policy (CFSP). In short, EU sanctions aim to foster peace and democracy and to uphold EU values.[6] The EU sanctions play a significant role in

[3] Alain Pellet and Alina Miron, 'Sanctions', Max Planck Encyclopaedia of Public International Law, https://opil.ouplaw.com/display/10.1093/law:epil/9780199231690/law-9780199231690-e984.

[4] Joined cases C-402/05 P and C-415/05 P *Yassin Abdullah Kadi and Al Barakaat International Foundation v Council of the European Union and Commission of the European Communities* EU:C:2008:461.

[5] ibid.

[6] Arts 2 and 21 TEU.

EU law as a form of hybrid warfare by putting significant economic pressure on a third state that, in one way or another, breaches human rights. According to the EU Commission, in response to Russia's full-scale invasion of Ukraine, the EU greatly expanded sanctions by adding numerous individuals and organisations to the sanctions list and implementing unprecedented measures to 'weaken Russia's economy, deprive it of critical technologies and markets, and severely limit its ability to wage war'.[7]

As noted above, EU sanctions are intended to promote peace and democracy, human rights, and safeguard EU values, but some inevitably have adverse effects.[8] The EU has for a time long imposed sanctions for human rights breaches and other trade violations. The EU External Action Service has stated that the 'EU has close to 50 sanctions regimes in place, and almost 5,000 individuals and entities worldwide are subject to EU sanctions. Geographical sanctions regimes address the specific situation of third countries and currently apply to over 40 countries.'[9] Moreover, the EU commonly adopts targeted sectoral sanctions, such as economic and financial measures (eg, restrictions on banking services) or arms embargoes to prohibit exporting weapons and other goods that could be used in conflicts or for internal repression.[10] While the EU has had in place a regime for the adoption of sanctions for a while, it should be noted that the Lisbon Treaty has drastically restructured the legal architecture of the EU legal system by merging the previous complex pillar structure. While largely maintaining the existing normative framework for the imposition of restrictive measures, the Lisbon Treaty has introduced several significant changes to address the EU's challenges and resolve past problems.[11]

EU sanctions in external relations are often referred to as restrictive measures. The term 'restrictive measures' appears in Part V, Title IV, as well as in Articles 215 and 275 Treaty on the Functioning of the European Union (TFEU), in official EU acts – particularly in decisions (formerly known as common positions) and related regulations. However, the term 'restrictive measures' may be considered equivalent to 'sanctions' if a functional definition of the latter is accepted. Furthermore, the EU Commission has clarified that although restrictive measures are often referred to as sanctions, they are not criminal law but administrative measures that aim to induce a change in policy or activity by targeting entities and individuals in non-EU countries responsible for such harmful conduct. According to the EU Commission, 'Restrictive measures (sanctions) are an essential tool in the EU's common foreign and security policy …, through

[7] https://finance.ec.europa.eu/eu-and-world/sanctions-restrictive-measures/sanctions-adopted-following-russias-military-aggression-against-ukraine_en. See also the chapters by Cardwell, and Kaunert and Deus Pereira.

[8] Anton Moiseienko, *The Future of EU Sanctions against Russia: Objectives, Frozen Assets, and Humanitarian Impact*, (2022) 2 *Eucrim* 130.

[9] www.eeas.europa.eu/eeas/sanctions-what-types_en.

[10] ibid.

[11] See also chapters by Cardwell and Södersten in this edited volume.

which the EU can intervene where necessary to prevent conflict or respond to emerging or ongoing crises.' Despite their colloquial name – 'sanctions' – EU restrictive measures are not considered punitive. They are designed to induce a policy or activity change by targeting entities and individuals outside the EU responsible for such harmful actions.[12]

The effectiveness of the EU sanctions, or restricted measures, has been challenged by some scholars either because they oppose sanctions or because they believe the sanctions are insufficient and more action is needed. The unilateral sanction regime in international law has long been debated.[13] The EU Commission has, however, maintained its position and views the sanctions as effective and as necessary.[14] In the EU context, this is not about a unilateral regime, but a multilateral one which encompasses the Member States. The EU Commission is firm on imposing sanctions as an important statement against the Russian aggression and for tracking down human rights breaches as a result of the Russian invasion. Furthermore, sanctions are important in EU law as a way of 'hybrid warfare'.[15] The EU has now adopted 19 sanctions packages.[16] The EU Commission states that:

> After 24 February 2022, in response to Russia's military aggression against Ukraine, the EU massively expanded the sanctions. It added a significant number of individuals and organizations to the sanctions list. It adopted unprecedented measures to weaken Russia's economic base, depriving it of critical technologies and markets, and significantly curtail its ability to wage war.[17]

In addition, recently there has been an added dimension to the question of EU sanctions. More specifically, the EU has adopted measures based on Article 122 TFEU. On 12 December 2025, the Council of the EU used Article 122 TFEU, a legal basis allowing for a vote by qualified majority and to bypass the Hungarian veto.[18] The proposal stipulates that 'Preventing that funds are transferred to Russia is urgently required to limit the damage to the Union's economy'.[19] The

[12] https://ec.europa.eu/commission/presscorner/detail/en/qanda_22_1401.

[13] James G Devaney, 'On Sanctions and the Enforcement of International Law: A Rule of Law Analysis' (2025) 94 *Nordic Journal of International Law* 217.

[14] https://ec.europa.eu/commission/presscorner/detail/en/qanda_22_1401.

[15] Emmet Foley and Christian Kaunert, 'Russian Private Military and Ukraine: Hybrid Surrogate Warfare and Russian State Policy by Other Means' (2022) 16 *Central European Journal of International and Security Studies* 172.

[16] Council Decision (CFSP) 2020/1999 of 7 December 2020 concerning restrictive measures against serious human rights violations and abuses.

[17] https://finance.ec.europa.eu/eu-and-world/sanctions-restrictive-measures/sanctions-adopted-following-russias-military-aggression-against-ukraine_en.

[18] Valentin Kreilinger, 'Article 122 TFEU, The legal workaround to freeze Russian assets and possible repercussions'. Policy analysis 19epa (SIEPS, December 2025), available at https://sieps.se/media/ndzouhj3/2025_19epa.pdf.

[19] For a critical analysis, see Til Leichsenring and Julia Popp 'From Security to Economics: Freezing Russian Assets under Article 122(1) TFEU Violates the Treaties', VerfBlog (23 December 2025), available at https://verfassungsblog.de/from-security-to-economics.

EU has agreed to indefinitely immobilise the Russian Central Bank's assets, which are considered a central element of the reparations loan to Ukraine.[20] The EU adopted Regulation 2025/2600 of 12 December (Russian Assets Regulation), and the Council effectively froze Russian state assets permanently.[21] In the recital to the Russian Assets Regulation,[22] the EU states that in § 29:

> The need to ensure the financial stability of the Union and to safeguard the systemic importance of central securities depositories for the functioning of securities markets should be taken into consideration in the application of this Regulation.

There are thus a number of concerns in the EU raised in connection with security and the adoption of sanctions – not only security concerns, but also the need to maintain a security regime and the concern about too divergent application and enforcement across the Member States. An interesting cross-over between external and internal security is the new Directive on the criminalisation of breaches of restrictive measures adopted in 2024. Indeed, there is an underexplored and important relationship between criminal law sanctions adopted under Article 83 TFEU and those under Article 215 TFEU and Article 29 TEU when placed in a broader context of EU policy choices. The next section will try to tie the external sanctioning regime to internal matters in EU sanctioning law. The EU has recently extended its sanctions regime also to involve the Area of Freedom, Security and Justice (AFSJ). The reason for extending the sanctioning regime is, on the one hand, to ensure that external action sanctions are effectively enforced, and, on the other hand, to avoid divergent application and enforcement that could harm the smooth functioning of the EU market.

3.3 THE EU CRIMINALISATION OF BREACHES OF RESTRICTIVE MEASURES AND FROZEN ASSETS, AND ITS ENFORCEMENT

An interesting cross-policy dimension regarding EU sanctions is the overlap between the AFSJ and external relations in securing security and human rights. In 2024, the EU adopted a Directive criminalising violations of restricted measures adopted under the CFSP based on Article 83(1) TFEU.[23] The new Directive makes it clear that the implementation of Union restrictive measures is not as

[20] www.euronews.com/my-europe/2025/12/11/eu-triggers-emergency-clause-to-indefinitely-immobilise-russian-assets.

[21] See chapter by Moishenko in this volume.

[22] Council Regulation (EU) 2025/2600 of 12 December 2025 on emergency measures addressing the serious economic difficulties caused by Russia's actions in the context of the war of aggression against Ukraine.

[23] COM(2022) 247 final, Proposal for a Council decision on adding the violation of Union restrictive measures to the areas of crime laid down in Article 83(1) of the Treaty on the Functioning of the European Union.

uniform across the Union as it ought to be.[24] Article 3 of the Directive sets out a detailed list of criminal offences related to violations of EU sanctions. Such offenses address violations of individual measures (ie, asset freezes and travel bans), breaches of economic and financial sectoral measures, arms embargoes, and circumvention of EU sanctions.[25] According to the EU, restrictive measures are an essential tool for promoting the objective of the CFSP, as set out in Article 21 TEU. They are concerned with the EU's role in the wider world. These objectives include safeguarding the Union's values, maintaining international peace and security, and consolidating and supporting democracy, the rule of law, and human rights.

Furthermore, according to the EU, the implementation of sanctions and restrictive measures is not as uniform across the Union as it ought to be to ensure the effective implementation of EU sanctions policies.[26] In the recital to the Directive, it is stated that the divergent application in the Member States 'creates distortions in the Single Market, as Union companies, including EU subsidiaries of foreign companies, can find means to circumvent the restrictive measures'. These restrictive measures are intended to increase pressure on Russia. The EU also sanctions human rights breaches in Russia, such as systematic and 'intensifying repression against civil society and human rights defenders, as well as the unabated crackdown on independent media, individual journalists and media workers, political opposition members and other critical voices active throughout the Russian Federation and outside the country'.[27]

Another topical discussion concerns the practical implications of criminalisation, i.e., what to do with the frozen funds emanating from the sanctioning regime, and whether these funds can be confiscated to pay for Ukraine's reconstruction. This concerns the money that has been frozen. As mentioned above, the EU has recently agreed on the use of the internal emergency clause, Article 122 TFEU.[28] This provision enables the Council to adopt measures based on a European Commission proposal without involving the European Parliament.[29] While Article 122 TFEU is an emergency provision in the context of sanctions, it concerns whether the entire amount of already frozen Russian assets can be spent on Ukraine as reparations.[30] The Commission links Article 122 TFEU to Article 2 TEU, which sets out the Union's common values of human dignity,

[24] Directive (EU) 2024/1226 of the European Parliament and of the Council of 24 April 2024 on the definition of criminal offences and penalties for the violation of Union restrictive measures and amending Directive (EU) 2018/1673.

[25] Peter Csonka and Lucia Zoli, 'The New Directive on the Violation of Union Restrictive Measures in the Context of the EPPO' (2024) 1 *Eucrim* 76, https://doi.org/10.30709/eu-crim-2024-006.

[26] See also the chapter by Finelli and Öberg in this volume.

[27] www.consilium.europa.eu/en/policies/sanctions-against-russia/#human-rights.

[28] Csonka and Zoli (n 24).

[29] www.europarl.europa.eu/thinktank/sv/document/EPRS_BRI(2025)769579.

[30] Anton Moiseienko *Frozen Russian State Assets: The Key to Enforcing the Largest Financial Debt of Our Times,* VerfBlog (4 April 2025), available at https://verfassungsblog.de/frozen-russian-state-asset.

freedom, democracy, equality, the rule of law, and respect for human rights. The Commission also points out that the implementation of Union restrictive measures is not as uniform across the Union as it ought to be. This creates distortions in the Single Market, as Union companies, including EU subsidiaries of foreign companies, can find means to circumvent the restrictive measures.[31]

Finally, regarding enforcement, as Peter Csonka and Lucia Zoli point out, another key goal of the new Directive is to facilitate the confiscation of assets and resources subject to EU sanctions when linked to criminal activity.[32] This is primarily achieved through the linkage between this Directive and the new Directive on asset recovery and confiscation. Additionally, they argue that there may be good reasons to expand the European Public Prosecutor's Office competence to include criminal offences harmonised by the new Directive. First, as mentioned earlier, Union restrictive measures are a crucial tool for advancing the objectives of the CFSP. Therefore, like the fraud against the EU budget, the effective enforcement of sanctions against breaches of restricted measures can be viewed as an interest of the Union itself, justifying criminal enforcement at the EU level.[33]

3.4 HUMAN RIGHTS JUSTIFICATIONS, PROPORTIONALITY AND SANCTIONS

As noted above, the EU has long imposed sanctions for human rights breaches and other trade violations. The EU's global sanctioning system is rooted in human rights concerns, and the measures taken are primarily justified by human rights reasons. For example, in EU external relations, the EU's Global Human Rights Sanctions Regime, which imposes sanctions for human rights violations abroad, exemplifies how human rights justifications are used to pass new EU-level laws rather than relying solely on Member State actions.[34] Under this regime, the EU is supposed to impose sanctions on human rights violations in third countries. It 'targets both state and non-state actors, regardless of their location or whether they commit violations within their own country, in other states, or across borders'. Based on Article 21 TEU, one goal of the Global Human Rights Regime is for the EU to 'foster the sustainable economic, social, and environmental development of developing countries, with the primary aim of eradicating poverty'. Although it could be questioned whether the EU should have such (universal) jurisdiction, it reflects the EU's ambitions in this domain and how serious the current security situation is.

[31] www.consilium.europa.eu/en/policies/sanctions-against-russia/#human-rights
[32] Csonka and Zoli (n 24).
[33] ibid.
[34] www.consilium.europa.eu/en/press/press-releases/2025/12/04/eu-global-human-rights-sanctions-regime-listings-prolonged-for-a-year.

As noted above, the EU Global Sanctioning regime is focused on targeting individuals and entities responsible for serious human rights violations and abuses worldwide. The EU sanctions are similar to the US Global Magnitsky act,

> which imposes sanctions on any foreign person determined by the Secretary of the Treasury, in consultation with the Secretary of State and the Attorney General, to be responsible for or complicit in, or to have directly or indirectly engaged in, serious human rights abuse.[35]

When the EU global human right regime was adopted, it was ironically criticised for a lack of human rights protection despite aiming to protect human rights.[36]

The Directive on the criminalisation of breaches against restricted measures, discussed above, introduces a specific exclusion from criminal liability for the provision of 'humanitarian assistance'. In recital 20 and Article 3(5) of the Directive, it is stated that the 'Directive does not intend to criminalise humanitarian assistance for persons in need or activities in support of basic human needs provided in accordance with the principles of impartiality, humanity, neutrality and independence, and where applicable, with international humanitarian law'.

It has been suggested that this provision is especially necessary to provide clear legal guidance and predictability for every citizen, particularly humanitarian actors, regarding any potential (criminal) consequences of their actions. [37] This is to prevent discouraging the delivery of humanitarian aid when it is needed and to avoid unintended spillover effects that EU sanctions might cause.[38]

A question that has arisen concerns the proportionality of sanctions, with regard to any interference with fundamental rights such as access to a lawyer, the measures, and the scope of Article 47 of the EU Charter regarding the right to an effective remedy in EU law and the right to a hearing. In several cases, the EU Court has ruled that the targeted sanctions against individuals and against the Russian state are not disproportionate. In cases such as *Ordre néerlandais des avocats du bureau de Bruxelles and Others v Council*, the General Court of the EU held that limitations may be placed on the right to access a lawyer under certain circumstances to ensure compliance with and defend the rule of law.[39] Furthermore, the Court stated that the sanctions in question pursue objectives of general interest without impairing the fundamental role of lawyers in a democratic society, as the measures also allowed natural persons to consult lawyers. Regarding their effectiveness, critics argue that sanctions also serve a rhetorical purpose by accompanying public condemnations of human rights violations,

[35] www.state.gov/global-magnitsky-act.

[36] https://europeandemocracyhub.epd.eu/sharpening-the-eus-global-human-rights-sanctions-regime.

[37] Csonka and Zoli (n 24).

[38] ibid.

[39] Case T-797/22, *Ordre néerlandais des avocats du bureau de Bruxelles and Others v Council* EU:T:2024:670.

highlighting the consequences of the perpetrators' actions, and showing support for human rights defenders and affected communities. The EU, on the other hand, contends that the sanctions have been effective and carry an important symbolic significance.[40]

3.4.1 Human Rights Justifications in the Context of Dignity and Kantian Theory

It is interesting to reflect on dignity in this context of EU sanctions. The value of dignity is always at the heart of any discussions of what forms the constitutional law process at the EU level, as it is one of the EU's core values, and this is also intrinsic to any EU criminalisation. As Anthony Duff has argued,

> a polity that takes the moral status of its citizens seriously must treat and address them as responsible agents, even when they have done wrong: its responses to wrongdoing must still respect the wrongdoer's dignity as a citizen – that is, they must be such that citizens can impose them on each other, and can subject themselves to them, without thereby losing their civic status.[41]

For example, the criminal law process seeks to guarantee justice and fairness, and dignity is an umbrella concept in this regard. A protected interest can be either the individual victim's right to human dignity, or human dignity as an objective common value anchored in the relevant political community.[42] In the context of EU criminal law, scholars have referred to public good and the use of criminal law.[43]

Kantian theory is interesting in the context of sanctions, dignity and criminal law. Interestingly, the discussion of human dignity took place within Kant's doctrine of ethics and does not appear in his jurisprudence (*rechtlere*).[44] Kant reminds us that criminal law must be used to preserve and strengthen civic society.[45] This ethical aspect of criminal law explains why we have criminal law in the first place, and the question of civility and what it means to live in a decent society. For a very long time, the harm principle has navigated the criminal law

[40] See also Ester Herlin-Karnell, 'The Multifaceted Concept of Security in EU Law' (2026, forthcoming) *Columbia Journal of European Law*.

[41] Anthoney R Duff and Sandra Marshall, 'Crimes, Public Wrongs, and Civil Order' (2019) 13 *Criminal Law and Philosophy* 27.

[42] Tatjana Hörnle and Mordechai Kremnitzer, 'Human Dignity as a Protected Interest in Criminal Law' (2011) 44 *Israel Law Review* 143.

[43] Jacob Öberg, The Normative Foundations for EU Criminal Justice: Powers, Limits and Justifications (Hart Publishing, 2024); Stephen Coutts, 'Supranational public wrongs: The limitations and possibilities of European criminal law and a European community' (2017) 54 *Common Market Law Review* 771.

[44] Ahron Barak, *Proportionality* (Cambridge University Press, 2015).

[45] Ekoh N Yankah, 'Crime, Freedom and Civic Bonds: Arthur Ripstein's Force and Freedom: Kant's Legal and Political Philosophy' (2012) 6 *Criminal Law and Philosophy* 255.

terrain as to what ought to be criminalised. The assumption is that criminalisation is aimed at protecting interests from harm. But if neither the notion of harm, and relatedly human welfare, nor the notion of lack of consent, can explain the wrong, the notion of dignity is relevant.[46] Likewise, Anthony Duff and Sandra Marshall have suggested a public wrong principle rather than the harm principle.[47] The Kantian position is that to enter into a rightful condition is to exit the state of nature and enter into a civil society governed by law, where one submits one's unilateral view of how things should be to officials and institutions that govern in the name of us all.[48] For Kant we cannot adequately respect our own humanity unless we respect humanity in others.[49]

As noted above, the EU has adopted unprecedented measures to significantly weaken Russia's economic base,[50] depriving it of critical technologies and markets, and significantly curtailing its ability to wage war.[51] The effects of the sanctions have been contested, and the EU action seems to involve as much about taking values seriously and the stance taken as any actual effectiveness of the measures taken, as well as the methods of addressing threats emanating from Russia. Sanctions are intended to apply pressure to those engaged in aggressive war.[52] For example, Oona Hathaway and Scott Shapiro argue that sanctions have to be the outcome of multilateral decision-making; otherwise, it is just unilateral economic and political pressure, with economic and political might replacing military might.[53] Moreover, Arthur Ripstein argues that indiscriminate sanctions, like indiscriminate weapons, hit people who are not part of the conflict, which is why targeted sanctions are often used.[54] So even if they are targeted, they impose coercion that may or may not be justified in the individual case. According to Ripstein, the only answer from a Kantian perspective is multilateral action.[55] The EU fulfils this if regional (multilateral) action is one way of achieving multilateral action. The EU Council, by unanimity, decides

[46] Meir Dan-Cohen, 'Dignity, Crime, and Punishment: A Kantian Perspective' in Markus D Dubber (ed), *Foundational Texts in Modern Criminal Law* (Oxford, 2014; online edn, Oxford Academic, 20 November 2014), doi.org/10.1093/acprof:oso/9780199673612.003.000.

[47] Anthony Duff and Sandra Marshall, 'Public and Private Wrongs' in James Chalmers, Fiona Leverick and Lindsay Farmer (eds), *Essays in Criminal Law in Honour of Sir Gerald Gordon.* (Edinburgh University Press, 2010) 70–85.

[48] Yankah (n 44).

[49] ibid, 29–30.

[50] www.consilium.europa.eu/en/policies/sanctions/restrictive-measures-against-russia-over-ukraine/sanctions-against-russia-explained/#sanctions.

[51] See Moiseienko and Deus Pereira in this volume. See also the information given at the EU Commission website available at https://ec.europa.eu/info/business-economy-euro/banking-and-finance/international-relations/restrictive-measures-sanctions/sanctions-adopted-following-russias-military-aggression-against-ukraine_en.

[52] Arthur Ripstein, *Kant and the Law of War* (Oxford University Press, 2021). Also discussed in Ester Herlin-Karnell, 'The Constitutional Concepts of Sustainability and Dignity' (2023) 5 *Jus Cogens* 125,doi.org/10.1007/s42439-023-00078-9.

[53] Oona Hathaway and Scott Shapiro *The Internationalist* (Simon & Schuster, 2017).

[54] Ripstein (n 51).

[55] ibid.

to adopt, renew, or lift EU restrictive measures (sanctions) based on legislative proposals from the EU High Representative.[56]

3.4.2 Sanctions as a Market Correcting Measure

As mentioned above, sanctions are an important foreign policy tool. In the wake of the Russian full-scale invasion of Ukraine, the EU has stepped up its fight against organised and serious crime to help EU Member States 'tackle criminal networks and individuals who are exploiting the war in Ukraine'.[57] Moreover, as was briefly discussed above, some emergency actions were introduced in the EU crime priorities, such as trafficking in human beings, criminal finance, money laundering, asset recovery, new psychoactive substances and synthetic drugs, and high-risk criminal networks. However, as briefly discussed above, there is an economic dimension to the EU sanctions regime: for example, the EU has frozen assets under Article 122 TFEU, which will be important in supporting Ukraine in reparations. Article 122 TFEU concerns emergency and economic stability, which helps the EU to adopt measures using a qualified majority even when Hungary uses a veto.[58] To uphold EU values and promote peace, the Union may impose restrictive measures on third countries, entities, or individuals. The EU relates this to broader efforts at the EU level to combat serious and organised crime. It complements a set of laws that define offences and penalties related to criminal activities. It also includes measures aimed at preventing or combating related illegal activities, such as counterfeiting, trafficking in cultural goods, tax crimes, and the forging of administrative documents.[59]

The market dimension of criminal law is, however, interesting. As Lindsay Farmer has explained, markets of political economy have shaped much of our thinking about the criminal law. While markets were traditionally assumed to be self-regulating, criminal law was public.[60] According to this understanding, the market is self-regulating, and so what might be termed 'market crimes' are no longer integral to modern criminal law. This might raise familiar questions such as: by what criteria are rules recognised as part of criminal law rather than another body of regulations, for example, tort law or administrative law?[61] Today, however, the market-oriented path often calls for sanctions and criminal law and adopts parallel systems with administrative and sanctions through

[56] https://ec.europa.eu/commission/presscorner/detail/en/qanda_22_1401.
[57] www.consilium.europa.eu/en/policies/eu-fight-against-crime/#priorities.
[58] See also chapters in this volume by Cardwell, Moishenko and Södersten.
[59] www.consilium.europa.eu/en/policies/eu-fight-against-crime/#priorities.
[60] Lindsay Farmer, *Making the Modern Criminal Law: Criminalization and Civil Order* (Oxford University Press, 2016) and Lindsay Farmer, 'Civil order, markets, and the intelligibility of the criminal law' (2020) 70 *University of Toronto Law Journal* 123.
[61] For an analysis of sanctions in the context of Art 83 TFEU, see Jacob Öberg, 'The definition of criminal sanctions in the EU' (2013) *European Criminal Law Review* 273.

external relations. The argument here is not that sanctions are bad or not effective at all. Sanctions offer an important source of putting pressure and they have a symbolic function that should not be underestimated.

3.5 CONCLUSION

In this chapter, some of the key questions related to EU sanctions and the strategies taken against Russia's full-scale invasion of Ukraine has been accounted for. The chapter also looked more broadly at the relationship between AFSJ policies, external relations, and the links between security and criminal law. Additionally, the broader justification of adopting sanctions was examined. The EU has already enacted over 19 packages of sanctions. Furthermore, the EU has adopted the Directive on sanctions against violations of restricted measures. The adoption of sanctions by the EU shows that the internal and external aspects of security are closely connected. The issue of restrictive measures against Russia, adopted under the CFSP, is also closely linked to criminal sanctions implemented under the AFSJ framework in Article 83 TFEU. The EU's sanction regime and criminalisation theory, which are partly based on security concerns, partly on dignity and values, and partly on market considerations, highlight the complexity of these issues. While EU sanctions are motivated by human rights concerns, they are sometimes also accused of infringing on rights, such as limiting access to a lawyer. However, the EU court has not found such restrictions to be disproportionate.[62] The freezing of assets, the implementation of sanctions through both internal and external powers, as well as the use of Article 122 TFEU and measures related to economic emergency and solidarity, indicate a strong market dimension, along with enforcement challenges and the willingness of some Member States, like Hungary, to veto sanctions against Russia.[63] The EU strives to avoid inconsistencies among Member States that could harm the market, but security concerns are also at stake. It is about addressing two issues with one unified effort from the EU's perspective.

[62] Case T-797/22, *Ordre néerlandais des avocats du bureau de Bruxelles and Others v Council* EU:T:2024:670.

[63] On Hungary and sanctions see Armin von Bogdandy and Luke Dimitrios Speiker 'Overcoming the Hungarian Veto: Advancing Europe's Geopolitical Agency' (2025) VerfBlog, 13 June 2025 https://verfassungsblog.de/hungarian-veto-russian-central-bank-assets.

Part II

External Dimension of EU Sanctions

4

Sanctions as a Cornerstone of EU Foreign Policy in the Twenty-first Century

PAUL JAMES CARDWELL

4.1 INTRODUCTION

> The rules of engagement between global powers are changing. We should not take anything for granted. And while some in Europe may not like this new reality, we are ready to deal with it.
>
> Our values do not change. But to defend these values in a changing world, we must change the way we act.
>
> We must look for new opportunities wherever they arise. This is the moment to engage beyond blocs and taboos. And Europe is ready for change.
>
> Ursula von der Leyen, European Commission President, January 2025.[1]

Since the full-scale invasion of Ukraine by the Russian Federation in 2022, there has been a notable shift in the way the institutions and the Member States talk about EU foreign policy. The threat posed to the EU itself by an aggressive neighbour willing to use force has focused minds on the ways in which the EU can respond, which entails both a shift in thinking about the aims of the European integration project and how to confront the legal, institutional and material challenges to make EU foreign policy a reality.

The main vehicle for EU foreign policy is the Common Foreign and Security Policy (CFSP). The CFSP has, since its difficult birth in the Treaty of Maastricht in 1992, been dogged by accusations of a lack of coherence, identity and – crucially – effectiveness. These criticisms were well founded, given that the EU's response to the break-up of Yugoslavia and genocide in Rwanda in the 1990s

[1] Davos 2025: Special Address by Ursula von der Leyen, President of the European Commission, 21 January 2025, www.weforum.org/stories/2025/01/davos-2025-special-address-by-ursela-von-der-leyen-president-of-the-european-commission.

fell far short of the ambitions for foreign policy coordination as laid down in the Treaty. Since Maastricht, numerous attempts have been made to forge an institutional path forward between making the EU both visible and effective in foreign policy and respecting the hesitancy for further integration of some of the Member States in this core area of state sovereignty.

The ability of the EU to impose sanctions on third countries and individuals has, however, come to the fore in the past two decades. The stated objectives of autonomous sanctions – those which have not originated in the UN – are to support 'efforts to fight terrorism and the proliferation of weapons of mass destruction and as a restrictive measure to uphold respect for human rights, democracy, the rule of law and good governance'.[2]

Sanctions have become a 'go to' mechanism which, for the EU, have the characteristics of being both a foreign policy instrument and reliant on the EU's status as a trade powerhouse. Over 30 EU sanctions regimes are in place across the globe and the EU has developed 'extensive experience in designing, implementing, enforcing and monitoring restrictive measures'.[3] Beyond the legal instruments used to put sanctions in place, the EU's system of governance incorporates soft law mechanisms, such as whistleblowing procedures for violations of sanctions regimes.[4] The growth of the EU via waves of enlargement, has been supplemented by a process of inviting non-EU states in Europe to align with the EU's sanctions regimes.[5] Sanctions on the Russian Federation were placed in 2014, and since the full-scale invasion of Ukraine in 2022, a total of 19 packages had been agreed by the Member States by the end of 2025.

This chapter places sanctions in the context of the struggle for the EU to put in place a meaningful foreign policy, and investigates the extent to which sanctions might demonstrate that the EU has succeeded in creating a common foreign policy, as suggested by the terms of the Treaty. It argues that the legalisation of the CFSP, the familiarity of the use of sanctions and their increasing complexity, has allowed the EU and its Member States to forge a path which allows for agreement and consensus but whilst respecting differences. This path is predicated, however, on the Member States continuing to have the broadly the same views on those states and individuals on whom sanctions have been placed and highlights the risk that sanctions – whilst held up as an example of successful cooperation – could very easily turn to the opposite example. As such, this chapter contributes

[2] Council of the EU, Basic Principles on the Use of Restrictive Measures (Sanctions), 7 June 2004, 10198/1/04 REV 1, 2.

[3] Council of the EU, Sanctions Guidelines, 4 May 2018, 5664/18, https://data.consilium.europa.eu/doc/document/ST-5664-2018-INIT/en/pdf.

[4] See, for example, the procedure outlined by the Commission at https://finance.ec.europa.eu/eu-and-world/sanctions-restrictive-measures/overview-sanctions-and-related-resources/eu-sanctions-whistleblower-tool_en.

[5] Paul James Cardwell and Erica Moret, 'The EU, Sanctions and Regional Leadership' (2022) 32 *European Security* 1; Viktor Szép and Peter Van Elsuwege, 'EU Sanctions Policy and the Alignment of Third Countries: Relevant Experiences for the UK?' in Juan Santos Vara and Ramses A Wessel (eds), *The Routledge Handbook on the International Dimension of Brexit* (Routledge, 2020).

to the growing, interdisciplinary body of literature on sanctions and how to understand the EU's response to the full-scale invasion of Ukraine.[6]

The chapter begins with an outline of the difficulties in putting in place a foreign policy for non-state entity in a world built around, and for, nation states. It then considers how sanctions have come to the fore as a tool used by the EU, and how the institutional and legal challenges to putting sanctions regimes in place have been overcome. Finally, the chapter makes the case that the putting in place of sanctions represents a success for the EU in finding its 'niche' in global affairs insofar as sanctions occupy a distinct space between the EU's economic power and foreign policy aims.

4.2 DEFINING AND OPERATIONALISING AN EU 'FOREIGN POLICY'

Sanctions are essentially a foreign policy tool, operationalised via a legal process. In that respect, before considering what the nature of EU sanctions tell us, further exploration of the challenges of creating a foreign policy is necessary.

The development of the EU's foreign policy has been gradual and complex, shaped by the evolving nature of the EU itself and the changing dynamics of international relations. Foreign policy is not a new idea in the EU integration process, having its roots in the 1970s. In 1970 the Council of Ministers adopted the Davignon Report[7] which in time led to European Political Cooperation (EPC), a mechanism which promoted foreign policy dialogue among Member States but without a Treaty basis, defined competences or the involvement of the EU institutions beyond the Member States sitting in the Council.[8] Nevertheless, EPC laid the groundwork for strengthening cooperation and integration on a gradual basis, providing an opportunity for Member States to consult each other on international issues.

The lack of enforcement mechanisms and institutional depth, coupled with both the need and desire to move the EU beyond the stages of economic integration following the Europe 1992 programme on the completion of the single

[6] See, inter alia, Francesco Giumelli, Fabian Hoffmann and Anna Książczaková, 'The when, what, where and why of European Union sanctions' (2021) 30 *European Security* 1; Katharina Meissner, 'How to sanction international wrongdoing? The design of EU restrictive measures' (2023) 18 *Review of International Organizations* 61; Clara Portela, Paulina Pospieszna, Joanna Skrzypczyńska and Dawid Walentek, 'Consensus against all odds: explaining the persistence of EU sanctions on Russia' (2020) 43 *Journal of European Integration* 683; Helene Sjursen and Guri Rosén, 'Arguing Sanctions: On the EU's Response to the Crisis in Ukraine' (2017) 55 *JCMS: Journal of Common Market Studies* 20; Jan Lepeu, 'Ukraine, the de-targetization of EU sanctions, and the rise of the European commission as architect of EU foreign policy' (2025) 62 *International Politics* 975.

[7] Report by the Foreign Ministers of the Member States on the problems of political unification (Davignon Report), *Bulletin of the European Communities*, no 11 (Office for Official Publications of the European Communities, 1970) 9–14.

[8] Simon Nutall, *European Political Cooperation* (Oxford University Pree, 1992).

market, provided the basis for the creation of the CFSP in the Treaty on European Union (TEU) 1992. According to the TEU:

> The Union's competence in matters of common foreign and security policy shall cover all areas of foreign policy and all questions relating to the Union's security, including the progressive framing of a common defence policy that might lead to a common defence.[9]

This stated ambition is thus the one by which the current state of foreign policy can be judged. As one of the EU's three 'pillars', the CFSP aimed to provide the EU with the competences and tools to form unified voice in global affairs, albeit one which relied on intergovernmental cooperation rather than integration. The Commission, Parliament and Court of Justice did not have substantive roles in the CFSP pillar. The legal qualities of the instruments which could be adopted under the CFSP were uncertain, making the CFSP substantially different from the (then) first pillar competences that have driven forward the integration process.[10]

The ability of the Member States to forge a common foreign policy via the CFSP and live up to the expectations created and written into the Treaty was immediately put to the test in the break-up of Yugoslavia. Despite this taking place just beyond the EU's borders, the Member States failed to engage the mechanisms they had agreed to in the Treaty to – at the very least – coordinate their respective positions. The lack of ability to live up to the goals of the Treaty has haunted the drive for an EU foreign policy ever since. For proponents of EU integration, the failure was due to a lack of will in the Member States to commit to genuine integration as they had done in the single market and so many other policy areas, meaning that the CFSP was doomed without the Commission as the motor of integration and the potential for enforcement. A more charitable view is that the EU was trying to forge a role in international relations which – by its very nomenclature – is a set of relationships between *states*, of which the EU is not one.

An apt and oft-cited characterisation was provided by Christopher Hill, who in 1993 noted the scale of the tasks expected of the EU in the post-Cold War world:

> [S]tability and democracy for eastern Europe, a 'solution' for the Yugoslav crisis, relief for Third World poverty, all loom dauntingly on the horizon. Even with a clear strategy, which the Community demonstrably lacks over at least eastern Europe and the enlargement question, it would be difficult to cope with this flood-tide.[11]

[9] Art 24(1) TEU.

[10] Eileen Denza, *The Intergovernmental Pillars of the European Union* (Oxford University Press, 2002) 132–33; Alan Dashwood, 'The Law and Practice of CFSP Joint Actions' in Marise Cremona and Bruno De Witte (eds), *EU Foreign Relations Law: Constitutional Fundamentals* (Hart Publishing, 2008).

[11] Christopher Hill, 'The Capability-Expectations Gap, or Conceptualizing Europe's International Role' (1993) 31 *JCMS: Journal of Common Market Studies* 305, 315–16.

The EU's lack of resources and legal-political structures to deal with rapidly changing circumstances – which are materially different from the step-by-step, progressive building of an internal market – meant that the expectations of the EU acting as we would expect of a nation state were highly unlikely to be met by its limited capabilities of doing so.

This characterisation has thus stuck with the EU ever since. Subsequent treaties, including the Treaties of Amsterdam (1997) and Nice (2001) have grappled with the question of how to refine the CFSP, by making it more meaningful and able to engage on the world stage – but in the face of Member State reticent to use tools of integration – with its strong intergovernmental hallmark maintained.[12]

As a result, some of the institutional initiatives have been to mimic the arrangements of a nation state but adapted for the EU. The creation of the role of the High Representative for CFSP was designed to enhance the visibility and coherence of EU foreign policy, akin to a foreign minister.[13] Yet, given the high-profile splits between the Member States over the US-led invasion of Iraq in 2003, the idea of an EU foreign policy has been dogged by accusations that unless there is a mechanism to agree positions – and enforce them – it will remain a theoretical proposition only.

Nevertheless, renewed efforts to operationalise foreign policy occurred in the Treaty of Lisbon (2009). The Treaty merged the roles of the High Representative and the European Commissioner for External Relations into a High Representative of the Union for Foreign Affairs and Security Policy. The High Representative would be supported by a newly created European External Action Service (EEAS). The High Representative has emerged as a central figure, particularly in the context of sanctions policy. The prominence of this role, however, often depends on the skills and personality of the incumbent occupying it. Strong leadership can elevate the EU's visibility and effectiveness, but it also highlights the fragility of institutional continuity. Without structural reforms, the EU's foreign policy may remain overly reliant on individual agency rather than systemic strength. This institutional innovation of the EEAS aimed to streamline EU diplomacy and provide a more unified external representation, drawing on the strengths (and personnel) of the Member States which forging a distinct, and reliable, EU foreign policy. The creation of the EEAS laid bare the complexities of trying to fit the EU, as a non-state actor, into a system of international relations for which it was not built. Concurrently, a variety of civilian and military

[12] Marise Cremona, 'The Union as a Global Actor: Roles, Models, Identity' (2004) *Common Market Law Review* 553.

[13] Hylke Dijkstra, 'EU External Representation in Conflict Resolution: When does the Presidency or the High Representative Speak for Europe?' (2011) 15 *European Integration online Papers* 1; Niklas Helwig, 'The high representative of the union: The quest for leadership in EU foreign policy' in *The European External Action Service: European Diplomacy Post-Westphalia* (Palgrave Macmillan UK, 2015) 87–104; Lisbeth Aggestam and Elsa Hedling, 'Leaderisation in foreign policy: performing the role of EU High Representative' (2020) 29 *European Security* 301.

missions were launched under the Common Security and Defence Policy (CSDP) as a subset of CFSP, in regions including the Balkans, Africa, and the Middle East. The Treaty nevertheless maintained a strong intergovernmental flavour to the specific set of provisions of Title V, which attempted to ensure that the CFSP was 'ring-fenced'[14] from the (assumed) integrationist Commission and Court of Justice, and to prevent reading across of legal provisions from elsewhere in the Treaty.[15] This aim has only partly been achieved.[16] There remains resistance amongst Member States to move to a qualified majority voting in CFSP, leaving the unanimity requirement an ever-present danger to forging positions.[17] Since sanctions emerge from an agreement between the Member States within the framework of the CFSP, the intergovernmental/supranational tension permeates the policy.

Successive strategic documents reveal the gradual shift in how to characterise EU foreign policy, but also how its institutional and legal limitations structure where the emphasis should be placed. Although the EU Member States are required to assist others via the mutual assistance clause in case of an attack,[18] the EU does not have a military force to deploy. Its relationship with NATO is complex, partly due to the lack of NATO membership of four EU Member States.[19] As such, focussing on the high-level geopolitics only tells part of the story where EU foreign policy has taken shape. EU foreign policy has expanded to encompass a wide range of issues, including conflict prevention, human rights, development cooperation, and crisis management. Sanctions, as explored below, have become an integral part of this story.

Much emphasis has been placed in recent years on the EU becoming more *geopolitical*. This has become a hallmark of the Commission's view on foreign policy under Commission President Ursula von der Leyen, and sanctions play a key role in meeting this objective. The concept of strategic autonomy borrows from military discourse despite the military dimension being largely absent from the EU integration process. In the EU, the concept came to the CFSP initially via

[14] Paul James Cardwell, 'On "ring-fencing" the Common Foreign and Security Policy in the legal order of the European Union' (2013) 64 *Northern Ireland Legal Quarterly* 443.

[15] As per the Court in the 'third pillar' area of C-105/03, *Criminal Proceedings against Maria Pupino* EU:C:2005:386. The principle was read across from C-144/04, *Mangold v Helm* EU:C:2005:709 and C-555/07, *Kücükdeveci v Swedex GmbH* EU:C:2010:21. See further Valsamis Mitselegas, *EU Criminal Law* (Hart Publishing, 2009) 26 and Maria Fletcher, 'Extending "Indirect Effect" to the Third Pillar: the Significance of *Pupino*' (2005) 30 *European Law Review* 862.

[16] See, for instance, Christoph Hillion, 'A Powerless Court? The European Court of Justice and the Common Foreign and Security Policy' in Marise Cremona and Anne Thies (eds), *The European Court of Justice and External Relations Law* (Hart Publishing, 2014) 65.

[17] See further, Karolina Pomorska and Ramses A Wessel, 'Qualified Majority Voting in CFSP: A Solution to the Wrong Problem?' (2021) 26 *European Foreign Affairs Review* 351.

[18] Art 42(7) TEU.

[19] Austria, Cyprus, Ireland and Malta. It is worth noting here that the number of EU states who are not NATO members has diminished since Finland and Sweden joined NATO in the aftermath of the full-scale Russian invasion of Ukraine.

European Security and Defence Policy from around 2013. It became fully prominent in CFSP in the Global Strategy paper of June 2016.[20] Much of this centred on the EU's own actorness in a changing and challenging world rather than the legal conditions of the objectives to be pursued. [21]

The adoption of the Strategic Compass in 2022 marked an effort to define the EU's security ambitions more clearly. This touches on more than foreign policy, but represented a shift in attempting to confront 'the global threat landscape' and promote its values, including multilateralism.[22] Concluded only a month after the full-scale invasion of Ukraine by Russia in 2022, there is little doubt that the war has focused attention on how the EU can overcome institutional obstacles, including taking decisions to more rapidly deploy resources at its disposal and bringing together various tools in a response to a crisis. Initiatives including the European Peace Facility, Rapid Deployment Capacity and Crisis Management Military Exercises are practical demonstrations of the Strategic Compass.[23] Coupled with other trends in EU policy-making in the past decade – include the COVID-19 pandemic and migration – there has been a gradual characterisation as 'crisification'.[24] EU foreign policy can be said to have 'matured' and been brought within the same frame of the need for responses to intersecting crises.[25]

Central to all these strategic documents has been the role played by sanctions on third countries as a means of expressing EU foreign policy and as a tool with tangible, legal effects. Thus, they are both an expression of political will – since all sanctions are the result of a political response to a particular issue or set of circumstances – and of operational ability. Yet, although the large number of sanctions regimes in place demonstrates, as argued here, a successful ability of the EU to forge consensus and put its words into action, it remains highly dependent on the will of the Member States to do so. The following sections explore in more detail how sanctions regimes have emerged from the EU's institutional machinery and evolved over time.

[20] European External Action Service (EEAS), Global Strategy for the EU's Foreign and Security Policy (June 2016).

[21] Charlotte Beaucillon, 'Strategic Autonomy: A New Identity for the EU as a Global Actor' (2023) 8 *European Papers* 417, www.europeanpapers.eu/europeanforum/strategic-autonomy-new-identity-eu-global-actor.

[22] European External Action Service, 'A Strategic Compass for Security and Defence (24 March 2022), www.eeas.europa.eu/eeas/strategic-compass-security-and-defence-0_en.

[23] See further, the European Union External Action Service: www.eeas.europa.eu/eeas/strategic-compass-security-and-defence-1_en.

[24] Mark Rhinard, 'The Crisisification of Policy-Making in the European Union' (2019) 57 *Journal of Common Market Studies* 627.

[25] Marianne Riddervold and Pernille Rieker, 'Finally Coming of Age? EU Foreign and Security Policy after Ukraine' (2024) 33 *European Security* 497.

4.3 SANCTIONS AND FOREIGN POLICY

Sanctions, or 'restrictive measures' to give them their proper term in EU law,[26] have long been visible on the international legal horizon. Sanctions agreed through the United Nations Security Council (UNSC), which all UN members should enforce, began to emerge in the 1960s, although these were rather few and far between.[27] Initially, EU Member States implemented UNSC sanctions without the involvement of EU institutions. This was due to the absence of obligations under the UN Charter for the EU, as a non-state actor, and no indication in the Treaties at the time of any transfer of competence in this area.

This fragmented approach led to inconsistencies among Member States' national measures, resulting in distortions – actual or potential – within the common market;[28] and the Common Commercial Policy, where the Union already held significant competence. A related debate emerged around whether obligations had been transferred from Member States to the EU under the theory of state succession. The General Court (formerly the Court of First Instance) addressed this in the *Kadi* and *Yusuf* cases, drawing on the EU's experience with General Agreement on Tariffs and Trade obligations.[29]

The post-Cold War era, marked by diminished ideological divisions within the UNSC, saw a shift towards the greater use of unilateral sanctions in response to serious breaches of international law. During the 1990s, often termed the 'sanctions decade',[30] the UNSC imposed sanctions on Libya, Sudan and Afghanistan, often led by the United States and increasingly targeting states accused of supporting terrorism, even before the events of 9/11. Unilateral, or autonomous sanctions, had already become a tool of the EU, as demonstrated by its own sanctions on the USSR and Argentina in the early 1980s. The 1990s also thus saw a large increase in the use of unilateral sanctions, led by the US.[31] The EU has also embraced sanctions as a tool, but at the outset of the decade, given the lack of competence in foreign policy, the EU lacked the institutional

[26] See Art 215 TFEU.

[27] Sanctions on Rhodesia (1966–1979) and South Africa (1977–1994) are notable examples. See further: Thomas J Biersteker and Zuzana Hudáková, 'UN Targeted Sanctions: Historical Development and Current Challenges' in Peter AG van Bergeijk (ed), *Research Handbook on Economic Sanctions* (Edward Elgar Publishing, 2021) 107–24.

[28] Paul James Cardwell, 'The Legalisation of European Union Foreign Policy and the Use of Sanctions' (2015) 17 *Cambridge Yearbook of European Legal Studies* 287.

[29] T-306/01, *Ahmed Ali Yusuf and Al Barakaat International Foundation v Council and Commission* EU:T:2005:331 and T-315/06, *Yassin Abdullah Kadi v Council and Commission* EU:T:2005:332. For comment see: Paul James Cardwell, Duncan French and Nigel White, 'Casenote: Yassin Abdullah Kadi and Al Barakaat International Foundation v Council and Commission' (2009) 58 *International and Comparative Law Quarterly* 229–40.

[30] David Cortright and George A Lopez, *The Sanctions Decade: Assessing UN Strategies in the 1990s* (Lynne Rienner, 2000).

[31] Cécile Fabre, *Economic Statecraft: Human Rights, Sanctions, and Conditionality* (Harvard University Press, 2018).

architecture to allow for such political decision-making, even if measures could be taken under the common market competences.

The introduction of the CFSP enabled the EU to adopt a more proactive stance in projecting its values through sanctions. However, this raised questions about how to connect the CFSP with the EU's legal framework, given that the CFSP was contained as a separate pillar explicitly designed to avoid the institutions and processes associated with harmonisation. A partial solution had emerged from workaround practices developed in the 1980s: a decision under European Political Cooperation (EPC)[32] would be followed by a Regulation adopted via the Community Method under the Common Commercial Policy. The TEU formalised this approach, establishing a dual mechanism whereby a CFSP decision then results in a Regulation under the (then) first pillar.

The mechanism introduced at Maastricht remains largely intact today. The Treaty states:

> Where a decision, adopted in accordance with Chapter 2 of Title V of the Treaty on European Union, provides for the interruption or reduction, in part or completely, of economic and financial relations with one or more third countries, the Council, acting by a qualified majority on a joint proposal from the High Representative and the Commission, shall adopt the necessary measures. It shall inform the European Parliament thereof.[33]

This provision created a legal link between the 'political' CFSP and the 'regular' EU legal order, resulting in an innovative combination of legal bases upon which sanctions can be based.[34] This structure remains the same today. In spite of the critique of the CFSP since its inception, the linkage between the different legal mechanisms here can be understood as an example of coherence. The 9/11 attacks marked a turning point, prompting both the UNSC and the EU to impose sanctions on individuals and entities.[35] These targeted sanctions have become central to the EU's sanctions regime and a cornerstone of the CFSP. Some have led to significant legal challenges, with the Court of Justice refining its approach to the circumstances in which sanctions against individuals may be annulled.[36]

The Council thus remains in charge as the ultimate decision-making body, although it is far from the case that the EU's foreign policy can any longer

[32] European Political Cooperation was a discussion framework on foreign policy issues outwith the general competences of the EU. Its incremental development led to recognition in the Treaty via the Single European Act (1986).

[33] Art 215 TFEU.

[34] Christina Eckes, 'The Law and Practice of EU Sanctions' in Steven Blockmans and Panos Koutrakos (eds), *Research Handbook on the EU's Common Foreign and Security Policy* (Edward Elgar Publishing, 2018) , pp. 206–29.

[35] Mikael Eriksson, *Targeting Peace: understanding UN and EU Targeted Sanctions* (Routledge, 2016).

[36] See, for example, Marek Jaśkowski, 'Formal and Procedural Aspects of Individual Sanctions Adopted by the European Union in Reaction to Armed Conflicts: Analysis of Recent Case Law' (2025) 27 *International Community Law Review* 417.

be characterised as 'purely' intergovernmental.[37] As Koutrakos has observed, the requirement for a foreign policy measure as part of the sanctions process reflects the maturity of the EU's foreign policy framework.[38] The CJEU's decision in *Centro Com*[39]reinforced this, holding that a Regulation implementing a UN embargo had established mutual confidence among Member States in enforcing restrictive measures. The Court further ruled that even when measures are adopted under national foreign policy competence, they must comply with EU rules under the Common Commercial Policy. Embedding CFSP decisions with the EU's legal order ensures that the Union leverages both its economic power, often referred to as 'market power Europe',[40] and its competences where there is no doubt about legal enforceability. Sanctions sit at the intersection between foreign policy, trade and development, of which the latter is an area (often referred to as 'low politics') where the EU has gradually become a major player.[41]

Thus, even though CFSP decisions must be followed by a Regulation under Article 215 Treaty on the Functioning of the European Union (TFEU) – which mandates rather than permits Council action – Member States operate within a legalised framework. In the case of autonomous sanctions, this framework ensures that foreign policy decisions lead to enforceable legal outcomes, forming part of the CFSP *acquis*. The process of deciding whether and how to impose sanctions is, therefore, fundamentally legal in nature. Again, whether the sanctions actually fulfil their intended goals is highly contested[42] – the argument here is that a legal outcome demonstrates a high level of convergence between the Member States in terms of principle, form and shape of each of the different sanctions regimes.

With the legal mechanisms and processes in place, the EU has been able to demonstrate foreign policy 'in action'. The actual decision to do so remains a largely political one, but the extent to which sanctions regimes have been put in place against third states and individuals across the globe is insightful.

[37] Viktor Szép, 'New Intergovernmentalism Meets EU Sanctions Policy: The European Council Orchestrates the Restrictive Measures Imposed against Russia' (2020) 42 *Journal of European Integration* 855.

[38] Panos Koutrakos, *EU International Relations Law*, 2nd edn (Hart Publishing, 2015) 497.

[39] C-124/95, *The Queen, ex parte Centro-Com Srl v HM Treasury and Bank of England* EU:C:1997:8.

[40] Chad Damro, 'Market Power Europe' (2012) 19 *Journal of European Public Policy* 682.

[41] Katharina Meissner and Clara Portela, 'Beyond Foreign Policy? EU Sanctions at the Intersection of Development, Trade, and CFSP' (2022) 10 *Politics and Governance*, doi.org/10.17645/pag.v10i1.5118.

[42] See, inter alia, Niccolò Ridi and Veronika Fikfak, 'Sanctioning to Change State Behaviour' (2022) 13 *Journal of International Dispute Settlement* 210; Lee Jones and Clara Portela, 'Evaluating the Success of International Sanctions: a New Research Agenda' (2020) 125 *Revista CIDOB d'Afers Internacionals* 39.

4.4 SANCTIONS AS THE 'GO TO' FOREIGN POLICY TOOL

When any international crisis arises, it is generally not too long before 'sanctions' enter into the discourse as part of any potential response – at least by Western states and the EU.[43] Since the 1990s, both the UNSC and autonomous sanctions have become so widespread that it is often forgotten that their use is a relatively recent phenomenon. For the EU, sanctions have been used extensively – and creatively – as a means of furthering foreign policy goals. Indeed, sanctions have become central EU foreign policy, growing more than threefold in the past 30 years.[44] The total number of all EU sanctions regimes in place against third countries or thematic issues is around 35, although not all sanctions regimes are comprehensive.[45] Even where sanctions regimes have not been put in place on a third state, it is likely that there will be calls to do so and will – at the very least – be a subject of discussion amongst the Commission and the Member States in the European Council. Sanctions are not the only foreign policy instrument at the EU's disposal, but they are a visible sign that Member States have agreed to a specific course of action.

Before 2014, the stated uses of the restrictive measures were to promote international peace and security, uphold human rights, and support democratic governance.[46] EU sanctions before 2014 were characterised by a strong emphasis on multilateralism. While the EU's sanctions regime expanded significantly after 2014, particularly in response to Russia's annexation of Crimea, its pre-2014 history reveals a steady evolution in both scope and legal sophistication. Before 2014, the EU had already developed a dual-track approach: targeted sanctions (such as asset freezes and travel bans on individuals) and sectoral sanctions (such as arms embargoes or restrictions on trade and financial services). The emphasis was on targeted measures aiming to minimise humanitarian impact and avoid unnecessary harm to broader civilian populations, generally called 'smart' sanctions.[47] As with all sanctions regimes, no matter how 'smart', there remains a

[43] It should be noted here that China and India, in particular, take a remarkably different approach to sanctions. See Sarah Tzinieris and Rishika Chauhan, 'China's Arrival in the Great Sanctions Game: A Learnt Response, Made by America' (2024) 12 *Journal of Asian Security and International Affairs* 81 and Rishika Chauhan, 'Emerging India and Sanctions: Balancing Norms and Interests' in Ksenia Kirkham (ed), *The Routledge Handbook of the Political Economy of Sanctions* (Routledge, 2024).

[44] Giumelli, Hoffmann and Książczaková (n 6).

[45] A complete list, including legal acts and guidance documents, is provided at: www.sanctionsmap.eu.

[46] Council of the EU (n 2).

[47] Daniel W. Drezner, 'Sanctions Sometimes Smart: Targeted Sanctions in Theory and Practice' (2011) 13 *International Studies Review* 96.

vigorous debate as to whether the impact on populations can be minimised[48] and whether they do in fact meet their objectives.[49]

Until 2014, a look at the map of sanctions regimes[50] reveals that most of these were in place towards relatively small countries, especially in Africa. Once a sanctions regime is in place, it is relatively uncommon for it to be lifted, as the long-standing sanctions on countries such as North Korea demonstrate. Whilst some sanctions measures on countries including Zimbabwe, Myanmar and Syria have been lifted in part, it is relatively uncommon for a full lifting of sanctions, even if these only apply to former rulers of a state rather than the current leadership.[51]

One of the most extensive sanctions regimes in place before 2014 was that on the Islamic Republic of Iran, in response to concerns over its nuclear programme. Sanctions included asset freezes, visa bans, and restrictions on trade in sensitive technologies. The measures were coordinated with UNSC resolutions but often went further, reflecting the EU's commitment to non-proliferation.[52] For Libya, sanctions were imposed during the Gaddafi regime and intensified during the 2011 uprising. These included arms embargoes, asset freezes, and travel bans targeting regime figures. The EU also supported post-conflict stabilisation through the lifting and adjustment of measures. A point to note despite the wide-ranging nature of sanctions on Libya, which continue to be in place, is that this has not prevented functional cooperation on other foreign policy matters such as migration control.[53] EU sanctions regimes vary considerably, and

[48] See, for example, Jiyoun Park and Hyun Jin Choi, 'Are Smart Sanctions Smart Enough? An Inquiry into When Leaders Oppress Civilians under UN Targeted Sanctions' (2020) 43 *International Political Science Review* 433; Francisco Rodríguez, 'The Human Consequences of Economic Sanctions' (2024) 51 *Journal of Economic Studies* 942; Matteo Pinna Pintor, Marc Suhrcke and Christoph Hamelmann, 'The Impact of Economic Sanctions on Health and Health Systems in Low-income and Middle-income Countries: a Systematic Review and Narrative Synthesis (2023) 8 *BMJ Global Health* e010968, doi.org/10.1136/bmjgh-2022-010968.

[49] See, for example, Clara Portela and Juan S Mora-Sanguinetti, 'Sanctions Effectiveness, Development and Regime Type. Are Aid Suspensions and Economic Sanctions Alike?' (2023) 172 *World Development* 106370; George Tsouloufas and Matthew Rochat, 'Revisiting the Effectiveness of Economic Sanctions in the Context of Russia's Invasion of Ukraine' (2023) 29 *Canadian Foreign Policy Journal* 285, doi:10.1080/11926422.2023.2198247; Bryan R Early, 'Making Sanctions Work: Promoting Compliance, Punishing Violations, and Discouraging Sanctions Busting' in Peter AG van Bergeijk (ed), *Research Handbook on Economic Sanctions* (Edward Elgar Publishing, 2021) 167–86.

[50] www.sanctionsmap.eu/#/main.

[51] As in, for example, the case of Ukraine where sanctions apply to members of the former government for misappropriation of state funds. The original decision (since amended) is: Council Decision 2014/119/CFSP of 5 March 2014 concerning restrictive measures directed against certain persons, entities and bodies in view of the situation in Ukraine.

[52] Inter alia, Council Decision of 26 July 2010 concerning restrictive measures against Iran and repealing Common Position 2007/140/CFSP and Council Regulation (EU) No 267/2012 of 23 March 2012 concerning restrictive measures against Iran and repealing Regulation (EU) No 961/2010.

[53] See, for example, Sara Hamood, 'EU–Libya Cooperation on Migration: A Raw Deal for Refugees and Migrants? (2008) 21 *Journal of Refugee Studies* 19–42; Michela Ceccorulli, 'Triangular Migration Diplomacy: the Case of EU–Italian Cooperation with Libya' (2022) 52 *Italian Political Science Review/Rivista Italiana di Scienza Politica* 328; Agnese Pacciardi and Joakim Berndtsson

categorising them relies on a number of factors, including whether sanctions are also imposed by the US.[54]

The growth in sanctions, coupled with their complexity and targeting of individuals for suspected involvement in terrorism, chemical weapons development, cyber attacks or human rights abuse,[55] led consequently to a greater number of challenges, including legal disputes over listings. At present, the caseload of the General Court is in a large part made up of individuals challenging their inclusion on sanctions lists and to which the EU's legal system has had to adapt in terms of legal process as well as case management.[56]

The imposition of autonomous sanctions necessarily indicates that the Member States have formed a common view in the Council and used the legal procedure outlined above to impose the sanctions. However, the impact of the sanctions on the EU itself – especially economically – can be assumed to be relatively minor. In sum, the EU's pre-2014 sanctions regime laid the groundwork for its more assertive post-2014 posture. It reflected a cautious but increasingly confident use of economic and legal tools to pursue foreign policy objectives, balancing normative commitments with strategic interests. Nevertheless, questions about effectiveness, and the need for greater coherence in implementation and enforcement across Member States, have remained a constant feature.[57]

In 2014, the invasion and occupation of Crimea and parts of southeast Ukraine presented a strong challenge to EU foreign policy. The EU was now faced with what to do with an aggressive, large, and economically powerful neighbour that, inter alia, provided a significant amount of Europe's energy. The imposing of sanctions on the Russian Federation for restrictive measures for the stated rationale of 'Russia's actions destabilising the situation in Ukraine' was, at the very least, a success in the Member States agreeing a common cause of action.[58] The imposition of sanctions at this point meant that further sanctions were largely inevitable following the full-scale invasion of Ukraine in 2022. Yet, despite these sanctions which exhibited a level of political unity that defied some expectations, it did not prevent some Member States from cooperating with

'EU border externalisation and security outsourcing: exploring the migration industry in Libya' (2022) 48 *Journal of Ethnic and Migration Studies* 4010.

[54] For a fuller analysis, see Katharina Meissner, 'How to Sanction International Wrongdoing? The Design of EU Restrictive Measures' (2023) 18 *Review of International Organizations* 61.

[55] These are the four 'thematic' sanctions regimes which can apply to any individual rather than a nation state.

[56] See further, Yuliya Miadzvetskaya, 'Leaving the EU Sanctions List: How Evidence-based Judicial Review Facilitates Opportunistic Changes in Circumstances' (2025) *European Law Review.*

[57] Nina M Hart, 'Economic Sanctions and the Geopolitical Commission: Evaluating the Effects of Decentralized Sanctions Enforcement on the EU's Global Actorness' (2025) 30 *European Foreign Affairs Review* 507.

[58] Council Regulation (EU) 2022/328 of 25 February 2022 amending Regulation (EU) No 833/2014 concerning restrictive measures in view of Russia's actions destabilising the situation in Ukraine [2022] OJ L49/1; Portela, Pospieszna, Skrzypczyńska and Walentek (n 6); Helene Sjursen and Guri Rosén, 'Arguing Sanctions: On the EU's Response to the Crisis in Ukraine' (2017) 55 *JCMS: Journal of Common Market Studies* 20.

Russia in a variety of fields, including energy and even allowing military access to ports. For Orenstein and Kelemen, these instances demonstrated a limitation to the EU's overall foreign policy on Russia despite the discourse around the imposition of sanctions.[59]

Between the full-scale invasion of Ukraine in February 2022 and September 2025, 19 sanctions packages have been adopted by the EU on Russia. The workforce devoted to the drafting and impositions of sanctions has grown in the EU institutions, as has the ways in which sanctions evasion can be addressed. As would be expected, the number of challenges before the Court of Justice by sanctioned individuals has grown, alongside cases where the Court has considered the relationship between sanctions and fundamental rights. An example of the latter was a Regulation banning legal representation for 'legal persons, entities or bodies established in Russia'[60] was considered lawful by the court. In this case, the Regulation was unsuccessfully challenged by various national Bar organisations of Member States.[61]

Three points are worth noting regarding the experience of sanctions-making and enforcement since 2022. First, the extent of the sanctions placed on Russia as a third state is unprecedented. The speed at which the packages have been agreed and put in place is remarkable, especially given the complexities of the texts and the commercial sectors and individuals targeted. Speed is crucial if sanctions stand a chance of being effective, especially for asset freezes, but the EU's institutional machinery was not created with rapid decision-making in mind and is thus generally ill-equipped to do so. Similar, the range of sanctions in place go beyond what applies to any other states. For example, the banning of audio-visual services (including Russia Today and Sputnik) from operating within the EU has not previously been explored.[62]

As a consequence, the continuous cycle of drafting and implementing new sanctions regimes has also provided a valuable learning process for the EU. Not only the speed, but the place of the EU at the heart of the coalition sanctioning Russia and other states, has made it a target for retaliatory measures and 'hybrid' forms of warfare.[63] Led by sanctions, the EU institutions – and not the Member States – thus find themselves in the spotlight and geopolitical frontline.

[59] https://onlinelibrary.wiley.com/action/showCitFormats?doi=10.1111%2Fjcms.12441.

[60] Council Regulation (EU) 2022/1904 of 6 October 2022 amending Regulation (EU) No 833/2014 concerning restrictive measures in view of Russia's actions destabilising the situation in Ukraine, Art 1(12).

[61] T-797/22 *Ordre néerlandais des avocats du barreau de Bruxelles and Others v Council* EU:T:2024:670.

[62] Council Regulation (EU) 2022/350 of 1 March 2022 amending Regulation (EU) No 833/2014 concerning restrictive measures in view of Russia's actions destabilising the situation in Ukraine. See also Council of the EU, 'EU imposes sanctions on state-owned outlets RT/Russia Today and Sputnik's broadcasting in the EU' Press release (2 March 2022), www.consilium.europa.eu/en/press/press-releases/2022/03/02/eu-imposes-sanctions-on-state-owned-outlets-rtrussia-today-and-sputnik-s-broadcasting-in-the-eu.

[63] See, for example, Politico, 'Cyber spying on the rise, EU agency warns' (1 October 2025) www.politico.eu/article/eu-institutions-target-more-hacking-espionage-campaigns-cyber-agency-warns.

Second, there can be little doubt over the central, strategic place of sanctions in EU discourse. This had already begun to be a core feature of EU discourse post 2014. The EU's Global Strategy (2016), noted in the previous section, was an attempt to forge a renewed, strategic voice for EU foreign policy in the twenty-first century. It noted that:

> Restrictive measures, coupled with diplomacy, are key tools to bring about peaceful change. They can play a pivotal role in deterrence, conflict prevention and resolution. Smart sanctions, in compliance with international and EU law, will be carefully calibrated and monitored to support the legitimate economy and avoid harming local societies.[64]

As a general statement, this likely remains valid as to the EU's general approach to sanctions. Now, however, the emphasis is squarely placed on the role of sanctions in meeting the EU's geopolitical goals. The full-scale invasion of Ukraine has underlined the need for more streamlined processes, so although sanctions may still seek longer-term change in targeted state, the rapid putting together of sanctions packages coupled with a more assertive discourse about the EU's role has provided an opportunity for the Commission.[65] The increased devoting of resources to sanctions implementation and enforcement within the EU institutions flows from the importance placed on sanctions.

Third, the extensive use of sanctions has had a strong impact on other areas of EU policy-making, especially in the external relations field. The full-scale invasion of Ukraine has spurred on the enlargement process, with not only Ukraine but also Moldova and Georgia applying for EU membership, and the EU institutions and Member States seemingly recovering from the enlargement 'fatigue' of recent years[66] to use membership as a tool in the battle for influence in the EU's eastern neighbourhood. The potential for enlargement has become framed as a means to ensure that would-be members are within the EU's orbit, rather than those of Moscow.

Alongside this renewed enthusiasm for the growth of the EU, for existing candidate states, the place of foreign policy in the enlargement process has shifted dramatically. The Copenhagen Criteria remain the guiding principles for adopting the EU *acquis*, but whereas alignment with the CFSP was a comparatively minor consideration alongside criteria such as a functioning market economy, it is now front and centre. The most recent enlargement reports on all

[64] Council of the EU, 'Shared Vision, Common Action - A Stronger Europe; a Global Strategy for the European Union's Foreign and Security Policy' (2016) 16, www.eeas.europa.eu/top_stories/pdf/eugs_review_web.pdf.

[65] Yulija Miadzvetskaya, 'EU Sanctions Decision-Making in Times of War: Procedural Changes and Rise of the Commission' (2025) *Maastricht Journal of European and Comparative Law*, doi.org/10.1177/1023263X251345672; Jan Lepeu, 'Ukraine, the De-targetization of EU Sanctions, and the Rise of the European Commission as Architect of EU Foreign Policy' (2025) *International Politics* (early view), doi.org/10.1057/s41311-024-00649-.

[66] John O'Brennan, 'On the Slow Train to Nowhere?' The European Union, "enlargement fatigue" and the Western Balkans' (2014) 19 *European Foreign Affairs Review* 221.

the candidates underline the importance of whether the candidate has aligned with the EU and adopted sanctions on Russia as a demonstration of the sharing of (or perhaps, adherence to) EU values. As a point of comparison, the following appears on the first page of each of the 2024 reports on Albania and Serbia respectively, which underlines the centrality of CFSP and sanctions for the enlargement process:

> Albania maintained its record of full alignment with the EU's common foreign and security policy. … including on restrictive measures and sanctions against Russia. Albania's stance sends a strong signal of its strategic choice of EU accession and of its role as a reliable partner.[67]

And:

> Following Russia's war of aggression against Ukraine, Serbia aligned with some EU positions in international forums (including in the UN General Assembly). Serbia has continued to cooperate with the EU on sanctions circumvention and providing financial and humanitarian support to Ukraine. However, it still does not align with any restrictive measures against the Russian Federation and has not aligned with most of the High Representative statements on this matter. It has maintained high-level relations with the Russian Federation and intensified its relations with China, raising questions about Serbia's strategic direction. Under the EU-Serbia negotiating framework, Serbia is expected to progressively align its policies towards third countries with the policies and positions adopted by the EU, including restrictive measure.[68]

The extent to which states who have applied for EU membership can be evaluated as to their adhere to foreign policy norms and sanctions can be seen through an established practice of public alignment. In the run-up to the 2004 enlargement, the Council began to invite enlargement states to align with CFSP declarations. This practice became more regularised in 2007, and non-EU states included enlargement/pre-enlargement states in the Western Balkans, those in the EEA (Iceland, Liechtenstein and Norway), and other Eastern Partnership states including Moldova and Ukraine, with invitations to Armenia, Azerbaijan and Georgia following a short time later. The CFSP Declarations ranged from general statements marking international days relating to human rights, to condemnation of the use of the death penalty in states including Iran and the United States.[69] Increasingly, declarations have noted a fresh imposition of sanctions against a third state, and thus it is possible to evaluate the extent to which these 14 invited states take up the opportunity on an individual basis.[70] Evidence shows that in the majority of cases around six to eight third states

[67] Commission, 'Staff Working Document: Albania Report 2024' COM(2024) 690 final.

[68] ibid.

[69] Paul James Cardwell, 'Values in the European Union's Foreign Policy: An Analysis and Assessment of CFSP Declarations' (2016) 21 *European Foreign Affairs Review* 601.

[70] Croatia was invited to align before its EU accession in 2013. The UK is not invited to align, but since Brexit, EU and UK sanctions regimes remain broadly the same.

explicitly align with EU sanctions. Whilst higher numbers have generally been seen for sanctions regimes against smaller African countries, there alignment rate fluctuates according to the views of the third state government and the general progress of alignment. Full alignment on sanctions on Russia can be observed with some of the third states in questions, whilst others have declined to do.[71] This is an example of both a wider convergence of European (not only EU) values with leadership which cannot only be explained by the 'pull' of the enlargement process but which reflects a 'European' (and not only the 'EU') approach, meeting the Treaty-based requirements to share values within the special relationships with neighbouring countries .[72]

4.5 CONCLUSION

The full-scale invasion of Ukraine has served as a profound catalyst for re-evaluating the EU's foreign policy. For decades, the EU has grappled with the question of whether it can, as a non-state actor, truly act as a unified and strategic global player. Faced with the greatest security threat to the EU and its Member States since the Treaty-based competences in foreign policy, the war has prompted renewed discussions about the institutional architecture of the EU, and its future direction. Much of this discussion has centred on whether EU foreign policy has finally 'come of age'.[73] There are two aspects to whether this is the case, and what it means. The first speaks to whether the EU has managed to live up to the expectations set out in the Treaty. The second is whether foreign policy has moved from a peripheral area of the EU integration process to front-and-centre. The volume and frequency of sanctions imposed on a wide variety of third states suggest that that the answer to both of these is a (tentative) yes.

At the heart of the EU's foreign policy challenges lies a resistance to integration and an overall final goal for cooperation. Whilst it is untrue to say that foreign and security policy remains solely in the hands of the Member States, it nevertheless retains a strong intergovernmental flavour running through the Treaty provisions and the institutional practices. The fundamental distinction between the EU and a nation state is found in its institutional arrangements and actors, and the need for consensus, resulting in often slow, reactive, and diluted responses. In foreign policy, the absence of a strong integration reflex is

[71] Albania, Montenegro and Norway are in the first category, with Serbia and Türkiye in the latter. For an analysis before the full-scale invasion, see Elin Hellquist, 'Either With Us or against Us? Third-country Alignment with EU Sanctions against Russia/Ukraine' (2016) 29 *Cambridge Review of International Affairs* 997.

[72] As per Art 8(1) TEU. For a fuller analysis, see Paul James Cardwell and Erica Moret, 'The EU, Sanctions and Regional Leadership' (2022) 32 *European Security* 1.

[73] Heidi Maurer, Kolja Raube, and Richard G Whitman, '"Zeitenwende" as Coming of Age? EU Foreign & Security Policy through War & Peace' (2024) 33 *European Security* 345, doi:10.1080/09662839.2024.2376604; Lepeu (n 65).

compounded by the increasing prevalence of differentiated integration across the EU. The rise of populist governments within the EU further complicates consensus. Populist leaders often challenge the legitimacy of supranational decision-making and resist foreign policy initiatives that conflict with national interests or ideological narratives. This internal contestation weakens the EU's coherence and credibility, especially when unanimity is required for key decisions in foreign and security policy.[74]

Taken together, the ever-present risk of fragmentation undermines the EU's ability to present a united front in international affairs, including in sanctions. Consensus-building, while a foundational principle of EU decision-making, is increasingly strained. Reflex coordination – where Member States align their positions in response to external pressures rather than through proactive strategy – has become commonplace. However, this reactive posture limits the EU's capacity to shape global events and instead forces it into a position of perpetual adjustment. Whilst enforceable 'law' in EU foreign policy is often cited as the answer, it seems unlikely in the present political context of widespread contestations of the EU's raison d'etre, including its role in international affairs, even by leaders of Member States.[75]

Recognition of the EU and its foreign policy as meaningful is not merely about self-perception but also how external actors view the EU's role in international affairs. The shift toward viewing the EU as a 'strategic actor' raises important questions about its traditional identity as a civilian power. Historically, the EU has emphasised normative influence – promoting democracy, human rights, and multilateralism – through soft power tools such as development aid, trade agreements, and diplomatic engagement. This civilian power model has been central to the EU's global image. The European Commission, under the leadership of Ursula von der Leyen, has taken deliberate steps to position itself as a strategic geopolitical actor. Von der Leyen's framing of the Commission's role is no accident – it reflects a conscious effort to redefine the EU's identity in global politics.[76] The EU is increasingly engaging with defence and 'hard' security issues, including military mobility, defence procurement, and strategic autonomy. This does not necessarily mean abandoning its normative foundations, but it does indicate a more pragmatic approach to power politics.

Sanctions exemplify this duality. They are a quintessential foreign policy tool, used to exert pressure on third countries in response to violations of international norms. Yet, their effectiveness relies heavily on the EU's internal market and other competences. By leveraging its economic power, the EU can

[74] Ana E Juncos and Karolina Pomorska, 'Populists in the Shadow of Unanimity: Contestation of EU Foreign and Security Policy' (2024) 12 *Politics and Governance*, doi.org/10.17645/pag.8099.

[75] See, for instance, the comments by the Prime Minister of Italy, Georgia Meloni: 'EU doomed to 'irrelevance' in face of US, Chinese competition, Meloni warns' (Politico, 27 August 2025), www.politico.eu/article/eu-doomed-irrelevance-facing-us-china-competition-italy-pm-giorgia-meloni-says.

[76] Calle Håkansson, 'The Ukraine War and the Emergence of the European Commission as a Geopolitical Actor' (2023) 46 *Journal of European Integration* 25.

impose significant costs on adversaries, effectively weaponising its strength as an international economic actor, even when there might be significant economic costs to bear. This intersection of internal and external policy underscores the complexity of EU foreign policy and its potential for strategic influence. All of this depends, of course, on whether the sanctions themselves are effective in meeting their goals. But given the possibility for political and institutional division amongst the Member States, a collective agreement to impose sanctions serves as a demonstration of the EU's ability to act on its words collectively and decisively, and putting to bed the critiques of the CFSP of the past. The success of sanctions depends not only on legal frameworks but also on political unity and enforcement capacity.

In short, the EU's foreign policy is at a pivotal moment. The invasion of Ukraine has forced a reckoning with long-standing structural and political challenges. While there are signs of maturation – such as increased strategic awareness, institutional visibility, and effective use of economic tools – significant obstacles remain. The path to becoming a fully fledged strategic actor requires more than crisis response; it demands institutional reform, political will, and a coherent vision for the future.

Whether the EU has truly 'come of age' in foreign policy and whether the EU can be considered to act alongside nation states on the same terms are still open questions. The current trajectory suggests progress, but the journey is far from complete, and always subject to a potential division of views between the Member States. The coming years will be critical in determining whether the EU can transform its potential into sustained global influence, balancing its civilian legacy with the demands of a changing geopolitical landscape.

5

The European Union's Unprecedented Sanctions against Russia: Legal and Institutional Implications

PETER VAN ELSUWEGE AND CELIA CHALLET

5.1 INTRODUCTION

The response of the EU to Russia's full-scale invasion of Ukraine in 2022 has been widely described as 'unprecedented' in both scale and character.[1] At the end of 2025, the EU had adopted 19 sanctions packages, introducing a wide variety of sanctions. This includes restrictive measures against individuals and entities, economic sanctions targeting Russia's financial, trade, energy, transport and defence sectors, and specific sanctions such as a broadcasting ban for state-sponsored Russian media outlets and a prohibition of providing certain services such as IT consultancy or legal advice.[2]

Significantly, the 19 sanctions packages build upon the list of sanctions that were adopted already in 2014 in response to the destabilising events in Eastern Ukraine and Russia's illegal annexation of Crimea.[3] As a result, the relevant legal instruments imposing the restrictive measures against Russia go back to this period and were gradually extended and supplemented with additional sanctions regimes. In essence, six sets of restrictive measures can be distinguished: (i) sanctions aimed at putting an end to 'actions undermining or threatening the territorial integrity, sovereignty and independence of Ukraine';[4] (ii) sanctions

[1] For instance, the EU Council's website refers to 'massive and unprecedented sanctions', www.consilium.europa.eu/en/policies/sanctions-against-russia-explained.

[2] ibid.

[3] Significantly, the post-2014 sanctions were already described as 'unprecedented in both target and scope'. See Sabine Fischer, 'European Union Sanctions Against Russia: Objectives, Impacts and Next Steps' *SWP Comments* (March 2014), www.swp-berlin.org/publications/products/comments/2015C17_fhs.pdf5.

[4] Council Decision 2014/145/CFSP and Council Regulation (EU) No 269/2014 of 17 March 2014 concerning restrictive measures in respect of actions undermining or threatening the territorial integrity, sovereignty and independence of Ukraine [2014] OJ L78/6.

adopted in view of 'Russia's actions destabilising the situation in Ukraine';[5] (iii) sanctions in response to the illegal annexation of Crimea and Sevastopol;[6] (iv) sanctions 'in response to the recognition of the non-government-controlled areas of the Donetsk and Luhansk oblasts of Ukraine and the ordering of Russian armed forces into those areas';[7] (v) sanctions in response to the accelerating and systemic repression in Russia;[8] and (vi) sanctions in response to Russia's destabilising activities against the EU and its Member States.[9]

The first three sets of restrictive measures were already established in 2014 and significantly extended with every new package of sanctions. The fourth set of measures was adopted after Russia's full-scale invasion of Ukraine in February 2022. The fifth set of measures was introduced in 2024 after the tragic death of opposition politician Alexey Navalny. The sixth set of measures – the last one adopted to date – was enacted in October 2024 in response to Russia's (attempts of) foreign interference in the EU through hybrid actions. In addition, the Council has listed several Russian individuals under the (horizontal) EU Global Human Rights Sanctions regime for their gross violations of human rights in Ukraine during the war (eg in Bucha).[10]

Taken together, the EU's sanctions against Russia may indeed be regarded as unprecedented for a number of reasons. First, from a quantitative point of view, Russia is the most sanctioned country by the EU in terms of listed persons and entities, exceeding by far the sanctions list of countries such as Syria, Iran and North Korea.[11] Russia is also the most sanctioned country in terms of EU sectoral restrictive measures, which have affected the import and export of an exceptionally wide and diversified range of products and services.

Second, from a qualitative perspective, the EU sanctions against Russia stand out in comparison to other sanctions regimes. While certain precedents may be found in other EU sanctions regimes (eg against Iran or North Korea) restrictive measures such as the broadcasting ban, the oil price cap or the ban on legal advisory services are novelties in the EU's sanctions practice. The immobilisation of

[5] Council Decision 2014/512/CFSP and Council Regulation (EU) No 833/2014 of 31 July 2014 concerning restrictive measures in view of Russia's actions destabilising the situation in Ukraine [2014] OJ L229/1.

[6] Council Decision 2014/386/CFSP and Council Regulation (EU) No 692/2014 of 23 June 2014 concerning restrictions on goods originating in Crimea or Sevastopol, in response to the illegal annexation of Crimea and Sevastopol [2014] OJ L183/9.

[7] Council Decision (CFSP) 2022/266 and Council Regulation (EU) 2022/263 of 23 February 2022 concerning restrictive measures in response to the recognition of the non-government controlled areas of the Donetsk and Luhansk oblasts of Ukraine and the ordering of Russian armed forces into those areas [2022] OJ L 42/77.

[8] Council Decision (CFSP) 2024/1484 of 27 and Council Regulation 2024/1485 of 27 May 2024 concerning restrictive measures in view of the situation in Russia [2024] OJ L1485.

[9] Council Decision (CFSP) 2024/2643 of 8 October 2024 and Council Regulation (EU) 2024/2642 of 8 October 2024 concerning restrictive measures in view of Russia's destabilizing activities [2024] OJ L2642.

[10] For an overview of sanctioned individuals, see www.sanctionsmap.eu.

[11] ibid.

the Russian Central Bank assets, while not the first freeze of this kind in history,[12] also marked a significant step within the EU's sanctions practice. The EU has displayed considerable legal creativity by devising mechanisms to channel immobilised revenues and tax windfall profits to finance Ukraine's reconstruction.[13] The discussions on a possible use of frozen Russian state assets to finance loans for Ukraine[14] and the EU's decision to immobilise those assets on the 'emergency' legal basis of Article 122 Treaty on the Functioning of the European Union (TFEU)[15] further illustrate the unprecedented developments triggered by the Russia sanctions.

Third, as a consequence of the quantitative and qualitative dimensions, the EU sanctions against Russia are also the most complex and most sophisticated, triggering an unprecedented list of implementation challenges. It is sufficient to look at the long list of 'frequently asked questions', prepared by the Commission services to guide national authorities, EU operators and citizens with the application of sanctions.[16] At the end of 2025, this document already counted more than 450 pages. Significantly, that guidance is non-binding since 'only the Court of Justice of the EU is competent to interpret EU law'.[17] Not surprisingly, the volume and scope of the EU sanctions against Russia also resulted in an unprecedented number of judicial proceedings before the Court of Justice of the European Union (CJEU).[18]

Proceeding from these observations, this contribution analyses the specific nature and long-term institutional implications of the EU's sanctions against Russia. How do those sanctions differ from previous EU sanctions regimes and

[12] See the United States' sanctions against Syria (US Executive Order 13582, Blocking Property of the Government of Syria and Prohibiting Certain Transactions with Respect to Syria, 2011), Iran (Executive Order 13599, Blocking Property of the Government of Iran and Iranian Financial Institutions, 2012), and Afghanistan (Executive Order 14064 2022, Protecting Certain Property of the Afghanistan Bank for the Benefit of the People of Afghanistan, 2022).

[13] 'Extraordinary revenues generated by immobilised Russian assets: Council greenlights the use of net windfall profits to support Ukraine's self-defence and reconstruction' Council Press release (27 March 2024); Anna Caprile and Tim Peters with Ana Luisa Melo Almeida, *Confiscation of immobilised Russian sovereign assets: State of play, arguments and scenarios*, European Parliament Research Service Briefing, September 2025.

[14] Peter Van Elsuwege, 'Walking a Tightrope: On the Legal Stakes of the EU's Proposed Reparations Loan for Ukraine' Verfassungsblog (8 December 2025).

[15] Council Regulation (EU) 2025/2600 of 12 December 2025 on emergency measures addressing the serious economic difficulties caused by Russia's actions in the context of the war of aggression against Ukraine [2025] OJ L2600.

[16] Commission Consolidated FAQs on the implementation of Council Regulation No 833/2014 and Council Regulation No 269/2014, at https://finance.ec.europa.eu/publications/consolidated-version_en.

[17] This caveat is explicitly mentioned in the Commission's FAQ document. See also the *Jemerak* case where the Court of Justice held that the authentication by a notary of a contract for the sale of immovable property belonging to a legal person established in Russia is not covered by the ban on legal services, whereas the Commission had suggested otherwise. See: Case C-109/03, *Jemerak* EU:C:2024:681.

[18] Celia Challet, *Sanctions against Russia and the Court of Justice of the EU* (Brill, 2026), forthcoming.

to what extent does this affect the EU's sanctions policy in practice? Various dimensions can be identified to answer this question. First, the chapter analyses the evolution towards broad designation criteria for the adoption of individual sanctions as well as the introduction of new sectoral sanctions. This evolution raises critical questions relating to the EU's compliance with fundamental rights, the principle of proportionality, and its own sanctions competence (section 5.2). Second, the unprecedented focus on ensuring sanctions effectiveness has led to new anti-circumvention mechanisms, some of which are also subject to legal debates (section 5.3). Third, the EU sanctions against Russia have triggered significant institutional innovations and an evolution towards the adoption of complementary measures outside the EU's Common Foreign and Security Policy (CFSP) (section 5.4). The combination of all these elements implies that the EU's sanctions against Russia may be regarded as a 'game-changer' in the EU's sanctions practice with long-term legal and institutional consequences. Sanctions are no longer merely a foreign policy instrument but increasingly permeate the entire EU legal order (section 5.5).

5.2 THE EVER-EXPANDING SCOPE OF EU SANCTIONS AGAINST RUSSIA: ARE THERE ANY LIMITS TO THE COUNCIL'S DISCRETION?

The dynamic evolution of the EU's sanctions against Russia triggered new legal questions that have been the subject of various cases before the EU courts. Broadly speaking, two main trends can be distinguished. On the one hand, the Council gradually developed and expanded the designation criteria for the sanctions listing of natural and legal persons. On the other hand, the EU's sanctions practice entered into uncharted territories with the adoption of new sectoral sanctions such as inter alia the banning of broadcasting and certain legal services. Both evolutions raise questions about the balance between the Council's discretion in adopting sanctions as an instrument of EU foreign policy and respect for fundamental rights in the EU legal order.

5.2.1 The Evolution of Sanctions Designations and the Role of the Court of Justice

According to the Council Sanctions Guidelines, 'the decision to subject a person or entity to targeted restrictive measures requires clear criteria, tailored to each specific case'.[19] Such a decision must be taken on 'a sufficiently solid factual basis'.[20] This implies that sanctions designations must be substantially motivated

[19] Council of the EU, *Sanctions Guidelines* (2018) doc 5664/18, 9.

[20] Joined Cases C584/10 P, C593/10 P and C595/10 P *Commission and Others v Yassin Adbullah Kadi* EU:C:2013:518 (*Kadi II*) para 119.

and based on verifiable information. Since the war in Ukraine makes it difficult in practice to access certain sources, designations are often based on indirect references, such as press articles and websites.[21] Whereas this practice is not exclusively related to the EU's sanctions against Russia,[22] the use of open-source material is now (more) widely accepted.[23]

Apart from the more flexible approach towards the gathering of relevant information, the actual reasons for adding persons and entities on the EU's sanctions list also evolved over time. The initial sanctions focused on the targets' support for the actions and policies undermining Ukraine's territorial integrity or evidence that they were benefiting from Russian decision-makers. Such conduct-based designations turned out to be difficult to prove when challenged before the CJEU. For instance, in the case of Aven and Fridman, the General Court found that the Council's evidence illustrated 'a degree of proximity' between the two oligarchs and Vladimir Putin, but that this was insufficient to conclude that they actually supported the regime's actions or policies.[24] Accordingly, the General Court annulled their initial listing, which was based on the 'support' criterion. The practical implications of this annulment turned out to be very minimal because the Council introduced additional, more broadly defined designation criteria. The so-called criterion (g) targeting 'leading businesspersons or legal persons, entities or bodies involved in economic sectors providing a substantial source of revenue to the Government of the Russian Federation' was an important game-changer. The core issue under this criterion is not the support of the targeted persons for Russia's actions against Ukraine or their close connections with the Russian leadership, but their activities in strategic economic sectors. This is a noticeable difference in comparison to the sanctions regime against Syria, where leading businesspersons were targeted because of their close links with the Syrian regime.[25] Under the Russia sanctions, the existence of a close connection with the Russian leadership is irrelevant because the reason for their targeting is related to their business activity in a sector that provides a substantial source of revenue for the Russian Government.[26] This makes it more difficult

[21] See eg Case T-193/22 *OT v Council* [2023] EU: T:2023:716 paras 116–20.

[22] With respect to the EU sanctions against Syria, the CJEU referred to 'the difficulty in obtaining more specific evidence in a state at civil war and having an authoritarian regime'. See Case C-630/13 P *Anbouba v Council* EU:C:2015:247, para 47; Case T-257/19 *Al Zoubi v Council* EU: T:2021:819, para 50.

[23] For a critical note on this evolution, see Antonino Ali, 'Examining the Legality of EU Restrictive Measures on the Russian Federation: The Information Gathering Process in Sanction Imposition' in Antonio Bultrini, Francesco Giumelli, Clara Portela and Mirko Sossai (eds), *International Sanctions in Practice: An Interdisciplinary Perspective* (Routledge, 2024) 35–36.

[24] Case T-301/22 *Aven v Council* EU:T:2024:214 and Case T-304/22 *Fridman v Council* EU:T:2024:215.

[25] Francesca Finelli, 'Countering Circumvention of Restrictive Measures: the EU Response' (2023) 60 *CML Review* 733.

[26] See the Opinion of Advocate General Medina in Case 696/23 P *Pumpayanski v Council* EU:C: 2025:409, para 72.

for Russian oligarchs to challenge the validity of the restrictive measures before the CJEU.[27]

Significantly, the scope of criterion (g) gradually extended to include also 'immediate family members' of leading businesspersons and 'other natural persons, benefitting from them' as well as other businesspersons providing revenue for the Government.[28] Moreover, additional listing criteria were added, inter alia for facilitating infringements on the prohibition against sanctions circumvention or for frustrating the relevant sanctions provisions.[29] Taken together, this expansion of the listing criteria in the Council's sanctions practice regarding Russia goes much further than in other sanctions regimes. It is based upon the dual objective to exert maximum pressure on the Russian Government to desist from it military aggression against Ukraine and to avoid the risk of sanctions circumvention.[30]

The impact of this evolution is mostly visible with respect to the targeting of family members of leading businesspersons. With respect to the category of 'associated' family members, the established case law clearly provides that individuals cannot be designated on the sole basis of their family ties with leading business figures in a targeted country.[31] Following a confirmation of this approach in cases such as *Prighozina*[32] and *Mazepin*,[33] the Council amended criterion (g) and introduced another significant evolution in the EU's targeting practice. As explained by the General Court in *Ezubov v Council*, the extended criterion (g) now includes two categories of family members: the ones that are deemed to be 'associated' with the leading businesspersons because of the existence of economic or business links and the ones that have benefited from them.[34] With this further extension, the Council again broadened the scope of its sanctions designations in response to the General Court's earlier case law. However, the new requirement also has its limitations. In view of the objective of avoiding sanctions circumvention, the General Court (GC) defined the beneficiary requirement as 'any benefit regardless of its nature, which is not necessarily undue, but which must be quantitatively or qualitatively non-negligible'.[35] Accordingly, the GC put some limits to a potentially very wide interpretation of this designation

[27] Francesca Finelli, 'Who are the Russian Oligarchs? Recent Developments in the Case Law of the European Court of Justice', (2023) 8 *European Papers* 1516.

[28] Art 2(1)(g) of Council Decision 2014/145/CFSP (consolidated version).

[29] ibid, Art 2(1)(h).

[30] Council Decision 2023/1094/CFSP of 5 June 2023 amending Decision 2014/145/CFSP concerning restrictive measures in respect of actions undermining or threatening the territorial integrity, sovereignty and independence of Ukraine [2023] OJ L146/20, recitals 4 and 5.

[31] Case C-376/10 P *Tay Za v Council* EU: 2012:138.

[32] Case T-212/22 *Prighozina v Council* EU: T:2023:104, para 95.

[33] Case T743/22 *Mazepin v Council* EU: T:2024:180, para 92.

[34] Case T-273/24 *Ezubov v Council* EU: T:2025:628, para 32.

[35] ibid, para 46.

criterion. In *Tokareva*, it also excluded the possibility for the Council to target a person who is not directly associated with a person on the sanctions list.[36]

Hence, the EU's sanctions practice reveals a constant 'back-and-forth' between the Council and the Court. Since the adoption of the initial sanctions against Russia in 2014, the designation criteria for listing individuals and entities have been constantly amended to address difficulties of compliance with the standards of judicial review. This has resulted in an expanded list of designation criteria, which is more far-reaching in comparison to previous sanctions regimes to address the flaws identified by the EU courts in the original sanctions listings. Whereas the Council has a broad discretion in defining and re-defining those criteria, the Court has to ensure that their application in practice is in line with their determined objectives and scope.

5.2.2 Entering Uncharted Territories: The Adoption of Innovative Sectoral Sanctions

Apart from the expanded listing of natural and legal persons, the EU sanctions against Russia also stand out because they introduced specific restrictions of a more general nature. The very nature of these measures have raised questions about the Council's competence to adopt such measures, as well as their compliance with fundamental rights. Two sectoral measures deserve particular attention in this respect: the broadcast ban against selected Russian media; and the ban on legal advisory services.

The broadcast ban against certain Russian media, introduced in the immediate aftermath of Russia's invasion of Ukraine,[37] was a particularly innovative measure adopted under the CFSP. For the first time, the Council adopted an EU-wide prohibition for EU operators and internet providers from broadcasting the contents of media from a specific country. This measure was complemented by, or perhaps paved the way for, an increased use of sanctions against journalists and a stand-alone regime responding to Russia's destabilising activities,[38] thereby signalling a broader effort to address propaganda and disinformation through EU sanctions.

At the time, the prohibition stood out as one of the most controversial EU restrictive measures against Russia. Some argued that the Council had

[36] Case T-744/22 *Tokareva v Council* EU: T:2024:608, para 49.

[37] Council Decision (CFSP) 2022/351 of 1 March 2022 amending Decision 2014/512/CFSP concerning restrictive measures in view of Russia's actions destabilising the situation in Ukraine [2022] OJ L65/5; Council Regulation (EU) 2022/350 of 1 March 2022 amending Regulation (EU) No 833/2014 concerning restrictive measures in view of Russia's actions destabilising the situation in Ukraine [2022] OJ L65/1.

[38] See Celia Challet, 'Politique étrangère et de sécurité commune et lutte contre la propagande: les sanctions de l'Union européenne à l'épreuve de la liberté d'expression' in Christophe Meaubernard, Sébastien Platon and Romain Tinière (eds), *Les mutations de la liberté d'expression dans l'Union européenne* (Bruylant, 2025) 221–38.

overstepped its CFSP competence by adopting a measure that pertained to media regulation and by precluding any control by an independent regulator.[39] Significant concerns were voiced as to the risk of arbitrariness raised by the ban[40] as well as its compliance with the freedom of expression and information in the meaning of Article 11(1) of the Charter of Fundamental Rights ('the Charter').[41]

These questions reached the General Court, whose landmark ruling in *RT France*[42] confirmed that the Council could adopt the broadcast ban under the CFSP and that the circumstances justified a restriction to the freedom of expression and information as entailed by the broadcast ban. With respect to the Council's competence, the General Court dismissed Russia Today's claim that only national regulatory authorities could impose sanctions on an audiovisual media outlet.[43] The broadcast ban aims to protect the EU 'against disinformation and destabilisation campaigns conducted by media outlets under the control of [Russia's leadership] which threatened the Union's public order and security, in a context marked by military aggression against Ukraine'.[44] It thus contributes to the objectives of peace and security under Article 3(1) and (5) Treaty on European Union (TEU) since 'propaganda and disinformation campaigns are capable of undermining the foundations of democratic societies and are an integral part of the arsenal of modern warfare'.[45] In any event, the General Court stressed that the national authorities' competence pursues different objectives and, unlike a CFSP action, it cannot guarantee a uniform and immediate intervention throughout the EU's territory.[46] This approach was further confirmed in *A2B Connect*: 'the competence attributed to the national administrative authorities by domestic law does not pursue the same objectives, is not based on the same premisses or the same values',[47] and the ban applies 'irrespective of the Member State in which [EU] operators are established and of the mode by which the content is broadcast'.[48] In other words, the effectiveness of the measure dictates an action at EU level and justifies the Council's competence to enact the ban.

[39] European Federation of Journalists, 'Fighting disinformation with censorship is a mistake' (1 March 2022), https://europeanjournalists.org/blog/2022/03/01/fighting-disinformation-with-censorship-is-a-mistake; Case T-307/22 *A2B Connect and Others v Council* EU:T:2025:331, paras 41–62.

[40] Viktor Szép and Ramses A Wessel, 'Balancing restrictive measures and media freedom: RT France v Council' (2023) 60 *CML Review* 1384.

[41] Igor Popovic, 'The EU Ban of RT and Sputnik: Concerns Regarding Freedom of Expressions' *EJIL:Talk* (30 March 2022); Ronan O Fathaigh and Dirk Voorhoof, 'Freedom of Expression and the EU's Ban on Russia Today: A Dangerous Rubicon Crossed' (2022) 27 *Communications Law* 186.

[42] Case T-125/22 *RT France v Council* EU:T:2022:483.

[43] ibid, para 46.

[44] ibid, para 55.

[45] ibid, para 56.

[46] ibid, para 58.

[47] *A2B Connect* (n 39) para 57.

[48] ibid.

Importantly, in *RT France* the General Court dismissed the applicant's claim that the broadcast ban entailed a disproportionate restriction of the freedom of expression and information under Article 11(1) of the Charter. The General Court recalled that, notwithstanding the essential role of audiovisual media in democratic societies, journalists have 'duties and responsibilities' to act in good faith and provide 'reliable and precise information'.[49] Applying a detailed several-step reasoning, the General Court first stated that the prohibition has clear legal bases in EU law (ie Article 29 TEU and Article 215 TFEU)[50] and that

> it was foreseeable that … the large-scale media support for the military aggression against Ukraine by [Russia], provided during television and internet broadcasts by a media outlet entirely funded by the Russian State budget, could be targeted by such broadcast ban.[51]

The Court also considered that the essence of the applicant's freedom of expression was not impaired. The broadcast is temporary since it may only be renewed if two conditions continue to be fulfilled: 1) the continuation of Russia's aggression against Ukraine; and 2) the continuation, by Russia and its associated media outlets, of 'propaganda actions against the Union and its Member States'.[52] The Court held that the measure also pursues an objective of general interest, notably given that it aims to protect the EU's public order and security against propaganda and disinformation.[53] Finally, the Court considered that the broadcast ban was proportionate. There was evidence that RT France was controlled by Russian leaders[54] and that it had engaged in propaganda in support of Russia's aggression against Ukraine,[55] notably by offering a 'manifest imbalance'[56] in the views expressed by its invited speakers.[57] Crucially, the Court held that the ban was both appropriate and necessary as at the time, in the context of extreme urgency of the Russian invasion, no other measure could have achieved the same outcome.[58]

The Court's reasoning, which it reiterated in *A2B Connect*, is thus particularly important for the Council's practice. While it has sparked legal discussions that would go beyond the scope of this chapter,[59] in the *RT France* judgment,

[49] *RT France* (n 42) paras 133–38. The General Court referred, in particular, to *NIT SRL v Republic of Moldova*, 28470/12, paras 177–82.
[50] *RT France* (n 42) para 149.
[51] ibid, para 151.
[52] ibid, para 155.
[53] ibid, paras 161–62.
[54] ibid, paras 171–74.
[55] ibid, paras 180–85.
[56] ibid, para 211.
[57] ibid, para 186.
[58] ibid, para 197.
[59] Björstern Baade, 'EU Sanctions Against Propaganda for War – Reflections on the General Court's Judgment in Case T-125/22 (RT France)' (2023) *ZaöRV* 257; Björnstern Baade, 'The EU's "Ban" of RT and Sputnik: A Lawful Measure Against Propaganda for War' *Verfassungsblog* (8 March 2022); Fathaigh and Voorhoof (n 41); Luigi Lonardo, 'Censorship in the EU as a Result of

the Court affirmed the Council's margin of discretion to address situations of conflict through restrictive measures which, though prima facie associated with other fields of EU law, are motivated by EU security objectives.

In another important strand of case law, the Court of Justice has examined the legal implications of the ban on legal advisory services and assessed its compatibility with fundamental rights. The latter was bound to be a core aspect of the cases given that the ban effectively prohibits any form of legal advice to Russian legal persons and entities, regardless of whether they are individually targeted or affected by sectoral restrictions. In three distinct actions for annulment against the prohibition,[60] several bar associations argued that the Council had infringed the right to consult a lawyer in order to obtain legal advice in the meaning of Articles 47 and 7 of the Charter.[61] According to them, these provisions protected a fundamental right of access to legal advice from a lawyer, in contentious but also non-contentious matters.[62] This argument did not convince the General Court. While it recalled the 'cardinal importance' of the right to effective judicial protection under Article 47 of the Charter,[63] which includes the possibility to be advised, defended and represented by a lawyer, the General Court stressed that this provision does not protect a right for legal advisory services. Notwithstanding the 'fundamental role of lawyers in a State governed by the rule of law',[64] neither the Charter, nor Member States' constitutional traditions provide a fundamental right for all persons to have access to and be advised by a lawyer other than in the context of existing or probable litigation.[65] The right of access to and advice from a lawyer is only to be guaranteed in the event of a 'link to judicial proceedings have already been commenced or can be pre-empted or anticipated, on the basis of tangible elements, at the stage at which the lawyer assesses his or her client's legal situation'.[66]

This outcome is particularly significant for the EU's sanctions practice. This unprecedented measure was conceived as a cornerstone of the EU's fight against sanctions circumvention, based on the understanding that lawyers may serve as an important vector (if not facilitator) of circumvention. It remains to be seen whether the judgments will be upheld by the Court of Justice (all first instance

the War in Ukraine. *RT France v Council of the European Union*' (2023) 48 *European Law Review* 707; Sara Poli and Francesca Finelli, 'Context specific and structural changes in EU restrictive measures adopted in reaction to Russia's aggression on Ukraine' (2023) 3 *Eurojus* 33.

[60] Case T-797/22 *Ordre néerlandais des avocats du barreau de Bruxelles v Council* EU:T:2024:670; Case T-798/22 *Ordre des avocats à la cour de Paris and Couturier v Council* EU:T:2024 :671; Case T-828/22 *ACE v Council* EU:T:2024:672.

[61] Case T-797/22 (n 60) para 30.

[62] ibid.

[63] ibid, para 40.

[64] ibid, para 43. The Court referred, in this respect, to Case 155/79, *AM & S Europe v Commission* EU:C:1982:157, para 18.

[65] ibid, paras 49–50.

[66] ibid, para 51.

judgments have been appealed).[67] In the affirmative, the appeal judgments would provide an important confirmation that the Council may explore new types of measures to step up its response to circumvention.

Admittedly, one may ponder whether the General Court sufficiently considered the legal consequences of the ban, which are unparallelled too. According to the applicants, it is 'artificial and inappropriate' to distinguish between legal advisory services that are necessary to exercise the right to an effective remedy and those that are not.[68] Until a piece of legal advice is provided, it cannot entirely be determined whether it relates to future litigation. The applicants also argued that the wording of the prohibition could lead to a form of self-censorship by lawyers, thereby restricting access to legal advice in practice.[69] The General Court did not really engage with these concerns. Neither did the Court of Justice address, in *Jemerak*, the referring court's concern that if the ban on legal advisory services were interpreted in such a broad way as to prohibit notaries from merely authenticating lawful transactions involving non-sanctioned Russian entities, there would be a significant restriction on the right to property.[70] While the Court eventually ruled that the ban does not apply to authenticating notarial acts, thereby sidelining the Commission's FAQs on the matter,[71] it based its reasoning on the objective to ensure internal consistency within the Russia sanctions and on the fact that the latter did not prohibit non-sanctioned entities from selling their property.[72] Either way, both sets of judgments have inherently upheld the premise that the Council might take innovative sectoral measures to respond to Russia's war against Ukraine.

5.3 TACKLING SANCTIONS CIRCUMVENTION AS A NEW PRIORITY

Another important feature of the EU's post-2022 Russia sanctions is the unprecedented attention to countering sanctions circumvention and closing loopholes to increase the effectiveness of the restrictive measures. Sanctions circumvention is by no means a new phenomenon and is an inevitable variable for each sanctions regime.[73] However, circumvention of the Russia sanctions has gained exceptional salience in the EU's sanctions practice due to several factors. First,

[67] Case C-865/24 P, *Ordre néerlandais des avocats du Barreau de Bruxelles and others v Council* (pending); Case C-866/24 P, *Ordre néerlandais des avocats à la cour de Paris et Couturier v Council* (pending); Case C-867/24 P, *ACE v Council* (pending).

[68] Case T-797/22 (n 60) para 32.

[69] ibid, paras 32–33.

[70] Case C-109/03, *Jemerak* EU:C:2024:681.

[71] ibid, para 30.

[72] ibid, para 49.

[73] On historical examples of sanctions circumvention, see Nicholas Mulder, *The Economic Weapon: The Rise of Sanctions as a Tool of Modern War* (Yale University Press, 2024) 1–24; Agathe Demarais, *Backfire: How Sanctions Reshape the World Against U.S. Interests* (Cambridge University

the scale of the EU's sanctions, coupled with the imperative to make them effective to constrain Russia's capacity to wage war against Ukraine and to safeguard the Union's security interests, has significantly raised the stakes.[74] Second, prior economic interdependence between the EU and Russia has made compliance particularly demanding. Third, Russia has engaged in systematic and coordinated efforts to circumvent the sanctions. The most emblematic example of that is Russia's so-called 'shadow fleet', a network of obscurely owned tankers that transport Russian oil illicitly, notably through ship-to-ship transfers. While the practice of using a shadow fleet long predates the post-2022 sanctions against Russia (notable examples include Iran, North Korea and Venezuela),[75] it has expanded dramatically since then.[76] Another form of circumvention implies the use of front or shell companies which act as intermediaries for sanctioned entities or obscure the end-users of restricted products.[77] Russia has also redirected trade through alternative routes such as Turkey, Kazakhstan and China.[78] Finally, there has been a marked increase in Russia's use of alternative payment systems, including crypto-assets, to mitigate the impact of EU financial restrictions and SWIFT-related measures.[79]

As a result of these combined factors, the EU's response to sanctions circumvention has been unprecedented legally, politically, and operationally. The EU has adopted a growing set of instruments which, taken together, represent a turning point for the law and practice of EU sanctions.

The *first tool* used by the EU is evidently based upon the CFSP. Since 2022, the EU has amended the restrictive measures to introduce new provisions targeting circumvention. This is particularly evident regarding sanctions involving individual listings, such as asset freezes. The Council has broadened the listing criteria to target a wider range of individuals and entities involved in circumvention (see section 5.2). This includes individuals who facilitate sanctions evasion,[80] those

Press, 2022); Keith A Prevle and Charmaine N Willis, 'Trading with Pariahs: North Korean Sanctions and the Challenge of Weaponized Interdependence' (2024) 4 *Global Studies Quarterly*.

[74] Anna Caprile and Cristina Cirlig, 'EU sanctions against Russia 2025: State of play, perspectives and challenges' EPRS Briefing (2025), www.europarl.europa.eu/RegData/etudes/BRIE/2025/767243/EPRS_BRI(2025)767243_EN.pdf.

[75] See John Frittelli, 'The Global Oil Tanker Market: An Overview as It Relates to Sanctions' (Congressional Research Service, 2024), www.congress.gov/crs-product/R47962.

[76] Anna Caprile and Cabija Leclerc, 'Russia's "shadow fleet": Bringing the threat to light' EPRS Briefing (2025), www.europarl.europa.eu/thinktank/en/document/EPRS_BRI(2024)766242.

[77] See, for instance, Elżbieta Kaca, 'Countering the circumvention of EU sanctions against Russia by foreign compagnies' (Polish Institute of International Affairs, 2025), www.pism.pl/publications/countering-the-circumvention-of-eu-sanctions-against-russia-by-foreign-companies?.

[78] Oliver Ruth, 'The Impact of Sanctions and Alliances on Russian Military Capabilities' (RUSI, 2025), www.rusi.org/explore-our-research/publications/commentary/impact-sanctions-and-alliances-russian-military-capabilities.

[79] 'Crypto coin for Russian shadow payment moves $9bn' *Financial Times* (2025), www.ft.com/content/1c71cac0-b86b-4361-8f54-ee5d3bb5a489; European Commission, 'EU adopts 19th package of sanctions against Russia' (2025), https://finance.ec.europa.eu/news/eu-adopts-19th-package-sanctions-against-russia-2025-10-23_en.

[80] Council Regulation 269/2014 (n 4) as amended by subsequent acts, Art 3(1)h.

who own or operate vessels in Russia's shadow fleet (particularly transporting crude oil or petroleum products),[81] and, under the so-called 'criterion g', leading businesspersons operating in Russia, their immediate family members, or other natural persons benefiting from them.[82]

It is on the basis of this criterion that the EU has targeted Russian oligarchs and their inner circle.[83] The Council has also introduced a reporting obligation for listed individuals: they must declare all resources located in each relevant Member State.[84] Failure to do so constitutes circumvention, which may potentially lead to confiscation.[85] In May 2025, to prevent the delisting of Russian oligarchs who resigned or sold their business interests in order to claim that they no longer fulfilled their designation grounds, the Council amended the restrictive measures. It is now specified that even if such persons resign from their position or sell their shares, they will continue to be considered leading businesspersons unless sufficient, recent, and reliable information demonstrates otherwise.[86] While this is legally questionable as it effectively reverses the burden of proof and introduces a form of presumption that listed targets continue to fulfil the listing criteria,[87] it aims to prevent a premature release of assets. Additionally, the Council has sanctioned entities located in third countries, including India, China, and Kazakhstan, which contribute to Russia's military and technological development, ensuring that alternative supply chains supporting Russia's defence capabilities are targeted.[88]

The EU's fight against circumvention is also visible with respect to the sectoral restrictions adopted under the CFSP. The EU has prohibited legal advisory services to Russian entities,[89] the transit of dual-use goods via Russia,[90] the re-export of sensitive goods to Russia (the so-called 'no Russia clause'),[91] and access to EU ports for vessels suspected of violating sanctions, including more than 500 vessels in Russia's shadow fleet transporting military equipment or stolen grain.[92] Furthermore, the EU included a provision to ban exports to third countries that have been 'identified by the Council as having systematically and

[81] ibid, Art 3(1)k.

[82] ibid, Art 3(1)g.

[83] Celia Challet, 'Op-Ed: No Links, Still Listed: Reflections on AG Medina's Opinions in Russian Leading Businesspersons Cases' EU Law Live (2025), https://eulawlive.com/op-ed-no-links-still-listed-reflections-on-ag-medinas-opinions-in-russian-leading-businesspersons-cases.

[84] Council Regulation 269/2014 as amended by Council Regulation 2022/1273 [2022] OJ L194/1, Art 9(2).

[85] See Council Regulation (EU) 2022/880 amending Regulation 269/2014 [2022] OJ L153/75.

[86] Council Decision 2025/904 amending Decision 2014/145/CFSP [2025] OJ L2025/904.

[87] Challet (n 18).

[88] Marco Sibona, 'Tackling Circumvention of EU Sanctions' (Jacques Delors Institute, 2024) 4, https://institutdelors.eu/content/uploads/2025/04/PB_241001_Sanctions_Sibona_EN_3.pdf.

[89] Council Regulation 833/2014 (n 5) as amended by Council Regulation 2022/1904 [2022] OJ LI259/3, Art 5n(a).

[90] Council Regulation 833/2014, as amended by subsequent acts, Art 2(1)a.

[91] ibid, Art 12g.

[92] ibid, Art 3s.

persistently failed to prevent [their] sale, ply, transfer or export to Russia'.[93] This provision signalled the EU's willingness to place the fight against circumvention at the forefront of its Russia sanctions. This was further illustrated by the nineteenth package of sanctions targeting Russia, adopted on 23 October 2025.[94] To disrupt the shadow fleet, the package expands listings across the entire maritime value chain – covering insurers, maritime registries providing false flags, shipbuilders, port operators, and key facilitators such as Lukoil's UAE-based trading arm. The reinsurance of vessels belonging to the shadow fleet is now also prohibited.[95] The EU also imposed a transaction ban on the state-backed stablecoin A7A5[96] as well as on several third-country banks that circumvent EU sanctions.[97] Finally, the EU has imposed restrictions on maintaining relationships with entities active in several Russian special economic zones.[98]

The *second tool* is based on EU criminal law. A Council decision in 2023 identified sanctions violations as an EU crime under Article 83(1) TFEU,[99] paving the way for a directive harmonising national offences and penalties.[100] This marks an important step toward integrating sanctions enforcement into the EU criminal law framework, which has been complemented by a parallel increase in the cooperation between the European Anti-Fraud Office (OLAF) and Europol.[101] The adoption of anti-money laundering directives and regulations in 2024 also aims to strengthen efforts to detect and prevent circumvention through financial channels.[102]

The *third tool* consists of multilateral cooperation and sanctions diplomacy. The appointment of an EU Sanctions Envoy strengthened outreach to third countries to close loopholes. The EU has established coordination mechanisms, including the Freeze and Seize Taskforce and the REPO Taskforce with G7 partners and Australia, to trace and freeze Russian assets.[103] Through the Global

[93] ibid, Art 12f. This option was first applied with respect to Kyrgyzstan as part of the 20th sanctions package, adopted in April 2026.

[94] Council Regulation 2025/2033 amending Regulation 833/2014 [2025] OJ L2025/2033.

[95] Council Regulation 833/2014 (n 5), as amended by Council Regulation 2025/2033 (n 94), Art 3s.

[96] ibid, annex LIII.

[97] ibid, annexes XLV and LVI.

[98] ibid, annex LII.

[99] Council Decision (EU) 2022/2332 on identifying the violation of Union restrictive measures as an area of crime that meets the criteria specified in Article 83(1) of the Treaty on the Functioning of the European Union [2022] OJ L308/18.

[100] Directive (EU) 2024/1226 on the definition of criminal offences and penalties for the violation of Union restrictive measures and amending Directive (EU) 2018/1673 [2024] OJ L2024/1226.

[101] OLAF 'OLAF and Europol join forces to strengthen the fight against circumvention' Press release (2025), https://anti-fraud.ec.europa.eu/media-corner/news/olaf-and-europol-join-forces-strengthen-fight-against-sanctions-circumvention-2025-11-20_en.

[102] For a detailed overview of this important anti-money laundering 'package' and the underpinning legal instruments, see Council of the EU, 'Anti-money laundering: Council adopts package of rules' Press release (2024), www.consilium.europa.eu/en/press/press-releases/2024/05/30/anti-money-laundering-council-adopts-package-of-rules.

[103] European Commission, 'Enforcing sanctions against listed Russian and Belarussian oligarchs: Commission's "Freeze and Seize" Task Force steps up work with international partners' Press release (2022), https://ec.europa.eu/commission/presscorner/detail/sv/ip_22_1828.

Export Control Coalition, which now comprises 39 countries, the EU participates in a Common High Priority List of critical items to harmonise export control requirements and limit international circumvention.[104]

The *last tool* comprises of additional operational measures targeting the Russian shadow fleet. In April 2025, the EU amended the 2022 Vessel Monitoring Directive to introduce a mandatory ship reporting system.[105] Some Member States, particularly in the Baltic region, have joined Operation Nordic Warden and NATO's Operation Baltic Sentry to monitor shadow fleet routes in real time and support the enforcement of the restrictions on access to EU ports.[106] These hard-security efforts have prompted an escalation with Russia, which dispatched fighter jets and missile-armed ships to escort certain tankers.[107] However, these developments precisely demonstrate the EU's willingness to act on an important pressure point for Russia.

Taken together, these measures reflect the EU's increasingly comprehensive approach to countering sanctions circumvention. At the same time, they also raise critical questions of legal certainty, proportionality and compliance with fundamental rights, particularly with respect to the measures adopted under the CFSP. The latter have led to several cases before the EU courts, in which the Council invoked the objective of preventing circumvention to justify the legality of the individual listings and of the sectoral measures (see section 5.2).

It was not necessarily obvious how the Court would approach this argument, especially as there was no judicial precedent for measures such as the reporting obligation and the ban on legal advisory services. While the developments within the case law have reflected a nuanced picture as to the weight of anti-circumvention objectives in the review of the legality of individual listings,[108] the Court has so far upheld the validity of some of the new sectoral measures aiming to respond to circumvention. In addition to upholding the ban on legal advisory services (see section 5.2.2), the General Court has ruled that the reporting obligation imposed on listed individuals subject to asset freezes complies with EU

[104] European Commission, 'EU and partners expand list of common high priority items to further weaken Russia's war effort' (2024), https://policy.trade.ec.europa.eu/news/eu-and-partners-expand-list-common-high-priority-items-further-weaken-russias-war-effort-2024-02-23_en.

[105] Commission Delegated Directive (EU) 2025/811 amending Annex I to Directive 2002/59/EC of the European Parliament and of the Council as regards information to be notified to ship reporting systems [2025] OJ L2025/811.

[106] See Gonzalo Saiz Erausquin and Tom Keatinge, 'Countering Shadow Fleet Activity through Flag State Reform' (RUSI, 2025), www.rusi.org/explore-our-research/publications/insights-papers/countering-shadow-fleet-activity-through-flag-state-reform.

[107] Joseph Ataman, 'Russian fighter jet protects "shadow fleet" vessel in first such move by Moscow, officials say' CNN (2025), https://edition.cnn.com/2025/05/20/europe/russian-fighter-jet-shadow-fleet-intl-cmd.

[108] Cases T-744/22, *Tokareva v Council* EU:T:2024:608; T-741/22; *Ezubov v Council* EU:T:2024:605; T-497/22, *Mordashova v Council* EU:T:2024:604. On these judgments, see Celia Challet, 'How far may the Council go to combat sanctions circumvention? Recent CJEU rulings on the restrictive measures against Russia' *EU Law Live* (2024), https://eulawlive.com/weekend-edition/weekend-edition-no207.

rules.[109] This obligation forms part of the EU's broader effort to enhance the effective and uniform implementation of sanctions and to counter increasingly sophisticated evasion schemes. Under this requirement, listed individuals must disclose the funds or economic resources within the territory of a Member State that belong to them or that they own, hold or control. Failure to report shall be considered as participating in the circumvention of asset freezes.[110]

Several Russian oligarchs challenged the legality of the reporting obligation before the General Court.[111] They claimed that the Council lacked a proper legal basis to impose such positive obligations on listed persons. According to the applicants, the Council had exceeded its competence under Article 215 TFEU – and, more broadly, within the CFSP framework – since such measures went beyond the mere implementation of CFSP decisions.[112] They further argued that the Council infringed Article 40 TEU and Article 83(1) TFEU: the execution of CFSP decisions lies with the Member States, not with the Council,[113] and any harmonisation of criminal penalties for breaches of restrictive measures must be carried out via directives adopted under the ordinary legislative procedure.[114] The applicants also claimed that the reporting obligation breached the principle of legal certainty, based on the premise that the notions of 'ownership' and 'control' are complex and subject to divergent interpretations from one Member State to another.[115]

The General Court dismissed these claims by placing the objective to ensure an effective and uniform implementation of the restrictive measures at the centre of its reasoning. On the question of legal basis, the General Court held that the reporting obligation fell squarely within the Council's competence under Article 215 TFEU. It recalled the implementing role of regulations adopted pursuant to CFSP decisions and found that the obligation followed the same logic: it aimed to ensure the effective and uniform implementation of restrictive measures in light of increasingly complex circumvention schemes.[116] The Court also referred to the unprecedented number of Russian listings, the persistence of circumvention practices, and the fact that when the reporting obligation was introduced, few domestic legislations already imposed it.[117] The measure thus complied with Article 215(2) TFEU. The General Court also dismissed the alleged infringement of Article 83(1) TFEU: non-compliance with the reporting obligation qualifies as circumvention and not as a crime, and Member States retain competence to

[109] Case T-635/22, *Fridman and Others v Council* EU:T:2024:620; Case T-644/22, *Timchenko v Council* EU:T:2024:621.
[110] Council Regulation 269/2014 (n 4), Art 9(3).
[111] *Fridman* (n 109); *Timchenko v Council* (n 109).
[112] *Fridman* (n 109) para 44; *Timchenko* (n 109) para 46.
[113] *Fridman* (n 109) para 49.
[114] ibid, para 6.
[115] *Timchenko* (n 109) paras 109–11.
[116] *Timchenko* (n 109) para 57.
[117] ibid, para 58.

determine the nature of the penalties applicable to breaches.[118] As to Article 40 TEU, the provision does not regulate the division of competences between the Union and the Member States and could not be relied upon in this context.[119]

With respect to legal certainty, the Court found that the notions of 'ownership' and 'control' constitute autonomous concepts of EU law, which do not display 'such ambiguity' as to create legal uncertainty in the procedures before national authorities.[120] The Court recalled its previous case law, according to which a company may be considered owned or controlled by another entity 'when it was in a situation where that other entity was in a position to influence its choices, even in the absence of any legal link of ownership or shareholding between either of those two economic entities'.[121]

The General Court's reasoning was recently confirmed by the Court of Justice in the *Timchenko* appeal case.[122] The Court not only confirmed the Council's competence to adopt the reporting obligation on the basis of Article 215(2) TFEU,[123] but it also stressed that this provision's reference to 'restrictive measures' does not limit the Council to adopting prohibitions only.[124] The Council may also impose positive obligations on listed persons when this is necessary to make sanctions effective.[125] The Court's appeal judgment is thus significant as it preserves the Council's discretion to adopt additional measures to strengthen the implementation of asset freezes.

5.4 THE CREEPING SUPRANATIONALISATION OF EU SANCTIONS POLICY

The scale and complexity of the EU's sanctions against Russia reveal a broader trend in the EU's sanctions practice. In essence, this implies that sanctions can no longer be seen as a typical foreign policy instrument that is subject to the classic intergovernmental mechanisms of the CFSP. This is particularly visible at the institutional level, with an increasingly dominant role for the European Commission in the sanctions policy cycle. In addition, the Russia sanctions triggered a diversification of legal bases, implying an increased use of qualified majority voting (QMV) in the Council. Taken together, these trends reveal a creeping supranationalisation of the EU's sanctions policy.

[118] ibid, paras 76–80.
[119] ibid, para 61.
[120] *Timchenko* (n 109) paras 117 and 123–24.
[121] ibid, para 119. The Court referred to Case C-123/18 P, *HTTS v Council* EU:C:2019:694, para 75.
[122] Case C-805/24 P *Gennady Timchenko and Elena Timchenko v Council* EU:C:2025:792.
[123] ibid, paras 20–27.
[124] ibid, para 28.
[125] ibid, paras 30–32.

5.4.1 The Evolving Institutional Architecture of the EU Sanctions Policy Cycle

The EU sanctions against Russia triggered important institutional evolutions in the entire policy cycle, from the preparation to the adoption and implementation of the sanctions. Most notably, the European Commission's role has grown significantly since the start of Russia's full-scale war against Ukraine. The increasingly technical nature of the sectoral sanctions, requiring the expertise of the Commission services, as well as the pressure to act swiftly in times of crises, implies that 'the Commission *de facto* leads the EU sanctions drafting process'.[126] The Directorate-General for Financial Stability, Financial Services and Capital Markets Union (DG FISMA) plays a central role in the preparation of the Council regulations implementing restrictive measures in the EU legal order. As foreseen under Article 215 TFEU, such proposals are designed by the Commission and the High Representative to implement the foreign policy decision imposing sanctions under Article 29 TEU (CFSP). Whereas it used to be the case in the past that the CFSP decision would be adopted first, this practice has now changed. The Commission prepares the new sanctions packages and drafts the regulations, which form the foundation of the CFSP Council decisions. Accordingly, the order of the so-called 'two-tier procedure' for the adoption of sanctions has been reversed, with the European Commission in the driving seat.[127]

DG FISMA is also in charge of monitoring the implementation and enforcement of EU sanctions in all Member States. It provides guidance through the publication of answers to frequently asked questions raised by national competent authorities and economic operators. The establishment of a Sanctions Whistleblower Tool and a Freeze and Seize Task Force strengthened its institutional role within the EU's sanctions policy. Moreover, the European Commission appointed a 'Special Envoy for the Implementation of EU Sanctions', to engage in high-level discussions with third countries to prevent sanctions evasion or circumvention. Taken together, these institutional evolutions put the European Commission at the forefront of the EU's sanctions policy. This may seem surprising in view of the essential political nature of sanctions as part of the EU's CFSP. Hence, the often shared perception that the CFSP is an essentially intergovernmental policy field has to be qualified.[128] The role of 'supranational' institutions

[126] Yulia Miadzvetskaya, 'EU Sanctions Decision-Making in Times of War: Procedural Changes and Rise of the Commission' (2025) *Maastricht Journal of European and Comparative Law* 284. See also Jan Lepeu, 'Ukraine, the De-targetization of EU Sanctions and the Rise of the European Commission as Architect of EU Foreign Policy' (2025) *International Politics* 975.

[127] ibid.

[128] Alvaravo de Elera, 'A Typology of Legal Acts in the European Union's Common Foreign and Security Policy' in Frank Hoffmeister and Lorant Havas (eds), *The High Representative of the Union for Foreign Affairs and Security Policy as a Legal Actor. Liber Amicorum in Honour of Stephan Marquart* (Brill-Nijhoff, 2025) 22.

such as the European Commission and the Court of Justice can hardly be underestimated.[129] Whereas this trend was already visible before the EU's sanctions against Russia and results from the integration of the CFSP in the post-Lisbon EU legal order, their unprecedented nature accelerated this evolution.

The expanded scope of the EU's sanctions policy also has an impact on other institutional actors. For instance, the High Representative and the European External Action Service (EEAS) are increasingly involved at various levels.[130] The High Representative intervened, amongst others, before the General Court to support the Council in defending restrictive measures such as the media broadcasting ban.[131] The new anti-circumvention tools (see section 5.3) reinforce the role of the European Anti-Fraud Office (OLAF), Europol and the European Public Prosecutors Office (EPPO).[132] The European Parliament, which typically has a limited role in traditional CFSP-based restrictive measures, is also increasingly involved through the adoption of sanctions on a non-CFSP legal basis (see section 5.4.2). To what extent the evolving institutional architecture of the EU sanctions policy cycle is only temporary and largely confined to the specific context of the Russia-related sanctions remains to be seen. Taking into account that institutional developments are rarely reversed, some lasting impact may well be expected.[133]

5.4.2 The Diversification of Legal Bases to Pursue EU Sanctions Objectives

The creeping supranationalism of the EU's sanctions policy is also visible with respect to the decision-making procedure in the Council. Whereas the basic principle of unanimity for the adoption of CFSP decisions is still upheld, significant evolutions restricting the role of veto-players can be observed. Initially, the introduction of exemptions proved helpful to ensure the smooth adoption of new sanctions packages. This was most visible with the sixth sanctions package introducing inter alia an embargo on imports of Russian oil and petroleum products. To overcome a potential veto of certain import-dependent landlocked Member States, most notably Hungary, Slovakia and the Czech

[129] See also: Peter Van Elsuwege, 'Judicial Review and the Common Foreign and Security Policy : Limits to the Gap-Filling Role of the Court of Justice' (2021) *CML Review* 1731–60.

[130] Calle Hakansson, 'Understanding the European Union's Response to the Russian War on Ukraine: The Role of the European External Action Service' (2025) *Defence Studies* 845.

[131] Madalena de Almeida Veiga, 'Combatting Foreign Manipulation and Interference Through EU Restrictive Measures' in Frank Hoffmeister and Lorant Havas (eds), *The High Representative of the Union for Foreign Affairs and Security Policy as a Legal Actor. Liber Amicorum in Honour of Stephan Marquart* (Brill-Nijhoff, 2025) 184–202.

[132] 'OLAF and Europol Join Forces to Strengthen the Fight against Sanctions Circumvention', https://anti-fraud.ec.europa.eu/media-corner/news/olaf-and-europol-join-forces-strengthen-fight-against-sanctions-circumvention-2025-11-20_en.

[133] Emilia Korkea-Aho and Luigi Lonardo, 'How Russia's War against Ukraine Changed EU Sanctions Decision-Making' (2025) *Journal of European Integration*.

Republic, Russian crude oil delivered by pipeline was exempted from the embargo.[134] Given the limitations of this consensual approach, the use of alternative, non-CFSP legal bases became a more common practice to overcome potential vetoes within the Council. A typical example concerns the use of trade measures, such as the introduction of increased customs duties applicable to the import of agricultural products and fertilisers from Russia and Belarus.[135] Such measures can be adopted under Article 207 TFEU, taking into account that the common commercial policy contributes to the EU's external action objectives.[136] Following a similar logic, the European Commission proposed a ban on Russian gas imports in June 2025 on the combined legal bases of Articles 207 and 194(2) TFEU, covering the respective fields of common commercial policy and energy, instead of Article 29 TEU (CFSP) and Article 215 TFEU (on restrictive measures).[137] Presenting the gas import ban as a trade measure instead of a foreign policy measure has significant institutional implications, since it does not require unanimity but qualified majority in the Council.[138]

Another example of the trend towards the use of non-CFSP legal bases within the EU's sanctions policy concerns the immobilisation of Russian Central Bank assets. This measure was first introduced within the framework of the CFSP and subject to six-monthly renewal, requiring unanimity in the Council.[139] In the context of the discussions surrounding the introduction of a 'reparations loan' to Ukraine,[140] the Council adopted a new regulation 'on emergency measures addressing the serious economic difficulties caused by Russia's actions in the context of the war of aggression against Ukraine' on the legal basis of Article 122(1) TFEU.[141] This regulation includes a prohibition of transactions

[134] Council Decision (CFSP) 2022/884 of 3 June 2022 amending Decision 2014/512/CFSP concerning restrictive measures in view of Russia's actions destabilising the situation in Ukraine [2022] OJ L153/128, recital 8 and Article 4o.

[135] Regulation (EU) 2025/1227 of the European Parliament and of the Council of 17 June 2025 on the modification of customs duties applicable to imports of certain goods originating in or exported from the Russian Federation and the Republic of Belarus [2025] OJ L1227.

[136] Art 207(1) TFEU provides that 'The common commercial policy shall be conducted in the context of the principles and objectives of the Union's external action.' The latter are included in Art 21 TEU and inter alia refer to the consolidation of respect for international law.

[137] European Commission, Proposal for a Regulation of the European Parliament and of the Council on phasing out Russian natural gas imports, improving monitoring of potential energy dependencies and amending Regulation (EU) 2017/1938, COM(2025) 828 final.

[138] Viktor Szep and Lukas Schaupp, 'Energy Sanctions Reloaded. Navigating the Trade-Based Sanctions Divide in the EU's Proposed Gas Ban' *Verfassungsblog* (25 June 2025).

[139] See Council Decision (CFSP) 2022/395 of 9 March 2022 amending Decision 2014/512/CFSP concerning restrictive measures in view of Russia's actions destabilising the situation in Ukraine [2022] OJ L81/8 and Council Regulation (EU) 2022/394 of 9 March 2022 amending Regulation (EU) No 833/2014 concerning restrictive measures in view of Russia's actions destabilising the situation in Ukraine [2022] OJ L81/1.

[140] See Peter Van Elsuwege, 'Walking a Tightrope: On the Legal Stakes of the EU's Proposed Reparations Loan for Ukraine' *Verfassungsblog* (8 December 2025).

[141] Council Regulation (EU) 2025/2600 of 12 December 2025 on emergency measures addressing the serious economic difficulties caused by Russia's actions in the context of the war of aggression against Ukraine [2025] OJ L 2600.

related to the management of reserves and assets of the Russian Central Bank. Accordingly, a measure that both in content (prohibiting the transfer of Russian assets) and objectives (countering Russia's war of aggression) traditionally falls with the scope of the CFSP is brought under a legal basis that is part of the EU economic policy chapter in the TFEU.[142] The motives for this bold move are clear: it is no longer required to regularly extend the restrictive measures on the basis of unanimity within the Council.

The question, however, is whether the recourse to Article 122(1) TFEU is legally justifiable. According to the Commission, the new emergency regulation complements the CFSP-based restrictive measures since it has a different scope and pursues 'objectives that are specific to the area of the economic stability of the Union'.[143] Reference is made to the macroeconomic implications of Russia's war of aggression against Ukraine and its implications for the EU. It is noteworthy that, in this respect, 'Ukraine is considered as an integral part of Europe's defence and security architecture and this latter is intrinsically connected with the economic situation in the Union'.[144] Moreover, it is argued that the economic stability of the Union is also affected by Russian hybrid threats against EU Member States. Whether this is sufficient to bring the freezing of Russian Central Bank assets under the scope of Article 122(1) TFEU is subject to discussion. It may well be argued that the measure essentially aims to address the security situation of Ukraine, and therefore mainly falls within the CFSP. This raises significant constitutional questions regarding the choice of legal basis within the EU legal order and the delimitation between CFSP and non-CFSP external action. Further litigation before the Court of Justice is on the agenda.[145]

Apart from potential cases about the choice of legal basis, there is a significant pending case brought by the European Parliament against the Council concerning the applicable voting rights for the definition of sanctions targets.[146] Such targets are to be defined in an annex to, in this case, Council Decision (CFSP) 2024/2643 concerning restrictive measures in view of Russia's destabilising activities. When the Decision was adopted, the Annex with the actual list of sanctioned natural and legal persons, entities and bodies was left blank. Article 4(1) of this Decision provides that 'The Council, acting by *unanimity* upon a

[142] See also Jan Dunin-Wasowicz, 'Leveraging Article 122 TFEU to Block Russian Central Bank Assets. The Emergence of Sanctions-Like Measures under EU Economic Emergency Powers', https://eusanctions.substack.com/p/leveraging-article-122-tfeu-to-block.

[143] European Commission, Proposal for a Council Regulation (EU) 2025/2600 of 12 December 2025 on emergency measures addressing the serious economic difficulties caused by Russia's actions in the context of the war of aggression against Ukraine, COM(2025) 3501 final, 2.

[144] ibid, 3.

[145] See Case C-46/26, *Hungary v European Parliament and Council*; Case T-150/26, *European Central Bank v Council*.

[146] Case C-883/24: Action brought on 19 December 2024 – *European Parliament v Council of the European Union* C 2025/889.

proposal of a Member State or the High Representative … shall decide to establish and amend the list in the Annex'.[147] According to the European Parliament, this approach contradicts the wording of Article 31(2) TEU, which provides that decisions implementing an established CFSP decision shall be adopted by qualified majority voting. It is also deemed to violate Article 40 TEU in the sense that the Council's insistence on unanimity for the determination of the sanctions targets adversely affects the subsequent decision-making procedure under Article 215 TFEU.[148]

Arguably, there is a lot of merit in the European Parliament's arguments. With its insistence on unanimity for the adoption and amendment of the actual sanctions lists, the Council precludes any meaningful implementation on the basis of QMV. This seems to contract the logic of the Treaties, which envisage unanimity for the adoption of truly political decisions, ie the adoption of sanctions and the designation criteria, whereas the actual application of those criteria is subject to QMV. When the Court of Justice follows this logic, this will have significant implications for the EU's sanctions practice. For instance, Member States would no longer be able to veto the adoption of sanctions against certain individuals or entities on the basis of their own national preferences. A notable example of such a case concerned the opposition of Hungary against the blacklisting of Russian Patriarch Kirill despite his support for the invasion of Ukraine and close links with Putin's regime.[149]

5.5 CONCLUSIONS

The EU's sanctions against Russia may well be regarded as a true 'game-changer' with long-term legal and institutional implications. From a legal perspective, the evolving case law of the CJEU has played a decisive role in shaping the contemporary EU sanctions policy. The Court has not only further clarified the procedural thresholds for individual listings but also triggered an evolution in the Council's designation practice, from conduct-based to status-based designations. The scope of EU (sectoral) sanctions has also entered into unchartered territories with the adoption of new types of restrictive measures such as the broadcast ban and multiple anti-circumvention measures, thereby significantly broadening the substantive and territorial reach of EU sanctions.

These developments also reveal an increasing interaction between the CFSP and other areas of EU law and policy. On the one hand, several restrictive measures adopted under the CFSP touch upon other areas such as criminal law or

[147] Council Decision (CFSP) 2024/2643 of 8 October 2024 concerning restrictive measures in view of Russia's destabilising activities L 2024/2643.

[148] Case C-883/24 (n 146).

[149] Leonie Kijewski and Jacopo Barigazzi, 'Orban wins again as furious EU envoys take church patriarch off Russian sanctions list' *Politico* (2 June 2022).

media regulation. Their adoption on a CFSP legal basis signals a shift towards a broader and more security-driven understanding of EU law and policies. On the other hand, certain sanctions are increasingly complemented, or even replaced, by instruments adopted on alternative legal bases such as trade, energy, and economic emergency provisions under the TFEU. The adoption of asset immobilisation measures on the basis of Article 122(1) TFEU clearly illustrates this dynamic.

While many of these legal innovations are closely linked to the specific context of the Russia-related sanctions, it may reasonably be assumed that they will leave a long-term impact on the EU's sanctions practice. This is particularly evident from an institutional perspective. The Russia sanctions have accelerated a significant reconfiguration of institutional roles, with the European Commission – and DG FISMA in particular – emerging as the central actor throughout the EU's sanctions policy cycle. The Commission not only carefully prepares the subsequent sanctions packages but is also in charge of monitoring the implementation and enforcement in EU Member States.

Accordingly, the EU's sanctions policy may no longer be regarded as an area of intergovernmental cooperation, despite its clear connection with the specific rules and procedures under the CFSP. The growing use of complementary measures adopted outside the CFSP, combined with the Commission's enhanced operational role, points towards a more integrated and cross-sectoral sanctions policy. Whereas some of the identified trends were already visible with respect to other sanctions regimes (such as the ones against Iran and Syria), the more comprehensive sanctions packages against Russia provided a significant quantum leap towards a more integrated EU sanctions policy that is permeating the entire EU legal order.

6

Frozen Russian State Assets and Reparations for Ukraine

ANTON MOISEIENKO

6.1 INTRODUCTION

In February 2022, a coalition of states including all G7 economies and other like-minded nations (G7+) froze approximately US$300 billion in Russian state assets[1] consisting of foreign currency reserves accumulated by the Central Bank of Russia (CBR).[2] By definition, CBR assets belong directly to the Russian state, as opposed to the US$60 billion or so in private property owned by sanctioned Russian public officials, generals and oligarchs.[3] This has propelled CBR assets into focus as the likeliest source for the provision of reparations that Russia owes Ukraine as a consequence of its aggression against Ukraine.[4]

To what extent CBR assets can be used in this fashion – and, if so, how this should be accomplished – has been a source of controversy since 2022 and the central question this chapter seeks to address. The chapter seeks to account for the principal legal, policy and economic points of contention. In doing so, it traces the evolution of the debate about the future fate of frozen Russian state assets through three main phases. The objective of this chapter is to provide a brief, accessible summary of the main issues involved, without laying claim to comprehensiveness of coverage. This is a rapidly developing

[1] For an overview of the amounts involved, see Yuliya Ziskina, Jamison Firestone and Anton Moiseienko, 'Resolving Accountability Over Russian State Assets: New Understandings of Jurisdiction and Policy Opportunities' (New Lines Institute for Strategy and Policy, 2025), https://newlinesinstitute.org/rules-based-international-order/resolving-accountability-over-russian-state-assets-new-understandings-of-jurisdiction-and-policy-opportunities.

[2] For details about the nature of central bank foreign currency reserves, see Anton Moiseienko, 'Seizing Foreign Central Bank Assets: A Lawful Response to Aggression?', SSRN Working Paper, 49–54 https://papers.ssrn.com/sol3/papers.cfm?abstract_id=4420459.

[3] US Department of Treasury, 'Joint Statement from the REPO Task Force' Press release (9 March 2023), https://home.treasury.gov/news/press-releases/jy1329.

[4] On Russia's obligation to pay reparations, see Furtherance of Remedy and Reparation for Aggression Against Ukraine, UN Doc A/ES-11/L6 (7 November 2022).

area, and the law and policy developments reflected here are current as of mid-December 2025.

This chapter begins by explaining the freezing measures taken in relation to Russian state assets (section 6.2). It then proceeds to discuss the three phases of freezing measures against the CBR. The first phase (section 6.3) involves the crystallisation of key disagreements in 2022–23. They involve international law considerations, primarily to do with the interaction between state immunities, reparations and countermeasures; policy concerns over Russia's escalatory actions should CBR assets be transferred to Ukraine; and the ramifications, if any, for global confidence in Western financial systems. The second phase, commencing in 2024, features the EU's rollout of a scheme seeking to utilise the interest generated on Russian state assets via the Extraordinary Revenue Acceleration (ERA) loan (section 6.4). Finally, the third phase, starting in 2025 centres around the proposed Reparations Loan, which appears to have garnered support of some of the key national capitals in the EU (section 6.5). This continues the trend of the EU resorting to financial engineering to sidestep the difficult questions associated with an outright transfer of Russian state assets. The final section concludes with thoughts on the factors that are likely to shape the ultimate disposal of frozen Russian assets.

6.2 FROZEN RUSSIAN STATE ASSETS

To understand the legal and policy issues involved, it is helpful to consider the nature and geographical distribution of frozen Russian state assets.

Prior to its full-scale invasion of Ukraine, Russia had accumulated a 'war chest' of US$600 billion in foreign currency reserves.[5] They were intended, in part, to blunt the effect of any economic sanctions that might be imposed on Russia in response to the aggression. Ironically, however, they themselves presented a target for Western sanctions – especially from the United States. Indeed, at various points in the past, the US Government had frozen the central bank reserves of Afghanistan, Cuba, Iran, Syria and Venezuela.

This risk was not lost on the Russian Government. In the lead-up to February 2022, the CBR had moved substantial amounts of its foreign reserves from the United States and Canada to Belgium.[6] This foresight proved partial. As a result of EU sanctions, US$300 billion of CBR assets ended up frozen within two days of the invasion, among it roughly US$200 billion held at Euroclear, a securities

[5] Bank of Russia, Foreign Exchange and Gold Asset Management Report (2022).

[6] Laura Dubois, 'EU Mulls Seizing Profits of $323b Frozen Russian Assets' *Financial Review* (25 May 2023), www.afr.com/policy/foreign-affairs/eu-mulls-seizing-profits-of-323b-frozen-russian-assets-20230525-p5dbcp; 'Why the EU will not seize Russian state assets to rebuild Ukraine' *The Economist* (20 July 2023), www.economist.com/europe/2023/07/20/why-the-eu-will-not-seize-russian-state-assets-to-rebuild-ukraine. See also Emidio Cocozza and others, 'In Search of Russia's Foreign Assets' CEPR (10 January 2023), https://cepr.org/voxeu/columns/search-russias-foreign-assets.

clearinghouse based in Belgium. This has turned Belgium, and by extension the EU, into a crucial focal point for the ensuing discussions.

6.2.1 Amounts and Distribution

It is worth dwelling on the issue of the amounts involved and their distribution. For these purposes, Russian state assets are largely synonymous with CBR assets.

Some fundamental facts are reasonably clear. While there is no comprehensive, publicly available accounting of frozen Russian state assets across the G7+, most estimates coalesce around the total figure of approximately US$300 billion.[7] The majority of this amount is frozen at Euroclear. At the time of writing, Euroclear's public reporting indicates US$214 billion (€185 billion) in frozen Russian state assets.[8]

Details of what is held outside Euroclear is less certain. This is especially so for some non-European countries. For example, some public reporting puts the amount of Russian state assets in Australia at AU$9 billion.[9] Euroclear itself estimates the amount of AU$-denominated assets that it holds on the CBR's behalf at two per cent of 'cash balances related to Russian sanctions', amounting to AU$6.6 billion.[10] Finally, the Australian Sanctions Office reports that the totality of frozen Russian assets in Australia – public and private – only comprises AU$100 million.[11]

One frequently cited source of information is the CBR's own pre-invasion annual report published in 2021. It indicated that the CBR was holding 12.2 per cent of its reserves in France, 9.5 per cent in Germany, 6.6 per cent in the United States, and 4.5 per cent in the UK, as well as a range of other countries.[12] Given the lack of reference to Belgium, where Euroclear is located, this is unlikely to be an accurate indication of the breakdown as of February 2022.

[7] European Parliament, 'MEPs to push for seizing Russian assets and phasing out Russian energy' (6 March 2025), www.europarl.europa.eu/news/en/agenda/briefing/2025-03-10/3/meps-to-push-for-seizing-russian-assets-and-phasing-out-russian-energy.

[8] Euroclear, Euroclear Holding Consolidated Annual Report 2024 (2024) 25–26 (indicating €217 billion in total assets under management, and €33 billion in assets under management excluding frozen Russian state assets, leaving €184 billion in frozen Russian state assets).

[9] Rob Harris, 'Australian elite seek to divert Russia's $9b "dirty money" to Ukraine' *Sydney Morning Herald* (9 April 2024), www.smh.com.au/world/europe/australian-elite-seek-to-divert-russia-s-9b-dirty-money-to-ukraine-20240408-p5fi55.html.

[10] 'Euroclear reports strong business income growth in Q1 2025' (14 May 2025), www.euroclear.com/newsandinsights/en/press/2025/mr-13-strong-first-quarter-results.html.

[11] 'Inquiry reveals shortcomings in Australia's sanctions regime' ABC News (23 February 2025), www.abc.net.au/news/2025-02-23/australia-sanction-regime-russia-ukraine-senate-inquiry/104937222.

[12] Bank of Russia (n 5). See also Charles Lichfield, 'The Russian Central Bank is Running Out of Options' Atlantic Council (4 March 2022), www.atlanticcouncil.org/blogs/new-atlanticist/the-russian-central-bank-is-running-out-of-options (citing slightly different figures).

This lack of clarity about the amounts and distribution of frozen Russian state assets impedes democratic scrutiny of governments' decision-making in relation to this property. In simple terms, it is not obvious which governments sit on significant amounts of frozen Russian money, what precisely those amounts are, and what if anything those governments are proposing to do with it. This abiding uncertainty is compounded by the manner in which frozen Russian state assets are held.

6.2.2 Euroclear-held and Directly Held Assets

On the surface, the statement that €185 billion has been frozen at Euroclear in Belgium is self-explanatory. However, it conceals a more complicated story. As a securities clearinghouse, Euroclear holds and manages assets in various countries on the CBR's behalf. This means that the abovementioned €185 billion is likely to comprise assets held in multiple locations around the world.

Specifically, Euroclear used to hold foreign government-issued bonds on the CBR's behalf. Following the imposition of G7+ sanctions, these securities matured. This resulted in coupon and principal payments accruing in bank accounts in respective states (eg Canadian banks for Canadian Government-issued securities, etc).[13] Describing these assets as Euroclear-held only tells part of the story. These funds are located in bank accounts around the world but managed by the Belgian-based Euroclear. They can therefore be affected by regulatory action, including sanctions, *both* in the country where the bank account is held (eg Canada) and, at the Euroclear level, in Belgium.[14]

This set-up has several important ramifications. Because these CBR assets will be held indirectly, in overseas bank accounts opened in Euroclear's name, it is possible that they are not formally identified as belonging to the CBR by the respective countries' governments. For instance, this would seem to be suggested by the Australian Government's estimate, mentioned above, that only AU$100 million in Russian assets have been frozen in Australia. By contrast, Euroclear's public reporting indicates it is holding AU$6.6 billion in AU$-denominated assets, which is most likely to refer to Australian-based bank accounts held by Euroclear on the CBR's behalf. This means that, while these assets are frozen as a result of EU sanctions that Euroclear must abide by, there is no separate freeze in place in relation to those assets at the Australian level. The same holds true for Canada and potentially other jurisdictions with Euroclear-held Russian state assets.

[13] 'Where possible, cash is principally redeposited with central banks in their own currency, reinvested in short-term reverse repos with highly rated counterparties or in government bonds through outright purchase': Euroclear SA/NV, Consolidated Annual Report 2024, 189.

[14] Ziskina, Firestone and Moiseienko (n 1).

In addition to this, the CBR holds some funds directly in overseas bank accounts without Euroclear's intermediation. These accounts will have been identified as the CBR's and frozen in respective countries, but there is no comprehensive public accounting of the amounts involved or their distribution across states. This compounds uncertainty around which governments hold the decision-making power over substantial CBR holdings, in the EU and beyond.

6.2.3 Freezing

The 'freezing' of Russian state assets means that Russia cannot use them, including by selling them, but remains their owner. By its legal nature, the 'freezing' involves a prohibition on any transactions involving these assets.[15] In official communications, the EU and the US describe frozen Russian state assets as 'immobilised': a term introduced specifically in connection with these assets.

It was meant to help US and EU sanctions officials present the unprecedented freezing of US$300 billion in central bank assets as essentially an anti-sanctions-evasion measure. Given the other sanctions imposed on Russia, the argument was that leaving CBR assets intact would allow the CBR to intervene to support Russia's economy. To prevent this, CBR assets had to be 'immobilised'.[16] Despite this rhetorical emphasis, there is no substantive difference whatsoever between freezing and immobilisation; the more familiar term 'freezing' will be employed her for clarity and consistency.

One important aspect of the EU's freeze is that it needs to be extended by unanimous agreement of all Member States every six months.[17] So far, the EU has managed to consistently secure Hungary and Slovakia's agreement to such extensions. Every time, however, the spectre of a potential veto from those two states looms large. A failure to extend EU sanctions would result in a return of now-frozen state assets to Russia and thus be a catastrophic setback to European foreign policy and credibility.[18] However, it was reported on 11 December 2025 that most EU Member States had 'handed emergency powers to the European

[15] Art 1a(4) of Council Decision 2014/512/CFSP of 31 July 2014; Executive Order 14024: Prohibitions Related to Transactions Involving the Central Bank of the Russian Federation, the National Wealth Fund of the Russian Federation, and the Ministry of Finance of the Russian Federation, 19 May 2023.

[16] Edward Fishman, *Chokepoints: American Power in the Age of Economic Warfare* (Penguin, 2025) 364.

[17] Art 9(1) of Council Decision 2014/512/CFSP of 31 July 2014 concerning restrictive measures in view of Russia's actions destabilising the situation in Ukraine, as amended.

[18] Anton Moiseienko and Yuliya Ziskina, 'The Impending Collapse of Russia Sanctions: The Cost of Inaction', *RUSI Commentary* (20 March 2025), www.rusi.org/explore-our-research/publications/commentary/impending-collapse-russia-sanctions-cost-inaction.

Commission' to be able to prolong EU sanctions against Russia without unanimity from then on.[19]

This brings us back to Euroclear-held assets in jurisdictions other than Belgium, such as Australia and Canada. Because those assets are not formally identified owned or controlled by Russia, Euroclear could withdraw them to repay the CBR if EU sanctions lapsed. Imposing separate Australian and Canadian freezes on those assets would eliminate this risk and maintain a 'double lock' of EU and Australian/Canadian sanctions.[20] The position is likely the same in other jurisdictions outside Europe.

6.3 PHASE I: FREEZE TO SEIZE

With the benefit of this understanding of the amounts involved, the manner in which CBR assets are held, and the challenges of maintaining EU sanctions against CBR assets, we can now turn to the substance of the 'freeze to seize' debates unfolding over the past three years. They centre around the question of whether, and if so how, CBR assets can be used to enforce Russia's obligation to pay reparations to Ukraine.

The obligation to pay reparations is the starting point for these conversations. Under international law, Russia must make full reparation for the damage caused by its war of aggression. This has been recognised, among others, by the UN General Assembly.[21] No comprehensive accounting of such damage is possible while the war goes on, but by most estimates it already far exceeds the amount of frozen assets.[22]

In other words, Russia owes Ukraine a financial debt that it is unwilling to discharge. This is a crucial, and occasionally overlooked, part of the background to the 'freeze to seize' debate. One of Russia's habitual narratives is that Western nations are contemplating a 'theft' of its reserves.[23] What is really at stake is designing a mechanism to enforce the largest inter-state financial obligation of

[19] Gregorio Sorgi, 'EU approves legal workaround to sideline Orbán, keep Russian assets frozen forever' Politico (11 December 2025).

[20] Bill Browder, Marcus Kolga and Aaron Gasch Burnett, 'Canada cannot wait for Europe and must act alone to "double-freeze" Russian assets' *Globe and Mail* (15 October 2025), www.theglobeandmail.com/business/commentary/article-canada-europe-double-freeze-russian-assets.

[21] Furtherance of Remedy and Reparation for Aggression Against Ukraine (n 4).

[22] Darryl Coote, 'Rebuilding Ukraine will cost $600B, says Prime Minister Denys Shmyhal' *UPI* (22 April 2022), www.upi.com/Top_News/World-News/2022/04/22/ukraine-600-billion-rebuild-country/5451650610486; Simon Johnson and Oleg Ustenko, 'A Basic Income for Ukrainians, Paid for with Frozen Russian Assets' Politico (2 March 2022), www.politico.com/news/magazine/2022/03/02/frozen-russian-assets-humanitarian-relief-00013286; Robert E Litan, 'Russia Can be Made to Pay for Ukraine Damage Now' Brookings Institution (17 March 2022), www.brookings.edu/opinions/russia-can-be-made-to-pay-for-ukraine-damage-now.

[23] 'Russia says EU frozen assets plan is theft, will lead to decades of lawsuits' Reuters (21 March 2024), www.reuters.com/world/europe/russia-says-eu-frozen-assets-plan-is-theft-will-lead-decades-lawsuits-2024-03-20.

modern times. As adumbrated earlier, the development of such a mechanism enlivens a range of legal, economic and policy considerations.

6.3.1 Legal Considerations

Like with freezing, there is some variability in the terminology one might encounter. 'Seizing', 'confiscation', 'transfer' and 'repurposing' are all used interchangeably. The choice of one of these terms over the others makes no difference as a matter of international law. Politically, though, they may have different connotations. While 'seizure' and 'confiscation' foreground the taking of assets, 'transfer' and 'repurposing' focus on making them available to Ukraine.

The main legal obstacle to a change in the title of CBR assets lies in state immunities. In the ordinary course of events, state immunities preclude seizure of state property. In this instance, however, much depends on the proper application of the law of state responsibility, as well as its relationship with the law of state immunities.

The law of state responsibility allows states to take countermeasures, ie engage in acts that would otherwise be contrary to international law in order to respond to another state's breach of international law. Countermeasures must aim to restore the state of compliance with international law between the parties and be proportionate and non-punitive. Some argue, therefore, that they could be used to transfer the aggressor state's property to the victim of its aggression.[24]

There are three main counterarguments. The first one stems from the wording of the International Law Commission's Articles on the Responsibility of States for Internationally Wrongful Acts (ARSIWA).[25] The ARSIWA posit that countermeasures must aim to 'induce' the state in breach to comply with its obligations.[26] Some contend that this allows for the freezing of another state's property until it agrees to pay its debt, but not for its transfer in satisfaction of the debt.[27] It has been argued elsewhere that this reads far too much into a single word in the ARSIWA in a way more suitable to the interpretation of a domestic statute than of a document reflecting customary international law.[28]

The second counterargument has to do with the ARSIWA's following requirement: 'Countermeasures shall, as far as possible, be taken in such a way as to

[24] Tom Grant, 'Multilateral Action Model on Reparations: Developing an Effective System for Reparations and Compensation for Ukraine and Ukrainians for Damage Caused by the Russian Federation' (New Lines Institute for Strategy and Policy, 2022).

[25] International Law Commission, *Draft Articles on Responsibility of States for Internationally Wrongful Acts, with Commentary*, UN Doc A/56/10 (24 October 2001).

[26] Art 49(1) ARSIWA.

[27] Oona Hathaway, Maggie Mills and Thomas Poston, 'War Reparations: The Case for Countermeasures' (2024) 76 *Stanford Law Review* 10.

[28] Anton Moiseienko, 'Sanctions, Confiscation and the Rule of Law' (2023) 4 *Revue Européenne du Droit* 33.

permit the resumption of performance of the obligations in question.'[29] This is often referred to as the reversibility requirement. The disagreement comes down to whether a transfer of financial assets is irreversible. Some argue that, unlike a (temporary) freeze, a (permanent) transfer is by definition irreversible; others point out that a financial transfer can always be unwound – unlike, say, the destruction of a physical asset.[30]

The third counterargument pertains to the longstanding disagreement over the lawfulness of 'third-party' countermeasures, ie countermeasures taken by a state other than the directly aggrieved state. Their legality determines whether states other than Ukraine can lawfully rely on countermeasures to seize, or transfer, Russian state assets. This particular debate has been well traversed over the decades but continues to command no consensus.[31]

This controversy can have repercussions for freezing, not only seizing. Since state immunities preclude attachment of state property, if third-party countermeasures are not available, then one might query the lawfulness of the ongoing freezing of Russian state assets.[32] This is where the notion of 'immobilisation' comes in again. The EU's argument, articulated more often in private than in public, is that 'immobilising' assets only entails directing Western financial intermediaries to avoid any transactions with them – therefore rendering such assets effectively untouchable – without formally interfering with the owner's property rights at all. This distinction is entirely artificial: there is no way of disposing of one's financial assets other than through financial intermediaries. Therefore, states would be on firmer ground if they explicitly invoked third-party countermeasures. That, however, would entail committing to a view on the lawfulness of third-party countermeasures.

Views continue to differ on the issues outlined above. Leading international law scholars and practitioners from all G7 jurisdictions argue in favour of the lawfulness of the seizure on the basis of its constituting lawful countermeasures.[33] So does Philippa Webb in a study commissioned by the European Parliament.[34] Dissenters include the Dutch Advisory Committee on Public International Law,

[29] Art 49(3) ARSIWA.

[30] For detailed analysis, see Moiseienko (n 2) 49–54, https://papers.ssrn.com/sol3/papers.cfm?abstract_id=4420459.

[31] See Martin Dawidowicz, *Third-Party Countermeasures in International Law* (Cambridge University Press, 2017); Christian J Tams, *Enforcing Obligations Erga Omnes in International Law* (Cambridge University Press, 2009) (both arguing in favour of third-party countermeasures).

[32] Ron van der Horst, 'Illegal, Unless: Freezing the Assets of Russia's Central Bank' (2023) 34 *European Journal of International Law* 1.

[33] Dapo Akande and others, 'On Proposed Countermeasures Against Russia to Compensate Injured States for Losses Caused by Russia's War of Aggression Against Ukraine' (The International Institute for Strategic Studies, 20 November 2023).

[34] Philippa Webb, 'Legal Options for Confiscation of Russian state Assets to Support the Reconstruction of Ukraine' (European Parliamentary Research Service, 2024).

coordinated by Cedric Ryngaert; Ingrid Brunk; and several other scholars, who view central bank immunity as absolute.[35]

With the weight of authority balanced but tilting towards the legality of seizure, it is difficult to escape the conclusion that, if G7 governments mustered the political will to act, no plausible challenge could be mounted against the international legality of a potential transfer.

This is true conceptually as well as practically. Since Russia does not recognise the jurisdiction of the International Court of Justice under the Optional Clause,[36] and the CBR as a state agency is unlikely to qualify for protection under applicable investment treaties,[37] there is no obvious forum for Russia to contest the validity of such measures – although some are still wary of the prospect of investment disputes.[38] Meanwhile, the EU has legally precluded the recognition and enforcement in the EU of any Russian court judgments purporting to award damages for losses incurred in connection with EU sanctions.[39]

6.3.2 Economic Considerations

The considerations that are likely to weigh most heavily on governments' minds are economic and political, not legal. They include, first and foremost, the potential impact of confiscatory measures on foreign investors' confidence in the European financial system. The issue can also be framed in terms of the precedent that such a step would set, namely whether it would presage the seizure of central bank reserves for other breaches of international law. Some governments, such as that of Saudi Arabia, are reported to have threatened the EU with withdrawal of their funds should Russian assets be taken.[40]

In this discussion, it is useful to distinguish between several groups of states. Some states have already repeatedly committed to minimising their reliance on 'Western' financial systems: especially, China and Russia.[41] Over the past

[35] Commissie van advies inzake volkenrechtelijke vraagstukken (Dutch Advisory Committee on Public International Law), 'Confiscatie van eigendommen van vreemde staten' (Confiscation of foreign state assets) (December 2024); Ingrid Brunk, 'Central Bank Immunity, Sanctions, and Sovereign Wealth Funds' (2023) 91 *George Washington Law Review* 1616.

[36] www.icj-cij.org/declarations.

[37] Moiseienko (n 2) 33–37.

[38] Philipp Kehl, 'Seizing Russia's Frozen Assets: Quis iudicabit?' *EJIL: Talk!* (24 January 2024), www.ejiltalk.org/seizing-russias-frozen-assets-quis-iudicabit.

[39] Art 7a of Council Decision 2014/512/CFSP of 31 July 2014 concerning restrictive measures in view of Russia's actions destabilising the situation in Ukraine, as amended.

[40] Dmytro Basmat, 'Saudi Arabia issued vague threats to G7 against seizing frozen Russian assets, Bloomberg reports' *The Kyiv Independent* (10 July 2024), https://kyivindependent.com/saudi-arabia-warned-g7-against-seizing-russian-assets-bloomberg-reports.

[41] Juan Zarate, *Treasury's War: The Unleashing of a New Era of Financial Warfare* (Public Affairs, 2013) 400; Laurence H Tribe and others, 'The Legal, Practical, and Moral Case for Transferring Russian Sovereign Assets to Ukraine' (*Renew Democracy Initiative*, 2023) 170–79.

10 years, this trend has not abated.[42] While China, Russia, and other like-minded states continue to rely on the US dollar, this is not for want of seeking alternatives.[43] It is not evident that the fate of CBR assets would make a meaningful difference to those states' wish to extricate themselves from the Western financial infrastructure.

The position of other countries is less clear-cut. On the one hand, other states, which would otherwise be content to keep significant holdings in the US, EU, UK and Japan, could be alarmed by the potential for their property to be taken in response to real or perceived wrongdoing.[44] On the other hand, the freezing of CBR assets was itself unprecedented in terms of scale, yet it did not appear to have caused any major ruptures to global finance. Reflecting these sentiments, the global bank Morgan Stanley concluded as follows in December 2025:

> Usage of Russian assets may not necessarily weaken investors' perception of robust legal guardrails and investor protections if usage is viewed as prudent, measured, and firmly in line with existing legal standards and due process. The current situation may also be viewed as exceptional and exigent, which may reduce investor concerns of its probability of future usage.[45]

In essence, the disagreement comes down to whether the move from freeze to seize would in this instance be seen as undermining the reliability of Western financial systems. One would expect a clear legal and policy rationale behind any potential transfer to mitigate this risk. Furthermore, any threats of mass withdrawal of foreign assets from the EU beg the question of where exactly they might be placed instead: can jurisdictions such as China, suffering from their own rule of law deficits, really be a safe and attractive alternative?

6.3.3 Policy Considerations

There are broader policy issues involved, too. Most fundamentally, there is a certain tension between, on the one hand, treating a potential transfer of CBR assets as a unique, *sui generis* measure and, on the other hand, presenting it

[42] See, eg, Serkan Arslanalp, Barry Eichengreen and Chima Simpson-Bell, 'Dollar Dominance and the Rise of Nontraditional Reserve Currencies' (International Monetary Fund, 1 June 2022), www.imf.org/en/Blogs/Articles/2022/06/01/blog-dollar-dominance-and-the-rise-of-nontraditional-reserve-currencies.

[43] Agathe Demarais, *Backfire: How Sanctions Reshape the World Against US Interests* (Columbia University Press, 2023).

[44] See Joseph Stiglitz and Andrew Kosenko, 'Russia Must be Held Accountable Over Ukraine – We Should Seize its Assets' *The Guardian* (8 January 2024), www.theguardian.com/business/2024/jan/08/russia-ukraine-seize-assets-us-eu. *cf* Teuta Franjkovich, 'Seizing $300B of Russian Assets May Be a "Cataclysm" for Dollar System, Nobel Prize Winner Says' CCN (27 December 2023), www.ccn.com/news/seizing-300b-russian-assets-cataclysm-dollar-nobel-prize.

[45] Morgan Stanley, 'Market Implications of Possible Use of Frozen Assets' (11 December 2025).

as a precedent for accountability and the payment of reparations. The former approach might make the idea more politically palatable for cautious governments. The latter stance is more principled, consistent and avoids the charge of exceptionalism in the global community's treatment of the Russo-Ukrainian war. It is also more likely to serve as a deterrent for other would-be aggressors. But, precisely because of its more far-reaching systemic implications, this approach is less likely to command broad international support for now.

Another policy consideration giving rise to considerable consternation in G7+ capitals is the potential for further Russian escalation. As previously discussed, there are few options for legal recourse on Russia's part. The greater concern therefore pertains to extra-legal actions. Since 2022, Russia has expropriated the property of multiple Western companies operating in Russia.[46] It has also indicated its readiness to carry on in the same vein. Whether this threat should alter the course of G7+ policies depends largely on the view that one takes of the prudence, or recklessness, of continued business presence in Russia post-2022.

There may also be fears that are not of a strictly economic nature at all. For instance, Russia has been known to detain Western citizens in so-called 'hostage diplomacy'. It has also been accused of orchestrating drone incursions that caused the repeat shutdown of multiple European airports in autumn 2025.[47] These intimidation tactics are likely to be aimed at undermining support for Ukraine writ large, including but not only as relates to the disposal of frozen Russian state assets.

6.4 PHASE 2: USING THE INTEREST

The legal, economic and policy considerations outlined above have prompted the G7+, and the EU in particular, to look for alternative solutions that would leverage frozen Russian state assets for Ukraine's benefit without transferring title in these assets. Despite the seeming impossibility of achieving this, some progress has been made on this front by using the interest accruing on Euroclear-held CBR assets.

The core of the EU's position is that, while those assets themselves continue to be Russia's property, Russia is not entitled to ownership of the interest that has been accruing on these assets since February 2022. As we shall see, this approach, while innovative, comes with significant limitations. To appreciate

[46] Guy Faulconbridge, 'Russia seizes $50 billion in assets as economy shifts during war in Ukraine' Reuters (11 July 2025), www.reuters.com/world/europe/fortress-russia-has-confiscated-50-billion-assets-over-three-years-kommersant-2025-07-09.

[47] Frank Gardner, 'Mysterious drones have been spotted at night at airports across Europe. How worried should we be?' BBC News (17 November 2025), www.bbc.com/news/articles/crkl3d6pegpo.

them, it is convenient to begin by considering the legal rationale the EU relies on, before discussing the EU's Extraordinary Revenue Acceleration loan.

6.4.1 Legal Rationale

The EU's proposals to treat the interest accruing on Euroclear-held CBR assets as distinct from the principal first emerged in late 2022. They were not accompanied by any detailed explanation of their legal rationale. For instance, legal analysis was conspicuously absent from the leaked Options Paper prepared by the Freeze and Seize Task Force, the EU's Russia sanctions task force, in November 2022.[48] The seemingly arbitrary distinction drawn by the EU between the principal and the interest originally prompted widespread criticism.[49]

It has turned out that the EU's legal position has more substance than was initially appreciated.[50] Originally, Euroclear was contractually bound to manage the CBR's assets on its behalf. Once sanctions were put in place, those contracts either became invalid or expired with time. Therefore, Euroclear found itself in the position of holding approximately €200 billion in CBR assets. These assets – bank accounts and securities – continue to generate interest. Euroclear has neither any obligation nor even the legal ability to remit it to Russia, and therefore the interest accrues to Euroclear itself in what the EU describes as 'extraordinary' or 'windfall' profits.[51]

Consistent with this explanation, Euroclear has reflected the profits from investing CBR assets in its financial reporting.[52] In 2024, the EU adopted rules requiring Euroclear to segregate extraordinary profits in its financial reporting

[48] *Options Paper by the European Commission on the Use of Frozen Assets to Support Ukraine's Reconstruction*, European Commission (undated), www.politico.eu/wp-content/uploads/2023/02/07/Use-of-assets-option-paper_19-Nov-2022_final_clean.docx (unauthenticated and published by Politico); For commentary, see Lorin-Johannes Wagner, 'Investing Immobilized Russian Assets, Monetarizing the Common Foreign and Security Policy' Verfassungsblog (25 April 2023), https://verfassungsblog.de/investing-immobilized-russian-assets-monetarizing-the-common-foreign-and-security-policy.

[49] See, eg, Eleanor Rundle, 'Why the European Commission's Proposal for Russian State Asset Seizure Should be Abandoned' Just Security (23 March 2023), www.justsecurity.org/85661/why-the-european-commissions-proposal-for-russian-state-asset-seizure-should-be-abandoned; Hathaway, Mills and Poston (n 27) 33; 'Roundtable: Making Putin Pay: The Case for Transferring Russian Sovereign Assets to Ukraine' House Foreign Affairs Committee (18 October 2023), www.youtube.com/watch?v=_-jMJMQ8LBU (including Philip Zelikow's critique of the EU's proposal to confiscate the interest generated on CBR assets).

[50] Dr Bart Szewczyk's remarks at the seminar 'Freeze to Seize: Do Sovereign Immunities Preclude the Seizure of Central Bank Assets?' (Graduate Institute, 25 January 2024).

[51] Gregorio Sorgi, 'EU Takes First Step to Raise Money for Ukraine from Russian Frozen Assets' Politico (12 December 2023, www.politico.eu/article/eu-takes-first-step-to-raise-money-for-ukraine-from-russian-frozen-assets.

[52] Julia Payne, 'Belgium Expects to Use $2.4 Billion in Tax on Frozen Russian Assets to Fund Ukraine' Reuters (12 October 2023), www.reuters.com/world/europe/belgium-expects-use-24-bln-tax-frozen-russian-assets-fund-ukraine-2023-10-11.

and abstain from distributing them to Euroclear's shareholders (who, curiously, include China's sovereign wealth fund).[53] Such profits have been taxed at Belgium's 25 per cent corporate income tax rate, generating several billion Euros per annum in tax payments. Belgium has shared some, but not all, of these tax revenues with Ukraine.[54]

This unique arrangement has prompted questions about various parties' incentives and motivations. For instance, Włodzimierz Cimoszewicz, a European MP and Poland's former prime minister, suggested there might be a reluctance on Euroclear's behalf to part with the windfall from CBR assets: 'Euroclear's position is that this wartime profit — around a hefty €4 billion in 2023 — is its own private property'.[55] While this is not the position that Euroclear has adopted in public, it has argued that the extraordinary revenues, or a substantial part of them, should remain in its hands as a strategic reserve for litigation costs should Russia sue it. This view has been backed up by the Belgian Government.

International law does not provide any assistance in determining whether the interest accruing on CBR assets in fact belongs to the CBR or Euroclear. As Zachary Douglas observes, 'General international law contains no substantive rules of property law'.[56] So, while international law sets out the protections that apply to certain categories of property once property rights arise under domestic laws (eg sovereign immunities or investment protections), whether a particular property right arises remains the province of domestic law, in this case Belgian law.[57]

Based on its assessment of Belgian law, the EU has achieved consensus that the interest on frozen Russian assets should be used for Ukraine's benefit. Some of the funds generated have already been transferred to Ukraine. However, the amounts involved – €1.5 billion via the first tranche – are small in the grand scheme of what Ukraine requires or the damage that Russia has caused.[58] This has paved the way for considering the opportunities to frontload the amount that will be generated by frozen Russian state assets over the future years.

[53] Council of the EU, 'Immobilised Russian assets: Council decides to set aside extraordinary revenues' (12 February 2024), www.consilium.europa.eu/en/press/press-releases/2024/02/12/immobilised-russian-assets-council-decides-to-set-aside-extraordinary-revenues.

[54] Gregorio Sorgi, 'Greedy Belgian taxman should keep hands off Russian assets, West tells Brussels' Politico (14 April 2024), www.politico.eu/article/russian-assets-belgian-tax-authorities-ukraine-aid-eu-g7-euroclear.

[55] Włodzimierz Cimoszewicz, 'Europe Must Seize Russia's State Assets Now' Politico (24 January 2024), www.politico.eu/article/europe-must-seize-russia-state-assets-now.

[56] Zachary Douglas, *The International Law of Investment Claims* (Cambridge University Press, 2009) 52.

[57] ibid.

[58] Tribe and others (n 41) 168.

6.4.2 Extraordinary Revenue Acceleration

In 2024, the G7 agreed to issue a $50 billion loan for Ukraine's benefit backed by recourse to the stream of revenue generated from frozen Russian assets over the next 10 years.[59] This converts future earnings into a sum available here and now, as reflected in the name of the initiative: Extraordinary Revenue Acceleration (ERA).

The ERA scheme advances the EU's now preferred approach of drawing on the interest without encroaching on the principal. One of the main obstacles to the scheme is that, for it to work, Russian state assets need to remain frozen long-term. This cannot be guaranteed because EU sanctions against Russia need to be regularly renewed, as discussed previously, subject to the workaround that has been reportedly agreed on in mid-December as this chapter is being finalised.

This state of affairs has led to the emergence of proposals to place frozen Russian state assets into a distinct, special purpose vehicle (SPV) – in essence, a Ukraine compensation fund.[60] If this could be done on a permanent basis, this one-off action could obviate the need for further periodic renewals of EU freezing measures. It could also enable the EU to preserve the principal but seek to invest and manage it more actively to generate a greater stream of revenues for Ukraine's benefit, endowment-style. This would have the effect of alleviating any concerns about the reversibility of countermeasures because the principal could be returned to Russia should it comply with its obligation to pay reparations.[61]

As we shall see, the SPV idea ultimately became subsumed within a larger set of proposals to do with the lending of the entire amount of frozen Russian state assets to Ukraine. Like so much in these discussions, the idea of 'lending' these assets without formally confiscating them might strike one as paradoxical. However, in a testament to the European Commission's ingenuity, it may well present a successful solution to the seemingly impossible task of making Russia pay *without* confiscating its property.

6.5 PHASE 3: REPARATIONS LOAN

For some time, it appeared that, short of a fundamental change in the EU's appetite to take on the legal, economic and policy considerations involved in an outright transfer of CBR assets to Ukraine, the ERA scheme would be the

[59] 'G7 Leaders' Statement on Extraordinary Revenue Acceleration (ERA) Loans' (25 October 2024), www.g7italy.it/wp-content/uploads/G7-Leaders-Statement-on-Extraordinary-Revenue-Acceleration-ERA-Loans.pdf.

[60] Philip Zelikow, 'A Fresh Look at the Russian Assets: A Proposal for International Resolution of Sanctioned Accounts' Hoover Institution (9 January 2025), www.hoover.org/research/fresh-look-russian-assets-proposal-international-resolution-sanctioned-accounts.

[61] Tom Keatinge and Kinga Redlowska, 'How to use Russia's central bank assets for Ukraine' Politico (1 April 2025), www.politico.eu/article/russia-central-bank-assets-ukraine.

proverbial 'only game in town'. This has changed in 2025 with the EU's proposal of a Reparations Loan that could provide Ukraine with approximately €135 billion in short order.[62]

The details of the proposal were made public in early December 2025.[63] The proposal formed a central part of the European Council's meeting on 17–18 December.[64] The chances of the proposal succeeding appeared high given the support from the German Chancellor, Friedrich Merz.[65] Berlin and Paris had been widely identified as the two national capitals whose agreement was crucial for securing EU action and overcoming any Belgian misgivings.

In the end, the proposal failed due to last-minute opposition by France and Italy.[66] Instead, a €90 billion loan to Ukraine was approved in principle that did *not* involve frozen Russian assets, but its disbursement is blocked by Hungary at the time of writing.[67] The other crucial outcome of the European Council's December 2025 meeting was the decision to extend the freezing of Russian state assets for an indefinite period of time, without requirement for further biannual renewals, based on Article 122 of the Treaty on the Functioning of the European Union.[68]

This means that the issue of disposal of frozen Russian state assets remains unresolved, and the Reparations Loan model could be considered again further down the line, although Friedrich Merz has recently been quoted as discounting that option. Still, in light of the Reparations Loan being the only concrete proposal as to the future of frozen Russian state assets considered by the EU, it is useful to explain its main features.

[62] Ursula von der Leyen, 'State of the Union Speech' (10 September 2025), www.europarl.europa.eu/doceo/document/CRE-10-2025-09-10-ITM-002_EN.html.

[63] Proposal for a Regulation of the European Parliament and of the Council establishing the Reparations Loan to Ukraine and amending Regulation (EU) 2024/792 of the European Parliament and of the Council of 29 February 2024 establishing the Ukraine Facility, 2025/3502 (COD), 3 December 2025, https://commission.europa.eu/document/download/ceae8dde-0291-4ee3-8519-80b30317bf35_en.

[64] Alastair McCready, 'EU proposes using Russian assets, loans to fund $105bn package to Ukraine' Al Jazeera (4 December 2025), www.aljazeera.com/news/2025/12/4/eu-proposes-using-russian-assets-loans-to-fund-105bn-package-to-ukraine.

[65] Jon Shelton, 'Merz says Germany and EU must "bring its power to bear"' DW (16 October 2025), www.dw.com/en/merz-says-germany-and-eu-must-bring-its-power-to-bear/a-74383436.

[66] Gregorio Sorgi, 'EU heavyweight Italy joins Belgium in opposing Russian frozen assets plan' Politico (12 December 2025), www.politico.eu/article/eu-italy-joins-belgium-opposing-russia-frozen-assets-plan; Oksana Kovalenko and Kateryna Kobernyk, 'How Western partners one by one buried Ukraine's hopes for a reparations loan — behind the scenes of the negotiations, which were not without surprises and threats from the Russians. Negotiator Mykola Yurlov tells the story' Babel (14 January 2026), https://babel.ua/en/texts/124290-how-western-partners-one-by-one-buried-ukraine-s-hopes-for-a-reparations-loan-behind-the-scenes-of-the-negotiations-which-were-not-without-surprises-and-threats-from-the-russians-negotiator-mykola-yur.

[67] Noa Schumann and Tamsin Paternoster, 'Fact check: Did the EU bypass Hungary's veto on Ukraine's €90 billion loan?' Euronews (27 February 2026), www.euronews.com/my-europe/2026/02/27/fact-check-did-the-eu-bypass-hungarys-veto-on-ukraines-90-billion-loan.

[68] Council Regulation (EU) 2025/2600 of 12 December 2025 on emergency measures addressing the serious economic difficulties caused by Russia's actions in the context of the war of aggression against Ukraine.

6.5.1 Reparations Loan Mechanics

The Reparations Loan would involve Euroclear transferring, or lending, CBR assets to Ukraine.[69] To receive this funding, Ukraine would have to present to the European Commission, and have the European Commission approve, a Ukrainian Financing Strategy.[70] The Ukrainian Financing Strategy would need to cover certain predetermined expenditures, including €45 billion for the repayment of the ERA loan.[71] Crucially, Ukraine will only be required to repay the Reparations Loan once it receives full reparations from Russia:[72]

> Given the difficult situation of Ukraine caused by Russia's war of aggression and in order to support Ukraine on its long-term stability path, it is appropriate for the Union to provide the Reparations Loan to Ukraine as a limited recourse loan that is to become due and payable when Ukraine receives from Russia cash or non-monetary assets for war reparations, indemnities or any financial settlement from Russia, other than territory.

If this were all that the Reparations Loan would entail, it would essentially amount to a transfer of frozen Russian state assets to Ukraine. Here comes the crucial detail. In exchange for the transfer of CBR assets from Euroclear to Ukraine, the EU will issue zero-per-cent bonds that Euroclear will hold for the CBR's benefit. These bonds will be equal in the amount to the assets that the CBR held via Euroclear. In other words, the EU will guarantee that it will repay Russia that total amount once Russia makes full reparations to Ukraine.[73]

It is worth taking a moment to contemplate what this scheme, circuitous though it is, might accomplish. From the EU's perspective, the Reparations Loan enables a plausible argument that CBR assets are not in any way expropriated. In legal terms, the CBR's Euroclear holdings comprise the CBR's claims on Euroclear, which are backed up by Euroclear's own claims on overseas banks where Euroclear holds its accounts (Euroclear's underlying assets). The transfer or loan of Euroclear's underlying assets to Ukraine does not extinguish or alter the CBR's claims on Euroclear. Furthermore, in economic terms, those claims are backed up by the EU's promise to pay €185 billion to enable Euroclear on deliver on its obligations vis-a-vis the CBR.

As a result, the Reparations Loan does not meaningfully alter the CBR's position compared to the status quo. It continues to own €185 billion in Euroclear

[69] Proposal 2025/3502 (COD) (n 63) 16.
[70] ibid, 18.
[71] ibid, 20, 22.
[72] ibid, 10. See also Bjarke Smith-Meyer and Gregorio Sorgi, 'Commission proposes €140B loan to Ukraine using Russian frozen assets' Politico (25 September 2025), www.politico.eu/article/european-commission-loan-ukraine-frozen-russian-assets.
[73] ibid.

but, as is the case at present, the EU's stance is that these funds will only be unfrozen if and when the CBR complies with its obligation to pay reparations to Ukraine. Should that happen, Ukraine will use the reparations funds it obtains from Russia to repay the EU, and the EU in turn will repay Russia. In that situation, the Reparations Loan will have caused Russia – or, in the language of the ARSIWA, 'induced' it – to comply with its international law obligation to provide reparations to Ukraine. On this basis, a recent report commissioned by the European Parliament concludes that the Reparations Loan presents the safest legal option for the use of frozen Russian state assets for Ukraine's benefit.[74]

An important consequence of this arrangement is mitigating the risk of Russia's non-payment. As things stand, Ukraine has a legal claim for reparations vis-a-vis Russia without any mechanism to enforce it. The Reparations Loan would provide Ukraine with €135 billion, which falls substantially short of the full reparations owed but is significant nonetheless, and mitigates the risk of non-payment in that amount. While legally the EU undertakes the obligation to repay that amount to Russia, that obligation will only be triggered by Russia's payment of full reparations, and therefore the EU's acceptance of that obligation would appear to be close to risk-free in practical terms.

Belgium has however insisted on there being substantial litigation risks stemming from any use of frozen Russian state assets.[75] In light of this, the law firm Covington and Burling LLP prepared a memorandum on the (very limited) Russian options for legal recourse and, consistent with the analysis presented earlier in this paper, concluded as follows:

> The argument that the EU should not proceed with the Reparations Loan because it involves unjustified legal risk should be given no weight by EU policymakers. In reality, it would be well-nigh impossible for Russia to persuade an international court or tribunal to find and exercise jurisdiction over such a claim. And, in the unlikely event that it succeeded in doing so, its claim would likely be defeated by one or more of the other practical challenges confronting it.[76]

6.5.2 Use of the Reparations Loan

One notable factor that has prompted the EU's discussion of the Reparations Loan is Ukraine's ongoing budgetary deficits. To sustain Ukraine's economic

[74] Maruša Veber, 'EU Sanctions and Russia's Frozen Assets' (European Parliament, November 2025) 72.

[75] Nick Beake, 'Belgium urges Europe to drop plan for frozen Russian assets to aid Ukraine' BBC News (3 December 2025), www.bbc.com/news/articles/cz7n95wzl9lo.

[76] Covington and Burling LLP, 'The Minimal Litigation Risk to EU Member States of the EU's Reparations Loan' (8 December 2025).

viability, new infusions of EU support would be required. There is therefore the possibility that the Reparations Loan will be used in lieu of EU economic aid to Ukraine. There are also reports of the EU contemplating the use of the loan for the purchase of military equipment for Ukraine.[77]

This raises questions that tend to surface in any discussion of a potential transfer, or some other use, of frozen Russian state assets for Ukraine's benefits. They pertain to the objectives towards which such funds can be put. While military purchases are vital to Ukraine's defensive effort, the allocation of these funds towards military expenditure would deplete the amount available to compensate the victims of Russia's war crimes or rebuild destroyed civilian infrastructure.

These discussions highlight an uncomfortable political reality. The strongest impetus for EU action on frozen Russian state assets is the prospect of defraying or minimising the EU's expenses in supporting Ukraine. Doing so would recognise and address the abiding absurdities of the status quo, which is that the EU has been spending its taxpayers' money on Ukraine while shielding hundreds of billions in Russian state money held within the EU. Self-evidently, though, this would detract from the funds that are badly needed to compensate Ukraine's population and rebuild civilian infrastructure, and therefore not fully advance the pursuit of reparations properly so called.

6.6 CONCLUSION

This chapter has sought to shed light on some of the manifold complexities involved in the debates about whether, and how, frozen Russian state assets can be used to deliver reparations for Ukraine. Understanding the evolution of these discussions is critical to a full appreciation of where we stand.

The fundamental question of whether frozen Russian state assets should be transferred to Ukraine in satisfaction of Russia's obligation to pay reparations is still central. However, the EU has demonstrated remarkable ingenuity and persistence in trying to leverage those assets for Ukraine's benefit without resorting to an outright transfer. This has generated challenges and opportunities alike.

One of the crucial challenges is the prospect of EU sanctions lapsing if a periodic six-month renewal is not secured. This has changed the complexion of the debates. In addition to the question of whether frozen Russian state assets can be transferred to Ukraine, a very real concern has emerged around the risks of their unintended return to Russia prior to any reparations being paid. These

[77] 'Ukraine could use reparations loan to buy weapons outside Europe, document shows' Reuters (18 October 2025), www.reuters.com/business/ukraine-could-use-reparations-loan-buy-weapons-outside-europe-document-shows-2025-10-17.

fears, coupled with Ukraine's budgetary woes, resulted in the development of the ultimately unsuccessful Reparations Loan proposal.

Had it been adopted, the Reparations Loan would have represented a culmination of the EU's resolve to deliver Russian state funds to Ukraine without transferring them – a seeming contradiction in terms. It appeared to present a credible, coherent and creative solution to the dilemmas with which the EU has been grappling. However, it would have required considerable further thought given to the details, including permissible uses to which the funds raised through the Reparations Loan can be put.

Following the EU's failure to agree on the Reparations Loan, the future of frozen Russian state assets remains uncertain. Their open-ended freezing from December 2025 onwards ensures that their imminent return to Russia is no longer likely. Equally, however, it is not entirely clear when, if ever, the EU may return to the fraught question of whether these assets could be utilised for Ukraine's benefit. Past experience suggests that the issue is likely to resurface once the financial pressures of defending Ukraine against Russia's aggression begin to be felt again.

With the EU continuing to be the locus of most activity, other G7+ nations, including Australia, Canada and Japan, do not yet appear to be willing or able to actively contribute to discussions over the fate of frozen Russian assets. Nor is there much hope for any leadership role for the United States under Donald Trump's second administration. This means that, somewhat unusually for global sanctions developments, the EU is likely to shape the future in this most important area of sanctions law and practice.

7

EU Sanctions on Russia – the War against Ukraine

CHRISTIAN KAUNERT AND JOANA DE DEUS PEREIRA

7.1 INTRODUCTION

IN THE WAKE of the fall of the Berlin Wall and the dissolution of the USSR, Europe found itself on the cusp of transformation, envisioning a future characterised by unity and prosperity among its neighbouring states. This aspiration set the stage for the European Neighbourhood Policy (ENP) and the Eastern Partnership (EaP), which aimed to foster stability and cooperation in countries such as Armenia, Azerbaijan, Belarus, Georgia, Moldova, and Ukraine.[1] However, the unfolding of recent events, particularly Russia''s ongoing aggression towards Ukraine, has fundamentally recalibrated the security landscape of Europe.[2] This recalibration marked a decisive break with the EU's earlier neighbourhood paradigm, which had been premised on gradual integration, conditional cooperation, and the diffusion of stability beyond the Union's borders. As Russia's actions increasingly challenged these assumptions, the EU's policy response shifted from engagement-centred instruments towards security-oriented measures. In this context, economic sanctions emerged as a central tool through which the EU sought not only to constrain Russian behaviour but also to signal normative boundaries, reaffirm its values, and redefine the meaning of security in its eastern neighbourhood.

This chapter analyses the impact of Russia's actions on European security, beginning with the sanctions regime imposed on Russia in response to its military incursions. It will assess the ontological securitisation process whereby

[1] Marek Dabrowski, 'A Special Historical Analysis: Europe's 35-Year Journey since the Fall of the Berlin Wall' Bruegel (6 November 2024); Judith Kelley, 'New Wine in Old Wineskins: Promoting Political Reforms through the New European Neighbourhood Policy' (2006) 44 *Journal of Common Market Studies* 29; Elena A Korosteleva, 'Change or Continuity: Is the Eastern Partnership an Adequate Tool for the European Neighbourhood?' (2011) 25 *International Relations* 243.

[2] Christian Kaunert and Joana de Deus Pereira, 'EU Eastern Partnership, Ontological Security and EU-Ukraine/Russian Warfare' (2023) *Journal of Contemporary European Studies* 1.

Ukraine and Europe are perceived as threats due to Russia's provocative behaviour. Under the leadership of Vladimir Putin, a calculated narrative has been crafted that invokes feelings of disruption and insecurity; this is realised through acts, imagery, and the deft manipulation of cognitive and normative frameworks[3] that elevate Russia as an ontologically stronger actor while undermining the EU. Unlike the ideological battles of the Cold War, where the spread of communism was central, Russia's current agenda seeks to destabilise and redefine the liberal and security order of the continent, reshaping it to its advantage rather than pursuing total military dominance.[4] As European leaders grapple with the implications of this renewed threat, it is clear that the relationship between the EU, its Eastern neighbours, and Russia must be re-evaluated to address the complexities of the contemporary geopolitical environment. The Eastern Partnership, initially envisioned as a vehicle for cooperation, has become increasingly challenged by a 'ring of fire' encompassing both the Eastern and Southern neighbours of the EU, prompting a critical reassessment of security cooperation and policies in light of the ever-evolving conflict in Ukraine.

The Ukrainian conflict has had a profound impact on the EU's Eastern Partnership, particularly in terms of its relationship with Russia. Zwolski identifies two contentious perspectives arising from this discussion: the first portrays Europe as being 'threatened by an expansionist Russia', leading to more proactive responses from the EU to counter this perceived threat.[5] Sakwa connects this viewpoint with the broader concept of a united Europe, which is encompassed within a larger Atlantic community.[6] The second perspective argues for a more 'inclusive approach towards Russia', which Sakwa relates to the notion of a greater Europe that would include not just Russia but also Turkey and Ukraine in a concentric arrangement.[7] Zwolski emphasises the consequences of these contrasting visions: Russia has shown expansionist tendencies, despite the EU and NATO's attempts to strengthen ties with neighbouring countries. This situation suggests a need for the EU to stand firm against Russia's aggressive behaviour towards its neighbours, as discussed in the 2015 House of Lords review on future

[3] Catarina Kinnvall, 'European Trauma: Governance and the Psychological Moment' (2012) 27 *Alternatives* 266; C Kinnvall, 'The Postcolonial Has Moved Into Europe: Bordering, Security and Ethno-Cultural Belonging' (2016) 54 *Journal of Common Market Studies* 152; Catarina Kinnvall, 'Ontological Insecurities and Postcolonial Imaginaries: The Emotional Appeal of Populism' (2018) 42 *Humanity & Society* 523; Catarina Kinnvall, 'Feeling Ontologically (In)Secure: States, Traumas, and the Governing of Gendered Space' (2017) 52 *Cooperation and Conflict* 90.

[4] Richard Sakwa, *Russia against the Rest: The Post-Cold War Crisis of World Order* (Cambridge University Press, 2017); Andrei P Tsygankov, 'Finding a Civilisational Idea: "West," "Eurasia," and "Euro-East" in Russia's Foreign Policy' (2007) 12 *Geopolitics* 375;

[5] Kamil Zwolski, 'Wider Europe, Greater Europe? David Mitrany on European Security Order' (2017) 55 *Journal of Common Market Studies* 645.

[6] Richard Sakwa, 'The Death of Europe? Continental Fates after Ukraine' (2015) 91 *International Affairs* 553.

[7] ibid.

EU–Russia relations).[8] Scholarly debates on EU–Russia relations and the war in Ukraine are extensive and encompass competing interpretations of responsibility, intent, and systemic change. For the purposes of this chapter, however, two core perspectives are particularly relevant. One emphasises Russia's revisionist behaviour and views the conflict as a catalyst for a more assertive EU security posture.[9] The other frames Russia as reacting to European and Euro-Atlantic expansion, highlighting Moscow's perceived security concerns and the failure of post-Cold War institutional inclusivity.[10]

This chapter engages selectively with these perspectives to advance a different analytical focus, and explores how anxieties and fears have influenced the policy agendas of both the EU and Russia in the Eastern Neighbourhood, particularly concerning Ukraine, this chapter is structured as follows: it will first investigate the ontological securitisation process in the relationship between Europe and Russia (section 7.2), subsequently analysing how both sides have articulated their fears and anxieties throughout the Ukrainian conflict in two phases: 2014 and from 2022 onward (section 7.3). Additionally, the chapter will assess the interactions between the EU and Russia during the war in Ukraine from 2014 onwards, and from 2022 (section 7.4) and how these evolving dynamics pose ongoing threats to the stability and resilience of the Eastern Neighbourhood. Finally, the chapter integrates the case of EU sanctions against Russia within this theoretical framework (section 7.5) with a brief summary and reflections on key findings of the chapter (section 7.6).

7.2 ONTOLOGICAL SECURITISATION BETWEEN THE EU AND RUSSIA

This section sets out the conceptual foundations of the chapter, drawing on ontological security and securitisation theory to examine the identity-based dynamics underpinning EU–Russia security relations.

Ontological security, a concept rooted in sociology and psychology, refers to a state of stable self-identity and continuity in the perception of self-existence. It encompasses an individual's or a collective entity's ability to maintain a coherent and consistent narrative of self over time, which is crucial for psychological well-being and social functioning.[11] In International Relations (IR), the concept

[8] House of Lords, 'The EU and Russia: Before and beyond the Crisis in Ukraine - European Union Committee' (UK Parliament, March 2015), https://publications.parliament.uk/pa/ld201415/ldselect/ldeucom/115/11510.htm.

[9] Matthias Matthijs and R Daniel Kelemen, 'Europe Reborn' 94 *Foreign Affairs*, www.foreignaffairs.com/articles/europe/europe-reborn; Jolyon Howorth and Anand Menon, 'Wake up, Europe!' (2015) 1 *Global Affairs* 11.

[10] Sakwa (n 6).

[11] Kinnvall, 'European Trauma' (n 3); Kinnvall, 'The Postcolonial Has Moved Into Europe' (n 3); Kinnvall, 'Feeling Ontologically (In)Secure' (n 3); Catarina Kinnvall, Ian Manners and Jennifer

of ontological security has been extended to understand how states and societies seek a stable sense of their identity amid an uncertain and changing international environment. This involves managing anxieties arising from existential threats to their narrative continuity and sense of self-coherence.[12] The significance of ontological security lies in its ability to provide a deeper explanation for behaviour beyond material or rational calculations, emphasising how individuals and states construct and maintain existential narratives that enable them to navigate uncertainties.[13] These narratives function as a framework that helps agents make sense of the social world, maintaining a sense of 'being' that is essential for their ontological stability. The failure to sustain ontological security can trigger crises that permeate both internal socio-political orders and external relations

Securitisation theory is a framework for understanding how issues come to be framed as existential threats that require extraordinary measures beyond routine political procedures. Rather than treating threats as objective, the framework highlights securitisation as a discursive process in which actors frame referent objects as under threat and seek audience acceptance for extraordinary responses.[14] This focus on speech acts and audience reception is particularly relevant for analysing EU–Russia relations, where security policies, including sanctions, are embedded in contested narratives of threat, legitimacy, and identity. In this context, securitisation helps explain how the EU has progressively framed Russia's actions as warranting exceptional policy responses, and how these framings have been accepted, contested, or reinforced across different audiences.[15] The amalgamation of ontological security with securitisation theory creates a robust analytical lens wherein the focus expands from purely political processes to include psychological and identity-based drivers of securitising moves.[16] While securitisation theory elucidates how security threats are socially constructed and politically legitimised, it traditionally underexplores the deeper motivations behind why individuals and collectives assent to these constructions.[17] Ontological security bridges this gap by explaining that identities – both individual and collective – seek existential continuity and reassurance, making

---

Mitzen, 'Introduction to 2018 Special Issue of European Security: "Ontological (in) Security in the European Union"' (2018) 27 *European Security* 249.

[12] Kinnvall, 'European Trauma' (n 3); Kinnvall, 'The Postcolonial Has Moved Into Europe' (n 3).

[13] Christopher S Browning and Pertti Joenniemi, 'Ontological Security, Self-Articulation and the Securitization of Identity' (2016) 52 *Cooperation and Conflict* 31.

[14] Thierry Balzacq, 'The Three Faces of Securitization: Political Agency, Audience and Context'' (2005) 11 *European Journal of International Relations* 171; Thierry Balzacq (ed), 'Securitization Theory: How Security Problems Emerge and Dissolve' (Routledge, 2010).

[15] Phillippe Bourbeau, *The Securitization of Migration: A Study of Movement and Order* (Routledge, 2011); Sarah Leonard and Christian Kaunert, *Refugees, Security and the European Union* (Routledge, 2019).

[16] Christian Kaunert and Edwin Ezeokafor, 'Securitization Outside the West: West African Security Reconceptualised' (Routledge, 2022).

[17] Christian Kaunert and Ori Wertman, 'The Securitisation of Hybrid Warfare through Practices within the Iran-Israel Conflict - Israel's Practices to Securitize Hezbollah's Proxy War' (2020) 31 *Security and Defence Quarterly* 99.

audiences predisposed to accept securitisation when it aligns with their need to maintain ontological stability.[18] Ontological security thus complements securitisation theory by addressing why securitising moves resonate emotionally and cognitively with audiences, and why groups might request or encourage securitisation from powerful elites.[19] This theoretical synergy enriches our understanding of the securitisation process by situating identity management and anxiety reduction as core drivers behind security politics rather than viewing securitisation as merely a top-down discursive manoeuvre.[20]

Originally developed by Giddens and subsequently adapted in IR, the concept has been used to explain how states seek to preserve a stable sense of self in the face of uncertainty and disruption.[21] In this context, security practices are not only responses to material threats but also means of stabilising identity and managing anxiety. This perspective is useful for analysing EU–Russia relations, as it helps illuminate how policies such as sanctions serve to reaffirm normative boundaries, political agency, and the EU's self-understanding as a security actor.

Ontological insecurity, stemming from threats to identity continuity and coherence, drives audiences to seek reassurance in securitisation narratives that promise protection and order.[22] Reflexivity, or self-awareness, becomes pivotal as actors interpret threat claims through the lens of identity preservation, rendering securitisation outcomes contingent on this identity work.[23]w Proposals for a multidimensional approach argue that securitisation should not be viewed solely as a discursive act but also as a process imbued with emotional and psychological undercurrents that bind audiences to threat constructions. This comprehensive framework acknowledges emotional investments, cultural insecurities, and anxiety management as synergistic mechanisms reinforcing securitisation.[24]

7.2.1 The Role of Identity in Ontological Securitisation

Ontological security fundamentally depends on stable narratives that provide continuity for both individual and collective identities. These narratives serve as cognitive frameworks enabling actors to navigate uncertainty by anchoring

[18] Browning and Joenniemi (n 13).

[19] Bourbeau (n 15); Phillippe Bourbeau, 'Moving Forward Together: Logics of the Securitisation Process' (2014) 43 *Millennium: Journal of International Studies* 187.

[20] Kaunert and Ezeokafor (n 16).

[21] Browning and Joenniemi (n 13); Brent J Steele, *Ontological Security in International Relations: Self-Identity and the IR State* (Routledge, 2008).

[22] Eteri Tsintsadze-Maass, 'Ontological Crisis and the Compartmentalization of Insecurities' (2024) 4 *Global Studies Quarterly* ksae003.

[23] Thierry Balzacq, Sarah Léonard and Jan Ruzicka, '"Securitization" Revisited: Theory and Cases' (2016) 30 *International Relations* 494; Bourbeau (n 15).

[24] Browning and Joenniemi (n 13).

their sense of self in a predictable social reality.[25] For states and societies, sustaining ontological security entails the preservation and reinforcement of collective identity through symbolic practices, rituals, and discourse.[26] The state plays a critical role in this process by acting as an institutional referent that manages internal identity coherence and negotiates external recognition. Failures of recognition, or misrecognition, introduce ontological insecurity and prompt defensive reactions to safeguard the integrity of one's identity.[27] This dynamic clearly showcases the interdependence between identity, ontological security, and political actions, especially in foreign policy and conflict contexts.[28]

Perceived threats to identity act as powerful catalysts for securitisation, as they destabilise ontological security and trigger collective anxiety.[29] These threats are not merely material but exist as challenges to the ontological continuity of self and group narratives. Fear and anxiety become the emotional substrate upon which securitising actors build their claims, mobilising support by emphasising existential stakes tied to identity survival.[30] Ethnic tensions, nationalism, and intergroup conflicts vividly illustrate how identity threats precipitate securitisation, especially when framed as attacks on the group's core being or cultural essence.[31] Such framings mobilise insecurities that make audiences more receptive to exceptional measures presented as necessary for identity continuity.

Narratives and collective memory are central to ontological securitisation, shaping the interpretative frames through which identities are constructed and existential threats assessed.[32] Mnemonic securitisation pertains to the politicisation and instrumentalisation of collective memories to legitimise security claims and delegitimise alternative perspectives. Selective remembrance serves to reinforce in-group identity and ontological security by sacralising certain historical

[25] Kinnvall, 'European Trauma' (n 3); Kinnvall, 'The Postcolonial Has Moved Into Europe' (n 3); Kinnvall, 'Feeling Ontologically (In)Secure' (n 3); Kinnvall, 'Ontological Insecurities and Postcolonial Imaginaries' (n 3).

[26] Jennifer Mitzen, 'Ontological Security in World Politics: State Identity and the Security Dilemma' (2006) 12 *European Journal of International Relations* 341; Steele (n 21).

[27] Matt McDonald, 'Securitization and the Construction of Security' (2008) 14 *European Journal of International Relations* 563.

[28] Steele (n 21).

[29] Kaunert and de Deus Pereira (n 2).

[30] Kaunert and Wertman (n 17).

[31] Tugba Basaran, 'Security, Law, Borders: Spaces of Exclusion' (2008) 2 *International Political Sociology* 339; Stuart Croft and Nick Vaughan-Williams, 'Fit for Purpose? Fitting Ontological Security Studies "into" the Discipline of International Relations: Towards a Vernacular Turn' (2017) 52 *Cooperation and Conflict* 12; Vincent Della Sala, 'Narrating Europe: The EU's Ontological Security Dilemma' (2018) 27 *European Security* 266; Rita Floyd, 'Can Securitization Theory Be Used in Normative Analysis? Towards a Just Securitization Theory' (2011) 42 *Security Dialogue* 427; Rita Floyd, 'Extraordinary or Ordinary Emergency Measures: What, and Who, Defines the "Success" of Securitization?' (2016) 29 *Cambridge Review of International Affairs* 677.

[32] Mitzen (n 26); Steele (n 21).

experiences while marginalising or criminalising others.[33] Political myths and mnemonic narratives, such as those surrounding wartime heroes or the concept of victimhood, become ontological strategies that sustain identity coherence during times of crisis. These affect peacebuilding by either entrenching conflict through exclusionary narratives or facilitating resolution through inclusive remembrance and narrative pluralism.[34]

Securitisation may be driven by a range of actors, including states, political elites, and non-state groups such as nationalist movements or social.[35] These actors act as securitising agents by framing issues as existential threats to ontological security, thereby legitimising exceptional measures that depart from ordinary political practices. The involvement of non-state actors complicates state-centric approaches to securitisation and highlights how identity-based or localised groups may articulate security claims within contested political contexts.[36]

Audiences play a decisive role in ontological securitisation, as their acceptance transforms threat narratives into legitimate security practice.[37] Such acceptance is more likely when securitising narratives resonate with identity concerns and provide reassurance in the face of uncertainty. Audience engagement involves both cognitive and emotional investment, with fear and anxiety shaping receptivity to securitising claims. As a result, securitisation remains a contingent and contested process, dependent on sustained resonance between threat constructions and collective affective states.[38]

7.2.2 Processes and Dynamics of Ontological Securitisation

Ontological insecurity often motivates securitising moves, as actors seek to stabilise identity and continuity in situations of uncertainty or crisis.[39] Justifications for ontological securitisation typically invoke the need to preserve the coherence and stability of identity narratives, framing exceptional measures as both necessary and legitimate. In this sense, securitisation functions not only as a response to perceived threats but also as a mechanism for reinforcing political authority and identity coherence.

Once initiated, securitisation is maintained through repeated speech acts, symbolic practices, and institutionalised narratives that reinforce dominant threat

[33] Amir Lupovici, 'The Limits of Securitization Theory: Observational Criticism and the Curious Absence of Israel' (2014) 16 *International Studies Review*.

[34] Croft and Vaughan-Williams (n 31); Della Sala (n 31).

[35] Balzacq, 'The Three Faces of Securitization' (n 14); Balzacq, 'Securitization Theory' (n 14); Kaunert and Ezeokafor (n 16).

[36] Floyd, 'Securitization Theory' (n 33); Floyd, 'Extraordinary or Ordinary Emergency Measures' (n 33).

[37] Mitzen (n 26); Steele (n 21).

[38] Balzacq, Léonard and Ruzicka (n 23).

[39] Mitzen (n 26); Steele (n 21).

perceptions and marginalise alternative interpretations.[40] These mechanisms, ranging from mnemonic practices to media and institutional representation, help manage anxiety and uncertainty while sustaining exceptional policy responses over time. In doing so, ontological securitisation contributes to the durability of security frameworks even in the absence of immediate or escalating material threats.

Building on this analytical framework, the following section turns to the empirical context of Russia's war against Ukraine, examining the geopolitical conditions and security dynamics that shaped EU–Russia relations before and after 2014.

7.3 RUSSIA'S WAR AGAINST UKRAINE

7.3.1 Geopolitical Landscape before 2014

Before the outbreak of the conflict in 2014, EU–Russia relations were characterised by a complex mixture of cooperation and tension, embedded within a wider regional security framework that was framed by the post-Cold War order in Europe.[41] The EU maintained substantial economic and political ties with Russia, seeing it as a strategic partner in areas such as energy, trade, and diplomacy. However, these cooperative aspects were underpinned by simmering geopolitical tensions, most notably surrounding the eastward enlargement of NATO, which Russia perceived as a direct encroachment on its sphere of influence.[42] This perception shaped Russia's geopolitical posture, reflecting a broader strategic concern to prevent deeper Western integration of post-Soviet states. Ukraine's positioning was inherently delicate, situated geopolitically and symbolically between aspirations for closer EU integration and historic, cultural, and economic ties with Russia.[43] This liminal status contributed to Ukraine becoming a focal point of competing influence between the Western bloc, spearheaded by the EU and the US, and Russia's efforts to maintain its regional hegemony.[44] Russia's increasing suspicion and anxiety about the EU's Eastern Partnership initiative and NATO's open-door policy towards countries in its vicinity heightened the risk of confrontation. These dynamics set the stage for the Ukrainian crisis, with Russia's anxieties over NATO enlargement being a persistent thread in Moscow's strategic

[40] Balzacq, 'The Three Faces of Securitization' (n 14); Balzacq, 'Securitization Theory' (n 14); Balzacq, Léonard and Ruzicka (n 23).

[41] Zwolski (n 5); Stefan Auer, 'Carl Schmitt in the Kremlin: The Ukraine Crisis and the Return of Geopolitics' (2015) 91 *International Affairs* 953; Howorth and Menon (n 9); Sakwa (n 6).

[42] Sakwa (n 6).

[43] Zwolski (n 5).

[44] Kaunert and de Deus Pereira (n 2).

calculus.[45] Nonetheless, the EU and Russia continued engaging in dialogue, with hopes for stable coexistence shaping official approaches until tensions escalated dramatically in 2014. The broader security architecture, which since the Cold War had rested on a series of normative taboos against the use of force to redraw borders in Europe, was being tested by the convergence of expanding EU integration, NATO enlargement, and Russian assertiveness.[46]

The year 2014 marked a decisive turning point with Russia's annexation of Crimea, swiftly followed by the onset of armed conflict in Eastern Ukraine's Donetsk and Luhansk regions.[47] The seizure of Crimea represented a blatant violation of international law and Ukraine's territorial sovereignty, radically altering the European security environment.[48] This act was accompanied by covert and overt support for separatist forces in Eastern Ukraine, leading to a protracted low-intensity conflict.[49] The international reaction was immediate and intense, with the EU instituting its first sanctions regime targeting individuals and entities directly involved in or supporting Russia's actions.[50] These measures included travel bans, asset freezes, and restrictions on key economic sectors closely linked to the annexation and destabilisation efforts. The sanctions framework was designed to exert targeted pressure on Russia while minimising broader humanitarian consequences. Domestically, Ukraine underwent dramatic political shifts as the Maidan Revolution ousted pro-Russian President Yanukovych, signifying an overt pivot towards European integration aspirations.[51] However, Ukraine faced immense security challenges as fighting broke out in the East and Russian-backed actors undermined the country's sovereignty.[52] The resulting conflict created a prolonged humanitarian crisis and significant strain on Ukraine's evolving state institutions. The EU and international

[45] Sakwa (n 6).

[46] Auer (n 41); Howorth and Menon (n 9); Zwolski (n 5).

[47] Auer (n 41); Howorth and Menon (n 9).

[48] Thomas D Grant, 'Annexation of Crimea' (2015) 109 *American Journal of International Law* 68; John Biersack and Shannon O'Lear, 'The Geopolitics of Russia's Annexation of Crimea: Narratives, Identity, Silences, and Energy' (2014) 55 *Eurasian Geography and Economics* 247; *Ukraine v Russia; (Re Crimea)* (2023) 202 International Law Reports 292.

[49] Anna Matveeva, 'Donbas: The Post-Soviet Conflict That Changed Europe' (2022) 23 *European Politics and Society* 410; Andrew Wilson, 'The Donbas in 2014: Explaining Civil Conflict Perhaps, but Not Civil War' (2016) 68 *Europe-Asia Studies* 631.

[50] Council Regulation (EU) No 269/2014 of 17 March 2014 concerning restrictive measures in respect of actions undermining or threatening the territorial integrity, sovereignty and independence of Ukraine [2014] OJ L 78/6; Council Regulation (EU) No 692/2014 of 23 June 2014 concerning restrictions on the import into the Union of goods originating in Crimea or Sevastopol, in response to the illegal annexation of Crimea and Sevastopol [2014] OJ L 183/9; Council Regulation (EU) No 825/2014 of 30 July 2014 amending Regulation (EU) No 692/2014 concerning restrictions on the import into the Union of goods originating in Crimea or Sevastopol, in response to the illegal annexation of Crimea and Sevastopol [2014] OJ L 226/2.

[51] Volodymyr Ishchenko, *Towards the Abyss: Ukraine from Maidan to War* (Verso Books, 2024); Taras Kuzio, *Ukraine: Democratization, Corruption, and the New Russian Imperialism* (Praeger, 2015).

[52] Richard Sakwa, *Frontline Ukraine: Crisis in the Borderlands* (Bloomsbury Publishing, 2014); Wilson (n 49).

institutions endeavoured diplomatic channels, such as the Minsk agreements, to broker a ceasefire and peace, though with limited success.[53] These efforts were complicated by the asymmetry of power and strategic ambiguity surrounding Russia's true objectives and level of direct involvement, setting the groundwork for the conflict's continuation.

7.3.2 Overview of the Two-Phase Conflict Framework

The protracted conflict in Ukraine is best understood within a two-phase framework.[54] The first phase, spanning from 2014 to 2022, was marked by a low-intensity conflict characterised by hybrid warfare tactics, support for separatists, and gradual escalation of sanctions and diplomatic pressure by the EU and its allies.[55] During this period, the EU's response evolved from symbolic political measures to more substantive economic sanctions targeting critical sectors of the Russian economy.[56] Military engagements remained predominantly localised in Eastern Ukraine, underscoring a conflict that, while severe, had not erupted into full-scale war.[57]

The second phase commenced in February 2022 with Russia's full-scale invasion of Ukraine, which dramatically escalated the conflict in terms of military operations, territorial control ambitions, and humanitarian impact.[58] This phase also witnessed an intensified and broadened sanctions regime by the EU, extending into areas previously considered sacrosanct, such as energy and financial sectors. The operational context shifted from a frozen or low-intensity conflict to an active war front, compelling recalibration of military, diplomatic, and economic strategies. This phase also catalysed significant geopolitical shifts within Europe and beyond, redefining security alliances, EU defence policies, and enlargement trajectories.[59]

[53] Cindy Wittke, 'The Minsk Agreements – More than 'Scraps of Paper'?' (2019) 35 *East European Politics* 264.

[54] Hiski Haukkala, 'From Cooperative to Contested Europe? The Conflict in Ukraine as a Culmination of a Long-Term Crisis in EU–Russia Relations' (2015) 23 *Journal of Contemporary European Studies* 1; Kaunert and de Deus Pereira (n 2).

[55] Roy Allison, 'Russian "Deniable" Intervention in Ukraine: How and Why Russia Broke the Rules' (2014) 90 *International Affairs* 1255; Bettina Renz, 'Russia and "Hybrid Warfare"' (2016) 22 *Contemporary Politics* 283; Andrew Monaghan, *The New Politics of Russia: Interpreting Change* (Manchester University Press, 2016), https://library.oapen.org/handle/20.500.12657/32305.

[56] Clara Portela and others, 'Consensus against All Odds: Explaining the Persistence of EU Sanctions on Russia' (2021) 43 *Journal of European Integration* 683.

[57] Andrey Makarychev, 'Beyond Geopolitics: Russian Soft Power, Conservatism, and Biopolitics' (2018) 3 *Russian Politics* 135.

[58] Petro Sukhorolskyi, 'Russian Aggression against Ukraine: Past, Present, and Futures (2022) 26 *Journal of Futures Studies*, https://jfsdigital.org/2022-2/vol-26-no-4-june-2022/russian-aggression-against-ukraine-past-present-and-futures; Kaunert and de Deus Pereira (n 2).

[59] Center for Preventive Action, 'War in Ukraine' (Global Conflict Tracker, 16 December 2025), https://cfr.org/global-conflict-tracker/conflict/conflict-ukraine; Sukhorolskyi (n 58).

7.3.2.1 *Phase 1: Conflict Dynamics from 2014 to 2022*

In the initial phase, Russia's military and paramilitary activities centred on Crimea and the Donetsk and Luhansk regions of Eastern Ukraine.[60] The annexation of Crimea was complemented by Russian military presence and the empowerment of separatist militias in Donbas. The warfare tactics combined conventional military operations with hybrid elements, including information warfare, covert deployments, and irregular forces, blending deniability with strategic objectives aimed at destabilising Ukraine.[61] The Minsk agreements, brokered in 2014 and 2015, sought to institute ceasefire arrangements and a political roadmap to resolve the conflict. These agreements included provisions for a ceasefire, withdrawal of heavy weapons, amnesty, and constitutional reforms in Ukraine to grant special status to the conflict regions.[62] Despite these frameworks, implementation stalled repeatedly due to violations and escalating skirmishes, effectively freezing the conflict but not resolving the underlying tensions. This stalemate prolonged the instability and prevented meaningful peace. Throughout this period, Russian hybrid warfare methods intensified, as Moscow employed economic coercion, information campaigns, and diplomatic pressure to maintain leverage.[63] The conflict formed a persistent security challenge to Ukraine's sovereignty, eroding trust and sharpening divisions within the EU and NATO about how to balance deterrence, engagement, and escalation risks.[64]

The EU's political and diplomatic response over this period involved multi-layered sanction packages alongside sustained diplomatic engagement.[65] Sanctions evolved gradually, targeting key sectors such as finance, energy, and defence, while also focusing on individuals involved in the aggression.[66] This phased approach reflected efforts to calibrate between signalling condemnation and maintaining a dialogue potential.[67] The EU attempted to coordinate with other international actors, including the United States and multilateral institutions, to maximise the impact of the sanctions. However, instituting these measures revealed institutional challenges, including the traditionally slow and

[60] Uygar Baspehlivan, 'Putin & Russian Heritage: Russia's Foreign Policy Identity Since Napoleon' (E-International Relations, 5 March 2016), www.e-ir.info/2016/03/05/putin-russian-heritage-russias-foreign-policy-identity-since-napoleon; Zbigniew Brzezinski, *The Grand Chessboard: American Primacy and Its Geostrategic Imperatives*, 2nd edn (Basic Books, 2016).

[61] Flemming Splidsboel Hansen, 'Russia's Relations with the West: Ontological Security through Conflict' (2016) 22 *Contemporary Politics* 359; Howorth and Menon (n 9).

[62] Council of Europe, Agreements Establishing the Commonwealth of Independent States 1994 (CDL (94) 54) 138; Makarychev (n 57).

[63] Brian Whitmore, 'Is This the End of Ukraine's Peace Process?' *The Atlantic* (5 August 2015), www.theatlantic.com/international/archive/2015/08/russia-ukraine-conflict-minsk-ceasefire-passports/400505.

[64] Kaunert and de Deus Pereira (n 2).

[65] Clara Portela, 'Are European Union Sanctions "Targeted"?' (2016) 29 *Cambridge Review of International Affairs* 912.

[66] Portela and others (n 56).

[67] Kaunert and de Deus Pereira (n 2).

consensus-driven Common Foreign and Security Policy (CFSP) decision-making process.[68] Despite such structural constraints, the EU managed to establish increasingly robust enforcement mechanisms and improve coordination between supranational and Member State levels, especially toward the latter years of the first phase.[69]

Diplomatic efforts ran in parallel with sanctions, with initiatives aimed at conflict resolution and political stabilisation, involving negotiations under formats such as the Normandy process.[70] These efforts were hindered by divergent interests among stakeholders and Russia's strategic objectives, which prevented the development of rapid or comprehensive solutions. Moreover, the EU faced ongoing pressure to balance internal policy coherence with external political commitments.[71] The sanctions inflicted measurable economic effects on Russia. Key sectors, including banking, finance, and energy, experienced constraints that led to capital flight, reduced access to global markets, and technological embargoes.[72] These measures contributed to a decline in investment inflows and industrial output, pressuring the Russian economy. However, the effect was mitigated by Russia's countermeasures, such as import substitution policies, repositioning toward Asian markets, and utilising alternative financial mechanisms.[73]

Ukraine, meanwhile, demonstrated notable resilience, mobilising its society and institutions despite ongoing military and economic hardships.[74] The socio-economic toll was severe, especially in conflict-affected regions, with displacement, infrastructural damage, and contraction of economic activity.[75] Nonetheless, Ukraine leveraged international support and reforms to sustain critical functions, adapt its economy, and maintain a strategic orientation towards

[68] Daniel Fiott and Giulia Tercovich, *Qualified Majority Voting in Common Foreign and Security Policy: A Cost of Non Europe Report* (Publications Office, 2023), https://data.europa.eu/doi/10.2861/509043.

[69] Della Sala (n 31).

[70] Andrew Lohsen and Pierre Morcos, 'Understanding the Normandy Format and Its Relation to the Current Standoff with Russia' (CSIS, 9 February 2022), www.csis.org/analysis/understanding-normandy-format-and-its-relation-current-standoff-russia.

[71] Gerard Toal, *Near Abroad: Putin, the West and the Contest over Ukraine and the Caucasus* (Oxford University Press, 2017).

[72] Christian Dreger and others, 'Between the Hammer and the Anvil: The Impact of Economic Sanctions and Oil Prices on Russia's Ruble' (2016) 44 *Journal of Comparative Economics* 295.

[73] Richard Connolly, *Russia's Response to Sanctions: How Western Economic Statecraft Is Reshaping Political Economy in Russia* (Cambridge University Press, 2018); Richard Connolly and Cecilie Sendstad, 'Russian Rearmament: An Assessment of Defense-Industrial Performance' (2018) 65 *Problems of Post-Communism* 143.

[74] Karina Korostelina, 'National Resilience to Protracted Violence in Ukraine' (2020) 27 *Peace and Conflict Studies*, https://nsuworks.nova.edu/pcs/vol27/iss2/4.

[75] Gwendolyn Sasse, 'War and Displacement: The Case of Ukraine' (2020) 72 *Europe-Asia Studies* 347; Valeria Lazarenko, 'Conflict in Ukraine: Multiplicity of Narratives about the War and Displacement' (2019) 20 *European Politics and Society* 550.

Western integration.[76] Russia's adaptive capacity, including the utilisation of its sovereign wealth fund and tighter fiscal controls, mitigated the long-term impact of sanctions. Economic diversification efforts, although constrained, allowed Russia to mitigate some immediate shocks but could not fully compensate for restrictions on technology and finance.[77]

7.3.2.2 Phase 2: Full-Scale Invasion from 2022 to Present

The transition to full-scale warfare in 2022 marked an unprecedented expansion of hostilities.[78] Russia undertook coordinated offensives on multiple fronts across Ukraine, deploying massive conventional forces aiming to seize territorial control, notably targeting Kyiv, Kharkiv, and southern regions. The scale, speed, and intensity of military operations starkly contrasted the previous phase's hybrid and limited engagements.[79] Ukrainian forces, supported by extensive international military aid and internal mobilisation, mounted robust territorial defences and successive counteroffensives. This defensive resilience not only inflicted significant material and personnel losses on Russian forces but also galvanised Ukrainian society and the international community around the conflict's stakes. The humanitarian toll was staggering, with millions displaced internally and abroad, widespread civilian casualties, and infrastructure devastation of urban and rural areas alike.[80] The war thus precipitated a severe crisis with profound social and demographic implications, extending into neighbouring EU states through refugee flows and economic strain.[81]

[76] Christoph Trebesch and others, 'The Ukraine Support Tracker: Which Countries Help Ukraine and How?' (Kiel Working Paper, 2023) Working Paper 2218, www.econstor.eu/handle/10419/270853; Maryna Rabinovych and Andrea Gawrich, 'The Conflict in Eastern Ukraine and International Support for the Decentralization Reform (2014–2022): Theory-Guided Observations' (2023) 37 *East European Politics and Societies* 1036.

[77] Iwona Wiśniewska, 'A Game of Cat and Mouse. How Russia Is Circumventing Sanctions' (OSW, April 2025); Cristina Popa, 'Ten Years of Economic Sanctions and Their Macroeconomic Impact on the Russian Federation' (2024) 12 *Expert Journal of Economics* 37.

[78] Hardy Hanappi, 'Russia. The Background of The Russian Invasion of Ukraine' (2022) XIII *Theoretical and Practical Research in Economic Fields* 116; Taras Kuzio, 'Why Russia Invaded Ukraine' (2022) *Horizons: Journal of International Relations and Sustainable Development* 40.

[79] Markus Balázs Göransson, 'Russia's Thinking on New Wars and Its Full-Scale Invasion of Ukraine' (2024) 24 *Defence Studies* 449; Steven L Chadwick, John A Nagl and Katie Crombe, 'Russia-Ukraine War Lessons for Multidomain Operations' (Strategic Studies Institute, US Army War College, 2024), www.jstor.org/stable/resrep61511.20; Roman Knubel, Marcel Berni and Moritz Nepomuk Kueng, 'From Chechnya to Ukraine: Russian Military Adaptation in a Comparative Perspective' (2025) *Journal of Strategic Studies* 1.

[80] Jack Watling and Nik Reynolds, 'Ukraine at War: Paving the Road From Survival to Victory' RUSI Special Report (4 July 2022), www.rusi.orghttps://www.rusi.org.

[81] European Commission, 'The Cost of EU Member States' Proximity to the War - Economy and Finance' (17 November 2025), https://economy-finance.ec.europa.eu/cost-eu-member-states-proximity-war_en; Ryhor Nizhnikau and Arkady Moshes, 'The War in Ukraine, the EU's Geopolitical Awakening and Implications for the "Contested Neighbourhood"' (2024) 45 *Policy*

In response to the invasion, the EU dramatically expanded and intensified its sanctions, unprecedented both in scope and scale. The EU adopted comprehensive restrictions targeting sectors central to Russia's war capabilities, including a phased embargo on oil and coal imports, exclusion of Russian banks from SWIFT, capital market closures, and severe export controls on technology and dual-use goods vital for military and industrial applications.[82] This escalation of sanctions mirrored a strategic shift toward economic warfare aimed at crippling Russia's ability to finance continuous military operations. EU institutions underwent a functional restructuring, with greater roles assigned to the European Commission in sanction design and enforcement, enabling swifter and more coherent action, and signalling an evolution beyond traditional intergovernmentalism in the CFSP framework. The energy sanctions, given Europe's prior reliance on Russian supplies, also triggered an accelerated transition in the EU's energy policy, fostering diversification of sources, investment in renewables, and measures such as the RePowerEU plan to reduce dependency.[83]

The war catalysed profound geopolitical realignments. The EU articulated a strategic *Zeitenwende*, a historic reorientation toward enhanced defence capability, strategic autonomy, and deeper security integration. NATO significantly reinforced its eastern flank, while transatlantic cooperation intensified to coordinate military, economic, and diplomatic pressure on Russia. [84] Internationally, the conflict highlighted existing fractures and new alignments, with the EU accelerating Ukraine's candidacy status, reviving its enlargement policy focus, and managing relations with Eastern Partnership countries amid the war's repercussions. [85] This set the stage for a recalibrated European power projection and reflects evolving global balance-of-power dynamics.

Studies 489; Wojciech Pac, 'Demographic And Social Consequences Of The Russo-Ukrainian War For Ukraine' (2024) 9 *Politics & Security* 53.

[82] Francesco Giumelli, 'A Comprehensive Approach to Sanctions Effectiveness: Lessons Learned from Sanctions on Russia' (2024) 30 *European Journal on Criminal Policy and Research* 211; Peter AG van Bergeijk, 'Sanctions and the Russian-Ukraine Conflict: A Critical Appraisal' (15 March 2022), available at SSRN 4058559; 'EU Sanctions against Russia' (Consilium), www.consilium.europa.eu/en/policies/sanctions-against-russia.

[83] Tetiana Vasylieva, 'From Energy Dependency to Energy Security: How the War in Ukraine Accelerated Renewable Deployment in Europe' (2025) 18 *Economics and Sociology* 229; Caroline Kuzemko and others, 'Russia's War on Ukraine, European Energy Policy Responses & Implications for Sustainable Transformations' (2022) 93 *Energy Research & Social Science* 102842; Rosalba Famà, 'REPowerEU' in Federico Fabbrini and Christy A Petit (eds), *Research Handbook on Post-Pandemic EU Economic Governance and NGEU Law* (Edward Elgar Publishing, 2024), www.elgaronline.com/edcollchap/book/9781035328161/book-part-9781035328161-17.xml.

[84] Ivan Bakalov, 'Explaining the Russian Invasion in Ukraine: Between Geopolitics, Civilisational Choice, and Dead-End Capitalist Transition' (2024) 21 *Globalizations* 1215; Stefanie Ortmann, 'Russian Spatial Imaginaries and the Invasion of Ukraine: Geopolitics and Nationalist Fantasies' (2023) 101 *Political Geography* 102784.

[85] Dmytro Panchuk, 'The Impact of the Russian Invasion of Ukraine on Public Support for EU Enlargement' (2024) 31 *Journal of European Public Policy* 3128; Roman Petrov, 'Bumpy Road of Ukraine Towards the EU Membership in Time of War: "Accession Through War" v "Gradual Integration"' (2023) 2023 8 *European Papers* 1057.

7.4 EU SANCTIONS ON RUSSIA

The EU sanctions against Russia serve not just as an economic coercive measure but also as a fundamental instrument via which the Union aims to stabilise its ontological security against a significant threat to the European security framework.[86] The imposition of restrictive measures following the 2014 annexation of Crimea was significantly transformed by Russia's comprehensive invasion of Ukraine in February 2022. Sanctions transitioned from being calibrated signalling mechanisms to integral components of a comprehensive economic strategy designed to limit Russia's ability to conduct high-intensity warfare and to reinforce the EU's identity as a security entity dedicated to territorial sovereignty and international law.[87]

The post-2022 sanctions system signifies a shift from targeted restraint to structural disruption. The EU shifted its focus from solely promoting behavioural change through elite pressure to undermining the material underpinnings of Russia's war economy by limiting access to finance, advanced technologies, logistics, and energy revenues. Within an ontological securitisation framework, these policies have served to both materially undermine Russia and symbolically delineate it as outside the European normative system, so strengthening the EU's self-perception as the custodian of that order.

The efficacy of sanctions must hence be evaluated along two dimensions: material restraint and ontological stabilisation. Sanctions have exerted continuous pressure on Russia's access to cash, technology, and export markets, especially in industries associated with defence production and energy infrastructure.[88] Russia's adaptive capacity via import substitution, alternative payment systems, and selective decoupling has alleviated immediate shocks but has not eradicated enduring limitations on productivity and military-industrial rejuvenation.[89] This pattern highlights a fundamental finding of sanctions scholarship: sanctions seldom achieve immediate coercive success; rather, they function as cumulative limitations whose political impacts develop gradually over time.[90]

Simultaneously, sanctions have fulfilled a vital intra-EU role. The escalation following 2022 prompted institutional transformation by augmenting the European Commission's operational role in sanctions coordination, enforcement, and anti-circumvention initiatives, thereby partially supplanting

[86] Calle Håkansson, 'The Ukraine War and the Emergence of the European Commission as a Geopolitical Actor' (2024) 46 *Journal of European Integration* 25; Clara Portela, 'Sanctions and the Geopolitical Commission: The War over Ukraine and the Transformation of EU Governance' (2024) 2023 8 *European Papers* 1125.

[87] Portela and others (n 56); Giumelli (n 82).

[88] Giumelli (n 82).

[89] Wiśniewska (n 77).

[90] Dominika Studzińska, Julia Dunaj and VIktor Pashkov, 'The (in)Effectiveness of Sanctions: An Attempt at Evaluating the Effectiveness of the Sanction Policy against Russia' (2024) 14 *Journal of Geography, Politics and Society* 14; Giumelli (n 82).

conventional intergovernmental authority within the CFSP.[91] This transition illustrates the dynamics of extraordinary politics linked to securitisation: after Russia was characterised as an existential threat to European order, the EU sanctioned increasingly centralised and invasive governance techniques to maintain credibility and coherence. Sanctions thereby facilitated the strengthening of EU actorness clarifying responsibility and power in crisis management.

Furthermore, energy sanctions have also mirrored the extensive structural ramifications of this securitisation shift. The limitations on Russian energy earnings, coupled with Moscow's manipulation of supply, hastened a strategic shift in EU energy strategy towards diversification, demand reduction, and investment in renewables.[92] This transition has been perceived as a security-oriented reconfiguration of dependency rather than a solely economic adjustment.[93]

Ultimately, EU sanctions have facilitated broader geopolitical realignment. They have enhanced transatlantic cooperation, strengthened NATO–EU complementarity, and engaged with the resurgence of EU enlargement as a strategic tool, particularly through Ukraine's expedited candidature. These developments highlight that sanctions are not a singular policy reaction but rather an integral component of a comprehensive process of delineating boundaries and establishing order. Their ability to persuade Russia to conclude the conflict is unknown; but, their importance is evident in the manner they have reshaped European security practices and identity in the face of an ontological threat.

To sustain this expanded sanction regime and its geopolitical objectives, the EU simultaneously adapted its legal and institutional framework governing the adoption, implementation, and enforcement of restrictive measures, which the following section will briefly describe.

7.5 EVOLUTION AND LEGAL FRAMEWORK

The translation of these identity-shaping and geopolitical effects into durable policy practice required parallel adjustments to the EU's legal and institutional architecture. As sanctions evolved from temporary crisis instruments into a core component of the EU's security posture, their effectiveness increasingly depended on the capacity of existing legal frameworks to sustain prolonged exceptional measures.[94] This development exposed structural tensions within

[91] Jacopo Giraudo, 'EU Restrictive Measures: How to Make Them More Efficient and Effective'CEPOB (March 2024); Marco Sibona, 'Tackling Circumvention of EU Sanctions' Policy Brief (Jacques Delors Institute, October 2024).

[92] Famà (n 83); Vasylieva (n 83).

[93] Andreas Goldthau and Nick Sitter, 'Whither the Liberal European Union Energy Model?: The Public Policy Consequences of Russia's Weaponization of Energy' (2022) 23 *EconPol Forum* 4.

[94] Katharina Meissner and Chiara Graziani, 'The Transformation and Design of EU Restrictive Measures against Russia' (2023) 45 *Journal of European Integration* 377.

the CFSP, particularly between the requirements of rapid collective action, legal certainty, and the preservation of member state sovereignty.[95]

From an ontological securitisation perspective, legal frameworks are not neutral conduits for policy implementation. Rather, they function as mechanisms through which exceptional security practices are stabilised and normalised. Embedding these identity-driven and geopolitical shifts into durable policy practice required corresponding adaptations in the EU's legal and institutional architecture. Council decisions and implementing regulations thus serve not only to ensure compliance, but also to codify threat perceptions, reinforce identity boundaries, and sustain EU actorness under conditions of persistent insecurity.

7.5.1 Typology of EU Sanctions

The EU sanctions regime against Russia is structured around a differentiated typology that reflects both strategic intent and legal constraint. This layered design enables the EU to calibrate pressure while maintaining internal cohesion and legal proportionality.[96]

- *Individual sanctions*, including travel bans and asset freezes, target political elites, military officials, oligarchs, and entities deemed responsible for undermining Ukraine's sovereignty. Legally grounded in CFSP Council decisions and implemented through binding regulations, these measures aim to personalise responsibility and signal normative condemnation without directly penalising the wider population. Analytically, individual sanctions perform a symbolic function within ontological securitisation by identifying specific agents as threats to European order, thereby reinforcing a moral boundary between legitimate and illegitimate actors.
- *Sectoral economic sanctions* represent a more structural form of coercion. These measures restrict access to EU capital markets, prohibit transactions with key financial institutions, and limit investment and services in strategic sectors such as energy and defence. By targeting the infrastructural foundations of Russia's war economy, sectoral sanctions reflect a shift from behavioural signalling towards long-term constraint. Within the EU's legal framework, their expansion required increasingly detailed regulations and monitoring mechanisms, underscoring the move from episodic response to sustained economic statecraft.

[95] Clara Portela and Kim B Olsen, 'Implementation and Monitoring of the EU Sanctions' Regimes, Including Recommendations to Reinforce the EU's Capacities to Implement and Monitor Sanctions' (European Parliament, 2023), www.europarl.europa.eu/RegData/etudes/STUD/2023/702603/EXPO_STU(2023)702603_EN.pdf.

[96] 'EU Sanctions against Russia: Questions and Answers' (Consilium), www.consilium.europa.eu/en/policies/sanctions-against-russia-explained.

- *Trade and technology controls* further deepen this logic by restricting exports of dual-use goods, advanced technologies, semiconductors, aerospace components, and military-relevant equipment. These measures are explicitly designed to erode Russia's future military and industrial capabilities rather than to compel immediate policy reversal. Their legal complexity reflects the EU's attempt to reconcile security imperatives with obligations under international trade law, highlighting how ontological insecurity reshapes regulatory priorities.
- *Financial and monetary restrictions*, including the exclusion of major Russian banks from SWIFT and limitations on dealings with the Central Bank of Russia, represent some of the most far-reaching measures adopted after 2022. These sanctions illustrate how legal innovation has been mobilised to disrupt systemic financial access while remaining formally compliant with EU competences. Politically, they mark a decisive escalation in the EU's willingness to accept economic risk in defence of security identity.
- *Transport and media sanctions* extend the regime beyond economic coercion. Airspace bans and restrictions on Russian carriers aim to isolate Russia physically and symbolically, while prohibitions on state-backed media outlets address the informational dimension of hybrid warfare. These measures demonstrate how the EU's sanctions framework has expanded to encompass cognitive and communicative domains, reinforcing ontological boundaries through the regulation of movement and narrative.

7.5.2 Enforcement, Normalisation, and Limits

The durability of this typology depends on enforcement. Since 2022, the European Commission has assumed a more prominent role in coordination, monitoring, and anti-circumvention efforts, signalling a partial shift away from strict intergovernmentalism. Enhanced customs cooperation, information sharing, and legal instruments addressing sanctions evasion reflect attempts to close implementation gaps that threaten the credibility of the regime.

Yet this evolution also exposes enduring constraints. Divergent national capacities, uneven enforcement, and legal challenges concerning proportionality and competence[97] reveal the limits of a framework originally designed for short-term restrictive measures. The EU's sanctions architecture thus embodies a paradox: sanctions have become indispensable to the Union's security identity, yet their effectiveness remains contingent on legal coherence, institutional coordination, and sustained political consent across a heterogeneous polity.

[97] See further on this the chapters by Finelli and Öberg and Van Elsuwege and Challet in this volume.

Table 7.1 Summary of key EU sanction measures against Russia post-2022

Sanction category	Measures	Targeted effects
Individual sanctions	Travel bans, asset freezes on officials, oligarchs	Restrict Kremlin affiliates' movement and finances
Energy sector	Embargoes and price caps on oil, bans on coal imports, tech embargo	Reduce Russia's energy export revenues
Financial sector	SWIFT bans for banks, freezing Central Bank reserves, trading bans	Isolate Russian financial institutions
Trade controls	Export restrictions on dual-use goods, high-tech equipment	Limit military and technological advancement
Transportation	Ban on Russian airlines, transport restrictions	Limit Russia's connectivity and economic activity
Media	Ban on state-backed Russian media outlets	Combat disinformation
Trade embargoes	Bans on coal, steel, gold, imports from occupied territories	Disrupt key sectors and annexation-related imports
Compliance enforcement	Customs risk management, sanctions evasion legislation	Ensure uniform application and counter evasion

7.6 CONCLUSION

EU sanctions have become a cornerstone of the Union's response to Russia's war against Ukraine and its challenge to the post-Cold War European security order. The analysis shows that sanctions cannot be reduced to an instrument of economic coercion alone. They have also functioned as a repertoire of identity-affirming practices through which the EU has sought to restore narrative continuity, stabilise agency, and reassert a boundary between a rules-based European order and Russia's challenge to that order.

Viewed through ontological securitisation, the key dynamic is not simply whether sanctions compel compliance, but how they institutionalise threat perceptions and enable the EU to sustain a coherent sense of 'self' under conditions of disruption. Russia's actions from 2014 onward, and especially after February 2022, produced a profound rupture in the EU's neighbourhood paradigm and in the assumptions that underpinned engagement with Moscow. In response, sanctions served three interlocking functions. First, they operated as *boundary-making devices*, designating Russia as an illegitimate actor outside the normative space of European order and thereby reaffirming the EU's identity commitments to sovereignty and territorial integrity. Secondly, they became instruments of *exceptional politics normalised over time*: what began as reactive restrictive measures evolved into a durable security practice embedded in EU governance, with intensified coordination, enforcement, and anti-circumvention measures. Thirdly, sanctions strengthened *EU actorness* by consolidating internal authority structures, clarifying responsibility, and enabling collective action in ways that partially offset longstanding CFSP constraints.

This ontological reading also helps clarify why debates over sanctions 'effectiveness' frequently generate ambivalent conclusions. The evidence suggests that sanctions have imposed meaningful constraints on Russia's access to finance, technology and markets, yet they have not produced immediate coercive success. Rather, their impact has been cumulative, interacting with Russia's adaptive strategies and with the broader trajectory of the war. From the perspective advanced here, this does not render sanctions analytically marginal. Their significance lies in how they have reshaped European security practice: accelerating the securitisation of interdependence (particularly in energy), reinforcing transatlantic coordination, and linking economic statecraft to wider projects of European order-making, including the renewed strategic salience of enlargement and Ukraine's candidacy.

Finally, the chapter highlights that sanctions have contributed to a *cycle of mutual securitisation*. As the EU has codified Russia as a threat to European order, Russia has reciprocally intensified narratives of external encirclement and civilisational antagonism. This feedback loop is likely to entrench long-term confrontation and constrain future pathways back to cooperative security arrangements. The implication is that sanctions should be analysed not merely as a tool used within EU foreign policy, but as part of a deeper transformation in the EU's identity and security governance. Future research should therefore move beyond narrow coercion-centred evaluations and examine more systematically how sanctions reshape institutions, narratives, and audience expectations – both within the EU and in the target state – over time.

8

The WTO Law Dimension of Unilateral Economic Sanctions: The EU Economic Sanctions against Russia – A Case Study

RACHEL FRID*

8.1 INTRODUCTION: UNILATERAL ECONOMIC SANCTIONS AND THE WTO LEGAL FRAMEWORK

Recent years have witnessed a substantial increase in the implementation of unilateral economic sanctions for non-trade objectives.[1] The definition and the legality of unilateral economic sanctions under international law remain undetermined.[2] Generally speaking, unilateral economic sanctions are understood to be direct trade-restricting policies between sovereign states,

* The author wishes to thank Professor Jacob Öberg (University of Southern Denmark) and Professor Ester Herlin-Karnell (University of Gothenburg) for their insightful comments on earlier drafts of this chapter. It was first presented at SNELS Conference on Sanctions in EU Policy and Law at Lund University 16–17 May 2024.

[1] The term 'unilateral economic sanctions', which is relevant for this chapter, will be used interchangeably with the terms 'economic sanctions' and 'trade sanctions'. The term 'states' will be used to include the EU, as an entity that has the competence to impose economic sanctions under EU law that are binding on its member states.

[2] The definition of 'economic sanctions' is outside the scope of this chapter. For different views on definitions of the term see eg Alain Pellet and Alina Miron, 'Sanctions' in Rüdiger Wolfrum (ed), *Max Planck Encyclopedia of Public International Law* (Oxford University Press, 2013); Alain Pellet, 'Unilateral Sanctions and International Law' (2015) 76 *Yearbook of the Institute of International Law* 723; Tom Ruys, 'Sanctions, Retorsions and Countermeasures: Concepts and International Legal Framework' in Larissa Van den Herik (ed), *Research Handbook on UN Sanctions and International Law* (Edward Elgar, 2017); Tom Ruys, 'Immunity, Inviolability and Countermeasures: A Closer Look at Non-UN Targeted Sanctions' in Tom Ruys and Nicolas Angelet (eds), *The Cambridge Handbook of Immunities and International Law* (Cambridge University Press, 2019); Devika Hovell, 'Unfinished Business of International Law: The Questionable Legality of Autonomous Sanctions' (2019) 113 *AJIL Unbound* 140.

without prior authorisation from an international forum, based on domestic legal frameworks.[3]

The objective of economic sanctions is generally related to achieving changes in the internal or foreign policy of the target country. Economic sanctions are thus an economic instrument that aims to achieve political objectives. Sanctions are widely seen as being part of international diplomacy and as providing an alternative to war. While the use of economic sanctions can politically be an attractive policy tool, their effectiveness is arguable, and they often entail harmful effects.[4]

This chapter focuses on examining the legality of comprehensive economic sanctions, such as trade bans, under World Trade Organization (WTO) law[5] and the effects sanctions might have on the rule of international trade law. From an international trade law perspective, the growing tendency of using economic sanctions by WTO members may raise concern regarding the potential harmful consequences to the rule of international trade law, primarily because economic sanctions that affect trade allegedly violate WTO rules. Article XXI of the General Agreement on Tariffs and Trade (GATT) provides WTO members with exceptional powers to deviate from their WTO obligations when essential security interests are at stake, and is commonly used as legal basis for applying economic sanctions among WTO members. This tendency has prompted targeted states to increasingly challenge the legal validity of economic sanctions within the WTO legal system, generating important jurisprudential developments.[6]

To assess the WTO consistency of unilateral economic sanctions taken under Article XXI GATT, the chapter examines the lawfulness under WTO law of EU

[3] Economic sanctions appear in the form of financial or investment restrictions, import and export restrictions including so-called 'boycotts' and 'embargoes', sectoral restrictions, asset freezes, and travel bans. Boycotts are generally associated with the refusal to purchase goods and services from a supplier, and embargoes imply that no goods and services will be supplied to the buyer. Other variations of sanctions include novel type sanctions, so-called 'smart sanctions', that are targeted against certain individuals or entities (private or governmental) or a policy to completely isolate a country and break off economic and trade relations. For a useful distinction between sanctions according to their degree of discrimination see Thomas J Biersteker and others, 'Thinking About United Nations Targeted Sanctions' in Thomas Biersteker and others (eds), *Targeted Sanctions: The Impacts and Effectiveness of United Nations Action* (Cambridge University Press, 2016).

[4] See eg Maarten Smeets, 'Can Economic Sanctions be Effective?' (WTO Staff Working Paper ERSD-2018-03, 15 March 2018); Peter Egger, Constantinos Syropoulos and Yoto V Yotov, 'Analyzing the Effects of Economic Sanctions: Recent Theory, Data, and Quantification' (2024) 32 *Review of International Economics* 1; Peter AG van Bergeijk (ed), *Research Handbook on Economic Sanctions* (Edward Elgar, 2021); Clara Portela and Andrea Charron, 'The Evolution of Databases in the Age of Targeted Sanctions' (2023) 25 *International Studies Review* viac061; Alena F Douhan, 'Unilateral Coercive Measures: Effects and Legality Issues' (Yale Journal of International Law Online, 20 June 2023), https://campuspress.yale.edu/yjil/unilateral-coercive-measures-effects-and-legality-issues; Andreas Hofer, 'The EU's "Massive and Targeted" Sanctions in Response to Russian Aggression, a Contradiction in Terms' (2023) 25 *Cambridge Yearbook of European Legal Studies* 19.

[5] Some targeted or 'smart' sanctions like assets freezes and travel restrictions on individuals and entities fall outside the scope of WTO law. Ton Notermans, 'Are EU Trade Sanctions on Russia WTO Compatible?' (10 June 2022) https://ssrn.com/abstract=4141568.

[6] See section 8.2.3.

sanctions against Russia as a case study. The EU's sanctions present a useful case study given the EU's big share in world trade, its commitment to WTO rules and the increasing application of economic sanctions by the EU as a tool of EU foreign policy.

This chapter contends that even if, from a legal standpoint, unilateral trade sanctions imposed by the EU or any other WTO member would seem to satisfy the WTO''s legal requirements, this would nonetheless necessitate scrutiny of the potentially detrimental impact on the WTO legal regime, and more broadly, on the rule of international trade law as embodied by the WTO legal system.

The chapter deals with these issues in the following manner: section 8.2 provides a thorough analysis of the scope, interpretation, and evolving jurisprudence of the national security exception under Article XXI GATT. Based on this analysis, section 8.3 offers a case study examining the WTO compatibility of EU sanctions against Russia following the Russia–Ukraine war. If the EU sanctions should appear to deviate from the EU's WTO obligations, the question of whether the EU sanctions would withstand WTO scrutiny under Article XXI GATT will be examined. Section 8.4 will draw conclusions and provide recommendations for the way ahead.

8.2 THE NATIONAL SECURITY EXCEPTION: ARTICLE XXI GATT

The growing application of economic sanctions under Article XXI GATT by WTO members calls for a thorough examination of their WTO law consistency. This section offers an analysis of the scope, interpretation, and evolving jurisprudence of the national security exception under Article XXI GATT.

8.2.1 Unilateral Economic Sanctions and WTO Law

Unilateral economic sanctions that affect trade allegedly violate WTO rules. Article XXI GATT provides WTO members with exceptional powers to deviate from their WTO obligations when essential security interests are at stake and is commonly used as legal basis for applying economic sanctions among WTO members. These security exceptions represent a delicate balance between on the one hand, respecting 'members' sovereignty in security matters and on the other hand, maintaining the integrity of the multilateral trading system and the jurisdiction of the WTO Dispute Settlement Mechanism (DSM) to review members' use of their discretion.

Within the WTO legal architecture, two principal deviations from WTO obligations may be legally justified:

- The first category concerns authorised measures. The Dispute Settlement Body (DSB) may authorise retaliatory measures that deviate from the principle of non-discrimination. The DSB may authorise the complainant to withdraw concessions to compensate for losses sustained as a result of an unjustified trade action by the respondent.[7]

- The second category concerns unauthorised measures where WTO members may adopt certain emergency measures that deviate from WTO obligations without the authorisation of the DSB. Such unauthorised measures are permissible only as WTO exceptions and must satisfy specific conditions stipulated under WTO provisions.[8]

It is important to draw a distinction between (un)authorised measures and unilateral economic sanctions.

Both unauthorised emergency measures and unilateral sanctions deviate from WTO rules, they are not authorised by WTO organs, and both may be justified under various exceptions. However, while unauthorised emergency and defensive trade measures serve to protect the economy of the imposing member, the objective of unilateral sanctions is usually to change the political behaviour of the targeted member, an objective that is remote from trade considerations. Furthermore, the member applying unauthorised emergency measures is under certain surveillance in accordance with WTO rules, while the sanctioning member acting under the national security exception has a very broad discretion for performing its actions.

The differences between authorised retaliatory measures and unilateral sanctions are more prominent. Retaliatory measures are authorised by the DSM as a result of a legal process and are under the DSM surveillance. Importantly, the aim of such measures is to restore compliance with WTO obligations and trade balance. Contrary to that, unilateral sanctions are decided unilaterally by the sanctioning member. Moreover, economic sanctions sustain the violation of WTO rules by the sanctioning member, because they are often used for non-economic interests where the targeted member did not violate its WTO obligations.

There is clearly a tension between unilateral economic sanctions and the fundamental objective of the WTO. The WTO's principled aim is to liberalise trade between its members and reduce trade restrictions internationally,

[7] Marrakesh Agreement Establishing the World Trade Organization (adopted 15 April 1994, entered into force 1 January 1995) 1867 UNTS 154, Annex 2 (Understanding on Rules and Procedures Governing the Settlement of Disputes) (DSU) Arts 21 and 22.

[8] For example: to protect or restore an adequate level of foreign currency reserves (Arts XII and XVIII:B GATT; Understanding on the Balance-of-Payments Provisions of the General Agreement on Tariffs and Trade 1994); to provide temporary protection for domestic industries in case of an unforeseen surge in import causing serious injury (Art XIX GATT); or when confronted with unfair trading practices (Agreement on Implementation of Article VI of GATT 1994; Agreement on Subsidies and Countervailing Measures). In addition, the WTO framework includes three escape clauses. Art XXXV GATT allows for non-application of the agreement only at the time of accession of a new Member State. For an overview of the other waivers and exceptions in the WTO agreements see David Kramer, 'Exceptions to WTO Rules' in Daniel Bethlehem and others (eds), *The Oxford Handbook of International Trade Law*, 2nd edn (Oxford University Press, 2021).

whereas economic sanctions are aimed to restrict trade with targeted states and in essence add trade restrictions, mostly for non-economic reasons, in order to deprive them from trade gains.[9] For as long as unilateral sanctions are in force certain trade concessions no longer apply. This nullifies the concessions that were exchanged between the parties and are contained in legally binding schedules of concessions. This goes to the very heart of the WTO system to ensure predictable and growing access to markets.[10]

The drastic increase in the use of unilateral economic sanctions for non-trade policy goals, and the growing tendency by the imposing states to invoke national security exceptions contained in Article XXI GATT in defence of violations of WTO obligations, calls for a thorough consideration.[11]

Article XXI GATT provides WTO members with exceptional powers to deviate from their WTO obligations when essential security interests are at stake. These security exceptions represent a delicate balance between on the one hand, respecting members' sovereignty in security matters and on the other hand, maintaining the integrity of the multilateral trading system and the jurisdiction of the WTO DSM to review members' use of their discretion.

Next the scope, interpretation, and evolving jurisprudence of Article XXI GATT will be examined.

8.2.2 The Text and Structure of Article XXI GATT

The language employed in Article XXI GATT appears to grant WTO members extraordinarily broad discretion, particularly through the qualifying phrase 'which it considers' in paragraphs (a) and (b).[12] This wording suggests that the determination of what constitutes 'essential security interests' and what actions

[9] Smeets, 'Conflicting Goals: Economic Sanctions and the WTO' (2000) 2 *Global Policy Dialogue*.

[10] Comprehensive economic sanctions directly affect the quantity of trade and are therefore causing more trade distortion than the imposition of import duties. Import duties define the price level of a product and might result in a high price but contrary to trade bans such duties leave the choice to the consumer and do not block trade. This is the rationale of Art XI.1 GATT that prohibits trade restrictions other than duties, taxes or other charges, with some exceptions defined in Art XI.2.

[11] The national security exceptions contained in Art XXI GATT are mirrored in Art XIV bis General Agreement on Trade in Services (GATS) and Art 73 Agreement on Trade-Related Aspects of Intellectual Property Rights (TRIPS), which will not be analysed in this chapter.

[12] Art XXI GATT reads as follows: 'Nothing in this Agreement shall be construed (a) to require any contracting party to furnish any information the disclosure of which it considers contrary to its essential security interests; or (b) to prevent any contracting party from taking any action which it considers necessary for the protection of its essential security interests (i) relating to fissionable materials or the materials from which they are derived; (ii) relating to the traffic in arms, ammunition and implements of war and to such traffic in other goods and materials as is carried on directly or indirectly for the purpose of supplying a military establishment; (iii) taken in time of war or other emergency in international relations; or (c) to prevent any contracting party from taking any action in pursuance of its obligations under the United Nations Charter for the maintenance of international peace and security.'

are 'necessary' for their protection is left largely to the invoking member's judgment.

Unlike other GATT exceptions, Article XXI does not explicitly establish prior notification requirements or procedural safeguards for its invocation. This gap was partially addressed by the 1982 Decision Concerning Article XXI of the General Agreement ('the 1982 Decision') which requires members to notify other members of measures taken under Article XXI.[13] It is notable that the 1982 Decision sets a notification requirement but not a prior notification requirement. Article 1 of the 1982 Decision reads, 'contracting parties should be informed to the fullest extent possible of trade measures taken under Article XXI', thus referring to measures already taken and not prior to imposing such measures. In addition, the notification requirement under the 1982 Decision is qualified by Article XXI(a), which exempts members from disclosing information they consider contrary to their essential security interests. Furthermore, the language 'should be informed to the fullest extent *possible*' (emphasis added) under Article 1 of the Decision maintains significant discretion for the invoking member regarding the timing and content of notifications.

The national security exceptions stand in stark contrast to other GATT exceptions that are allowed without a DSM authorisation. For example, general exceptions that may justify violation of the non-discrimination principle by legitimate domestic regulatory purposes are found under Article XX GATT. While Article XX begins with a *chapeau* requiring that measures 'are not applied in a manner which would constitute a means of arbitrary or unjustifiable discrimination between countries where the same conditions prevail, or a disguised restriction on international trade', Article XXI contains no comparable constraint. This difference might significantly broaden the scope of permissible measures under Article XXI and reduce the grounds upon which they might be challenged.

Thus, the provisions in Article XXI, read together with the 1982 Decision, would appear to suggest that a WTO member may interrupt its trade relations with WTO members and allegedly violate WTO rules, whenever it deems it necessary for its security interests, without prior notice and with no comparable constraints to other WTO exceptions, subject to its unilateral discretion. As a result, a targeted member has no possibility in real time to dispute the measures before the DSM. De facto it means that measures under Article XXI can be imposed unilaterally by a WTO member without prior DSM review and authorisation.

[13] The Decision states: '1. Subject to the exception in Article XXI(a), contracting parties should be informed to the fullest extent possible of trade measures taken under Article XXI; 2. When action is taken under Article XXI, all contracting parties affected by such action retain their full rights under the General Agreement; 3. The Council may be requested to give further consideration to this matter in due course.'

The growing use of Article XXI GATT security exceptions to justify economic sanctions, entailed a substantial increase in challenging the legal validity of such sanctions within the WTO legal system.

8.2.3 Jurisprudential Developments on Article XXI GATT

The WTO's DSM appears to be the most suitable international forum to adjudicate claims regarding the WTO consistency of economic sanctions between WTO members.[14] Notably, a potential WTO challenge of the legality of sanctions could not comprise the entire scope of sanctions but only comprehensive sanctions affecting trade and regulated under the WTO rules thus falling within the purview of the DSM jurisdiction.[15]

In the past, from the inception of GATT in 1947 until the establishment of the WTO in 1995, only five cases concerning Article XXI were brought before the DSM, none of which resulted in a binding panel report.[16] The scarcity of jurisprudence caused a substantial uncertainty concerning the scope of Article XXI, particularly its prima facie self-judging nature. In principle, sanctions could be challenged under the DSM, but since there was not much room for a legal review of the GATT compatibility of those measures,[17] such recourse to the DSM had only limited value for the targeted member.

In recent years the legal situation has changed. The increased use of Article XXI GATT security exceptions to justify economic sanctions by WTO members has precipitated a corresponding increase in challenges to such measures under the DSM, generating important jurisprudential developments.

[14] Since unilateral economic sanctions are based on the domestic legislation of the states imposing them, their legality may be challenged before the domestic courts of these states and under their domestic law. This option is hardly ever applied by states. The WTO's DSM is the common option for challenging sanctions also due to the scarcity and difficulty to bring such claims before other international forums. There are only a few examples: Iran initiated two disputes against the United States before the International Court of Justice (ICJ): Certain Iranian Assets (*Islamic Republic of Iran v United States of America*) and Alleged Violations of the 1955 Treaty of Amity, Economic Relations, and Consular Rights (*Islamic Republic of Iran v United States of America*). Qatar questions the legality of economic sanctions imposed against it before the ICJ (Application of the International Convention on the Elimination of All Forms of Racial Discrimination (*Qatar v United Arab Emirates*)) as well as before the WTO (DS526 is an ongoing dispute and in DS567 the panel report was issued, yet it is under appeal). Nevertheless, one of the main obstacles for bringing a claim before the ICJ are the rules on the court's jurisdiction. Iryna Bogdanova, 'Targeted Economic Sanctions and WTO Law: Examining the Adequacy of the National Security Exception' (2021) 48 *Legal Issues of Economic Integration* 171, 171–72.

[15] Some targeted or 'smart' sanctions like assets freezes and travel restrictions on individuals and entities fall outside the scope of WTO law. Notermans (n 5).

[16] US – Export Restrictions (Czechoslovakia) (June 1949); Sweden – Import Restrictions on Certain Footwear (17 November 1975); US – Imports of Sugar from Nicaragua (13 March 1984); US – Nicaraguan Trade (13 October 1986); EC – Trade Measures against the Socialist Federal Republic of Yugoslavia (2 December 1991); see Michael J Hahn, 'Vital Interests and the Law of GATT An Analysis of GATTs Security Exception' (1991) 2 *Michigan Journal of International Law* 558.

[17] Roger P Alford, 'The Self-Judging WTO Security Exception' (2011) *Utah Law Review* 697.

8.2.3.1 *General Guidelines for Interpreting Article XXI GATT*

The Panel in *US – Origin Marking (Hong Kong, China)* underlined the important balance between members' flexibility to take unilateral actions for protecting their security interests and the limits of the use of such flexibility:

> [T]he reading discussed here serves the security and predictability of the multilateral trading system by allowing for sufficient flexibility for members to adopt the measures they consider necessary for the protection of their security interests, while at the same time ensuring that this flexibility is exercised within the limits intended by the drafters.[18]

The Panel noted the limited scope in which security-related issues may be addressed by the DSM:

> [T]he WTO should not become a forum to discuss security issues generally. Rather, the WTO Agreement and its annexes set forth the limited circumstances under which the WTO and its dispute settlement mechanism have been tasked with addressing security matters linked to international trade. Only in those circumstances, would it be appropriate for those issues to be addressed.[19]

8.2.3.2 *The Justiciability Question: Scope of Panels Jurisdiction to Review Article XXI GATT*

Challenges to the justiciability of members actions under Article XXI represents a fundamental question in Article XXI jurisprudence. The 'justiciability' question under Article XXI(b)(iii) was definitively addressed in *Russia – Traffic in Transit*. The Panel asserted that WTO panels have 'the power to determine all matters arising in relation to the exercise of their own substantive jurisdiction'.[20] The Panel noted that the DSU contains no special provisions regarding disputes involving Article XXI and therefore found that the respondent's invocation of this provision fell within its terms of reference.[21]
Similarly, in *US – Steel and Aluminium Products (Turkey)*, the panel concluded that

> the entirety of Article XXI(b) of the GATT 1994 is to be given meaning and effect in a manner that preserves the right and discretion of a member to take action it considers necessary for the protection of its essential security interests under the conditions and circumstances described in subparagraphs (i) to (iii). The Panel does not consider that Article XXI(b) of the GATT 1994 is 'self-judging' or 'non-justiciable' …[22]

[18] Panel Report, United States – Origin Marking Requirement WT/DS597/R (adopted 23 July 2021) para 7.148.
[19] ibid, para 7.149.
[20] Panel Report, Russia – Measures Concerning Traffic in Transit WT/DS512/R (adopted 26 April 2019) para 7.5.3.
[21] ibid, para 7.56.
[22] Panel Report, United States – Steel and Aluminium Products WT/DS564/R (adopted 14 December 2022) para 7.143.

The panel further emphasised that the absence of any provision in the text of Article XXI(b) regarding the review of actions taken pursuant to this provision is not determinative. 'The absence of explicit provision or elaboration in Article XXI(b) of the GATT 1994 as to whether and how its invocation may be reviewed does not, in itself, preclude or otherwise determine the review of that provision in dispute settlement proceedings.[23] Rather, the scope and nature of such review derives from the terms of Article XXI(b) and the requirements of the DSU, which acknowledges *inter alia* the role of the WTO dispute settlement system in "providing security and predictability to the multilateral trading system". If Article XXI(b) of the GATT 1994 is raised in dispute settlement proceedings, the DSU requires that it be addressed in accordance with the terms of the provision itself and within an objective assessment of the relevant measures and claims to make findings that will assist the DSB to make recommendations provided for in the covered agreements.'[24]

The Panel in *US – Origin Marking (Hong Kong, China)* underscored that 'the political nature of essential security interests does not in itself warrant the exclusion of any evaluation thereof by a panel'.[25]

8.2.3.3 *The Chapeau of Article XXI(b): 'which it Considers'*

A crucial interpretive question concerns the scope of discretion endowed to WTO members by the phrase 'which it considers' in the *chapeau* of Article XXI(b).

The principle was set by the Panel in *US – Steel and Aluminium Products (Turkey)* establishing that factors and domestic legal provisions considered by members as essential national security interests cannot be directly transposed to the requirements of Article XXI(b)(iii) GATT without an objective assessment by the panel.[26]

Further elaboration of what constitutes an objective assessment was laid down in *Russia – Traffic in Transit*. The Panel held that the three sets of circumstances under Article XXI(b)(i)–(iii) operate as limitative qualifying clauses, ie they qualify and limit the exercise of the discretion accorded to members under the chapeau to these circumstances. The Panel laid down that 'for an action to fall within the scope of Article XXI(b), it must objectively meet the requirements in one of the enumerated subparagraphs of that provision'.[27] 'It follows

[23] (*footnote original*) 'The Panel notes that the invocation of Article XX of the GATT 1994 titled 'General Exceptions' has been reviewed in WTO dispute settlement proceedings notwithstanding the absence of an explicit provision in Article XX on whether and how its invocation may be reviewed.'

[24] ibid, para 7.140.

[25] Panel Report, United States – Origin Marking Requirement (n 18) para 7.147.

[26] The Panel underlined that 'the factors treated cumulatively by US domestic authorities under Section 232 may not be regarded as having commensurate relevance or weight in the Panel's objective assessment as to whether the measures were taken "in time of war or other emergency in international relations" under Article XXI(b)(iii) of the GATT 1994': para. 7.161.

[27] Panel Report, Russia – Measures Concerning Traffic in Transit (n 20) para 7.101.

from the Panel's interpretation of Article XXI(b), as vesting in panels the power to review whether the requirements of the enumerated subparagraphs are met, rather than leaving it to the unfettered discretion of the invoking Member'.[28]

In *US – Origin Marking (Hong Kong, China)* the panel elaborated on this interpretation, noting that Article XXI(b) clearly provides for a unilateral determination by the invoking member, but the question is what that determination covers. The panel concluded that

> what is in the subparagraphs is not subject to the invoking member's own determination but is instead subject to objective determination by a panel. The role of the subparagraphs, thus, would be to circumscribe (and limit) the circumstances in which the invoking Member may take action which it considers necessary for the protection of its essential security interests.[29]

8.2.3.4 The Chapeau of Article XXI(b): 'Essential Security Interests'

The panel in *Russia – Traffic in Transit* described 'essential security interests' as 'a narrower concept than "security interests"' that 'may generally be understood to refer to those interests relating to the quintessential functions of the state, namely, the protection of its territory and its population from external threats, and the maintenance of law and public order internally'.[30]

The panel cautioned against labelling trade interests as essential security interests.

> It is therefore incumbent on the invoking member to articulate the essential security interests said to arise from the emergency in international relations sufficiently enough to demonstrate their veracity. ... the less characteristic is the 'emergency in international relations' invoked by the Member, i.e., the further it is removed from armed conflict, or a situation of breakdown of law and public order ... the less obvious are the defence or military interests, or maintenance of law and public order interests, that can be generally expected to arise.[31]

While acknowledging that each WTO member has discretion to define its essential security interests, the panel emphasised that this discretion is limited by two elements:

1. *The principle of good faith* – the obligation to interpret and apply Article XXI(b)(iii) in good faith. This obligation requires that members may not use the exceptions in Article XXI as a means to circumvent their obligations under the GATT 1994.[32]

[28] ibid, paras 7.102–7.103.
[29] Panel Report, United States – Origin Marking Requirement (n 18) paras 7.88–7.89.
[30] Panel Report, Russia – Measures Concerning Traffic in Transit (n 20) para 7.130.
[31] ibid, paras 7.134–7.135.
[32] ibid, paras 7.131–7.132.

2. *Minimum plausibility* – The panel pointed out that the principle of good faith applies not only to the definition of essential security interests but also, and most importantly, to their connection with the challenged measures:

> Thus, as concerns the application of Article XXI(b)(iii), this obligation is crystallized in demanding that the measures at issue meet a minimum requirement of plausibility in relation to the proffered essential security interests, i.e. that they are not implausible as measures protective of these interests.[33]

The question of proportionality in applying Article XXI(b)(iii) is evolving. While panels have generally avoided establishing an explicit proportionality test comparable to that in Article XX, the panel in Russia – Traffic in Transit established a test of 'reasonable nexus' between measures taken and essential security interests. The panel stated that the requirement of good faith in applying Article XXI implies that measures should not be unreasonable or arbitrary, suggesting a form of proportionality assessment.[34] In Saudi Arabia – IPRs, the panel indicated that measures must be 'genuinely related' to security interests, suggesting that measures should not be excessive relative to their objective.[35]

8.2.3.5 Article XXI(b)(i)–(ii)

The panel in *Russia – Traffic in Transit* stated that:

> The connection between the action and the materials or the traffic described in subparagraphs (i) and (ii) is specified by the phrase 'relating to'. The phrase 'relating to', as used in Article XX(g) of the GATT 1994, has been interpreted by the Appellate Body to require a 'close and genuine relationship of ends and means' between the measure and the objective of the Member adopting the measure. This is an objective relationship between the ends and the means, subject to objective determination.[36]

Regarding the term 'implements of war' in subparagraph (ii), panels have recognised that this term is not limited to traditional weapons and should evolve with technological developments. Members can broadly determine which products are considered to be of security importance, including dual-use technologies, as long as the decision is made in good faith and there is a reasonable connection between the technology and military capabilities.[37]

[33] ibid, para 7.138.
[34] ibid, paras 7.132–7.133.
[35] Panel Report, Saudi Arabia – Measures Concerning the Protection of Intellectual Property Rights WT/DS567/R (adopted 16 June 2020); see also Alexandr Svetlicinii, 'WTO Clarifies Rules on Security Exceptions in Trade Disputes' (CGTN, 22 June 2020), https://news.cgtn.com/news/2020-06-22/WTO-clarifies-rules-on-security-exceptions-in-trade-disputes-Rx98zc67yU/index.html.
[36] Panel Report, Russia – Measures Concerning Traffic in Transit (n 20) para 7.69.
[37] In Russia – Measures Concerning Traffic in Transit WT/DS512; Saudi Arabia – Measures Concerning the Protection of Intellectual Property Rights WT/DS567; Brazil – Certain Measures Concerning Taxation and Charges WT/DS472.

8.2.3.6 *Article XXIb(iii): 'War or Other Emergency in International Relations'*

The phrase 'taken in time of war or other emergency in international relations' in Article XXI(b)(iii) requires chronological concurrence between the action and a war or other emergency in international relations, which represents an objective fact amenable to objective determination.[38]

The panel in *Russia – Traffic in Transit* interpreted 'war' as referring to armed conflict, whether international or non-international.[39] Regarding the broader category of 'emergency in international relations' the panel emphasised that

> political or economic differences between Members are not sufficient, of themselves, to constitute an emergency in international relations, ... unless they give rise to defence and military interests, or maintenance of law and public order interests. An emergency in international relations would, therefore, appear to refer generally to a situation of armed conflict, or of latent armed conflict, or of heightened tension or crisis, or of general instability engulfing or surrounding a state.[40]

The Panel in *US – Steel and Aluminium Products (Turkey)* further clarified that an 'emergency in international relations' must be comparable in gravity or severity to 'war' in terms of its impact on international relations.[41]

8.2.3.7 *Current Challenges to Article XXI(b): 'Essential Security Interests' 'War or Other Emergency in International Relations'*

The panel in *Russia – Traffic in Transit* acknowledged that the interpretation of Article XXI(b)(iii) regarding 'other emergency in international relations' must evolve temporally to accommodate emerging security paradigms. Two new or untraditional forms of war or other emergency in international relations may be considered to provide a challenge for interpreting and applying Article XXI(b)(iii).

First, novel types of sanctions[42] – even if some of these sanctions are related to national security concerns such as cyber sanctions, it is doubtful

[38] Panel Report, Russia – Measures Concerning Traffic in Transit (n 20) para 7.70.

[39] ibid, para 7.72.

[40] (*footnote original*) 'This interpretation of an emergency in international relations is consistent with the preparatory work, referred to in paragraph 7.92 below, which indicates that the United States, when proposing the provision of the Geneva Draft of the ITO Charter that was carried over into Article XXI of the GATT 1947, and in referring to an "emergency in international relations", had in mind particularly the situation that existed between 1939 and 1941. During this time, the United States had not yet participated in the Second World War, yet owing to that situation, had still found it necessary to take certain measures for the protection of its essential security interests.'

[41] Panel Report, United States – Steel and Aluminium Products (n 22) para 7.154.

[42] For example, targeted sanctions imposed on individuals or corporations in connection with grave human rights violations ('Magnitsky-style sanctions'), those targeting perpetrators of cyber-attacks, and sanctions impacting trade in information and communications technology and services (ICTS) (eg, Huawei sanctions) imply various types of economic restrictions and raise possible violations of WTO obligations. Iryna Bogdanova, 'Targeted Economic Sanctions and WTO Law: Examining the Adequacy of the National Security Exception' (2021) 48 *Legal Issues of Economic Integration* 171, 172.

whether the imposing states meet the requirements of 'war' or 'emergency in international relations'.[43] In practice, it might not discourage members from using such sanctions by justifying them under the national security exception.

Another very pressing issue is the Trump administration's new tariff policy. On 13 February 2025, President Trump released a memorandum announcing his intention to impose 'reciprocal tariffs' on goods imported from various states. Since then, the tariffs policy was implemented with frequent changes. The Trump administration justified the measures taken to combat illegal immigration and the opioid crisis/fentanyl trafficking that the administration classified as a national emergency.[44] However, the legality of these measures regarding their compliance with WTO law, in particular with Article XXI(b), is questionable.[45] Trump's tariff policy was already challenged before the DSM.[46] However, with previous US resistance tactics to avoid compliance with WTO rulings, enforcement is far from certain.[47] The attempt to use the national security exception as a WTO legal justification, even if doomed to fail, raises concerns about the (lack of) boundaries for strong WTO members and possible abuse of the exceptions on grounds of national security.[48]

[43] When imposing sanctions targeting perpetrators of cyber-attacks the sanctioning member will need to demonstrate that the attack constitutes a threat to essential security interests and that the imposed sanctions bear a reasonable relationship to safeguarding this interest. Specific elements might be challenging to demonstrate, for example: that the attack is attributable to the targeted WTO member; that it resulted in substantial damage or disruption to critical infrastructure; that it constitutes an element of adversarial interstate relations. For a thorough examination see Bogdanova (n 40).

[44] White House, 'Fact Sheet: President Donald J Trump Imposes Tariffs on Imports from Canada, Mexico, and China' (1 February 2025), www.whitehouse.gov.

[45] The DSM's interpretation of the national security exception may become highly relevant for restricting the wide application of security justifications, as seen in past disputes against the US over steel and aluminium tariffs; for example DS550 initiated by Canada, DS551 initiated by Mexico. Interestingly, the panel in US – Steel and Aluminium Products (Turkey) pointed out that 'an "emergency in international relations" within the meaning of Article XXI(b)(iii) must be, if not equally grave or severe, at least comparable in its gravity or severity to a "war" in terms of its impact on international relations' (para 7.154). The Panel underlined that 'the factors treated cumulatively by US domestic authorities under Section 232 may not be regarded as having commensurate relevance or weight in the Panel's objective assessment as to whether the measures were taken "in time of war or other emergency in international relations" under Article XXI(b)(iii) of the GATT 1994' (para 7.161). Based on this assessment, the panel concluded that the measures at issue had not been taken in time of war or other emergency in international relations, and that therefore were not justified under Art XXI(b)(iii).

[46] *United States – Additional Import Duties on Goods from Canada* WT/DS634; *United States – Additional Tariff Measures on Goods from China* WT/DS633.

[47] Even if the panel will conclude that the US is in breach of its WTO obligations and that its measures are not justified under the national security exception the US can 'appeal into the air', ie since the Appellate Body is non-functional and the US is not party to the IMPA agreement, such an appeal might freeze the legal situation.

[48] The Trump administration's conduct may be seen as a direct assault on multilateralism and on the WTO, as the US takes the right to impose tariffs on any country based on its national perception of what is fair and necessary. Trump's tariff policy has already triggered tariff war as China takes unauthorised retaliatory measures, the EU and other states are considering various counter actions. See Petros C Mavroidis, '"Reciprocal" Tariffs: What's in a Word?' (Bruegel, 27 February 2025), www.bruegel.org/analysis/reciprocal-tariffs-whats-word.

8.2.4 Interim Conclusion

Recent WTO case law has provided important clarifications establishing the principal justiciability of members actions under Article XXI GATT. For this purpose, the WTO case law introduced a framework to analyse the national security justification distinguishing between objective and subjective elements. The panels clarified that the subjective elements are under the discretion of WTO members, and that the objective elements allow for an examination of their correct application in DSM proceedings.

Regarding subjective elements, the *chapeau* of Article XXI provides a prominent example where members are endowed with broad discretion to decide their 'essential security interests'.

In respect of objective elements the panels held that it is for the panel to review whether a WTO member considered its 'essential security interests' in good faith and whether a minimum requirement of plausibility between imposed measures and declared national security interests is met. Moreover, the panels laid down that the three sets of circumstances under Article XXI(b)(i)–(iii) qualify and limit the exercise of the discretion accorded to members under the *chapeau*. Whether the requirements of the enumerated subparagraphs are met is not subject to the invoking member's own determination but is instead subject to objective determination by a panel.

The jurisprudential developments reflect an effort to reach a balance between respecting members' sovereign discretion in national security matters and simultaneously affirming panels' jurisdiction to review invocations of Article XXI GATT.

Nevertheless, recourse to the DSM is not available to the target member in real time due to lack of a prior notification requirement. Moreover, DSM proceedings offer limited practical value for targeted states, particularly those with weaker economies.[49] Even if targeted states succeed in their claims before the DSM the enforcement of remedies remains problematic.

Considering emergent security threats within an era of deepening globalisation the interpretation of Article XXI GATT requires substantial revision. Any reformed approach must navigate the delicate tension between state sovereignty in security matters and the preservation of a rules-based international trading system. This necessitates a framework grounded in transparency, proportionality, and objective threat evaluation, ensuring that the trading system's legitimacy and capacity to respond to twenty-first-century security challenges remain intact. Several avenues for reform or clarification of Article XXI can be identified.

[49] Power asymmetries within the system allow stronger countries to exploit the flexibility in interpreting Art XXI, with economically powerful states able to better withstand sanctions for extended periods. Additionally, the enforcement of remedies remains problematic, particularly for weaker economies that cannot impose effective retaliatory measures without assistance from other WTO members, which is currently prohibited.

To name but a few: establishing stronger transparency measures, including prior notification obligations, detailed justifications, and trade impact assessments before invoking the national security exception; creating a periodic review system for measures taken under Article XXI to ensure they remain necessary and proportionate over time; developing specific guidelines for using the security exception in emerging contexts such as cyber warfare, supply chain security, health security and more.

The implementation of such reforms, however, might face considerable obstacles. These include: the complexities inherent in achieving multilateral consensus given divergent national security interests; the anticipated reluctance of powerful states to accept limitations on their discretionary authority in security affairs; and the fundamental requirement to maintain institutional flexibility capable of accommodating novel and unanticipated security developments. In addition, the paralysis of the Appellate Body makes it difficult to further develop consistent and binding jurisprudence defining legal standards for the application of Article XXI GATT.[50]

Below, the WTO consistency of the EU's unilateral economic sanctions against Russia and the potential application of Article XXI GATT is examined as a case study.

8.3 WTO COMPATIBILITY OF EU ECONOMIC SANCTIONS AGAINST RUSSIA? A CASE STUDY

Since March 2014, the EU has progressively imposed restrictive measures on Russia in response to the illegal annexation of Crimea (2014), the full-scale invasion of Ukraine (2022), and the illegal annexation of the Donetsk, Luhansk, Zaporizhzhia and Kherson regions of Ukraine (2022). So far, 18 packages of sanctions have been adopted.[51] According to the EU the measures are designed to achieve the EU policy objective of ending Russia's war of aggression against Ukraine, through maximising pressure on Russia and using all tools available to diminish Russia's ability to wage its illegal war of aggression.

[50] The current procedural environment, where Members can effectively neutralize DSM decisions by appealing 'into the air' – submitting appeals to the non-functioning Appellate Body – presents a further challenge to the effective resolution of disputes involving security exceptions.

[51] The 18th package was adopted on 18 July 2025. For detailed information and analysis of EU sanctions against Russia see: the European Council and the Council of the EU, www.consilium.europa.eu/en/policies/sanctions-against-russia; European Parliament, 'EU Sanctions against Russia 2025: State of Play, Perspectives and Challenges' (2025), www.europarl.europa.eu/RegData/etudes/BRIE/2025/767243/EPRS_BRI(2025)767243_EN.pdf; Matej Belín and Jan Hanousek, 'Imposing Sanctions versus Posing in Sanctioners' Clothes: The EU Sanctions against Russia and the Russian Counter-sanctions' in Peter AG van Bergeijk (ed), *Research Handbook on Economic Sanctions* (Edward Elgar, 2021); Mads Andenas and others (eds), *EU External Action in International Economic Law: Recent Trends and Developments* (TMC Asser Press, 2020).

As both the EU and Russia are WTO members such sanctions need to be WTO compatible. This case study examines the WTO compatibility of EU sanctions against Russia and the extent to which the EU can justify these measures as exceptions under WTO law. This is a timely issue as Russia could potentially bring a claim before the DSM challenging these sanctions. While Russia has indicated intentions to challenge these sanctions before the WTO DSM, no formal consultation request has yet been recorded.[52]

8.3.1 EU Sanctions Potential Violations of WTO Obligations

A potential WTO challenge by Russia of the legality of the EU sanctions would not comprise the entire scope of EU sanctions but only comprehensive sanctions affecting trade and regulated under the WTO rules thus falling within the purview of the DSM jurisdiction.[53] The EU measures potentially subject to WTO scrutiny could include: i) prohibition on Russian coal imports; ii) restrictions on exports of oil refining technology and goods; iii) closure of EU airspace to Russian-owned and Russian-registered aircraft; iv) closure of EU ports to Russian vessels; v) prohibitions on exports of goods and technology in the aviation, maritime, and space industry; vi) prohibition on exports of dual-use goods and technology; vii) arms trade prohibition; viii) partial ban on Russian oil imports and more. From a potential Russian complainant's side, these EU trade sanctions are allegedly in violation of the core principle of non-discrimination and possibly other obligations under the WTO.[54]

The EU trade restrictions that are applied only to the Russian Federation, cover a broad range of products and services that equals almost complete bans. This might violate the Most Favoured Nation (MFN) principle in Article I:1

[52] WTO, 'Dispute settlement – Disputes by member', www.wto.org/english/tratop_e/dispu_e/dispu_by_country_e.htm. At the time of writing (June 2024) only four cases of Russian Federation complaints against the EU were reported, none are relevant for this case study.

[53] Individual 'smart sanctions' targeting specific Russian persons or entities are beyond the scope of the WTO rules. In response to the criticism that comprehensive sanctions are of little effect while causing substantial collateral damage, the EU has placed more emphasis on 'smart sanctions', though that movement has been somewhat reversed. For example: the prohibition of transactions with the Bank of Russia, the Suspension of European Investment Bank (EIB) and European Bank for Reconstruction and Development (EBRD) operations in Russia, the cancellation of visa facilitation provisions for Russian officials and businessmen, the freezing of Russian accession negotiations to the Organisation for Economic Cooperation and Development (OECD) and the International Atomic Energy Agency (IAEA), and the cancellation of bilateral EU–Russia summits. See European Council and Council of the EU (n 49); Luca Pantaleo, 'Sanctions Cases in the European Courts' in Matthew Happold and Paul Eden (eds), *Economic Sanctions and International Law* (Hart, 2016). Such sanctions are beyond WTO purview and would instead be possibly subject to challenge before EU courts.

[54] Notermans (n 5); Rostam J Neuwirth and Alexandr Svetlicinii, 'The Current EU/US–Russia Conflict Over Ukraine and the WTO: A Preliminary Note on (Trade) Restrictive Measures' (2016) 32 *Post-Soviet Affairs* 237.

of the GATT. To determine a violation of Article I:1 GATT,[55] the WTO DSM should establish the following four elements.

First, the measures at issue must fall within the scope of application of Article I:1. The first element of Article I:1 GATT – 'all rules and formalities in connection with importation and exportation' – was interpreted in a broad manner. Therefore, EU import and export bans on Russian goods would be covered by the scope of Article I:1 GATT.[56]

Secondly, the products at issue must be 'like' products. Given that economic sanctions mostly target generic products differentiated solely by origin the second element would be met. The sanctions are not product-specific and are not related to process and production methods. The sanctioned products are distinguished from other 'like' products solely based on their origin from Russia.

Thirdly, the measures at issue should confer an 'advantage, favour, privilege, or immunity' on a product originating in the territory of any country. Economic sanctions prohibiting trade with a targeted state, allow only non-targeted members to benefit from market access advantages. This would meet the third element.[57]

Fourthly, the advantage so accorded must be extended 'immediately' and 'unconditionally' to 'like' products originating in the territory of all members.[58] Given that the objective of economic sanctions is to deprive the targeted state from trade benefits and deliberately withholding advantages from Russian 'like' products would establish the breach of the fourth element.

Hence, it appears that the EU economic sanctions entailing import and/or export bans on Russian goods, might violate the MFN obligation under Article I:1 GATT. The EU measures might also constitute a violation of the National Treatment obligation under Article III GATT, as they discriminate between 'like' products of the targeted Russian Federation and EU domestic products.

Article XI GATT, which forbids the use of quantitative restrictions, was interpreted as also prohibiting restrictions that have a limiting effect on the quantity of products being imported or exported.[59] Therefore, quantitative restrictions

[55] Art I:1 GATT, in the relevant part, reads as follows: 'with respect to all rules and formalities in connection with importation and exportation … any advantage, favour, privilege or immunity granted by any contracting party to any product originating in or destined for any other country shall be accorded immediately and unconditionally to the like product originating in or destined for the territories of all other contracting parties'.

[56] WTO Analytical Index: Guide to WTO Law and Practice, GATT 1994 – Art. I (Jurisprudence) 1, 6–7.

[57] The third element was interpreted as creating more favourable import opportunities or affecting the commercial relationship between products of different origins. Panel Report, European Communities – Regime for the Importation, Sale and Distribution of Bananas (Complaint by Ecuador) WT/DS27/R/ECU (adopted 25 September 1997) para 7.239.

[58] Appellate Body Reports, European Communities – Measures Prohibiting the Importation and Marketing of Seal Products WT/DS400/AB/R, WT/DS401/AB/R (adopted 18 June 2014) para 5.86.

[59] Appellate Body Reports, China – Measures Related to the Exportation of Various Raw Materials WT/DS394/AB/R, WT/DS395/AB/R, WT/DS398/AB/R (adopted 22 February 2012) paras 319–20.

under EU sanctions having a limiting effect on the quantity of imported or exported Russian products might violate Article XI GATT.

EU restrictions on trade in services, such as the closure of EU airspace to Russian-owned and Russian-registered aircraft and the closure of EU ports to Russian vessels, might breach some General Agreement on Trade in Services (GATS) obligations, including the MFN obligation under Article II GATS, the National Treatment obligation under Article XVII GATS, and market access provisions under Article XVI GATS, depending on EU commitments in specific sectors.

Given alleged violations of WTO rules by EU sanctions, potential EU defence venues are discussed below.

8.3.2 EU Potential Defence under WTO Exceptions

This subsection examines the extent to which the EU can justify the sanctions against Russia under exceptions in WTO law and the likelihood of such defences standing up in a potential DSM proceeding. Potential EU defence could rely on national security exceptions under Articles XXI(b)(iii) and XXI(c) GATT,[60] and possibly on general exceptions under Article XX(a) GATT.

8.3.2.1 EU Potential Defence under Article XXI(b)(iii) GATT

The EU will not be able to avoid potential DSM proceedings with reference to the seemingly self-judging nature of Article XXI(b)(iii) given the interpretation in WTO case law of the term 'which it considers'.[61] Hence, in order to meet the requirements of Article XXI(b)(iii) the EU would need to demonstrate that both the objective and the subjective requirements are satisfied.

For meeting the objective requirements the EU would need to deal with two major elements. First, that 'war' or an 'emergency in international relations' exists.[62] The EU could definitely argue that Russia's invasion of Ukraine amounts to a state of war and has created an emergency in international relations threatening the EU. Second, that the measures have been 'taken in time of' such an emergency. Since the first package of EU restrictive measures was adopted during the Russia Ukraine war, it should fulfil also the second requirement.[63]

[60] Where relevant on Art XIVbis GATS, and Art 73 TRIPS.

[61] Art XXI(b)(iii) GATT 1994 reads as follows: 'Nothing in this Agreement shall be construed: … (b) to prevent any Member from taking any action which it considers necessary for the protection of its essential security interests … (iii) taken in time of war or other emergency in international relations.' See section 8.2.3.3.

[62] See the interpretation of these terms by the DSM, section 8.2.3.

[63] The first package of EU restrictive measures was adopted at a special European Council meeting of 24 February 2022 and Council Regulation No 833/2014 as amended by Council Regulation (EU) 2022/328 is dated 25 February 2022.

For meeting the subjective requirements, the EU would need to deal with two criteria. First, that it considered its 'essential security interests' in good faith. The EU could effectively argue that Russia's invasion represents an acute threat to international order, democracy, human rights, European cybersecurity, and food security. The absence of protectionist motives is evident as export bans on arms and dual-use goods disadvantage EU industries, while import restrictions on Russian energy increase European prices.[64] Second, it also appears that the minimum requirement of plausibility between imposed measures and declared national security interests is fulfilled. The EU could reasonably argue that sanctions are necessary and designed to limit Russia's war-making capacity, thereby establishing a plausible relationship between the measures and the EU's security interests.[65] Although panels have generally avoided establishing an explicit proportionality test, it may be considered whether the EU measures are not unreasonable or arbitrary.[66]

8.3.2.2 EU Potential Defence under Article XXI(c) GATT

To justify the economic sanctions against Russia under Article XXI(c) GATT,[67] the EU would have to prove that its measures, that are binding on its Member States, all of which are UN members and bound by UN obligations,[68] are in pursuance of relevant UN obligations.[69]

The United Nations Security Council (UNSC) is empowered to call upon Member States to implement 'a complete or partial interruption of economic relations' on another Member State to enforce the UNSC's decisions.[70] However, the veto power enjoyed by the Russian Federation in the UNSC prevented any such decision. A UN General Assembly (UNGA) resolution noted this impasse but did not explicitly recommend economic sanctions.[71] Even if there was an UNGA resolution recommending economic sanctions against Russia, precedents like the conflict diamond trade restrictions would seem to suggest that it would not satisfy Article XXI(c) requirements.[72] Therefore, Article XXI(c) appears less viable for justifying EU sanctions.

[64] See the European Council and the Council of the EU, www.consilium.europa.eu/en/policies/sanctions-against-russia.

[65] See ibid.

[66] See section 8.2.3.

[67] Or similar exceptions under Art XIV bis GATS and Art 73 TRIPS.

[68] Arts 2 and 103 of the UN Charter.

[69] Art XXI(c) GATT reads as follows: 'Nothing in this Agreement shall be construed: ... (c) to prevent any contracting party from taking any action in pursuance of its obligations under the United Nations Charter for the maintenance of international peace and security.'

[70] Art 41, Ch VII of the UN Charter.

[71] ES-11/12 of 2 March 2022.

[72] The Kimberley Process for the Certification of Rough Diamonds (KPCS) came into force in 2003 and was based on an UNGA resolution (55/56, 29 January 2000), followed by non-binding UNSC resolutions expressing support for a certification process (UNSC Resolutions 1385 (19 December 2001), 1446 (4 December 2002) and 1459 (28 January 2003)). Under the KPCS participating Member

8.3.2.3 *EU Potential Defence under Article XX(a) GATT: Public Morals*

Establishing a direct link between Russian products and threats to EU public morals would be challenging.[73] Whereas in the EU *Seal Products* case the link between the products and the way they were produced was argued to have a strong link to the public and thus hurt public morals, the same could not be said regarding consumption of, eg, Russian oil and gas or Russian air transport services.[74] Accepting such an EU argument might create an undesirable loophole for WTO members to justify trade sanctions that are unrelated to the nature of the product.[75]

An indirect argument could be made that consuming Russian products strengthens the Russian economy and the Russian ability to violate international law, thereby threatening EU public morals. However, the EU would need to address whether less restrictive alternatives exist, such as labelling or intense diplomatic efforts.[76]

8.3.3 Interim Conclusion

EU trade sanctions against Russia might be inconsistent with WTO obligations. Therefore, a potential claim before the DSM of the WTO could be eligible given that both parties are WTO members. A potential EU defence could rely on national security exceptions under Articles XXI(b)(iii) and XXI(c),[77] and possibly on Article XX(a) GATT. The analysis above indicates that the national security exception in Article XXI(b)(iii) GATT appears the most relevant defence

States banned trade in uncertified raw diamonds to dry up the funding of violent conflicts in several sub-Saharan states. The EU opined that an UNGA resolution followed by non-binding UNSC resolutions would satisfy the requirements of Art XI(c) GATT. Yet, the participation of several WTO Member States was sanctioned by a waiver of the General Council of the WTO from Arts I, XI and XIII GATT (WT/L/518, 27 May 2003). The fact that a waiver was used to authorise the participation in the KPCS may suggest that the scheme was in violation of the GATT, as the function of a WTO waiver, as defined under Art IX of the Agreement Establishing the WTO, is to relieve a member of an obligation it has under that agreement. See Andrew D Mitchell, 'Sanctions and the World Trade Organization' in Larissa van den Herik (ed), *Research Handbook on UN Sanctions and International Law* (Edward Elgar, 2017).

[73] Art XX(a) GATT: 'Subject to the requirement that such measures are not applied in a manner which would constitute a means of arbitrary or unjustifiable discrimination between countries where the same conditions prevail, or a disguised restriction on international trade, nothing in this Agreement shall be construed to prevent the adoption or enforcement by any contracting party of measures: (a) necessary to protect public morals'.

[74] Appellate Body Reports WT/DS400/AB/R, WT/DS401/AB/R (n 58).

[75] A long-standing WTO jurisprudence objected to it: see eg Panel Report, United States – Measures Concerning the Importation, Marketing and Sale of Tuna and Tuna Products WT/DS381/49/Rev 1 (2019).

[76] The WTO jurisprudence has generally adopted a strict interpretation requiring that other, less trade-restrictive approaches be exhausted: see eg Appellate Body Report, *United States – Import Prohibition of Certain Shrimp and Shrimp Products* WT/DS58/23 (2001).

[77] Where relevant on Art XIV bis GATS, and Art 73 TRIPS.

for the EU and that properly framed EU sanctions would likely withstand WTO scrutiny under Article XXI(b)(iii) GATT.

8.4 CONCLUSIONS AND THE WAY AHEAD

Since the WTO serves as the principal international trade law maker and adjudicator, the WTO DSM's assessment of unilateral economic sanctions substantially reflects the international trade law position regarding the legitimacy of economic sanctions.

There is clearly a tension between unilateral economic sanctions and the fundamental objectives of the WTO. The WTO's principled aim is to liberalise trade between its members and reduce trade restrictions internationally, whereas economic sanctions are aimed to restrict trade with targeted states and in essence add trade restrictions, mostly for non-economic reasons.[78] Moreover, economic sanctions sustain the violation of WTO rules by the sanctioning member, because they are often used for non-economic interests where the targeted member did not violate its WTO obligations. For as long as unilateral sanctions are in force certain trade concessions no longer apply and this goes to the very heart of the WTO system to ensure predictable and growing access to markets.[79]

On its face, the national security exception under Article XXI GATT endows WTO members with broad discretion to implement unilateral economic sanctions, that might contravene WTO commitments, when such members deem it necessary for protecting their essential security interests.

In recent years, the invocation of this exception has expanded significantly. This tendency has prompted targeted states to increasingly challenge the legal validity of economic sanctions within the WTO legal system, generating important jurisprudential developments. Recent WTO case law has provided important clarifications establishing the principal justiciability of members' actions under Article XXI GATT. WTO case law introduced a framework to analyse the national security justification distinguishing between subjective elements under the discretion of WTO members, and objective elements that allow for an examination of their correct application in DSM proceedings. Notably, this may be useful regarding comprehensive sanctions. However, Article XXI(b)(iii) has limited relevance, when used to provide justification for other types of unilateral economic sanctions such as 'smart sanctions' that fall outside the purview of

[78] Smeets (n 4).

[79] Comprehensive economic sanctions directly affect the quantity of trade and are therefore causing more trade distortion than the imposition of import duties. Import duties define the price level of a product and might result in a high price, but contrary to trade bans such duties leave the choice to the consumer and do not block trade. This is the rationale of Art XI.1 GATT that prohibits trade restrictions other than duties, taxes or other charges, with some exceptions defined in Art XI.2.

WTO law, and thus reinforces the general tendency of questioning the legality of unilateral economic sanctions.[80]

The jurisprudential developments concerning Article XXI GATT reflect an effort to reach a balance between respecting members' sovereign discretion in national security matters and simultaneously affirming panels' jurisdiction to review invocations of Article XXI. Nevertheless, the provisions in Article XXI GATT read together with the 1982 Decision, would appear to suggest that a WTO member may interrupt its trade relations with WTO members and allegedly violate WTO rules, whenever it deems it necessary for its security interests, without prior notice and with no comparable constraints to other WTO exceptions, subject to its unilateral discretion. As a result, a targeted member has no possibility in real time to dispute the measures before the DSM. De facto it means that challenging sanctions can occur mostly after they have already been imposed.[81] Furthermore, such recourse to the DSM offers limited practical value for targeted states, particularly those with weaker economies. Even if targeted states succeed in their claims before the DSM the enforcement of remedies remains problematic.[82] Regrettably, the DSM currently faces significant challenges which might affect its ability to effectively oversee the use of the security exception. These include a fundamental legitimacy dilemma where extensive judicial intervention in national security matters might raise questions about WTO authority boundaries, while insufficient oversight might invite abuse. In addition, the paralysis of the Appellate Body makes it difficult to further develop consistent and binding jurisprudence defining legal standards for the application of Article XXI GATT.[83]

The case study on the compatibility of EU comprehensive sanctions against Russia designed to achieve the EU policy objective of ending Russia's war of aggression against Ukraine provided a clear example for the problematic legal situation. The EU, a strong WTO member which is committed to WTO law, imposes unilateral sanctions that might be inconsistent with WTO obligations, for a political goal. However, the legal analysis of a potential Russian claim before the DSM demonstrated that properly framed EU sanctions against Russia would likely withstand potential WTO scrutiny under Article XXI(b)(iii) GATT. The EU sanctions following the Russian invasion of Ukraine highlight the fundamental challenges as EU sanctions have been used as one of the primary foreign policy tools by the EU to intervene in the political conflict. It remains to be seen whether the EU, as a leading WTO law advocate, would further reconsider its

[80] Bogdanova (n 42) 198–99.

[81] See section 8.2.2.

[82] Particularly for weaker economies that cannot impose effective retaliatory measures without assistance from other WTO members, which is currently prohibited.

[83] The current procedural environment, where Members can effectively neutralize DSM decisions by appealing 'into the air' – submitting appeals to the non-functioning Appellate Body – presents a further challenge to the effective resolution of disputes involving security exceptions.

sanctions policy given the growing criticism and the potential threat to the rule of international trade law.[84]

The growing reliance on the national security exception by the EU and other WTO members for justifying economic sanctions might represent a potential regression in the juridification of trade relations and a concerning return to utilising trade instruments for non-economic purposes. Consequently, it might point to potential concerning trends such as: a domino effect where widespread use of the security exception by one member encourages others to adopt similar measures; an expansion of the security concept beyond traditional military threats to include geopolitical conflicts, economic and technological threats, global health emergencies, energy security and more; a strategic use of Article XXI GATT by stronger members either to gain economic advantages under the guise of national security or to achieve political aims by exploiting the flexibility in interpreting Article XXI GATT. This is likely to damage trust and certainty, consequently undermining the credibility of the multilateral trading system, and resulting in a chilling effect on international trade, critical supply chains and investment.[85]

As geopolitical tensions and evolving forms of war waging continue to manifest in the application of economic sanctions, resulting in violations of WTO rules, the interpretation and application of Article XXI GATT will remain critical to the WTO's capacity to manage the intersection of security and trade concerns in a principled manner. For the way ahead, the development in the interpretation of Article XXI GATT should reflect profound changes in the conception of national security in an era of globalisation and emerging challenges. Maintaining the delicate balance between security sovereignty and preserving the integrity of the international trading system requires a renewed approach that recognises modern threats while preventing abuse. Effective reform of Article XXI GATT should be founded on principles of transparency, proportionality, and objective assessment of security threats to the extent possible, while safeguarding the legitimacy of the international trading system and its capacity to address twenty-first-century challenges. However, several significant obstacles might complicate the implementation of such reforms, including difficulty in achieving consensus among countries with divergent conceptions of national security; resistance from powerful countries to any limitation on their discretion in security matters; and the need to maintain sufficient flexibility to address unforeseen future threats. The EU may have a leading role in advancing

[84] In response to the criticism that comprehensive sanctions are of little effect while causing substantial collateral damage, the EU has placed more emphasis on 'smart sanctions', though that movement has been somewhat reversed. Notably, targeted or 'smart sanctions' fall outside the scope of WTO law. See European Council and Council of the EU (n 51); Pantaleo (n 53). Such sanctions are beyond WTO purview and would instead be possibly subject to challenge before EU courts.

[85] See eg Bogdanova (n 42) 198–99.

required reforms to strengthen and adapt WTO rules to the current intersection of security and trade concerns.[86]

Admittedly, debate on a legal reform of Article XXI GATT is not satisfactory in isolation. Given the limitations of legal tools, it is advisable that the discussion on such a reform will be conducted in an interdisciplinary framework. This debate must grapple with fundamental questions about the proper role of trade measures in advancing non-economic objectives, the effectiveness of economic sanctions compared to the damage they cause, the limits of national sovereignty in an interconnected global economy, and the future of the rules-based international trading system in an increasingly fragmented geopolitical landscape.

[86] See eg the EU's efforts to solve the Appellate Body crisis demonstrated by its initiative for the Multi-Party Interim Appeal Arbitration Arrangement pursuant to Article 25 of the Dispute Settlement Understanding (MPIA). Olga Starshinova, 'Is the MPIA a Solution to the WTO Appellate Body Crisis?' (2021) 55 *Journal of World Trade* 787.

Part III

Criminal Dimension of EU Sanctions

9

Criminalisation of EU Sanctions Violations

FRANCESCA FINELLI AND JACOB ÖBERG*

9.1 INTRODUCTION

Safeguarding international peace and security, preventing conflicts, upholding values in its relations with the wider world, are the primary objectives the Union's Common Foreign and Security Policy (CFSP).[1] These objectives shape the Union's global actorness, including the imposition of restrictive measures (sanctions) against third countries and foreign actors,[2] while they have not traditionally guided the use of EU criminal law. Nonetheless, this chapter intends to shed light on how recent geopolitical developments, particularly Russia's invasion of Ukraine and the urgent need to ensure an effective response to this full-scale aggression at the border with Europe, have led to new interconnections between CFSP objectives and EU criminal law. In this unprecedented context,[3] the effectiveness and credibility of restrictive measures have been intertwined with the resort to criminal law measures. Since February 2022, the imperative to impose tough sanctions on Russia has, in fact, been translated into the need to approximate national enforcement systems and harmonise criminal rules and penalties to counter violations, including circumvention tactics. In other words, the need to strengthen the impact of EU sanctions (and induce Russia to stop its war of aggression against Ukraine) has resulted into a new emphasis on criminal punishment and deterrence of sanctions breaches.

* The authors have jointly developed the ideas underpinning this chapter. Francesca Finelli has authored sections 9.1, 9.3 and 9.5; Jacob Öberg has authored sections 9.2 and 9.4. The conclusions in section 9.6 were jointly written by both authors.

[1] see Art 3(5) and 21 Treaty on European Union (TEU).

[2] see Art 29 TEU and Art 215 TFEU. The terms 'restrictive measures', 'economic sanctions' and 'sanctions' shall be intended as identifying decisions adopted by the Council of the EU according to those two legal basis.

[3] See Alexandra Hofer, 'The EU's "Massive and Targeted" Sanctions in Response to Russian Aggression, a Contradiction in Terms' (2023) 25 *Cambridge Yearbook of European Legal Studies* 19; Katharina Meissner and Chiara Graziani, 'The Transformation and Design of EU Restrictive Measures against Russia' (2023) 45 *Journal of European Integration* 377.

Although Member States have previously been entrusted with the task of designing 'effective, proportionate and dissuasive' penalties for sanctions violations within their respective jurisdictions,[4] in 2022, the EU legislator argued that it could no longer place full trust in national authorities. In light of a pressing geopolitical context, it proposed to enforce restrictive measures by (common) criminal law measures. In this manner, the war in Ukraine, the urgency to ensure the effective application of sanctions against Russia, and to counter the phenomenon of circumvention, has led the Union to conclude, for the first time, that the harmonisation of criminal rules and penalties was a pressing necessity. Undoubtedly, the criminalisation of sanctions violations has been driven by a specific political momentum – where the Union seeks to maximise the effectiveness and credibility of its foreign policy decisions with the view of constraining Russia's capacity to wage war. Yet, this process amounts to a *structural* reform that affects EU restrictive measures *tout court* – not only those related to Russia's aggression.[5]

This chapter seeks to critically examine the legal and normative justification for criminalising breaches of EU sanctions. It first looks at the fast-track criminalisation process pursuant to Article 83(1) Treaty on the Functioning of the European Union (TFEU), and the negotiation history of Directive (EU) 2024/1226 (section 9.2). Subsequently, it examines the rationale behind this criminalisation process (section 9.3), and illustrates the extent to which the introduction of a new Eurocrime is in line with the legal preconditions for exercising the competence in Article 83(1) TFEU (section 9.4). Then, this chapter analyses, in detail, the approximation of criminal offences and penalties in the new Directive (section 9.5). Finally, the chapter has some broader reflections on the impact and potential for this Directive being transposed into national laws (section 9.6).

9.2 THE FAST-TRACK CRIMINALISATION OF EU SANCTIONS VIOLATIONS

The criminalisation of sanctions violations can be defined as the process according to which the EU legislator defines (intentional) non-compliance with restrictive measures as a new criminal offence and requires Member States to punish it accordingly under their domestic laws.[6] This process creates a new

[4] According to the 'Greek Maize' formula, see Case C-68/88, *Commission v Greece* EU:C:1989:339, para 24. See also standard clause in Regulations imposing sanctions, such as Art 15(1) Council Regulation (EU) No 269/2014 of 17 March 2014 concerning restrictive measures in respect of actions undermining or threatening the territorial integrity, sovereignty and independence of Ukraine [2014] OJ L78/6.

[5] Sara Poli and Francesca Finelli, 'Context Specific and Structural Changes in EU Restrictive Measures Adopted in Reaction to Russia's Aggression on Ukraine' (2023) 3 *Eurojus* 19.

[6] For a more general account of the criminalization of restrictive measures see Jacob Öberg, 'Criminalisation of Sanctions Violations' in Clara Portela, Andrea Charron and Mirko Sossai (eds), *Elgar encyclopedia of international sanctions* (Edward Elgar Publishing, 2025).

legal environment where Member States are asked to engage in the investigations, prosecution and, ultimately, the imposition of criminal penalties against those responsible for violation of EU sanctions.

One of the key ideas behind criminalisation is to deter individuals and companies who contemplate breaching EU sanctions, including those who intentionally infringe import–export restrictions against Russia, participate in circumvention schemes with third countries, or fail to freeze the asset of designated oligarchs.[7] This criminalisation seeks to combat wilful non-compliance by raising the awareness of EU citizens and economic operators, exposing them to new enforcement risks. In particular, the approximation of criminal law measures is intended to fight impunity, by limiting the uneven implementation and enforcement of sanctions across 27 national jurisdictions. Such approximation is pursued by means of the legal basis of Article 83 TFEU which empowers the EU to harmonise domestic substantive criminal laws in relation to specific offences.[8]

According to this provision, the European Parliament and the Council may, by means of directives, establish minimum rules concerning the definition of criminal offences and penalties in the areas of *particularly serious crime* with a *cross-border dimension* resulting from the nature or impact of such offences or from a special need to combat them on a common basis (emphasis added). The Article already lists 10 offences,[9] which are considered to be of a particularly serious nature and a cross-border dimension, and for which the EU has a right to establish minimum rules concerning the definition of criminal offences and penalties. Violation of EU sanctions were not initially included in that list. Nonetheless, according to the final subsection of Article 83(1) TFEU, the Council may identify *other areas* of crime that meet the criteria specified in this provision – by acting unanimously and after obtaining the consent of the Parliament.

Following this procedure, in May 2022, the Commission put forward an unprecedented proposals to redesign the national enforcement of EU restrictive measures.[10] Furthermore, in November 2022, the Council unanimously decided[11]

[7] Francesca Finelli, 'Who Are the Russian Oligarchs? Recent Developments in the Case Law of the European Court of Justice' (2024) 2023 *European Papers*.

[8] Jacob Öberg, *Limits to EU Powers: A Case Study of EU Regulatory Criminal Law* (Hart Publishing, 2017); Petter Asp, *The Substantive Criminal Law Competence of the EU: Towards an Area of Freedom, Security & Justice - Part 1* (Jure, 2012).

[9] Terrorism, trafficking in human beings and sexual exploitation of women and children, illicit drug trafficking, illicit arms trafficking, money laundering, corruption, counterfeiting of means of payment, computer crime and organised crime.

[10] See 'Ukraine: The Commission proposes rules on freezing and confiscating assets of oligarchs violating restrictive measures and of criminals' Press release (25 May 2022). On the Commission's role of 'leading promoter of closer European integration' see A Bradford, *The Brussels Effect: How the European Union Rules the World*, 1st edn (Oxford University Press, 2020) 15.

[11] Council Decision (EU) 2022/2332 of 28 November 2022 on identifying the violation of Union restrictive measures as an area of crime that meets the criteria specified in Article 83(1) of the Treaty on the Functioning of the European Union [2022] OJ L308/18. The Council Decision followed the consent of the European Parliament, see document P9 TA (2022) 0295.

to extend the list of Eurocrimes, thereby adding the violation of EU restrictive measures to the areas of crime meeting the criteria imposed by Article 83(1) TFEU.[12] Subsequent to this, the Council together with the European Parliament, acting together as co-legislators, adopted Directive (EU) 2024/1226 harmonising the Member States' criminal laws in respect of those criminal offences.[13]

In little more than two years from the beginning of Russia's invasion against Ukraine, the EU legislator has not only progressively expanded the magnitude of restrictive measures imposed on the aggressor state,[14] but also introduced a new Eurocrime, and established minimum rules for the definition of criminal offences and penalties to counter sanctions violations and circumvention.[15] In this way, the Union has successfully completed, for the first time, the procedure set forth in Article 83(1) TFEU, and ultimately expanded its competences to address a new area of particularly serious crime with a cross-border dimension. According to this fast-track criminalisation process, the adoption of Directive (EU) 2024/1226 was rushed through to ensure that those responsible for violating EU sanctions are duly prosecuted and held accountable for their crimes.

As the Commission did not conduct an impact assessment, one may argue that the establishment of common criminal rules at the Union level was accelerated on the *assumption* that it was necessary to create a level playing field among the 27 Member States and enhance law enforcement and judicial cooperation in addressing the violation of restrictive measures. In the words of the Commission, 'given the exceptional urgency, no impact assessment could [have been] conducted, and the relevant obligation was lifted'.[16] However, as further illustrated in the next sections, the lack of such an assessment is problematic. As a matter of fact, the exceptional circumstances of the war in Ukraine appear to have eclipsed one the most important *ex ante* guarantees for the creation of evidence-based legislation, in particular, evidence-based criminalisation.[17] The absence of evidence to support the criminalisation process gives rise to

[12] See also the Commission's proposal for a Council Decision, COM(2022) 247 final, of 25 May 2022.

[13] Directive (EU) 2024/1226 of the European Parliament and of the Council of 24 April 2024 on the definition of criminal offences and penalties for the violation of Union restrictive measures and amending Directive (EU) 2018/1673 [2024] OJ L. See also the first European Commission's proposal for a Directive, COM(2022) 249 final, of 25 May 2022.

[14] For a full timeline of the restrictive measures adopted since 2022 see https://finance.ec.europa.eu/eu-and-world/sanctions-restrictive-measures/sanctions-adopted-following-russias-military-aggression-against-ukraine_en#measures-adopted-since-2022.

[15] On the two-step approach proposed by the Commission to end impunity see Wouter Van Ballegooij, 'Ending Impunity for the Violation of Sanctions through Criminal Law' (2022) 17 *The European Criminal Law Associations' Forum* 146.

[16] See COM(2022) 247 final (n 12).

[17] Jannemieke Ouwerkerk, 'Evidence-Based Criminalisation in EU Law: Evidence of What Exactly?' in Jannemieke Ouwerkerk and others (eds), *The Future of EU Criminal Justice Policy and Practice* (Brill Nijhoff, 2019). See also COM(2015) 215 final, 'Better Regulation for Better Results – An EU Agenda'.

many questions, particularly whether the resort to criminal law measures can positively contribute to the implementation of EU sanctions, thereby eradicating impunity and countering sanctions violations more effectively than other non-criminal enforcement tools.[18]

9.3 THE RATIONALE BEHIND THE CRIMINALISATION PROCESS

Since May 2022, the Commission has clearly indicated that the criminalisation process seeks to target one major problem – the ultimately weak enforcement of EU sanctions – which, so far, has not been able to deter circumvention, close legal loopholes, prevent forum shopping, and therefore ensure the Union's ability to speak with one voice.[19]

In this regard, the Commission has employed a 2021 report by Genocide Network[20] as pivotal evidence to illustrate the extent to which the enforcement of EU sanctions varies significantly across the Union, resulting in a situation where, in practice, very few individuals or legal persons responsible for the violation of Union restrictive measures are effectively held accountable. This comparative study illustrates that some countries categorise sanctions violation as a *criminal* offence, others consider it as an only *administrative* offence, whilst a third category of states envisage the possibility of sanctions violations being categorised *either* as criminal *or* administrative offences, depending on their gravity or repeated violations. In the EU, it is reported that 12 Member States fall into the first category, as they ensure that the violation of EU restrictive measures is a criminal offence,[21] whilst only two Member States (Spain and Slovakia) fall into the second category, punishing EU sanctions breaches as a mere administrative offence. Lastly, the violation of these sanctions amounts to *either* an administrative or a criminal offence in 13 Member States.[22] The criteria according to which the unlawful conduct amounts to an administrative or a criminal offence are different in each country, but they are usually related to the gravity (serious nature) of the violation, determined in qualitative (intent, serious negligence) and quantitative (damage) terms.[23] With regard to the severity of penalties, the criteria for punishing non-compliance also differ substantially across Member

[18] On this question see Jacob Öberg, 'Do We Really Need Criminal Sanctions for the Enforcement of EU Law?' (2014) 5 *New Journal of European Criminal Law* 370.

[19] See 'Ukraine: The Commission proposes rules on freezing and confiscating assets of oligarchs violating restrictive measures and of criminals' Press release (25 May 2022) https://ec.europa.eu/commission/presscorner/detail/en/ip_22_3264.

[20] Genocide Network Secretariat, 'Prosecution of Sanctions (Restrictive Measures) Violations in National Jurisdictions: A Comparative Analysis' (2021). See also COM(2022) 247 final (n 12).

[21] Denmark, France, Croatia, Cyprus, Latvia, Luxembourg, Hungary, Malta, the Netherlands, Portugal, Finland, and Sweden.

[22] Belgium, Bulgaria, Czech Republic, Germany, Estonia, Ireland, Greece, Italy, Lithuania, Austria, Poland, Romania and Slovenia.

[23] See COM(2022) 247 final (n 12).

States. Focusing on criminal penalties, in 14 Member States, the maximum length of imprisonment is between two and five years, whilst maximum prison sentences of between eight and 12 years are possible in eight Member States. In terms of legal persons, 14 Member States provide for criminal liability of such persons for the violation of EU restrictive measures, whereas 12 Member States provide for administrative penalties, notably fines, which may be imposed on legal persons when their employees or their management violate restrictive measures.

All this suggests that national legal systems differ significantly in terms of their criminalisation of sanctions violations. This is not surprising, since Member States have had the freedom to decide which competent authorities are in charge of the implementation and enforcement of EU sanctions,[24] and what penalties they can impose for punishing non-compliance (as far as they result in effective, proportionate and dissuasive penalties). Before 2022, the principle of subsidiarity[25] allowed national autonomy to overshadow harmonisation. In that context, the Union trusted Member States to counter sanctions breaches within their respective jurisdictions – without interfering with national laws or enforcement capabilities.

Yet, in light of the pressing geopolitical context post-February 2022, the Commission has firmly pointed to the divergent legal frameworks among Member States, the inconsistent enforcement of restrictive measures, and the deficit in criminal investigations and prosecutions.[26] Lacking appropriate and effective tools to counter sanctions violations, the Commission has highlighted the risk that non-compliance will remain unpunished and that circumvention will proliferate. For instance, designated individuals whose assets are supposed to be frozen in the Union (eg, designated Russian oligarchs whose funds are immobilised in EU financial institutions) may continue to benefit from their assets[27] or even support their governments, targeted by restrictive measures, thus frustrating the objectives of those measures. Similarly, the money generated by the exploitation of natural resources traded through the violation of Union restrictive measures may allow the regimes targeted by those restrictive measures to purchase arms and weapons with which they execute their crimes. These violations and circumvention tactics may, in fact, survive and even thrive in the absence of effective enforcement across the Union – thereby undermining the credibility of EU sanctions. Moreover, the Commission has

[24] Clara Portela and Kim Olsen, 'Implementation and Monitoring of the EU Sanctions' Regimes, Including Recommendations to Reinforce the EU's Capacities to Implement and Monitor Sanctions' (European Parliament, 2023). See also Francesco Giumelli and others, 'United in Diversity? A Study on the Implementation of Sanctions in the European Union' (2022) 10 *Politics and Governance* 36.

[25] Art 5(3) TEU. See also Jacob Öberg, 'Subsidiarity as a Limit to the Exercise of EU Competences' 36 (2017) *Yearbook of European Law* 391.

[26] See COM(2022) 247 final (n 12).

[27] On the legality of family-based designations under EU sanctions regimes see Francesca Finelli, 'Countering Circumvention of Restrictive Measures: The EU Response' (2023) 60 *Common Market Law Review*.

emphasised that the same infringement, or circumvention scheme, might be punished differently in different Member States.[28] This may lead to forum shopping by offenders and could ultimately result into their impunity in case they choose to conduct their activities in the Member State(s) that provide for less severe penalties or have a record of being lenient in the prosecution for sanctions violations.[29]

The Commission has considered such an inconsistent enforcement landscape to be unacceptable, particularly in the context of the sanctions regime imposed in response to Russia's invasion against Ukraine. This is due to the potential of such a situation to frustrate the (CFSP) objectives pursued by sanctions, including the safeguarding of international peace and security, and the promotion of EU common values in the wider world. Thus, in May 2022, the Commission concluded that 'there [was] a special need for common action at EU level, by means of criminal law to address the violation of Union restrictive measures'.[30]

The fundamental question that remains unanswered is why a criminal law response is needed to address these issues. Notwithstanding the uncontested urgency to enhance national enforcement strategies, the Commission regrettably has failed to provide a satisfactory explanation as to why criminal law measures were appointed as the best regulatory tool to ensure the effective application of EU sanctions across 27 countries. It does not explain why criminal law measures are perceived to be the most effective tool to investigate, prosecute and punish sanctions breaches. Rather,

> we do not have any evidence that a failure to criminalise the violation of sanctions in some Member States, or the existence of dual administrative and criminal regimes in others, is the reason for low levels of detection, prosecution and conviction for the offence.[31]

Whilst there seems to be a presumption at the EU level that criminal law is the most effective response to non-compliance, we lack clear data concerning investigations and punishment of sanctions breaches across the Union. The criminalisation process appears difficult to reconcile with evidence-based decision-making – as well as the *ultima ratio* principle, which requires the legislator to resort to criminal law only when alternative measures have proved insufficient to achieve the desired objectives.[32]

[28] ibid.

[29] ibid.

[30] COM(2022) 684 final, Proposal for a Directive on the definition of criminal offences and penalties for the violation of Union restrictive measures (Brussels, 2 December 2022).

[31] See Report of the European Parliament on the proposed Directive (A9-0235/2023), Minority position (Ms. Clare Daly on behalf of The Left).

[32] On the notion of *ultima ratio* in EU criminal law, see Sakari Melander, 'Ultima Ratio in European Criminal Law' (2013) 3 *Oñati Socio-legal Series* 42; Nils Jareborg, 'Criminalization as Last Resort (Ultima Ratio)' (2004) 2 *Ohio State Journal of Criminal Law* 521.

9.4 THE EU'S COMPETENCE TO CRIMINALISE SANCTIONS VIOLATIONS PURSUANT TO ARTICLE 83(1) TFEU

When proposing new criminal legislation, the EU legislator needs to conform to the criteria set out in Article 83 TFEU. This provision enshrines two key normative justifications for criminalisation: the 'particularly serious' criterion (also known as the harm principle);[33] and the 'cross-border' criterion. These two criteria are cumulative, and both need to be satisfied for all new offences that are added to the list of Eurocrimes.[34]

9.4.1 The 'Particularly Serious' Criterion

The wording of Article 83(1) TFEU suggests that certain behaviours are particularly serious, because of the significant harm caused to society, thus pointing to the need for criminalisation. The harm principle is also more generally accepted as a guiding principle by the EU institutions in respect of the EU's substantive criminal law competence. In this context, the Council affirms that 'criminal provisions should focus on conduct causing actual harm or seriously threatening the rights or essential interests which is the object of protection'.[35] The European Commission stresses that criminalisation should proceed based on clear factual evidence about the serious nature or grave effects of the crime in question.[36] The European Parliament further argues that criminalisation should focus on the conduct that causes 'significant pecuniary or non-pecuniary damage' to the society or individuals.[37] Accordingly, the EU legislator needs to substantiate the serious harm, damage and effects of a certain conduct before it can subject it to regulation.

In the enumeration of Eurocrimes, the harm principle evidently transpires through the crimes listed in Article 83(1) TFEU. It has been argued that the

[33] On the harm principle, see *ex multis* Joel Feinberg, *The Moral Limits of the Criminal Law Volume 1: Harm to Others*, 1st edn (Oxford University Press, 1987); Nina Persak, *Criminalising Harmful Conduct: The Harm Principle, Its Limits and Continental Counterparts* (Springer Science & Business Media, 2007); Andrew Perry Simester and Andreas von Hirsch, *Crimes, Harms, and Wrongs: On the Principles of Criminalisation* (Hart Publishing, 2011); Jacob Öberg, 'Public Goods and Harm as Justificatory Frameworks for Supranational Criminalisation' in Jannemieke Ouwerkerk and others (eds), *The boundaries of criminalisation: rethinking public goods and legal interests in domestic and transnational criminal law* (Brill Academic Publishers, 2026).

[34] Asp (n 8) 18–20.

[35] Council, 'Council Conclusions on model provisions, guiding the Council's criminal law deliberations' (2979th Justice and Home Affairs Council meeting, Brussels, 30 November 2009) 3.

[36] Commission, 'Communication from the Commission to the European Parliament, the Council, the European Economic and Social Committee and the Committee of the Regions - Towards an EU Criminal Policy: Ensuring the effective implementation of EU policies through criminal law' COM(2011) 573 final, 3, 7–10.

[37] European Parliament, 'Resolution of 22 May 2012 on an EU approach to criminal law' P7 TA (2012) 0208, 2.

particularly serious nature usually reflects an 'EU-wide consensus about the harmfulness of the crimes' registered therein as similar conduct has already been recognised as deserving of criminalisation in the predominant majority of the EU Member States.[38] In other words, the harm principle is usually satisfied when there is an EU-wide consensus regarding the necessity of criminalising a particular conduct. Nonetheless, this wide consensus *cannot* be found for the criminalisation of sanctions breaches. In fact, prior to legislative developments of 2022, the majority of Member States had *not* opted for exclusive criminal enforcement to tackle the violation of sanctions in their domestic jurisdiction. In 13 Member States, the violation of restrictive measures would amount to either an administrative or criminal offence, and in two Member States, it would only result in administrative penalties. Together, these 15 states chose not to rely solely on criminal enforcement. Accordingly, one may wonder whether Article 83(1) TFEU requires a *pre-existing* EU-wide consensus on the necessity of employing criminal law measures – or whether the particularly grave nature of specific conduct can be criminalised even in the absence of a unanimous decision by all individual Member States. The criminalisation of sanctions breaches under Article 83(1) TFEU proves that the second scenario is possible – yet, it does not clarify to what extent the harm principle can be stretched to safeguard the effectiveness of EU law (in this case, the effectiveness of EU restrictive measures).[39]

Regrettably, in its legislative proposals, the Commission does not clarify the extent to which criminalising sanctions violations satisfies the harm criterion. On the one hand, it simply states that the violation of EU sanctions

> is a particularly serious area of crime, which, in terms of gravity, is of a similar degree of seriousness to the areas of crime listed in Article 83(1) TFEU, since it can perpetuate threats to international peace and security, undermine the consolidation of and support for democracy, the rule of law and human rights and result in significant economic, social, societal and environmental damage.[40]

On the other hand, it claims that there are often no direct victims of the violation of restrictive measures.[41] In this way, the Commission has not identified who are the specific 'beneficiaries' of the criminalisation process.

The Commission has invoked very little evidence to substantiate its legislative proposals – reaching only the minimum threshold of Article 296 TFEU.[42]

[38] Nina Peršak, 'Principles of EU Criminalisation and Their Varied Normative Strength: Harm and Effectiveness' (2022) 27 *European Law Journal* 463, 475–76.

[39] Which would be required to legislate under Art 83(2) TFEU which demands that criminal laws are 'essential' for the enforcement of an EU policy. See Öberg (n 18).

[40] See COM(2022) 247 final (n 12). See also recital 10 Council Decision (EU) 2022/2332 of 28 November 2022.

[41] ibid.

[42] Martin Shapiro, 'The Giving Reasons Requirement' (1992) *University of Chicago Legal Forum* 179.

It has not illustrated the specific damage caused by sanctions violations, nor the specific victims. Rather, the criminalisation of sanctions breaches appears to protect *a wide community* – and supranational legal interests. Differently from other Eurocrimes, the criminalisation process looks at the impact that sanctions violations have on the international society, and ultimately identifies the need to protect peace and security in a broader sense – even beyond the EU borders. Ultimately, given, the quite limited demands imposed by the Court of Justice on the justification for EU legislation,[43] it seems that the Directive – if contested – will likely satisfy the threshold imposed by Article 83(1) TFEU in addressing a 'particularly serious' crime.

9.4.2 The 'Cross-border' Criterion

This criterion suggests that the offence in question may have a cross-border dimension resulting either from its *nature*, its *impact* or a special *need to combat them on a common basis*. This requirement is typically satisfied when the offence involves the crossing of borders, such as smuggling of goods or trafficking human beings. The cross-border dimension may also result from the impact of the offence in question where the offence affects more than one country, including serious environmental offences and forgeries of the euro (neither of these offences impact only one country, nor stop at national borders).[44]

In respect of sanctions violations, the Commission claims these violations have an inherently cross-border dimension. Not only are they usually committed by natural persons and legal entities operating on a global scale but, in some cases, the Union precisely prohibits cross-border operations (such as import and export restrictions between the Union and third countries).[45] By definition, these violations imply cross-border activities which, according to the Commission, require a common EU response.[46] To illustrate, circumvention schemes often involve multiple jurisdictions – and rarely concern one single country. In the realm of asset freezes, for instance, a bank in one Member State may unfreeze funds or approve transfers of economic resources owned by a designated person, for the benefit of a company located in another Member State. These assets may reach a family member, who can act on behalf of the sanctioned relative, and move the unfrozen assets outside the Union, thereby undermining the effectiveness (and credibility) of EU sanctions via multiple cross-border operations. This suggests that the consistent and effective application of EU sanctions can

[43] Jacob Öberg, 'The Rise Of The Procedural Paradigm - Judicial Review Of EU Legislation In Vertical Competence Disputes' (2017) 13 *European Constitutional Law Review* 248.

[44] For a more comprehensive analysis of this criterion, see Jacob Öberg, *The Normative Foundations for EU Criminal Justice: Powers, Limits, and Justifications* (Hart Publishing, 2024) ch 4.

[45] See COM(2022) 247 final (n 12). See also recital 13 Council Decision (EU) 2022/2332 of 28 November 2022.

[46] ibid.

be better achieved at EU level rather than Member State level, by reason of the effects of the conduct at stake. A common EU response can also prevent forum shopping by offenders because they can no longer choose to exploit Member States that provide for less severe penalties for sanctions violations.

Hence, there are quite plausible arguments for claiming that the criminalisation of EU sanctions breaches under Article 83(1) TFEU satisfy the cross-border criterion. First, it is difficult to deny that infringing restrictive measures is an attack against common EU policies, or more precisely, CFSP decisions taken at the unanimity of 27 Member States.[47] It has been argued that some crimes 'would simply not exist without the EU' (eg, fraud against the EU budget, misappropriation of EU funds, corruption of EU officials) and that the Union therefore has a responsibility to protect the interests underlying such crimes.[48] This could definitively apply to the criminalisation of EU sanctions breaches. Second, restrictive measures typically have a cross-border character. For instance, travel bans, prohibitions on arms exports, asset freezing, and restrictions on goods and services always involve multiple jurisdictions, and at least two countries (typically a Member State and a third country, or a third-country national). Therefore, sanctions violations have, by nature, a cross-border character, and the Union is better placed to combat them on a common basis. Overall, there is a sufficient justification to substantiate that the criminalisation process is in line with the cross-border criterion in Article 83(1) TFEU.

9.5 THE APPROXIMATION OF CRIMINAL OFFENCES AND PENALTIES FOR EU SANCTIONS VIOLATIONS

Adopted on 24 April 2024, Directive (EU) 2024/1226 establishes common minimum rules concerning the definition of criminal conduct and penalties for the violation of restrictive measures.[49] These rules require Member States to criminalise specific conduct when it is 'in violation of a prohibition or an obligation that constitutes a Union restrictive measure or that is set out in a national provision implementing a Union restrictive measure, where national implementation of that measure is required'.[50] Importantly, these are *minimum* rules – meaning that Member States can add to them as part of their criminal law and introduce further definition or higher penalties. In addition, they apply to breaches of sanctions as 'EU' foreign policy decisions while they do not give

[47] Art 29 TEU.

[48] Pedro Caeiro, 'Beyond Competence Issues: Why and How Should the EU Legislate on Criminal Sanctions?' in Robert Kert and Andrea Lehner (eds), *Vielfalt des Strafrechts im internationalen Kontext. Festschrift für Frank Höpfel zum 65. Geburtstag* (Neuer Wissenschaftlicher Verlag, 2018) 652.

[49] Directive (EU) 2024/1226 (n 13).

[50] See Recital 4, Directive (EU) 2024/1226 (n 13).

the Union the power to harmonise criminal law as regards the breach of purely 'national foreign' policy sanctions.

In terms of its material scope, the Directive addresses non-compliance in a fairly comprehensive way, covering violations of *all types* of EU sanctions: not only asset freezes and travel bans imposed against designated persons, but also sectoral restrictions (such as economic and financial restrictions), as well as arms embargoes against third countries. More precisely, the Directive requires Member States to criminalise *nine* types of violations, which encompass the following conduct: a) making funds or economic resources available to a designated person; b) failing to freeze assets belonging to or owned, held or controlled by a designated person; c) enabling the entry into, or transit through, the territory of the Union, of a designated person; d) entering into transactions with sanctioned entities, including sanctioned third countries; e) trading in goods or services covered by sanctions; f) providing financial services covered by sanctions; g) providing other-than-financial services covered by sanctions; h) circumventing sanctions; and lastly i) breaching authorisations granted by national competent authorities.[51] Member States will have the option to exempt from criminalisation breaches involving sums *less than* EUR 10,000 – presumably because such breaches are not considered to be worthy of criminal prosecution.[52] However, in instances where multiple minor breaches are linked, Member States are obliged to aggregate them in order to attain the EUR 10,000 threshold, thereby enabling criminal prosecution.[53]

In every case, it is important to note that only *intentional* breaches are subject to criminalisation. For instance, only intentional failures to freeze assets of a designated person or intentional facilitation of their entry in the EU territory. The Directive does not contemplate strict (criminal) liability for non-compliance, nor the prosecution of gross negligence. Similarly, it does not criminalise circumvention tactics *tout court* – but it requires an intentional participation in a certain structure or scheme that frustrates the effectiveness of EU sanctions. Although the Commission initially proposed that infringing sanctions should constitute a criminal offence 'when committed with intent *as well as with serious negligence*' (particularly in cases where the natural or legal person knew, or should have known, that their conduct would infringe EU sanctions),[54] the Directive ultimately leaves out the criminalisation of gross negligence. Only in one case – presumably the most serious violation of sanctions, namely intentional trade in arms or dual use goods subject to restrictive measures – 'serious negligence' resulting in that breach will have to be criminalised.[55] But, despite this single exception, the Directive's focus remains firmly on the *deliberate*

[51] ibid, Art 3(1).
[52] ibid, Art 3(2).
[53] ibid.
[54] See COM(2022) 684 final (n 30).
[55] Art 3(3) Directive (EU) 2024/1226 (n 13).

engagement in sanctions violation, including inciting, aiding, abetting, as well as attempting the commission of such a violation.[56]

By providing an extensive list of conduct to be subject to criminal prosecution, and clarifying the requirement of *dolus* (and, exceptionally, serious *culpa*), the Directive aims to overcome the previously illustrated fragmented, inconsistent and ultimately weak enforcement of EU sanctions. However, it remains to be seen whether the exhaustive list of criminal offences introduced by the Directive will be sufficiently broad to encompass all forms of sanctions violations, and circumvention tactics – or whether a non-exhaustive list could have offered greater adaptability in the fight against non-compliance. Moreover, the effectiveness of these common criminal rules will heavily rely on the ability of national authorities to investigate and prove the intent of sanctions breaches. In practice, this could become a real challenge, as obtaining direct evidence of deliberate violations necessitates significant human capabilities and resource-intensive investigations.

Moving to common criminal penalties, the Directive introduces minimum–maximum penalties for both natural and legal persons, seeking to advance deterrence and a more consistent approach to prosecution of sanctions violations across 27 jurisdictions. It identifies two distinct categories of penalties: lighter penalties for minor offences; and more severe penalties for serious offences.

With regard to *natural* persons, the Directive establishes minimum–maximum penalties, in the form of imprisonment, of at least one year for minor offences, and of at least five years for serious offences.[57] To illustrate, failure to provide the national competent authorities with information on frozen assets (where such information was obtained in the performance of a professional duty), which amounts to a minor offence, shall be punishable by a minimum–maximum of one year of imprisonment, while, providing false or misleading information to conceal the fact that a designated person owns or control those assets, which amounts to a serious offence, shall be punishable by a minimum–maximum of five years. In this context, the Directive requires Member States to take the necessary measures to criminalise conduct that involve goods, services, transactions or activities of a value of at least EUR 100,000 on the date the offence was committed. Violations that involve a lower value still fall under the scope of the Directive – and common criminal rules – but Member States are invited to design their own criminal penalties, as long as they are 'effective, proportionate and dissuasive criminal penalties'.[58]

With regard to *legal* persons, the Directive offers a wider spectrum of criminal and non-criminal penalties, including exclusion from public benefits or aid;

[56] ibid, Art 4 (n 13).

[57] ibid, Art 5.

[58] On the proportionality of these penalties see Lorenzo Bernardini, 'Criminalising the Violation of EU Restrictive Measures: Towards (Dis)Proportionate Punishments Vis-à-Vis Natural Persons?' (2024) 14 *European Criminal Law Review* 4.

disqualification from business activities; withdrawal of permits and authorisations to pursue the activities that have resulted in the criminal offence, etc.[59] The Directive also codifies monetary fines. For minor offences, the maximum level of such fines is set to at least one per cent of the total worldwide turnover, or EUR 8,000,000. For serious offences, the minimum–maximum is increased to at least five per cent of the total worldwide turnover, or EUR 40,000,000.[60] It is worth noting that the Commission's initial proposal only contained a reference to the percentages of the total worldwide turnover – not providing for any alternative.[61] But, in its final version, the Directive establishes two alternatives, leaving Member States the choice to set the minimum–maximum level of penalties for legal persons according to their national preferences. Accordingly, each Member State retains a margin of manoeuvre in transposing the new provisions, as the Directive does not offer a definitive solution to punish sanctions breaches and evasion when (intentionally) committed by legal persons.

Hence, the new Directive (EU) 2024/1226 introduces a comprehensive (and exhaustive) list of sanctions breaches to be subject to criminalisation, as well as minimum–maximum penalties for those breaches. Undoubtedly, it compels significant reforms across 27 jurisdictions, and Member States had until 20 May 2025 to transpose the Directive into their national law.[62] Nonetheless, it has been argued that each Member State retains a margin of manoeuvre,[63] as the Directive still leaves room 'for wide variance' across the Union.[64]

9.6 FINAL REFLECTIONS ON THE CRIMINALISATION PROCESS: A MORE EFFECTIVE ENFORCEMENT FOR EU SANCTIONS – OR A STILL FRAGMENTED ONE?

It has been illustrated that the criminalisation of sanctions violations pursuant to Article 83 TFEU is intended to address a new area of *particularly serious crime* with a *cross-border dimension*. Engaging in sanctions breaches now amounts to a new Eurocrime, and Directive (EU) 2024/1226 approximates rules and penalties to counter it. While the Directive introduces significant reforms and advancements in the effective enforcement of restrictive measures, legal

[59] Art 7 Directive (EU) 2024/1226 (n 13).

[60] On the proportionality of these penalties see Pedro Caeiro, 'Broadly Unknown, but Deservedly Unloved? Turnover-Based Fines and Their Transplant from Competition Law to EU Criminal Law' in Lorenzo Grossio, Valsamis Mitsilegas and Stefano Montaldo (eds), *Proportionality of Criminal Penalties in EU Law* (Bloomsbury Publishing, 2025).

[61] See COM(2022) 684 final (n 30).

[62] Art 20 Directive (EU) 2024/1226 (n 13).

[63] Jeff Nielsen, 'Considering the EU Commission's Proposal on Its Directive for Criminal Penalties for Violations of Restrictive Measures in the Context of a Comparative Analysis With US Sanctions Enforcement' (22 November 2022), papers.ssrn.com/sol3/papers.cfm?abstract_id=4283807.

[64] ibid, 6. For instance, with regard to penalties to legal persons, Art 7 affords considerable discretion to Member States. National legislators can, in fact, decide whether the maximum monetary penalty should be set according to a numerical cap or a percentage cap.

challenges and fragmentation still persist throughout the Union. Furthermore, the rapid criminalisation of sanction violations in the last couple of years gives rise to a number of unresolved issues. Chief among these is the question of whether the approximation of criminal rules and penalties will truly ensure a more effective implementation of EU sanctions across the Union.

9.6.1 A Symbolic (rather than Evidence-Based) Criminalisation

Following the Commission's proposal of May 2025, the Union has successfully completed, for the first time, the procedure set forth in Article 83(1) TFEU, thereby expanding its competences to address a new area of crime. This legislative process demonstrates that the Union's foreign policy and criminal law are now two *intertwined* areas of EU law. Together, they empower the Union to uphold and promote its values and interests, in its relations with the wider world. While sanctions *directly* contribute to the achievement of CFSP objectives, criminal law measures are now intended to support the Union's external action by ensuring the effective enforcement of its restrictive measures across the 27 Member States. Particularly in the context of Russia's war of aggression against Ukraine, the resort to criminal law measures has been presented as the optimal strategy to enhance deterrence against non-compliance with EU sanctions.

Yet, the EU legislator essentially relies on *one comparative study* (published by the Genocide Network in 2021) to prove the need to introduce common criminal rules in order to effectively counter sanctions breaches. The 2021 study illustrates how the enforcement of EU sanctions varies significantly across the Union. It shows inconsistencies, and indicates that only a limited number of violators have been held accountable at the national level. However, it does *not* present criminal law as the 'magical solution',[65] a panacea for ensuring that individuals and legal persons responsible for sanctions violations are held accountable.

Thus, it remains unclear to what extent criminal law is the most effective tool to counter sanctions breaches and deter circumvention tactics. In the absence of an impact assessment or any more detailed study exploring the advantages and disadvantages of difference enforcement strategies, it has not been proven than reliance on criminal law invariably results in enhanced deterrence or an increase in investigations throughout the Union. Rather, it seems that the exceptional circumstances of the war in Ukraine have overlooked any obligation to produce evidence-based criminal legislation, which risks leading to *over-criminalisation*, also referred to as 'precautionary criminalisation',[66] or 'purely symbolic crim-

[65] On the heavy reliance on the 'magic of criminal law' see SS Buisman, 'The Future of EU Substantive Criminal Law: Towards a Uniform Set of Criminalisation Principles at the EU Level' (2022) 30 *European Journal of Crime, Criminal Law and Criminal Justice* 161, 176.

[66] Ester Herlin-Karnell, 'The Development of EU Precautionary Criminalisation' (2011) 1 *European Criminal Law Review* 149. See also Douglas Husak, *Overcriminalization: The Limits of the Criminal Law*, 1st edn (Oxford University Press, 2007).

inalisation'.[67] In this way, criminal law appears to be presumed by the EU legislator to be the most effective means to correct deficiencies in the enforcement of restrictive measures – without any evidence to support this assertion.

The extension of EU competences and proliferation of legislative initiatives in this field is closely related to Russia's invasion of Ukraine. Moreover, while the use of those criminal law powers will not end the war, it is considered to contribute to the effective implementation of EU sanctions. Plus, it conveys a political message that the Union is stepping up their enforcement. This suggests, once again, that the criminalisation process has a strong *symbolic* and *communicative* dimension – rather than evidence-based one.[68] Consequently, it can be argued that the over-reliance on criminal law may ultimately conflict with the *ultima ratio* principle – and the obligation to resort to less intrusive means *before* resorting to criminal law, which shall 'always remain a measure of last resort'.[69] But, in the context of an ongoing war, the imperative to enhance sanctions effectiveness by criminal means appears to prevail over evidence-based criminalisation.

In conclusion, this chapter sheds light on how the criminalisation process appears *functional* 'to ensure the effective application of Union restrictive measure'. Although it has been traditionally argued that the Treaties put forward 'a dual model of criminalisation',[70] namely a *securitised* model (reflected in Article 83(1) TFEU), which allows the Union to combat certain areas particularly serious crime with a cross-border dimension, and a *functional* model (reflected in Article 83(2) TFEU), which grants the Union with the competence to harmonise national criminal laws if such approximation 'proves essential to ensure the effective implementation of a Union policy in an area which has been subject to harmonisation measures',[71] this chapter demonstrates that the criminalisation of sanctions breaches has blurred the traditional distinction between securitised and functionalised criminalisation.[72] The resort to EU criminal law, in fact,

[67] 'The stronger the pull of external factors, the stronger the necessity to have proper safeguards in place and, in particular, the stronger the need to follow a tailor-made, evidence-based approach. ... New initiatives should [not] be purely symbolic ...' See Nicholas Franssen and Anne Weyembergh, 'From Facts and Political Objectives to Legal Bases and Legal Provisions: Incremental European Integration in the Criminal Law Field' (2021) 27 *European Law Journal* 368, 376.

[68] Steve Peers, 'Foreign policy sanctions and criminal law harmonisation' EU Law Analysis, 18 January 2024, https://eulawanalysis.blogspot.com/2024/01/foreign-policy-sanctions-and-criminal.html.

[69] COM(2011) 573 final (n 36). See also Ester Herlin-Karnell, 'What Principles Drive (or Should Drive) European Criminal Law?' (2010) 11 *German Law Journal* 1115.

[70] Valsamis Mitsilegas, 'Substantive Criminal Law: From Securitised to Functional Criminalisation' in *EU Criminal Law* (Hart Publishing, 2022).

[71] See also Öberg (n 18); Vanessa Franssen, 'EU Criminal Law and Effet Utile: A Critical Examination of the Union's Use of Criminal Law to Achieve Effective Enforcement' in *EU Criminal Law and Policy: Values, Principles, and Methods* (Routledge, 2016).

[72] For preliminary reflections on the tension between *securitised* and *functionalised* criminalisation, see Lorenzo Bernardini and Francesca Finelli, 'Violations of EU Sanctions and Criminal Penalties: Proportionality at Peril?' in Lorenzo Grossio, Stefano Montaldo and Valsamis Mitsilegas (eds), *Proportionality of Criminal Penalties in EU Law* (Hart Publishing, 2025). See also Jörg

appears to be *a means to an end* (the end being the effective implementation of sanctions), rather than reflecting the securitised model traditionally enshrined in Article 83(1) TFEU.

9.6.2 Inevitable Fragmentation

Besides the illustrated criticisms with regard to the symbolic and functional dimension of the criminalisation process, in practice, the Directive (EU) 2024/1226 cannot completely eliminate fragmentation in the enforcement of EU sanctions – as Member States still remain free to adopt *different responses* against non-compliance and circumvention tactics. The Directive, in fact, offers a legal framework for the identification and punishment of *certain* criminal offences: it provides definitions and penalties intended to regulate intentional and serious violations of EU sanctions – presented in a closed, exhaustive list of crimes. But it does not fully regulate national responses to non-compliance.

Moreover, and most importantly, it does not harmonise national capabilities, resources, budgetary priorities and procedures to detect and prosecute sanctions violations.[73] In other words, enforcement capabilities remain fragmented in the 27 Member States, as well as the national appetite for (criminal) investigations. Furthermore, the Directive does not specify what should be the *interplay* between criminal *and* non-criminal enforcement actions. It does not regulate to what extent Member States can maintain non-criminal penalties (for instance, in case of serious negligence or wilful blindness), while resorting to criminal prosecution only for the most serious (and intentional) violations.[74] As a result, some countries may continue to rely on non-criminal enforcement actions – while referring to criminal prosecution only in limited circumstances.[75]

Since early spring 2022, some national authorities have reacted promptly to the drift towards criminalisation, strengthening their enforcement mechanisms (eg the Netherlands has conducted multiple arrests and investigations, and the Baltic states have shown a special commitment in the fight against circumvention). In contrast, other authorities appear to have been less proactive. In fact, in

---

Monar, 'Reflections on the place of criminal law in the European construction' (2021) 27 *European Law Journal* 356.

[73] 'Member states have, together, officially designated more than 160 national authorities involved in the enforcement of EU sanctions. These are all, in turn, subject to greatly varying mandates, and have very different human and technical resources, and methods'; see Kim B Olsen and Simon Fasterkjær Kjeldsen, 'Strict and Uniform: Improving EU Sanctions Enforcement' [2022] DGAP Policy Brief. See also René Smits, 'Financial Sanctions: The Development of an EU Practice' in *International Sanctions: Monetary and Financial Law Perspectives* (Brill Nijhoff, 2024) 92.

[74] Francesca Finelli, 'Non-Criminal Penalties for Sanctions Violation' in Clara Portela, Andrea Charron and Mirko Sossai (eds), *Elgar Encyclopedia of International Sanctions* (Edward Elgar Publishing, 2025).

[75] Similarly, in the US and the UK, the enforcement of sanctions is predominantly administered by specialised agencies (OFAC and OFSI, respectively) which impose penalties on a *civil liability* basis.

June 2025, the European Commission even decided to open infringement procedures against 18 Member States (Belgium, Bulgaria, Czechia, Germany, Ireland, Greece, Spain, France, Croatia, Italy, Cyprus, Hungary, Malta, Austria, Poland, Portugal, Romania and Slovenia) for failing to fully transpose the new Directive into national legislation by the 20 May 2025 deadline.[76] This shows that national enforcement systems are *still* not harmonised throughout the Union – even after the unprecedented commitment to ensure sanctions effectiveness through criminal law.[77] The political agreement (and the unanimity vote expressed within the Council) has not solved the inherent fragmentation in the implementation and enforcement of EU restrictive measures.

In conclusion, it remains to be seen what impact the criminalisation of sanctions violations will have in practice. Undoubtedly, the fragmentation of national willingness, resources and expertise to investigate and initiate prosecutions will not be easily resolved.

9.6.3 A Possible Way Forward: the Role of the EPPO

Directive (EU) 2024/1226 intends to foster supranational cooperation, providing for a stronger inter-institutional exchange of information among Member States' competent authorities, the Commission, Eurojust, Europol, and the European Public Prosecutor's Office (EPPO), whose respective roles would come into play within their respective competences, as well as competent authorities of third countries.[78] It fosters the creation of institutional networks to detect and punish non-compliance across the Union.

Moreover, the prospect of extending competence to the EPPO to include breaches of EU sanctions has been raised by some Member States and the European Parliament, and such a development would clearly entail much stronger and coordinated *criminal* enforcement.[79] Conferring powers to a centralised supranational prosecutor can be desirable in selected areas of transnational crime where there are compelling rationales to fight those crimes through common measures. If the EPPO could contribute to addressing complex

[76] See https://ec.europa.eu/commission/presscorner/detail/en/inf_25_1842.

[77] See data and graphics on the enforcement of Russia and Belarus sanctions across the Member States, at https://blogs.duanemorris.com/europeansanctionsenforcement/2024/09/27/europe-hits-300th-concluded-sanctions-enforcement-action-since-2017/?lctg=281740899. See also European Banking Authority (EBA), Opinion on money laundering and terrorist financing risks affecting the EU's financial sector, EBA/Op/2023/08, (13 July 2023), para 3.1.1, www.eba.europa.eu/sites/default/files/document_library/Publications/Opinions/2023/1058335/EBA%20Op%202023%2008%20Opinion%20on%20MLTF%20risks%20EBA%20REP%202023%2021.pdf.

[78] Art 20 Directive (EU) 2024/1226 (n 13).

[79] See 'L'appel des ministres français et allemand de la justice: « Nous souhaitons l'extension de la compétence du parquet européen aux violations des sanctions prises par l'UE »' *Le Monde* (29 November 2022); European Parliament resolution of 18 January 2023 on the implementation of the common foreign and security policy — annual report 2022 (2022/2048(INI)) [2023] OJ C 214/26, para 18.

violations of EU restrictive measures by pooling expertise, competencies and investigative resources that individual Member States cannot muster, there is a *prima facie* case for an extension of the EPPO's powers in this field. In other words, EPPO appears better placed to enforce this type of legislation – limiting national fragmentation.[80] Yet, once again, it would offer a centralised tool for the investigations of *certain* types of sanctions breaches, namely criminal offences as listed in the Directive (EU) 2024/1226 – though it could not centralise the imposition of non-criminal penalties.

Csonka and Zoli have argued that, from a substantive perspective, there may be grounds to expand the EPPO's authority to include criminal offences harmonised by the new Directive.[81] In fact, restrictive measures are a crucial tool for advancing the objectives of the CFSP and, like fraud against the EU budget, the effective detection and punishment of non-compliance with EU provisions can be viewed as an interest of the Union itself, justifying criminal enforcement at the EU level. It is admittedly true that the crimes the EPPO would be empowered to investigate (ie, sanctions violations) are not primarily of national concern. With binding enforcement powers, the EPPO is capable of directing prosecutions and investigations into all the sanctions violations in all participating jurisdictions, thus ensuring a coherent and efficient prosecution of such offences. In addition, it is maintained that protecting the effectiveness of EU sanctions regimes is a collective asset belonging to the whole community, since the enforcement of EU sanctions is about protecting the common values and objectives of the EU in the external context.[82] The protection of EU sanctions are thus rightly conceived as 'European public goods',[83] which by their nature (since states alone do not have the expertise and resources to deal with this issue)[84] can only be protected on a European level, thus surpassing the notion of 'territory' and national public goods.

The key objections to conferring powers to the EPPO relates to sovereignty and legitimacy. Political legitimacy considerations nonetheless suggest that the Member States' interest in preserving national autonomy in this field should not be disregarded.[85] It is well known that most EU citizens regard themselves primarily as citizens of a Member State rather than of the EU. From this perspective, it is clear that the nation state regarded as the most legitimate entity for

[80] Jacob Öberg, 'The European Public Prosecutor's Office - Supranationalism, Sovereignty and Legitimacy' (2025) 50 *European Law Review* 705.

[81] Peter Csonka and Luca Zoli, 'The New Directive on the Violation of Union Restrictive Measures in the Context of the EPPO' Eucrim (2024), doi.org/10.30709/eu-crim-2024-006.

[82] Art 2 TEU.

[83] See Öberg (n 44) ch 2. See also Stephen Coutts, 'Supranational Public Wrongs: The Limitations and Possibilities of European Criminal Law and a European Community' (2017) 54 *Common Market Law Review* 771.

[84] Art 5(3) TEU.

[85] Art 4(2) TEU expresses a clear notion of state sovereignty. See Paul Craig and Gráinne De Búrca, *EU Law: Text, Cases, and Materials* (Oxford University Press, 2011) 279–314. The authors offer an extensive analysis of primacy suggesting that whilst national courts in principle accepts the principle, there are limits imposed on this acceptance by national constitutional courts.

adopting legislation in the field of criminal justice.[86] Even though the traditional ('Bodian') notion of sovereignty[87] is not persuasive enough to reject the conferral of binding powers to the EPPO, criticism of the EPPO's legitimacy should be taken seriously.[88] This speaks to the issue of legitimacy and the (absence) of a strong fundamental rights framework encasing the operations of the EPPO. If we conjecture that the legitimacy of the EPPO is not only dependent on the success of its enforcement actions (ie, output legitimacy) but also its capacity to respect individual rights, there is a need for corresponding legal standards of rights of defence and judicial protection surrounding the operations of the EPPO to countenance the body's enforcement powers.[89] Stronger common EU measures for protecting the rights of the defendant particularly in respect of judicial remedies against the EPPO's actions, along with effective safeguards that form the basis for the exercise of the EPPO's powers, should be a central feature of a potential future amendment of the EPPO Regulation.[90] A robust legal framework surrounding the EPPO's operational action, combined with strong legal safeguards for individual defendants, is imperative for ensuring the overall legitimacy of this new unique supranational prosecutor. In the absence of such a framework it is highly doubtful whether it is justified to extend the EPPO's powers beyond Article 86 TFEU to also cover the prosecution of crimes against the EU's sanctioning regime.[91]

[86] The German Federal Constitutional Court has stated that nothing more strongly embodies the exercise of sovereign authority than the right to define and enforce the rules of criminal law, since a criminal justice system constitutes a legal community which expresses a code of conduct that is anchored in its moral values, see ('Lisbon' judgment) 2 BvE 2/08,2 BvE 5/08, 2 BvR 1010/08, 2 BvR 1022/08, 2 BvR 1259/08, 2 BvR 182/09 (2009), paras 252–53, 355–56.

[87] Jean Bodin, *Bodin: On Sovereignty* (Cambridge University Press, 2012); Daniel Lee, *The Right of Sovereignty: Jean Bodin on the Sovereign State and the Law of Nations* (Oxford University Press, 2021).

[88] Paul P Craig, 'Democracy and Rule-making Within the EC: An Empirical and Normative Assessment' (1997) 3 *European Law Journal* 105; Giandomenico Majone, 'Europe's "Democratic Deficit": The Question of Standards' (1998) 4 *European Law Journal* 5.

[89] Christoffer C Eriksen and Jørgen A Stubberud, 'Legitimacy and the Charter of Fundamental Rights Post-Lisbon' *The Reach of Free Movement* (Springer, 2017); Craig and De Búrca (n 85).

[90] According to Art 119 EPPO Regulation, the Commission shall conduct an evaluation on the implementation and the impact of the Regulation and produce a report envisaged to be published in 2026. For the purpose of this evaluation Spark Consulting has produced two reports: i) 'Measures adopted by the Member States to adapt their systems to Council Regulation (EU) 2017/1939 of 12 October 2017 implementing enhanced cooperation on the establishment of the European Public Prosecutor's Office ("the EPPO")' (September 2023), www.europarl.europa.eu/cmsdata/280160/Final%20Report%20-%20DG%20JUST%20Study%20on%20the%20EPPO%20-%2029.09.2023_en.pdf, and ii) 'Extension of the Compliance assessment of measures adopted by the Member States to adapt their systems to Council Regulation (EU) 2017/1939 of 12 October 2017 implementing enhanced cooperation on the establishment of the European Public Prosecutor's Office ("the EPPO") (JUST/2022/PR/JCOO/CRIM/0004)' (September 2023), www.europarl.europa.eu/cmsdata/280163/Final%20Report%20on%20Extension%20Findings%20DG%20JUST%20Study%20on%20the%20EPPO_en.pdf.

[91] Öberg (n 80).

10

Proportionality of EU Criminalisation Choices and Harmonised Sanctions: A Conceptual Appraisal

LORENZO GROSSIO

10.1 INTRODUCTION: AIM AND SCOPE OF THE RESEARCH

While the EU does not itself exercise *ius puniendi*, Article 83 of the Treaty on the Functioning of the European Union (TFEU) enables the Parliament and Council to lay down minimum rules on the definition of offences and penalties concerning some 'areas of particularly serious crime with a cross-border dimension'[1] or 'to ensure the effective implementation of a Union policy in an area which has been subject to harmonisation measures'.[2] The exercise of such EU competence involves supranational criminalisation choices, resulting in obligations for domestic legislatures to penalise specific behaviours on the basis of EU harmonising provisions.[3] Legal scholarship has extensively dealt with the need to develop normative justifications and criminalisation principles to drive the supranational approximation of offences and penalties.[4] However, the analysis

[1] Art 83(1) TFEU.

[2] ibid, Art 83(2).

[3] In some cases, the definition of the crime provided by the EU legislature is particularly precise, thus leading to almost verbatim transposition at the domestic level; on this point, see Irene Wieczorek, *The Legitimacy of EU Criminal Law* (Hart Publishing, 2020) 51. Therefore, the expression 'criminalisation choices' should also apply to EU action in substantive criminal law. For an in-depth account of the rationales underpinning harmonisation pursuant to Art 83 TFEU, among extensive scholarly analysis, see Valsamis Mitsilegas, *EU Criminal Law*, 2nd edn (Hart Publishing, 2022) 89 ff.

[4] In particular, see Jacob Öberg, *The Normative Foundations for EU Criminal Justice: Powers, Limits and Justifications* (Hart Publishing, 2024); Ester Herlin-Karnell, 'What Principles Drive (or Should Drive) European Criminal Law?' (2010) 11 *German Law Journal* 1115; Irene Wieczorek, 'The Normative Legitimacy of EU Criminal Law: A Focus on EU Criminalisation' in Valsamis Mitsilegas, Maria Bergström and Teresa Quintel (eds), *Research Handbook on EU Criminal Law*, 2nd edn (Edward Elgar Publishing, 2024); SS Buisman, 'The Future of EU Substantive Criminal Law: Towards a Uniform Set of Criminalisation Principles at the EU Level' (2022) 30 *European*

of the implications of the principle of proportionality for EU substantive criminal law has only recently gained momentum in this scholarly stream.[5]

In light of this emerging debate, the chapter theorises the principle of proportionality in the context of EU instruments harmonising Member States' substantive criminal law. More specifically, it assesses the proportionality constraints on EU criminalisation choices underpinning minimum rules on the definition of offences and the approximation of the type and level of sanctions pursuant to Article 83 TFEU. The chapter takes a conceptual approach. First, it frames the key theoretical features of proportionality in EU criminal law, depicting a peculiar interaction between the EU and criminal law understandings of proportionality (section 10.2). Against this premise, the chapter assesses whether the same theoretical features underpin the proportionality constraints to supranational criminalisation choices. To that aim, the chapter explores the relevant legislative practice to disclose how the EU legislature balances conflicting interests when formulating harmonising provisions on offences and penalties (section 10.3). Thirdly, the analysis outlines the Court of Justice of the European Union (CJEU)'s approach to the proportionality review of those harmonising provisions (section 10.4). In this regard, the chapter examines the extent of the Court's scrutiny and the interaction between the EU and criminal law understandings of proportionality in the context of EU substantive criminal law. The last section joins the dots of the analysis to answer the research question and provides some conclusive remarks (section 10.5).

10.2 ONE GENERAL PRINCIPLE, MULTIPLE DECLINATIONS: KEY FEATURES OF THE PRINCIPLE OF PROPORTIONALITY IN EU CRIMINAL LAW

Proportionality is a general principle of the EU legal order that shapes the exercise of EU powers and the compatibility of domestic measures with EU law.[6] On the one hand, as emphasised by Article 5(4) Treaty on European Union

Journal of Crime, Criminal Law and Criminal Justice 161; Nina Peršak, 'EU Criminal Law and Its Legitimation: In Search for a Substantive Principle of Criminalisation' (2018) 26 *European Journal of Crime, Criminal Law and Criminal Justice* 20; Lucille Micheletto, 'Towards an Integrated (and Possibly Pan-European?) Prima Facie Legitimacy Test: Merging the Rechtsgut Theory, the Offensività Principle, and the Harm Principle' (2021) 29 *European Journal of Crime, Criminal Law and Criminal Justice* 241.

[5] In this stream of analysis, among many, see Ester Herlin-Karnell, *The Constitutional Dimension of European Criminal Law* (Hart Publishing, 2012) 127; Irene Wieczorek, *The Legitimacy of EU Criminal Law* (Hart Publishing, 2022); as well as the wide-ranging contributions published in Lorenzo Grossio, Stefano Montaldo and Valsamis Mitsilegas (eds), *Proportionality of Criminal Penalties in EU Law* (Hart Publishing, 2025).

[6] Among extensive literature, see: Takis Tridimas, 'The General Principles of EU Law and the Europeanisation of National Laws' (2020) 13 *Review of European Administrative Law* 5; Koen Lenaerts, 'Proportionality as a Matrix Principle Promoting the Effectiveness of EU Law and the Legitimacy of EU Action – Keynote Speech' in *Continuity and change – how the challenges of*

(TEU), proportionality implies that 'the content and form of Union action shall not exceed what is necessary to achieve the objectives of the Treaties'. The Court of Justice has consistently interpreted this provision as postulating a proportionality assessment composed of the traditional suitability-necessity-proportionality *stricto sensu* test, derived from German administrative law.[7] Pursuant to the suitability and necessity requirements, EU actions must 'be appropriate for attaining the legitimate objectives pursued by the legislation at issue and must not go beyond what is necessary to achieve them'.[8] Moreover, under proportionality *stricto sensu*, 'the disadvantages caused must not be disproportionate to the aims pursued'.[9] On the other hand, the principle of proportionality underpins the clash between EU and domestic measures with individual rights and freedoms secured by EU law. According to Article 52(1) of the Charter of Fundamental Rights of the European Union ('the Charter'), any interference with the enjoyment of fundamental rights must respect the essence of those rights and be suitable, necessary, and proportionate *stricto sensu* to achieving a legitimate interest.[10] An analogous threefold test applies in assessing the legitimacy of measures that interfere with the enjoyment of internal market freedoms.[11] In both dimensions, the general principle of proportionality unveils a finalistic assessment. The legitimacy of the measure is evaluated in relation to achieving a legitimate goal: only arrangements that are suitable in that respect, entail the least sacrifice for the countervailing interests and ensure proper balancing between the interests at stake shall be deemed proportionate.

---

today prepare the ground for tomorrow. ECB Legal Conference 2021 (European Central Bank, 2022) 27; Grainne de Búrca, 'The Principle of Proportionality and its Application in EC Law' (1993) 13 *Yearbook of European Law* 105, 105.

[7] Among many, see Takis Tridimas, *The General Principles of EU Law*, 2nd edn (Oxford University Press 2007) 29–34; Paul Craig, *EU Administrative Law*, 2nd edn (Oxford University Press, 2012) 643 ff; Nicolas Emiliou, *The Principle of Proportionality in European Law: A Comparative Study* (Kluwer Law International, 1996) 16. On the evolution of the principle of proportionality, see Nestor Courakis and Vagia Polyzoidou, 'The Principle of Proportionality: Tracing Its Historical Evolution' in Emmanouil Billis, Nandor Knust and Jon Petter Rui (eds), *Proportionality in Crime Control and Criminal Justice* (Hart Publishing, 2021); Eric Engle, 'The History of the General Principle of Proportionality: An Overview' (2012) 10 *Dartmouth Law Journal 1*.

[8] Case C-58/08, *Vodafone and Others* EU:C:2010:321, para 51.

[9] Case C-128/17, *Poland v Parliament and Council* EU:C:2019:194, para 94.

[10] For an analysis of the proportionality test encapsulated in Art 52(1) of the Charter, see Steve Peers and Sacha Prechal, 'Article 52 - Scope and Interpretation of Rights and Principles' in Steve Peers, Tamara Hervey, Jeff Kenner and Angela Ward (eds), *The EU Charter of Fundamental Rights: A Commentary*, 2nd edn (Hart Publishing, 2021); Dimitris Triantafyllou, 'The European Charter of Fundamental Rights and the "Rule of Law": Restricting Fundamental Rights by Reference' (2002) 39 *CML Review* 53; Sébastien Van Drooghenbroeck and Cecilia Rizcallah, 'Article 52-1. Limitations aux droits garantis' in Fabrice Picod, Cecila Rizcallah and Sébastien Van Drooghenbroeck (eds), *Charte de droits fondamentaux de l'Union européenne: Commentire article par article* (Bruylant, 2023).

[11] See Arts 36, 45(3), 52(1) and 65(1)–(3) TFEU. In case law, among many, see Case C-663/18, *B S and C A [Commercialisation du cannabidiol (CBD)]* EU:C:2020:938, para 83; Case C-591/17, *Austria v Germany* EU:C:2019:504, para 122; Case C-126/15, *Commission v Portugal* EU:C:2017:504, para 64; Case C-727/17, *ECO-WIND Construction* EU:C:2020:393, para 81.

Nonetheless, the threefold test alone proves insufficient to frame the principle of proportionality of offences and penalties in EU law. Indeed, proportionality has a distinctive meaning in the criminal law domain, which is inextricably linked to theories of punishment.[12] Traditionally, the principle is matched with retributivism, which postulates a retrospective assessment: the punishment must not be disproportionate to the seriousness of the past wrongdoing.[13] However, consequentialist theories – such as positive and negative general prevention – also entail a relationship with proportionality. On the one hand, since criminalisation and the imposition of punishment aim at deterring potential offenders, proportionality constitutes a constraint in this respect.[14] On the other hand, from a positive perspective, a proportionate exercise of *ius puniendi* would ensure higher compliance with the law, since individuals would perceive it as fairer.[15]

EU criminal law is not impervious to these divergent understandings of proportionality, which stem from the theoretical paradigms inherent in two distinct legal disciplines – namely, EU and criminal law. Notably, retrospective proportionality is crystallised in Article 49(3) of the Charter, which states that 'the severity of penalties must not be disproportionate to the criminal offence'. Moreover, the CJEU case law manifests an intersection between the threefold proportionality test and the criminal law understandings of proportionality. In assessing the compatibility of domestic offences and penalties with EU law, the Court's scrutiny is not limited to the suitability, necessity and proportionality *stricto sensu* requirements. Indeed, the CJEU complements the review with proportionality paradigms derived from the criminal law dimension. Specifically, the severity of criminal sanctions 'must be commensurate with the seriousness of the infringements for which they are imposed'[16] (retrospective proportionality), 'in particular by ensuring a genuinely dissuasive effect, while respecting the general principle of proportionality'[17] (prospective proportionality). This compound assessment is of a hybrid nature, since the traditional theorisation of proportionality is complemented with schemes pertaining to

[12] Among many, see RA Duff, 'Proportionality and the Criminal Law: Proportionality of What to What?' in Emmanouil Billis, Nandor Knust and Jon Petter Rui (eds), *Proportionality in Crime Control and Criminal Justice* (Hart Publishing, 2021) 29; Adriano Martufi, 'Proportionality of Sanctions Under EU Law: Insights from Penal Theory' in Lorenzo Grossio, Stefano Montaldo and Valsamis Mitsilegas (eds), *Proportionality of Criminal Penalties in EU Law* (Hart Publishing, 2025) 42–43.

[13] Andrew von Hirsch, 'Proportionality in the Philosophy of Punishment' (1992) 16 *Crime and Justice* 55, 79.

[14] Among many, see Nils Jareborg, 'Criminalization as Last Resort (Ultima Ratio)' (2005) 2 *Ohio State Journal of Criminal Law* 521.

[15] von Hirsch (n 13) 68.

[16] Case C-544/19, *ECOTEX BULGARIA* EU:C:2021:803, para 100.

[17] ibid. On the coexistence between prospective and retrospective proportionality in the CJEU case law, see Stefano Montaldo, 'Handle with Care! The Direct Effect of the Requirement of Proportionality of Sanctions and the Remedy of Disapplication: NE v. Bezirkshauptmannschaft Hartberg-Fürstenfeld' (2023) 60 *CML Review* 863, 874–75.

the principle's criminal law dimension.[18] While the hybrid review is mainstreamed in the CJEU case law regarding domestic criminal measures,[19] should it also apply to EU harmonising provisions on substantive criminal law based on Article 83 TFEU?

The answer to this question is not self-evident for two main reasons. Firstly, proportionality constraints for EU criminalisation choices are twofold. Indeed, they may involve either an assessment of the intensity of the supranational legislative intervention under Article 5(4) TEU or the interference it causes with the enjoyment of fundamental rights pursuant to Article 52(1) of the Charter. Therefore, it remains doubtful whether these two distinct profiles elicit comparable proportionality paradigms. Secondly, and in connection with that, there is no conclusive indication from the case law. In light of a longstanding loophole in the CJEU jurisprudence, the 2023 reference for a preliminary ruling in *Kinsa* marked the very first case concerning proportionality constraints on the EU legislature for its criminalisation choices. In particular, the proceedings before the Court concerned the validity of Directive 2002/90/EC[20] and Framework Decision 2002/946/JHA,[21] which criminalise facilitation of unauthorised entry, transit, and residence, vis-a-vis the proportionality grounds outlined in Articles 52(1) and 49(3) of the Charter. In his conclusions, Advocate General Richard de la Tour applied the principle of proportionality for reviewing the validity of these EU acts, although without relying on the hybrid paradigm.[22] Instead, the Advocate General referenced prospective and retrospective schemes for a different issue: evaluating the proportionality of national provisions implementing Directive 2002/90/EC and Framework Decision 2002/946/JHA. Even more surprisingly, the Court followed a completely different path, thereby advancing a Charter-oriented interpretation of Directive 2002/90/EC without relying on proportionality considerations.[23] Therefore, the Court's ruling in *Kinsa* fell short of filling the gap in case law concerning the theorisation and application of proportionality constraints to EU substantive criminal law.

[18] On this contention, a reference may be allowed to Lorenzo Grossio, *Proportionality of Criminal Offences and Penalties in EU Law: A Hybrid Principle* (Hart Pubishing, 2025), with particular emphasis on ch 5 therein.

[19] Among manifold potential references in the CJEU case law, see Case C-77/20, *K. M. (Sanctions infligées au capitaine de navire)* EU:C:2021:112, para 38; Case C-255/14, *Chmielewski* EU:C:2015:475, para 23; Case C-81/12, *Asociaţia Accept* EU:C:2013:275, para 63; Case C-565/12, *LCL Le Crédit Lyonnais* EU:C:2014:190, para 45.

[20] Council Directive 2002/90/EC of 28 November 2002 defining the facilitation of unauthorised entry, transit and residence [2002] OJ L328/17.

[21] Council Framework Decision 2002/946/JHA of 28 November 2002 on the strengthening of the penal framework to prevent the facilitation of unauthorised entry, transit and residence [2002] OJ L328/1.

[22] Case C-460/23, *Kinsa*, Opinion of AG Richard de la Tour, EU:C:2024:941.

[23] Case C-460/23, *Kinsa* EU:C:2025:392. In scholarship, see Valsamis Mitsilegas, 'The Ruling of the Court of Justice in Kinsa: A First Step Towards the Decriminalisation of the Facilitation of Unauthorised Entry?' *Eurojus* (21 July 2025), https://rivista.eurojus.it/the-ruling-of-the-court-of-justice-in-kinsa-a-first-step-towards-the-decriminalisation-of-the-facilitation-of-unauthorised-entry.

10.3 ASSESSING THE LEGISLATIVE PROPORTIONALITY ASSESSMENT IN THE DEFINITION OF EU HARMONISED OFFENCES AND PENALTIES

Against the gap just outlined, some elements of legislative practice may help shed light on the limits dictated by the principle of proportionality in approximating offences and penalties. When the EU legislature enacts harmonising provisions on substantive criminal law, it undergoes a positive balancing exercise: it frames the relevant interests at stake and weighs them against opposing ones to ensure the action at stake is proportionate. This approach is reflected in both general policy orientations on EU substantive criminal law (section 10.3.1) and the *travaux préparatoires* of single directives and pre-Lisbon framework decisions harmonising domestic criminal law provisions (section 10.3.2). The practice reveals a coherent approach: the Commission and EU legislature consistently incorporate both prospective and retrospective considerations in their proportionality assessments of harmonised offences and penalties, aligning with the hybrid theorisation of the principle.

10.3.1 Insights from General Policy Orientations on EU Substantive Criminal Law

Since the early 2000s, the Commission, Council and Parliament have sought to frame their respective approach in substantive criminal law by adopting general policy orientations.

In particular, the Council's approach over time reflects the willingness to standardise the drafting EU substantive criminal law instruments by defining model provisions on offences and different levels of severity for harmonised penalties. These orientations also address proportionality. From the Council's side, the 2009 Conclusions on Model Provisions, Guiding the Council's Criminal Law Deliberations states that harmonised provisions on substantive criminal law 'should be introduced when they are considered essential in order for the interests to be protected'.[24] More specifically, supranational criminalisation shall be limited to conduct 'which cannot be addressed effectively by less severe measures'.[25] That consideration matches with the 'essentiality' requirement enshrined in Article 83(2) TFEU, according to which EU criminalisation is warranted insofar as 'proves essential to ensure the effective implementation of a Union policy in an area which has been subject to harmonisation measures', and unveils a necessity assessment in line with the requirements of the

[24] Council Conclusions on Model Provisions, Guiding the Council's Criminal Law Deliberations (30 November 2009) para 1.

[25] ibid, para 2.

proportionality test.[26] Indeed, as reaffirmed in 2024 by the Council Conclusions on 'The Future of EU Criminal Law – Recommendations on the Way Forward',[27] 'criminal law instruments and provisions should only be adopted when necessary to achieve the objective behind those instruments and provisions, when that objective cannot be achieved through other means'.[28] Against this background, the Council acknowledges that this assessment shall include retrospective proportionality, thereby evaluating the seriousness of the wrongdoing. Indeed, among the elements that ought to be considered when ascertaining the need for EU criminalisation, the Council points to the need to verify 'how serious and/or widespread and frequent the harmful conduct is, both regionally and locally within the EU'.[29]

The retrospective scheme also extends to the harmonisation of criminal penalties. In that respect, the 2002 Council Conclusions on the Approach Towards the Approximation of Penalties sought to systematise the harmonised level of severity of custodial penalties into four categories.[30] According to the method outlined therein, the Commission and EU legislature may opt between fixed penalty scales considering the seriousness of the wrongdoing at stake. As an example in this respect, the Explanatory Memorandum of the 2003 Proposal for a Framework Decision on Ship-Source Pollution affirms that 'the seriousness of imprisonable offences is such … that it would seem right to set a harmonisation threshold corresponding to level 3'.[31] Still, that is a rare example: there is just one additional legislative proposal that follows the rigid categorisation of penalties outlined by the 2002 Council Conclusions.[32]

Concerning the Commission's approach, the 2011 Communication 'Towards an EU Criminal Policy'[33] provides crucial indications on the structure of the

[26] For an analysis of the 'essentiality' criterion esnhrined in Art 83(2) TFEU, among many, see Jacob Öberg, 'Do We Really Need Criminal Sanctions for the Enforcement of EU Law?' (2014) 5 *New Journal of European Criminal Law* 370. In particular, see at 381–82, where the author warns about the shortcomings inherent in the CJEU potential approach in reviewing compliance with the 'essentiality' criterion if construed as a proportionality requirement. On the Court's standard for reviewing the proportionality of harmonised offences and penalties, see section 10.4.2.

[27] Council Conclusions on 'The Future of EU Criminal Law: Recommendations on the Way Forward' (14 June 2024).

[28] ibid, para 2.

[29] Council Conclusions on Model Provisions, para 3, second indent.

[30] Council Conclusions on the Approach to Apply Regarding Approximation of Penalties, 9141/02 LIMITE DROIPEN 33, 4: 'Level 1: Penalties of a maximum of at least between 1 and 3 years of imprisonment; Level 2: Penalties of a maximum of at least between 2 and 5 years of imprisonment; Level 3: Penalties of a maximum of at least between 5 and 10 years of imprisonment; Level 4: Penalties of a maximum of at least 10 years of imprisonment (cases where very serious penalties are required)'.

[31] Commission, 'Proposal for a Council Framework Decision to Strengthen the Criminal-law Framework for the Enforcement of the Law against Ship-source Pollution' COM(2003) 227 final, 5.

[32] Commission, 'Proposal for a Directive of the European Parliament and of the Council on the Protection of the Environment through Criminal Law' COM(2007) 51 final, 8.

[33] Commission, 'Towards an EU Criminal Policy: Ensuring the Effective Implementation of EU Policies Through Criminal Law' (Communication) COM(2011) 573 final.

positive proportionality assessment underpinning legislative proposals.[34] In this respect, the policy document at stake demonstrates that the definition of proportionality in EU substantive criminal law is not limited to the threefold suitability, necessity and proportionality *stricto sensu* test. Indeed, even the Commission incorporates prospective and retrospective schemes into its reasoning. On the one hand, criminalisation may be proportionate only 'when it is considered important to stress strong disapproval *in order to ensure deterrence* (emphasis added)'.[35] This affirmation reproduces a prospective scheme: criminalisation is justified insofar as it constitutes the necessary means to deter potential wrongdoers. On the other hand, retrospective proportionality complements the legislative assessment. Indeed, 'the seriousness and character of the breach of law must be taken into account'[36] to decide whether it should be subject to criminal penalties. The same finding emerges from the European Parliament's policy indications as crystallised in the 2012 Resolution on an EU Approach to Criminal Law.[37] As recalled in paragraph 3 therein, supranational criminalisation is proportionate insofar as 'the crime involved is of a particularly serious nature'.[38]

Building on the findings just analysed, it appears that the EU institutions' general policy orientations on substantive criminal law demonstrate the key role of prospective and retrospective schemes in the proportionality reasoning regarding offences and penalties. How do these paradigms interact with the threefold proportionality test underlying Article 5(4) TEU and Article 52(1) of the Charter in defining EU substantive criminal law provisions? The *travaux préparatoires* of relevant legislative instruments, analysed in the subsequent section, provide further insights in this respect.

10.3.2 Insights from the *Travaux Préparatoires* of EU Substantive Criminal Law Directives and Framework Decisions

The following findings on the practice of the Commission and EU legislature stem from the analysis of the *travaux préparatoires* of all directives and framework decisions harmonising offences and penalties in force, as well as the proposals currently pending before the Parliament and Council. In this context, the issue of proportionality of harmonising provisions on offences and penalties arises in a twofold dimension. When presenting a legislative proposal in

[34] For a comprehensive analysis, see Anne Weyembergh and Irene Wieczorek, 'Is There an EU Criminal Policy?' in Renaud Colson and Stewart Field (eds), *EU Criminal Justice and the Challenges of Legal Diversity: Legal Cultures in the Area of Freedom, Security and Justice* (Cambridge University Press, 2016).

[35] COM(2011) 573 final, 11.

[36] ibid.

[37] European Parliament Resolution of 22 May 2012 on an EU Approach to Criminal Law (2010/2310(INI)) [2013] OJ C264E/7.

[38] ibid, para 3, line 3.

the EU substantive criminal law domain, the Commission must justify adherence to the principle of proportionality concerning both the intensity of the EU intervention under Article 5(4) TEU and its impact on the protection of fundamental rights under Article 52(1) of the Charter. In the context of that latter assessment, the establishment of harmonised penalty levels also warrants compliance with retrospective proportionality as enshrined in Article 49(3) of the Charter.

Both aspects of proportionality can influence the EU legislature's action. However, the practice reveals that constraints in that respect primarily originate from the fundamental rights dimension of proportionality as defined by Articles 52(1) and 49(3) of the Charter. Indeed, explanations regarding how the EU's intervention adheres to Article 5(4) TEU are typically limited to broad considerations that echo the proportionality test underpinning that provision. For instance, the 2010 Proposal for a Directive on Attacks against Information Systems merely states that the Directive 'confines itself to the minimum required in order to achieve [the objectives pursued] and does not go beyond what is necessary for that purpose, taking into account the accuracy of criminal legislation'.[39] Such a general consideration falls short of contributing to a comprehensive analysis of the proportionality of the proposed criminalisation choices and the levels of penalties.

Conversely, proportionality constraints are addressed more profoundly through the angle of their impact on the protection of fundamental rights under the Charter. This choice is unsurprising. Indeed, recourse to criminal law has profound implications for fundamental rights, and these amount to a key limitation on excessive criminalisation.[40] Therefore, it is necessary for the Commission to thoroughly assess the proposed harmonisation of offences and corresponding level of penalties through the prism of Articles 52(1) and 49(1) of the Charter. In line with the general policy orientations previously analysed, this proportionality assessment entails prospective and retrospective considerations, as demonstrated by some examples.

Concerning the proportionality of criminalisation choices, extending the harmonised definition of the offence to a given conduct must be justified by the need to tackle a given wrongdoing by effective and deterrent measures.[41] This approach paves the way to prospective proportionality considerations in defining supranational criminalisation choices. Indeed, their interference with the enjoyment of fundamental rights shall be justified under Article 52(1) of the

[39] Commission, 'Proposal for a Directive of the European Parliament and of the Council on Attacks Against Information Systems and Repealing Council Framework Decision 2005/222/JHA' COM(2010) 517 final, 8.

[40] Among many, see Françoise Tulkens, 'The Paradoxical Relationship between Criminal Law and Human Rights' (2011) 9 *Journal of International Criminal Justice* 577.

[41] For instance, see Commission, 'Proposal for a Directive of the European Parliament and of the Council Amending Directive 2011/36/EU on Preventing and Combating Trafficking in Human Beings and Protecting its Victims' COM(2022) 732 final, 7.

Charter by a general interest recognised by the Union, such as the need to deter offenders from committing those wrongdoings.[42]

In that respect, the legislative practice advances a specific definition of 'deterrence' for the purposes of EU substantive criminal law. As the Impact Assessment accompanying the 2012 Proposal for a Directive on the Fight Against Fraud to the Union's Financial Interests clarifies, this objective entails the criminal measure at stake seeking 'to influence conduct in a way which results in voluntary refraining from the commission of illegal acts'.[43] While deterrence drives supranational criminalisation as a tool functional to enhancing the effectiveness of EU law from a general prevention standpoint, proportionality poses a limit in that respect. Indeed, prospective proportionality requires the Commission and EU legislature to 'ensur[e] that these measures do not go beyond what is necessary to achieve this objective and are thus proportionate'.[44] More specifically, as the 2003 Proposal for a Directive on Ship-source Pollution expressly clarifies, any EU criminalisation choice is legitimate insofar as 'only criminal sanctions will be sufficiently effective for ensuring the intended effects'.[45] For the purposes of that assessment, a comparison with the potential effects of administrative sanctioning schemes may be envisaged. That is the approach emerging, for instance, from the 2021 Proposal for a Directive on the Protection of the Environment through Criminal Law, which justifies recourse to criminalisation on grounds that criminal penalties entail a 'stronger form of social disapproval compared to administrative penalties'.[46]

A retrospective assessment of the worthiness of criminalisation compared to the seriousness of wrongdoings regularly complements the proportionality justification of the scope of harmonised offences. In line with the approach emerging from the general policy orientations previously analysed,[47] the Commission usually recalls that EU substantive criminal law shall be limited to conduct qualifying as 'serious'. As an illustrative example in this respect, the already cited 2021 Proposal for a Directive on the Protection of the Environment through Criminal Law clarifies that proportionality requires

[42] Commission, 'Proposal for a Directive of the European Parliament and of the Council on the Fight Against Fraud to the Union's Financial Interests by Means of Criminal Law' COM(2012) 363 final, 8.

[43] Commission, 'Impact Assessment Accompanying the Proposal for a Directive of the European Parliament and of the Council on the Fight Against Fraud to the Union's Financial Interests by Means of Criminal Law' (Staff Working Paper) SWD(2012) 195 final, 11.

[44] COM(2012) 363 final, 8. On the same point, see also Commission, 'Proposal for a Directive of the European Parliament and of the Council on the Protection of the Euro and Other Currencies Against Counterfeiting by Criminal Law' COM(2013) 042 final, 8.

[45] Commission, 'Proposal for a Directive of the European Parliament and of the Council on Ship-source Pollution and on the Introduction of Sanctions, Including Criminal Sanctions, for Pollution Offences' COM(2003) 92 final, 5.

[46] Commission, 'Proposal for a Directive of the European Parliament and of the Council on the Protection of the Environment through Criminal Law and Repealing Directive 2008/99/EC' COM(2021) 851 final, 6.

[47] See section 10.2.1 above.

the scope of harmonised offences to be limited to 'serious breaches of environmental law'.[48] Following this approach, the 2016 Proposal for a Directive on Countering Money Laundering by Criminal Law expressly recalls that 'the principle of proportionality is respected in limiting the scope of the offences to what is strictly necessary to allow for the effective prosecution of acts that pose a particular threat to the EU's internal security'.[49] This approach is streamlined in the legislative practice, as the very same consideration features in the 2017 Proposal for a Directive on Fraud and Counterfeiting of Non-cash Means of Payment[50] and 2015 Proposal for a Directive on Combating Terrorism.[51] Justifying criminalisation on grounds of the behaviour's 'seriousness' may well be framed as an expression of traditional criminalisation criteria, such as the harm principle.[52] However, similar findings also align with the theoretical understanding of retrospective proportionality: since penalisation must be commensurate with the seriousness of the wrongdoing, only sufficiently serious ones warrant a criminal law response.

Prospective and retrospective proportionality schemes are also crucial for the legislative justification for harmonised penalties. In this respect, the minimum rules on the type and amount of criminal penalties may be justified by the need to tackle inadequate sanctioning arrangements at the domestic level. This is apparent, for instance, from the reasoning elucidated by the 2011 Proposal for a Directive on Criminal Sanctions for Insider Dealing and Market Manipulation, which stresses that 'sanctions currently in place … are insufficiently dissuasive, which results in ineffective enforcement'.[53] Against the need to enhance dissuasiveness at the domestic level, prospective proportionality requires the Commission and EU legislature to opt for 'the lowest realistic penalty which still exerts a deterring effect in the sense of stigmatising and disrupting effect'.[54] According to the Commission, the provision of aggravating circumstances and accessory sanctions also contributes to ensuring prospective proportionality. Indeed, these harmonising rules on sanctions provide domestic judges with 'a

[48] COM(2021) 851 final, 4.

[49] Commission, 'Proposal for a Directive of the European Parliament and of the Council on Countering Money Laundering by Criminal Law' COM(2016) 826 final, 11.

[50] Commission, 'Proposal for a Directive of the European Parliament and of the Council on Combating Fraud and Counterfeiting of Non-cash Means of Payments and Replacing Council Framework Decision 2001/413/JHA' COM(2017) 489 final, 15.

[51] Commission, 'Proposal for a Directive of the European Parliament and of the Council on Combating Terrorism and Replacing Council Framework Decision 2002/475/JHA on Combating Terrorism' COM(2015) 625 final, 14.

[52] On the harm principle in EU criminal law, among many, see Peršak (n 4); Micheletto (n 4); Buisman (n 4).

[53] Commission, 'Proposal for a Directive of the European Parliament and of the Council on Criminal Sanctions for Insider Dealing and Market Manipulation' COM(2011) 654 final, 2. On the same profile, see also COM(2013) 042 final (n 44), 3.

[54] SWD(2012) 195 final, 35. For a comparative assessment of sanctioning levels in the Member States, see the Report of the 2015 ECLAN Research Project on Minimum Sanctions in the EU Member States (Robert Kert, Brigitte Slot, Gisele Vernimmen, Andrea Lehner and Joachim Schellekens, *Study on Minimum Sanctions in the EU Member States: Final Report* (European Commission, 2015).

toolbox which [they] could choose the most appropriate and dissuasive ones adapted to the individual case'.[55]

In defining the type and level of harmonised penalties, the legislative practice also considers the nature and seriousness of the offence to ensure retrospective proportionality.[56] In that respect, two techniques may be employed. On the one hand, the type and level of the sanction provided for a given offence may be compared to those tackling wrongdoings characterised by a different level of seriousness. Such a technique, known as ordinal proportionality, hinges upon the premise that comparable sanctioning levels are justified for equally serious wrongdoings, while less or more harmful conducts warrant different types and levels of penalties.[57] Thus construed, ordinal proportionality entails a relative relationship of commensurability between the offence and its sanction, as it depends upon a comparative analysis internal to a given criminal justice system.[58] The Commission and EU legislature have sometimes relied on this technique to substantiate the retrospective proportionality of harmonised penalties. That is the case, for instance, of the 2010 Proposal for a Directive on Combating the Sexual Abuse, Sexual Exploitation of Children and Child Pornography. In that document, the Commission outlined that '[t]o determine the degree of seriousness and attach penalties proportionate to it, … a number of relations between offences can be established'.[59] On those premises, the Commission applied ordinal proportionality to compare the relative seriousness of behaviours subject to the proposed supranational criminalisation and established five different categories of offences with different penalties.

On the other hand, EU institutions may seek to establish an absolute relationship of commensurability between the seriousness of wrongdoings and the type and level of penalties through the cardinal proportionality technique. Without relying on a comparison with other offences, this approach entails assessing the worthiness of sanctions' severity with respect to the inherent harmfulness of the offence.[60] By relying on cardinal proportionality, the 2010 Proposal for a Directive on Preventing and Combating Trafficking in Human Beings sought to justify the level of penalties on the basis of offences' harmful effects on victims. In particular,

[55] Commission, 'Impact Assessment Accompanying the Proposal for a Directive of the European Parliament and of the Council on the Protection of the Environment through Criminal Law and Replacing Directive 2008/99/EC' (Staff Working Document) SWD(2021) 465 final, 51.

[56] On this point, notably, see: COM(2017) 489 final (n 50) 15; COM(2003) 227 final (n 31) recital 6.

[57] On this point, among many, see Andrew von Hirsch and Andrew Ashworth, *Proportionate Sentencing: Exploring the Principle* (Oxford University Press, 2005) 139.

[58] von Hirsch (n 13) 77.

[59] Commission, 'Proposal for a Directive of the European Parliament and of the Council on Combating the Sexual Abuse, Sexual Exploitation of Children and Child Pornography, Repealing Framework Decision 2004/68/JHA' COM(2010) 94 final, 7.

[60] Among many, see: Andrew von Hirsch, 'Proportionality in the Philosophy of Punishment: From "Why Punish" to "How Much"' (1991) 25 *Israel Law Review* 549, 576; Francesco Viganò, *La proporzionalità della pena: profili di diritto penale e costituzionale* (Giappichelli, 2021) 169.

> when the offence is particularly grave, for example when the life of the victim has been endangered or the offence has involved serious violence or has caused particularly serious harm to the victim, this should be reflected in a particularly severe penalty.[61]

Conversely, in the case of organised crime, penalty scales are meant to reflect the offender's degree of participation in the association.[62]

In the same vein, retrospective proportionality may also be ensured by differentiating the level of penalties on the grounds of monetary thresholds. This arrangement has been recently advanced in the 2022 Proposal for a Directive on the Definition of Criminal Offences and Penalties for the Violation of Union Restrictive Measures, which set a threshold value of EUR 100,000 of the proceeds of the committed offence to distinguish between different terms of imprisonment.[63] In the same vein, the 2013 Proposal for a Directive on the Protection of the Euro and Other Currencies against Counterfeiting by Criminal Law stipulated that

> to guarantee that the severity of penalties is not disproportionate to the criminal offence, a specific safeguard for cases of lower amounts of counterfeits is being proposed i.e. one threshold below which a lower penalty of imprisonment can be imposed and another one below which also a fine can be imposed, unless the case features particularly serious circumstances.[64]

This brief analysis of EU legislative practice in the substantive criminal law field reveals that prospective and retrospective proportionality schemes are consistently employed at the legislative level to justify harmonising offences and penalties. On that basis, the legislative practice appears in line with the hybrid nature of proportionality in EU criminal law highlighted above. Indeed, the two schemes complement the proportionality assessment mandated by primary law, with particular emphasis on Article 52(1) of the Charter. More specifically, to assess whether the interferences caused by EU criminalisation choices and harmonised penalties on the enjoyment of fundamental rights are necessary and proportionate *stricto sensu* to the aim pursued, the Commission and EU legislature are called upon to rely on prospective and retrospective proportionality. Under the first scheme, the legitimacy of harmonised offences and penalties depends on whether they materialise the minimum level of severity necessary to ensure a genuinely dissuasive effect. From that perspective, proportionality acts as a constraint for criminalisation: while the latter is warranted to foster

[61] Commission, 'Proposal for a Directive of the European Parliament and of the Council on Preventing and Combating Trafficking in Human Beings, and Protecting Victims, Repealing Framework Decision 2002/629/JHA' COM(2010) 95, recital 6.

[62] Commission, 'Proposal for a Council framework Decision on the Fight Against Organised Crime' COM(2005) 6 final, 5.

[63] Commission, 'Proposal for a Directive of the European Parliament and of the Council on the Definition of Criminal Offences and Penalties for the Violation of Union Restrictive Measures' COM(2022) 684 final, 13.

[64] COM(2013) 042 final (n 44), 7.

compliance with – and, consequently, the effectiveness of – EU law, prospective proportionality ensures that it does not exceed what is necessary and proportionate *stricto sensu* to this respect. Under retrospective proportionality, the scope of offences and minimum rules on sanctions shall reflect the seriousness of the wrongdoings they sought to penalise. Therefore, a functional relationship characterises the nexus between the threefold proportionality test inherent in Article 52(1) of the Charter, on the one hand, and the prospective and retrospective schemes, on the other. In EU criminal law, the latter assessments are essential steps to verify whether harmonised offences and penalties are necessary and proportionate *stricto sensu*.

10.4 THE JUDICIAL REVIEW OF EU CRIMINALISATION CHOICES AND HARMONISED PENALTIES

As recalled in the introduction, *Kinsa* represented the very first reference for a preliminary ruling calling upon the CJEU to adjudicate on proportionality pleas against the validity of harmonising provisions on offences and penalties. The previous absence of case law on this point may appear surprising. Still, the important limits to judicial review on third pillar acts posed by the pre-Lisbon TEU[65] – provisionally extended until December 2014 by Protocol No 36[66] – may explain that circumstance. Before that date, the CJEU could hear preliminary questions only if referred by the courts of those Member States which expressly accepted its jurisdiction within the Third Pillar. Moreover, during the provisional regime, only the Member States, Commission, Parliament, and Council could lodge an action for annulment against those acts.[67] Even under the current primary law framework, it is quite difficult to envisage natural or legal persons challenging the proportionality of harmonised offences and penalties under Article 263 TFEU, given the restrictive conditions for private applicants in actions for annulment.[68] Indeed, it would be particularly arduous for them to comply with the so-called 'Plaumann formula', thereby demonstrating that those provisions concern them 'by reason of certain attributes which are peculiar to them or by reason of circumstances in which they are differentiated from all other persons'.[69]

Conversely, following the end of the provisional regime, proportionality arguments against EU substantive criminal law may now be envisaged in the context of preliminary references, as demonstrated by the referring court's preliminary

[65] Art 35(6) of the Consolidated Version of the Treaty on the European Union [2006] OJ CE321/1.

[66] Art 10(1) of the Consolidated Version of the Treaty on the Functioning of the European Union – Protocol (No 36) on Transitional Provisions [2016] OJ C202/321.

[67] ibid.

[68] Art 263(4) TFEU.

[69] Among many, see Case C-309/89, *Codorniu v Council* EU:C:1994:197, para 20; Case 25/62, *Plaumann v Commission of the EEC* EU:C:1963:17, p 107.

questions in *Kinsa*. While the CJEU finally relied on considerations other than proportionality in its judgment, this case testifies that the proportionality review of harmonised offences and penalties is not merely hypothetical. It amounts to a pressing issue that unveils the need for further reflection on the theorisation of the CJEU proportionality review of harmonised offences and penalties.

Therefore, the CJEU proportionality scrutiny of harmonised offences and penalties shall now be framed. It consists of partially different features compared to the positive legislative proportionality assessment previously analysed. Unlike the EU legislature, the CJEU conducts a negative proportionality review to evaluate the validity of the secondary law provisions in question. The Court cannot replace the legislative balancing that underpins those provisions; rather, it examines whether they exceed the limits of legislative discretion under the Treaties, thus resulting in disproportionate arrangements. Therefore, theorising this proportionality reasoning requires defining not only the relevant test (section 10.4.1) but also the standard of review (section 10.4.2).

10.4.1 The Interaction between Prospective and Retrospective Proportionality in the CJEU Review

Proportionality pleas against EU substantive criminal law may manifest either an excessive exercise of EU powers in violation of Article 5(4) TEU or, conversely, an illegitimate interference with the enjoyment of fundamental rights pursuant to Article 52(1) of the Charter. Both paradigms envisage a proportionality assessment based on the threefold suitability, necessity and proportionality *stricto sensu* paradigm. In legislative practice, the threefold test is complemented by prospective and retrospective proportionality schemes, aligning with the hybrid EU and criminal nature of the principle of proportionality of offences and penalties. Do the same features extend to the judicial review of harmonising provisions on substantive criminal law?

As anticipated in section 10.3 above, Advocate General Richard de la Tour's conclusions in *Kinsa* suggested a negative answer.[70] Indeed, they proposed a different conceptualisation for the proportionality review of supranational criminalisation choices and their compatibility with the Charter, respectively. In the first case, the Advocate General frames the proportionality test exclusively by recourse to the requirements of adequacy and necessity, thus avoiding any reference to not only proportionality *stricto sensu*[71] but also prospective and retrospective assessments. Conversely, those schemes are recalled to review the

[70] See n 19 above.

[71] As observed in Stefano Zirulia, 'Facilitating Irregular Immigration Under the Lens of the Proportionality Principle – Brief Notes on the Advocate General's Conclusions in the Kinsa Case (C-460/23)' EU Law Live (2024), https://eulawlive.com/op-ed-facilitating-irregular-immigration-under-the-lens-of-the-proportionality-principle-brief-notes-on-the-advocate-generals-conclusions-in-the-kinsa-case-c-460-23.

proportionality of Italian implementing provisions: 'the severity of the penalty must be commensurate with the seriousness of the infringement that it punishes, in particular by ensuring a genuinely deterrent effect, while not going beyond what is necessary to achieve the legitimate objectives pursued'.[72]

This approach seems unconvincing. Insofar as the Commission, Parliament, and Council employ prospective and retrospective schemes to drive criminalisation choices under Article 52(1) of the Charter, their review by the CJEU should warrant a similar compound proportionality paradigm. This approach would be essential to ensure symmetry between the proportionality justifications provided by the Union legislator and their scrutiny by Union courts, thus fostering a more in-depth judicial oversight over EU criminalisation choices and harmonised penalties. What is more, the approach suggested here would be in line with the CJEU practice on the proportionality scrutiny of domestic criminal offences and penalties. Indeed, the prospective and retrospective schemes are well established in that stream of case law,[73] as they characterise the review of both the constituent elements of offences and the related sanctions[74] pursuant to either Article 49(3) or 52(1) of the Charter.[75] On these grounds, there is arguably no theoretical reason not to rely on the same hybrid assessment in scrutinising the validity of EU provisions on offences and penalties under Article 52(1) of the Charter.

10.4.2 The Standard of Review: Should the CJEU Recognise Broad Discretion on the EU Legislature or Exercise a Strict Assessment?

The second critical issue concerns the intensity of the proportionality test on EU criminalisation choices and harmonised penalties. The conclusions of Advocate General Richard de la Tour in *Kinsa* did not provide precise indications on this point. Indeed, they addressed the issue of the intensity of the proportionality test only with respect to the scrutiny of the Italian transposition law, thus clarifying that the latter must leave domestic courts with sufficient room to impose sanctions limited 'to what is strictly necessary with regard to the seriousness of the offence committed'.[76] Conversely, the Advocate General did not clarify the

[72] Case C-460/23, *Kinsa* EU:C:2024:941, Opinion of AG Richard de la Tour, para 102. For a deeper analysis of the conclusions, a reference may be allowed to Lorenzo Grossio, 'Lo scrutinio di proporzionalità delle scelte di criminalizzazione sovranazionali: due interrogativi lasciati aperti dalle conclusioni dell'AG Richard de la Tour nella causa Kinsa' (2025) 2 *Rivista Quaderni AISDUE* 1.

[73] Among many, see Case C-544/19, *ECOTEX Bulgaria* EU:C:2021:803, para 100; Case C-77/20 *K. M. (Sanctions infligées au capitaine de navire)* EU:C:2021:112, para 38.

[74] On this point, see Case C-190/17, *Zheng* EU:C:2018:357, para 40; Case C-210/10, *Urbán* EU:C:2012:64, paras 53 and 54.

[75] Case C-384/17, *Link Logistik N&N* EU:C:2018:810, pt 42; Case C-544/19, *ECOTEX Bulgaria* EU:C:2021:803, para 97.

[76] Case C-460/23, *Kinsa*, EU:C:2024:941, Opinion of AG Richard de la Tour, para 113.

degree of severity the Court of Justice should apply to examine the proportionality of the criminalisation choices.

Against this open issue, a look at the CJEU approach to the proportionality scrutiny of Union acts at large provides useful insights. Indeed, that stream of case law discloses two opposing tendencies. On the one hand,

> the Court has accepted that in the exercise of the powers conferred on it the Community legislature must be allowed a broad discretion in areas in which its action involves political, economic and social choices and in which it is called upon to undertake complex assessments and evaluations.[77]

In similar circumstances,

> the criterion to be applied is not whether a measure adopted in such an area was the only or the best possible measure, since its legality can be affected only if the measure is manifestly inappropriate having regard to the objective which the competent institutions are seeking to pursue.[78]

It follows that the Union courts generally exercise self-restraint in the proportionality review of EU acts.[79]

On the other hand, recent CJEU case law features a stricter review in cases where supranational provisions give rise to a particularly serious interference with the enjoyment of the fundamental rights guaranteed by the Charter. In such cases, the judicial scrutiny of compliance with Article 52(1) of the Charter is more intense, as it aims to verify that such interference is limited to what is strictly necessary to achieve the objective pursued.[80] In that respect, it is interesting to note that the Court in *Digital Rights Ireland* has relied upon this strict standard to review EU provisions on data retention, as the CJEU considered that their interference with fundamental rights 'must be considered to be particularly serious'.[81] *Digital Rights Ireland* is of crucial importance for the analysis advanced in this section, since it sets a benchmark: if data retention techniques entail interferences with the enjoyment of fundamental rights so serious as to warrant strict proportionality review, the same standard shall apply to reviewing any measure giving rise to comparable or even more serious limitations to individual rights.

[77] Case C-58/08, *Vodafone and Others* EU:C:2010:321, para 52.

[78] Case C-151/17, *Swedish Match* EU:C:2018:938, para 36.

[79] On this point, among many, see Jannemieke W Ouwerkerk, 'Criminalization Powers of the European Union and the Risks of Cherry-Picking between Various Legal Bases: The Case for a Single Legal Framework for EU-Level Criminalization ' (2017) 23 *Columbia Journal of European Law* 503, 533–34.

[80] Joined Cases C-92/09 and C-93/09, *Volker und Markus Schecke and Eifert* EU:C:2010:662, para 77; Joined Cases C-293/12 and C-594/12, *Digital Rights Ireland and Others* EU:C:2014:238, para 48; Case C-817/19, *Ligue des droits humains* EU:C:2022:491, paras 115–17; Joined Cases C-37/20 and C-601/20, *Luxembourg Business Registers* EU:C:2022:912, paras 64–65.

[81] Joined Cases C-293/12 and C-594/12, *Digital Rights Ireland and Others* EU:C:2014:238, para 37.

These two streams of case law offer insights into how severe the CJEU proportionality review of harmonised offences and penalties ought to be. Whenever a proportionality plea raises an issue regarding the excessive exercise of legislative powers under Article 5(4) TEU, the CJEU will likely need to confine its scrutiny to 'manifestly inappropriate' arrangements.[82] As recent scholarship has highlighted,[83] the harmonisation of offences and penalties may well amount to a sector where the Union legislator must undertake complex and political assessments, potentially implying moderation in the severity of judicial scrutiny.

Conversely, proportionality pleas concerning the validity of EU substantive criminal law provisions vis-a-vis the enjoyment of fundamental rights deserve different considerations. Could the harmonisation of offences and penalties lead to particularly serious interferences with the rights guaranteed by the Charter, such as necessitating strict proportionality review? The answer to this question should indeed be positive. It is widely accepted in legal scholarship that recourse to criminal law constitutes the most profound form of interference with individual rights.[84] Therefore, if data retention qualifies as a sufficiently serious tool from a fundamental rights perspective to warrant strict proportionality scrutiny, as the Court recognised in *Digital Rights Ireland*,[85] there is all the more reason to apply the same standard for reviewing harmonising provisions on offences and penalties pursuant to Articles 52(1) and 49(3) of the Charter.

10.5 CONCLUSION

This chapter advanced a conceptual appraisal of the principle of proportionality of criminal offences and penalties in the context of the EU harmonisation of substantive criminal law. To that end, the analysis focused, on the one hand, on the legislative approach to defining minimum rules for offences and sanctions and, on the other hand, the judicial scrutiny of the proportionality of those harmonising provisions.

The legislative practice has shown that the Commission, Parliament and Council carry out an articulated proportionality assessment of proposed approximation of substantive criminal law, particularly through the prism of

[82] On the issues that the CJEU faces in reviewing proportionality under Art 5(4) TEU, among many, see Jacob Öberg, 'The Rise of the Procedural Paradigm: Judicial Review of EU Legislation in Vertical Competence Disputes' (2017) 13 *European Constitutional Law Review* 248.

[83] Jorg Monar, 'Reflections on the Place of Criminal Law in the European Construction' (2021) 27 *European Law Journal* 356, 360.

[84] Among many, see Maria Kaiafa-Gbandi, 'The Importance of Core Principles of Substantive Criminal Law for a European Criminal Policy Respecting Fundamental Rights and the Rule of Law' (2011) 1 *European Criminal Law Review* 6, 33; Nils Jareborg, 'Criminalization as Last Resort (Ultima Ratio)' (2005) 2 *Ohio State Journal of Criminal Law* 521, 527; Sakari Melander, 'Ultima Ratio in European Criminal Law' (2013) 3 *European Criminal Law Review* 45, 52.

[85] See n 81.

Article 52(1) of the Charter. In this context, said institutions conceive the principle of proportionality as a hybrid compound assessment. Indeed, the latter is not limited to the threefold suitability, necessity and proportionality *stricto sensu* test characterising the general proportionality principle under EU law. To verify whether supranational criminalisation choices and corresponding penalty levels are necessary and proportionate *stricto sensu*, regard must be had to the criminal law dimension of the principle, which gives rise to a double assessment. On the one hand, the proportionality of the legislative arrangement under scrutiny shall be verified prospectively, thereby assessing whether it constitutes the least severe measure that still ensures a genuinely dissuasive effect. On the other hand, the proposed legislative provisions are also evaluated from a retrospective viewpoint, namely, by verifying whether they adequately reflect the seriousness of the wrongdoing. Therefore, the principle of proportionality of offences and penalties in EU substantive criminal law involves a hybrid assessment, combining the threefold test typical of the EU understanding of proportionality with prospective and retrospective schemes derived from its criminal law dimension.

Against those hints from the legislative practice, the CJEU proportionality review on harmonised offences and penalties remains more difficult to grasp. That is the consequence of the bare absence of relevant case law, a gap which, unfortunately, the much-awaited Court's ruling in *Kinsa* did not help fill. This gap is particularly regrettable, as sound judicial scrutiny is crucial for framing robust proportionality constraints to EU criminalisation choices.

What is more, that circumstance may be read as evidence of the persisting difficulty in translating the principle of proportionality of criminal offences and penalties into rules of assessment capable of being operationalised in the CJEU review of supranational criminalisation choices and harmonised penalties. This difficulty is even more evident with regard to the cardinal declination of retrospective proportionality, which Asp defined as 'an obscure, tradition-bound standard for assessing sanctions'.[86] While understandable, such uneasiness should not be overrated, as a certain degree of openness or vagueness is inherent in any general principle, insofar as it posits an optimisation command which, as influentially clarified by Alexy, can be realised to a different extent.[87] General principles are key in shaping the boundaries of the EU legislative activity, as they are not only interpretative tools but also grounds for judicially reviewing the validity of secondary law. Against that premise, the question remains: can the principle of proportionality of criminal offences and penalties be 'taken seriously', thus framing a standard for assessing the validity of EU substantive criminal law?

[86] Petter Asp, *The Substantive Criminal Law Competence of the EU* (Stiftelsen Skrifter utgivna av Juridiska fakulteten vid Stockholms universitet, 2012) 201.

[87] Robert Alexy, *A Theory of Constitutional Rights* (Oxford University Press, 2002) 47-48.

The chapter advances a positive answer: proportionality of criminal offences and penalties shall be understood as a compound general principle capable of being operationalised for reviewing EU criminalisation choices and harmonised penalties. This chapter advanced some arguments in that respect, aiming to provide elements of discussion on how the Court should review the EU legislature's compliance with the principle of proportionality in the harmonisation of substantive criminal law. In particular, one crucial takeaway shall be stressed: the principle's hybrid nature itself constitutes the key for framing a coherent standard for judicial scrutiny of EU substantive criminal law. Indeed, the combination of the prospective and retrospective declinations of proportionality derived from the criminal law discourse provides the Court with a toolbox allowing to apply the threefold suitability, necessity and proportionality *stricto sensu* test against the specific features of the substantive criminal law domain, thus relying on prospective and retrospective schemes.

This finding is supported by the outcome of the analysis of the EU legislative practice previously recalled. If the EU political institutions themselves abide by the hybrid conceptualisation of proportionality when assessing the scope of supranational criminalisation choices and the severity of harmonised penalty levels, even judicial review by the CJEU should follow the same approach. Indeed, this approach from the Court would allow for an in-depth scrutiny of EU criminalisation choices and harmonised penalties, thus ensuring that all prospective and retrospective arguments underpinning the EU legislative action may be amenable to judicial review.

Still, meaningful judicial review also requires an appropriate standard of scrutiny. Against the proportionality considerations shaping EU substantive criminal law provisions, how much discretion should be left to the legislature in reviewing prospective and retrospective proportionality? While the CJEU has traditionally been quite deferential towards the legislative margin of appreciation when scrutinising the proportionality of legislative choices, the chapter argues that the review of EU substantive criminal law shall be strict insofar as proportionality scrutiny is invoked on fundamental rights grounds pursuant to Articles 52(1) and 49(3) of the Charter. This approach would be consistent with the trends emerging from the CJEU jurisprudence in cases involving EU acts posing serious interferences with fundamental rights. What is more, a strict proportionality review at the judicial level would uphold EU criminalisation as a tool having profound fundamental rights implications, thus warranting thorough judicial scrutiny. Even in this respect, the combination of the EU and criminal law understandings of proportionality is key to materialising the strict scrutiny envisaged. Indeed, a heavier reliance on prospective proportionality (rather than the retrospective declination of the principle) would allow the CJEU to verify whether EU criminalisation choices and harmonised sanctions are strictly necessary to attain the objective pursued.

Following these considerations, the road towards the conceptualisation and progressive refinement of the principle of proportionality of offences and penalties in EU substantive criminal law is still awaiting exploration by the CJEU. Notwithstanding its approach in *Kinsa*, it can be expected that the Court will again be confronted with proportionality issues affecting EU harmonising provisions on offences and penalties. In such circumstances, the CJEU should staunchly embrace that argumentative path, as its final destination is certain and appealing: proportionality does constitute a meaningful tool for tracing sound limits to EU criminalisation choices and harmonised penalty levels. In that perspective, this chapter can be understood as a preliminary map to go down that road towards such a destination.

11

Why Consider Standardisation of the Concept of Corporate Criminal Liability in the EU Sphere?

FRANCIEN RENSE AND BAS VAN BOCKEL

11.1 INTRODUCTION

Standards for corporate liability in relation to criminal acts in the EU are divergent. Some EU Member States do not recognise the concept of corporate criminal liability, while others accept the concept and acknowledge that criminal acts can be committed by individuals or legal entities. Yet other EU Member States have merely implemented criteria to hold corporations liable for criminal acts, without qualifying that concept and those criteria as establishing criminal liability.

In most legal systems in EU Member States, the focus in connection with criminal liability of corporations or corporate liability for criminal acts is on the actions of individuals in that respect. The concepts of corporate criminal liability basically deal with when and how to attribute whose individuals' acts or omissions to corporations rather than considering actions of the legal entities on their own.

While explaining the flexible and neutral concept of corporate criminal liability under Dutch criminal law, the authors explain that such concept is playing out most effectively and fairly: (i) if it is able and tailored to identify and assess actions of the legal entities itself, not necessarily focusing on individuals' actions; and (ii) if the concept is determining and establishing criminal liability of corporations indeed. An important side-effect, so the authors argue, would be some protection of the individuals working for the corporations, one layer at least, while not denying individual liability when reasonable and fair thresholds in that respect are met.

The paramount EU law driver of proportionate, effective and dissuasive sanctioning when applied to legal entities calls for considering the prevailing concept of corporate liability *ex crimine* under EU law. In addition, differences in various concepts throughout the whole of the EU hamper that driver. Even more so, they potentially carry negative implications for the protection of fundamental rights and the exercise of free movement rights by legal entities within the EU.

Therefore, this contribution aims to invite further reflection on the constituent conditions for and qualification of corporate liability *ex crimine* in the EU. In that respect, some relevant legal and criminological considerations are described, that, according to the authors, deserve to be taken into account if such liability is at some point stipulated.

In this chapter, the Dutch model of corporate criminal liability is firstly discussed, by way of introduction of the discussion. The argument that a legal entity cannot and must not simply be equated with the individuals it employs, or who own or lead it, is presented, referring to some basic legal and criminological stances and perspectives in that regard. After that, some of the various models of criminal liability or liability for criminal acts found in the EU Member States are briefly presented, based on responses to a questionnaire. In the next section, some of the current EU trends and standards in relation to corporate liability *ex crimine* are described, in connection with the main EU objectives in this regard, and the safeguards to be respected.

All in all, this contribution does not aim to offer an exhaustive discussion of the arguments for or against harmonisation of corporate criminal liability at EU level. Such an inquiry would inter alia entail an examination of the constitutional limits of EU competences in the field of criminal law, something which falls outside of the scope of this contribution. Nevertheless, a more thorough discussion of, and a stronger common understanding of and agreement on, a concept of corporate criminal liability which focuses not on individuals' liability principally but on entities and primarily their organisation, could lead to initiatives and developments that can benefit the proportionate, effective and dissuasive sanctioning, the functioning of the internal market and the protection of fundamental rights within the Area of Freedom, Security and Justice of corporations and individuals working for them. The authors conclude that there is a need for critical reflection on corporate criminal liability under EU law and for renewed debate on its basic tenets, leading to the development of corporate *criminal* liability standards which focus on the entities' own merits. The authors argue that aspects of the flexible and neutral concept of corporate criminal liability under Dutch criminal law might be worth considering in that regard.

11.2 THE DUTCH CONCEPT OF CORPORATE CRIMINAL LIABILITY

Dutch criminal law recognises the concept of corporate criminal liability, but this has not always been so. When the criminal code was originally established in the nineteenth century, the Dutch legislator did not introduce the concept.

However, during the last decades of the nineteenth century, corporate criminal liability found its way into various specific laws, mainly of a financial-economic and regulatory nature. A more general concept of corporate criminal liability was introduced in the Dutch Economic Criminal Act in the 1950s.[1]

In 1976, Article 51 of the Dutch Code of Criminal Law (DCC) was introduced, establishing the general principal rule that criminal acts can be committed by individuals and legal entities under Dutch law, regardless of the nature and scope of the prohibition at issue.[2] What this entails is that legal entities can, in theory, commit any criminal act. Although some crimes are much more difficult to imagine (viz the crime of rape), Dutch law to date does not rule out potential corporate criminal liability for certain areas or certain types of criminal acts.[3] It is for example not uncommon for legal entities to be prosecuted for the crime of manslaughter in cases where a safety incident caused fatal injuries, typically in addition to a failure to comply with other, specific financial-economic, administrative and/or regulatory requirements.

Article 51(1) DCC stipulates that 'criminal acts can be committed by individuals and legal entities', without specifying the specific criteria for attributing criminal acts (activities or omissions) to a legal entity. In a landmark decision from 21 October 2003, the Dutch Supreme Court ruled on the criteria for establishing corporate criminal liability.[4] It started with some more general considerations: [5]

> It follows from the foregoing considerations that it is left to the court to interpret the requirements that must be met in order to designate a legal entity as the perpetrator of a criminal offence.
>
> According to the legislative history, a legal entity (within the meaning of Article 51 of the Criminal Code) can be designated as the perpetrator of a criminal offence if the conduct in question can reasonably be attributed to it. This attribution has also been recognized in case law as the basis for the legal person's perpetration of the offence (see, inter alia, Supreme Court 23 February 1993, NJ 1993, 605 and Supreme Court 13 November 2001, NJ 2002, 219).
>
> This raises the question of when (prohibited) conduct can reasonably be attributed to a legal person.
>
> The answer to that question depends on the specific circumstances of the case, including the nature of the (prohibited) conduct. It is therefore difficult to formulate a general rule. However, an important point of reference for attribution is whether the conduct took place or was carried out within the sphere of the legal person. In principle, such conduct can be attributed to the legal person."

[1] The commentary to the Dutch Code of Criminal Law (DCC) (in Dutch), *Tekst & Commentaar Wetboek van Strafrecht* ('T&C'), Art 51, note 1.

[2] ibid.

[3] ibid, note 6.

[4] NL:HR:2003:AF7938, https://uitspraken.rechtspraak.nl/details?id=ECLI:NL:HR:2003:AF7938.

[5] Informal translation by the authors.

And it followed up with some specific examples and criteria:

> Conduct within the sphere of the legal entity may be deemed to have taken place if one or more of the following circumstances apply:
>
> - it concerns an act or omission by someone who works for the legal entity either on the basis of an employment relationship or on other grounds,
> - the conduct is in line with the normal business operations of the legal entity,
> - the conduct has been useful to the legal entity in the business it conducts,
> - the legal entity was able to decide whether or not the conduct would take place and, according to the actual course of events, such or similar conduct was accepted or customarily accepted by the legal entity. Acceptance in this sense also includes the failure to exercise the care that could reasonably be expected of the legal entity with a view to preventing the conduct. It should be noted that the latter criteria – which were developed in HR 23 February 1954, NJ 1954, 378 and which, in the case in question, are referred to as 'ijzerdraad-criteria' – were developed with a view to the functional perpetration of a natural person (i.e. with a view to the criminal liability of a natural person for the conduct of another natural person), but that in certain cases they can also serve as criteria for attributing the conduct of a natural person to a legal person (see Supreme Court 14 January 1992, NJ 1992, 413).

The Dutch Supreme Court obviously reasons from the starting point of the attribution of a '(criminal) act' to the entity. The framework and criteria do not necessarily stipulate the attribution of a certain, identified act of an individual to the entity. In principle, establishing and determining whether 'an act occurred within the sphere of the entity' suffices to attribute this act to the entity. Whether the act occurred in 'the sphere of the entity' could depend on the actual individual acting or omitting to act and the position of said individual in relation to the entity, but neither is per se required. Moreover, the last criterion – whether the entity had 'authority in relation to the act and accepted such or similar acts given the factual course of events' – does not require any certain specific act of an individual or of certain individuals.[6]

In particular, criminal acts committed by way of omission can be attributed to legal entities solely on the basis of failed compliance structures and measures.[7]

[6] This is even so, despite the fact that originally the Dutch Supreme Court still referred to this criterion as a criterion 'for attributing the conduct of a natural person to a legal person'.

[7] For a further analysis of this judgment and the Drijfmest-criteria espoused in it and a broad interpretation thereof, see (in Dutch): Mark Hornman, 'De strafrechtelijke aansprakelijkheid van leidinggevenden van ondernemingen Een beschouwing vanuit multidimensionaal perspectief' (Boom, 2016), paras 3.4–3.5, 45–50.

If a specific criminal act is attributed to a legal entity, this does not preempt the possibility of investigating and prosecuting individuals under Dutch law. Individuals can still qualify as the actual perpetrator, in addition to the entity. This holds true, even if their criminal acts essentially concern one and the same act.[8] In addition, a legal entity may commit a criminal act jointly with, or with the assistance of, individuals. The legal entity and the individuals may, in appropriate circumstances, be considered co-perpetrators or accomplices.[9]

Even more so, individuals may be regarded, whether directly or indirectly, as principal agents or 'factual directors' of the offence committed by the legal entity. In those cases, the individual is actually held criminally liable for the criminal act committed by the legal entity, namely as the one ordering or leading and instructing ('in fact directing') that act.[10]

The Dutch concept of corporate criminal liability has been guided by sheer pragmatism, rather than lofty doctrines or principles. The concept is mainly practical, enabling the Dutch authorities and Prosecution Office to also investigate and prosecute the over the years rapidly growing group of legal entities in relation to alleged criminal acts, more particularly in financial-economic and regulatory areas. Basically, it is considered practical that these participants to the Dutch society and the Dutch market can also be punished for criminal acts.[11]

Nonetheless, over the years, it has been established that legal entities also have recourse to fundamental rights which must be safeguarded.[12] From that perspective, it is worthwhile to reflect on why, and under precisely which circumstances, a legal entity should bear, or could reasonably expect to bear, the burden of criminal liability. It would not seem unreasonable to demand that the threshold for attribution of criminal liability should reflect, and be proportional to, the nature of the legal entity and its role within the legal order and society at large.[13]

The flexibility and neutrality of the Dutch approach to corporate criminal liability may present an opportunity in that regard. While the Dutch case-law-based criteria for corporate criminal liability are rather neutral and non-exhaustive, they could form a suitable framework to accommodate a more

[8] T&C, note 2.

[9] ibid.

[10] ibid, and Art 51(2) DCC.

[11] T&C, note 1. For some older and highly economically and financially rationalised ideas on corporate criminal liability or more ideological, ethical and philosophical contrary ideas in that respect, leading up to the almost complete rejection of the concept from an US law perspective, see, respectively, John T Byam, 'The Economic Inefficiency of Corporate Criminal Liability' (1982) 73 *Journal of Criminal Law and Criminology* 582 and Jeffrey S Parker, 'Doctrine of Destruction: The Case of Corporate Criminal Liability' (1996) 17 *Managerial and Decision Economics* 381.

[12] See eg *Capital Bank AD v Bulgaria* App no 49429/99 (ECtHR 24 November 2005) and *Comingersoll SA v Portugal* App no 35382/97 (ECtHR, 6 April 2000).

[13] For some earlier thoughts on the same subject, see (in Dutch): JF Rense, 'Rechtspersonen in het strafrecht' (2005) 3 *Delikt & Delinkwent* 272.

principle-based approach (even if they do at present not engender or require such).[14]

Against this background, the Dutch concept of corporate criminal liability may aspire to a framework capable of reconciling effective enforcement with normative fairness. In order to achieve such a framework, the legal construct of the corporation must be squared with the concept of corporate criminal liability. Although the corporation remains, in essence, a juridical fiction, it has assumed the status of a legal and societal actor whose presence and agency are manifested in the social and economic order. Corporations have become a social reality, and recognising this reality necessitates legal mechanisms capable of attributing liability to such entities within the criminal law domain as well. The same goes for a more criminological perspective focusing on effectiveness of liability of legal entities and related punishment. Yet this liability must remain circumscribed by the foundational principles of legality, culpability, and proportionality that safeguard the rule of law and preserve the legal integrity of both collective and individual actors within society.[15] Corporate entities amount to more than the sum of the individuals involved; they have an existence of their own that must come with distinct capabilities, legal obligations and liabilities.[16]

[14] T&C, note 1.

[15] See n 13. For a more in-depth analysis of effective liability of principals and 'factual directors', and a plea for an organisational approach in that regard, see Hornman (n 7). Dutch criminology scholars acknowledge the relevance and importance of approaching legal entities and organisations on their own (internal and external) merits too, eg (in Dutch): Wim Huisman, *Tussen Winst en Moraal* (Boom, 2001) 103, 133–34 and H van de Bunt and W Huisman, 'Organisatiecriminaliteit' (2004) 2 *Tijdschrift voor Criminologie* 106, esp 109–13. Further, see NL:GHDHA:2025:2436, https://uitspraken.rechtspraak.nl/details?id=ECLI:NL:GHDHA:2025:2436&showbutton=true&idx=2 in which the Dutch Court agreed with the Public Prosecutor's stance in a substantive decision explaining why not to prosecute the former CEO of a Dutch financial institution, taking into account organisational dynamics and the former CEO's position and role therein, ie the organisational specifics to determine who to (further) prosecute and why or why not. From an US law perspective, Jennifer Arlen and Reinier Kraakman, 'Controlling Corporate Misconduct: An Analysis of Corporate Liability Regimes' (1997) 72 *New York University Law Review* 687 described a mixed bag of perspectives and approaches to effectively and efficiently held corporations liable in the criminal arena, whilst taking individuals' liability as a basic starting point: 'However, when structuring a corporate liability regime, it is crucial to understand firms both for what they are – organizations in which agents sometimes commit misconduct – and for what they are not – autonomous entities that wholly control their own agents. Recognizing that firms are not themselves wrongdoers, but are organizations in a position to monitor and influence their own agents' (752). Some years later, Cristina de Maglie, 'Models of Corporate Criminal Liability in Comparative Law' (2005) 4 *Washington University Global Studies Law Review* 547 described different models of determining and establishing corporate liability, emphasising various concepts of liability not necessarily derivative and underlining the importance of also protecting the corporate to a certain extent. Successively, S. Sun Beale, 'A response to the critics of corporate criminal liability' (2009) 46 *American Criminal Law Review* 1481 strongly pleads for corporate criminal liability, emphasising the reality of corporations and their societal impact and power, together with worldwide developments endorsing the concept and even extension thereof.

[16] Known as the legal 'personality principle'.

This perspective also underlines the importance of differentiating the legal entity from the individuals working for or within the entity. They cannot and must not be equated with the entity for which they are working, nor do they deserve that. The surroundings in which they are acting are complex and affected by all kinds of interests and actions besides their own, without being integrally controlled by them. The often-heard political and societal call and alert to hold the individuals accountable for the entity's actions is overly simplistic and might even be unjust.[17] Those individuals, usually just doing their jobs, deserve to be protected by one additional layer at least, namely by the entity and the entity's structure and liabilities, before being confronted with the actions of the entity. All this is not intended as a denial of any legal responsibility and liability of individuals in relation to entity's criminal acts; the aim is to emphasise the importance of differentiating both, and approaching them with an effective and fair legal framework with appropriate thresholds for criminal liability that take due account of their respective positions.[18]

[17] See eg Van de Bunt and Huisman (n 15) 114 underlining the merely symbolic instead of effective function of the outcry for executives' liability, referring to the complexity and organisational context of corporate criminal crimes. Further, see Hornman (n 7) for a sophisticated approach of individuals' liability for corporate crimes recognising the reality or acting from within organisations, and also the case at n 15.The Yates Memorandum of the US Department of Justice in 2015 (www.justice.gov/archives/dag/individual-accountability) is often remembered as starting this trend. In The Netherlands, the trend is also recognisable in daily legal practice, mainly in political and societal debates about corporate crimes and their enforcement, and in the Dutch Public Prosecutor's approach. John C Coffee Jr, 'Crime and Corporation: Making the Punishment Fit the Corporation' (2022) 4 *The Journal of Corporation Law* 964 recognises the difficulties in aiming for individual liability, but seems to plead for a corporate internal competitive system in which the corporation is 'incentivized to turn in its managers and executives to protect its own interests', suggesting that otherwise an 'implicit understanding' will exist 'with its senior managers under which they will protect each other' (988–89). However, such a cynical perspective does not seem to acknowledge the other situations in which faults and related criminal acts occur without specific intentions, planning and active participation. It might be that this difference in approach and appreciation finds its source primarily in differences in legal systems and concepts under which, for example, criminal acts can only be committed with specific criminal intentions, planning and active participation in comparison to systems and concepts in which such conditions do not necessarily apply. The authors did not assess such possible differences for this contribution.

[18] For a positive example of assessing corporate wrongdoing separate from its management and de facto directors' wrongdoing via tailored and more appropriate methods differentiating them, see (in Dutch) eg the decisions of the Dutch Public Prosecutor's office in relation to further prosecution of board members of two major financial institutions already under criminal investigation for non -compliance with AML rules and regulations and related money laundering: 'OM: onvoldoende bewijs verdere strafrechtelijke vervolging Hamers' Openbaar Ministerie (18 December 2024), www.om.nl /actueel/nieuws/2024/12/18/om-onvoldoende-bewijs-verdere-strafrechtelijke-vervolging-hamers; and 'OM gaat voormalig bestuurders ABN AMRO niet vervolgen' Openbaar Ministerie (18 December 2024), www.om.nl/actueel/nieuws/2024/12/18/om-gaat-voormalig-bestuurders-abn-amro-niet-vervolgen. Recently, the Dutch Court agreed with the Public Prosecutor's stance in a substantive decision not to prosecute the former CEO of one of these banks, taking into account organisational dynamics and the former CEO's position and role therein: NL:GHDHA:2025:2436, Gerechtshof Den Haag, K25/220277.

11.3 THE CONCEPT OF CORPORATE CRIMINAL LIABILITY IN SOME EU MEMBER STATES

How do the various EU Member States and their legal systems deal with this concept and perspective? In this section, the authors describe the divergent concepts of corporate criminal liability in various jurisdictions in the EU, based on the responses to a questionnaire sent out to legal practitioners and researchers in various jurisdictions, as well as other legal experts.[19]

The following general questions merely led to a basic overview, from which many substantive concepts (like 'knowledge' and 'culpability') have been omitted for the sake of clarity and brevity.[20] The aim of the questionnaire was not to develop an exhaustive overview of legal systems in all Member States on this point nor to establish an overview of scientifical verified sources, but merely to provide an indication of the variations within the EU and the underlying rationale to date.[21]

The questionnaire contained the following questions:

- Does/do your law/laws recognise the concept of corporate criminal liability?
- If yes, does/do this/these law/laws recognise the concept for certain specific criminal acts or rules or is the concept recognised more in general?
- If yes, what are the actual criteria to establish corporate criminal liability?
- Do these criteria necessarily include attribution of individual's actions or omissions to establish such? If yes, how and whose actions or omissions are or could be relevant, eg only the higher management's actions and omissions or all employees?

[19] The questionnaire was sent out and answered in the summer of 2025. The following professional practitioners and researchers kindly provided answers to the authors' questions: Mrs J Logesová, Wolf Theiss Prague; Mrs L Tumova, Wolf Theiss Prague; Mr B Cova, Greenberg Traurig Italy; Mr L Franceschi, Greenberg Traurig Italy; Mr Th Steen Brandi, Schjødt Norway; Mr G El-Brouch, Schjødt Norway; Dr Hellen Schilling, Schilling Tute Germany; Mr S de Navacelle, Navacelle France; Mr G Arnoult, Navacelle France; Mrs L Gaudey-Montaland, Navacelle France; Prof Ch Beaucillon, Université Paris-Est Créteil France; Prof J Alix, Université Paris Nanterre France; Mr IG Anagnostopoulos, Anagnostopoulos Greece. The authors thank them wholeheartedly and gratefully!

[20] Legal concepts like 'knowledge' and 'culpability' in the context of corporate criminal law would ultimately of course also be of interest when integrally assessing and comparing the various concepts.

[21] For a more in-depth description and comparison of the various legal systems and approaches from the 2010s, see: Antonio Fiorella, *Corporate criminal liability and compliance programs, Volume I, Liability 'Ex crimine' of legal entities in Member States* (Jovene Editore, 2012). In Mihai Stefănoaia, 'The Evolution of Corporate Criminal Liability in Romanian and European Criminal law: A Comparative Study on the Effectiveness of Sanctions' (2025) 2 *Proceedings of the 18th International Conference on Psychology, Social Sciences & Humanities* 8, the still varying various systems and approaches throughout the EU and EU Member States are underlined.

11.3.1 Czech Republic

Czech criminal law recognises the concept of corporate criminal liability for, in principle, all criminal acts, with few explicit exemptions. Attribution of criminal acts to corporates is generally based on criminal misconduct of individuals holding a particular position in the corporate entity, of those exercising decisive control over the corporate entity, their employees, and anyone acting in the interest of the corporate entity or in the course of the corporate entity's business. There is a wide variety of personnel listed in the Corporate Criminal Liability Act – eg managers, employees, board managers, shadow directors – whose actions can be attributed to the corporate. The corporate entity can be excused criminally, if it proves that it has implemented required measures that could have prevented the criminal acts.

11.3.2 Austria

Austrian criminal law recognises the concept of corporate criminal liability for any criminal act stipulated under Austrian criminal law. For corporate criminal liability to occur, certain conditions must be met, namely the criminal act must be committed in corporate entity's favour or in breach of specific obligations of the entity (eg statutory, contractual or administrative obligations). Corporate entities can be held liable for acts committed by decision-makers and employees. The first category is interpreted broadly, including amongst others managing directors, board members, authorised signatories, other persons authorised to represent the corporate entity externally, supervisory board members and others that exercise controlling powers in managerial positions or otherwise exert significant influence on the management of the corporate entity. All other personnel are employees. For the first category of criminal actor's acts to be attributed to the corporate entity, the actor's acts must have committed the criminal act unlawfully and culpably. For the second category of criminal acts to be attributed to the corporate entity, the actor must have committed the criminal act unlawfully and culpably, the act having been enabled or facilitated by a decision-maker of the corporate entity, who failed to meet the required standard of diligence and care, particularly if essential technical, organisational, or personal measures to prevent the criminal acts were not taken.

11.3.3 Bulgaria

Bulgarian criminal law does not recognise the concept of corporate criminal liability. The law stipulates criminal liability in relation to natural persons only, while legal entities can be subject to administrative fines, including in case of certain criminal acts.[22] In order to join the OECD and to implement various EU rules and regulations, Bulgaria is currently considering introducing the concept of corporate criminal liability.

11.3.4 Croatia

The concept of corporate criminal liability is recognised under Croatian law, alongside and in addition to criminal liability of individuals. Although there is some distinct law regulating corporate criminal liability, corporates can generally be held criminally liable for all criminal acts. Criteria to attribute criminals acts to corporate entities are whether criminal acts are committed by its responsible person, managing the operations of the corporate entity or entrusted with performing tasks within the scope of the corporate entity's activities, if violating the corporate entity's duties or benefiting the corporate entity, even if the criminal act occurred due to the person's failure to supervise or control the activities.

11.3.5 Hungary

Since 2004, Hungarian criminal law recognises the concept of criminal liability for all criminal acts in principle, on an indirect and contributory basis, meaning that criminal measures against corporate entities are based on the criminal liability of an individual having been established. Criminal proceedings will be against the individual, while criminal measures against the corporate entity can also be ordered, if the stipulated conditions are met. Corporate entities cannot be prosecuted on their own. Measures can be imposed for intentional acts, if committed with the purpose or effect of obtaining an advantage for the corporate entity or if committed using the corporate entity, and if the act was committed by the corporate entity's directors, managers, employees with powers of representation, officers, directors, supervisory board members or their delegates in the course of the corporate entity's business, or by shareholders or employees in the course of the corporate entity's business and the fulfilment of the duty of management or supervision by the respective manager, corporate secretary or supervisory board member which could have prevented the act, or if the manager, shareholder, authorised representative, employee, officer, company secretary or supervisory board member knew that the act had been committed.

[22] See the Engel criteria of the ECtHR in the *Case of Engel and others v The Dutch* (App nos 5100/71; 5101/71; 5102/71; 5354/72; 5370/72) (8 June 1976) and the *Case of Öztürk v Germany* (App no 8544/79) (21 February 1984), in this respect as well, underlining, in short, that 'criminal' has an autonomous meaning in respect of the European Convention on Human Rights, not necessarily depending on the national law qualification.

11.3.6 Romania

In Romania, the concept of corporate criminal liability is recognised and introduced in Romanian law as from 2006 for all criminal acts in general. Briefly, under Romanian criminal law corporates may face criminal liability for criminal misconduct of individuals acting on behalf of, or in the interest of the corporate entity or in the course of the corporate entity's business based on the specific facts and circumstances of the matter at hand (eg taking into account the corporate and operational rules). The criminal acts need not necessarily be committed by higher management. At the same time, the existence of robust and functioning measures and compliance programmes can lead to exclusion or mitigation of corporate liability.

11.3.7 Serbia

Under Serbian law, the concept of corporate criminal liability is recognised for all criminal acts under Serbian law, if the conditions for corporate criminal liability are met. Such conditions being: the criminal act being committed by its authorised persons within the scope of the activities and/or authorisation of that person, establishing a gain for the corporate entity, or the criminal act being committed by an individual acting under the supervision and control of an authorised person within the company if the act resulted from the lack of supervision or control, carried out for the benefit of corporate entity. The term 'authorised person' is to be interpreted broadly, referring to any individual that has been legally or practically entrusted with a certain scope of activities as well as anyone that is authorised or considered to be authorised to act on behalf of the corporate entity.

11.3.8 Italy

Under Italian law, a form of corporate criminal liability is established, namely under the dedicated Legislative Decree 231/2001. The liability arises from the commission of certain predicate criminal acts, enumerated in said Legislative Decree, frequently updated and extended, encompassing the most serious forms of criminality (eg bribery, specific so-called corporate offences, market abuse, money laundering, and criminal acts in relation to health, safety and environment). Although corporate liability is formally administrative in nature, substantially it is to be considered criminal in nature according to the case law of the European Court of Human Rights.[23] The conditions for said corporate liability are:

[23] See n 22.

- the commission of a predicate offence;
- the perpetrator of a criminal act is a director, officer, representative or employee;
- the act was committed in the interest or to the benefit of the corporate entity;
- while the corporate entity failed to adopt, update and effectively implement adequate compliance procedures designed to prevent the commission of acts of the type that occurred;
- the corporate entity has not appointed a specific internal body vested with autonomous and effective powers to supervise over the implementation of the compliance procedures;
- the supervisory body has not effectively performed its duties.

The attribution of individual conduct is essential for establishing corporate liability in this concept. However, the corporate entity can be held liable irrespective of whether the individual has been identified or prosecuted. The conduct of both senior management and employees is relevant in this regard. The burden of proof as regards the adoption and effective implementation of compliance procedures varies depending on whether the predicate act was committed by senior management or employees.

11.3.9 Norway

Norwegian law recognises the concept of corporate criminal liability. It means that a corporate entity can be held criminally liable for criminal acts committed by someone acting on its behalf (on the basis of a legal relationship, not necessarily managerial) whenever an act is committed in the context of corporate entity's activities or operations, and not solely in the perpetrator's own interest. It is a general concept rather than limited to specific criminal acts. The purpose of the liability is to strengthen the preventive effect of criminal provisions urging corporations to organise their activities so as to prevent criminal acts. If there are justification grounds for the perpetrator, such as self-defence or necessity, these also apply to the corporate entity. Preventive and compliance measures might be relevant in determining, within the relevant discretionary powers, whether to punish the corporate entity (and how it must be punished).

11.3.10 Germany

German law does not recognise the concept of corporate criminal liability, in the sense that legal entities themselves cannot be held liable under German law. This is rooted primarily in a particular understanding of criminal 'guilt' as a specific form of individual responsibility which, under German doctrine, cannot be borne by such entity but solely by a natural person. However, there are statutory bases for corporate liability that relate to criminal acts of individuals that, while not constituting criminal penalties in the strict sense, could severely impact the corporate entity.[24] For example, administrative fines could be imposed attributing acts of a managerial person undertaking business-related duties or an owner of an operation or undertaking breaching supervisory duties.

11.3.11 France[25]

French law recognises the concept of corporate criminal liability for acts committed by their corporate bodies (official bodies of a corporation or acting as such) or representatives (the ones empowered to represent the corporate entity or de facto representatives) on behalf of the corporate entity. This is interpreted broadly, merely requiring acts committed in the exercise of activities aimed at ensuring the organisation, operation or objectives of the corporate entity which is typically the case when the corporate entity had a financial stake in the activities. The act must be committed by an individual – 'A legal entity can only act through a natural person, and can only omit to act because a natural person has failed to act'[26] – although the liabilities of corporate entities and individuals are distinct, so that eg the absence of guilt of the individual does not necessarily exonerate the corporate entity too. Since the end of 2005, corporate criminal liability is extended to cover all criminal acts under French law, provided these meet these requirements.

11.3.12 Greece

Until recently, the Greek legal system refused to adopt any concept of corporate criminal liability, adhering to the classical adage *societas delinquere non potest*. If an individual committed a criminal act for the benefit of a corporate entity, only administrative fines could be imposed on the corporate entity.[27] The need to harmonise legislation with international standards and practices, however, prompted the introduction of a hybrid model of corporate criminal

[24] See n 22.

[25] For further details and background information in relation to the concept of corporate criminal liability in France, see: J. Alix and P.-L. Sutton, French report on criminal liability, 'Corporate criminal liability in the European Union', co-funded by the European Law Institute, The Institute of Law Studies of the Polish Academy of Sciences, and the European Anti-Fraud Office, C. Nowak and F. Nicolicchia (eds.), 2023-2026, forthcoming. The project website (still under construction) is available at www.europeanlawinstitute.eu/projects-instruments/current-projects/current-projects/eli-corporate-criminal-liability-in-the-european-union.

[26] ibid, 4.

[27] See n 22.

liability, with a limited scope. A specific article under Greek law establishes criminal liability of corporates for bribery offences, committed for its benefit or on its behalf by individuals in a managerial position or who have the authority to represent it, to take decisions concerning it or to exercise control over it, or committed by a subordinate officer or person acting on its instruction provided that the commission of such acts results from the failure to exercise appropriate supervision by one of the individuals mentioned before. Liabilities of individuals and corporates are however distinguished. The concept is based on the attribution of liability to the corporate entity depending on whether it resulted from a failure of managerial or high-ranking personnel to exercise proper supervision, theorising they constitute the 'directing mind' of the corporate entity.

11.3.13 Interim Findings

In summary, the concept of corporate criminal liability is now broadly acknowledged across the EU. Nonetheless, while the concept is still not recognised throughout the whole of the EU, attribution criteria vary and in those jurisdictions that have embraced it, the concept generally takes the form of attribution of identified individual conduct to the legal entity. This mechanism is often regarded as a necessary precondition for holding corporations criminally liable, still reflecting traditional principles such as *societas delinquere non potest* and the (perceived) need to identify a concrete, identifiable 'directing mind' of the corporate.

11.4 CORPORATE LIABILITY *EX CRIMINE* IN EU LAW

While primarily rooted in national legal orders, the concept of corporate liability in EU law in criminal surroundings developed too, in tandem with the expansion of EU competences in areas such as financial regulation, environmental protection, and market integrity.

The adoption of the Convention on the Protection of the European Communities' Financial Interests ('the PIF Convention') in 1997, requiring the Member States to establish liability of legal persons for criminal offences affecting the financial interest of the EU,[28] formed a foundational step in that development of corporate liability in the EU's legal order in this field. The PIF Convention reflected a then already growing awareness that effective protection of the Union's financial interests could not rely

[28] See Second Protocol, drawn up on the basis of Article K.3 of the treaty on European Union, to the Convention on the protection of the European Communities' financial interests - Joint Declaration on Article 13 (2) - Commission Declaration on Article 7, [1997] OJ C221/12, Art 13.

solely on individuals' criminal liability, given the reality of and increasingly complex structures of corporate actors involved in transnational economic activities. Corporate liability in EU law in this field of criminally qualified violations and enforcement has since expanded through subsequent directives and instruments, in areas such as corruption, money laundering, environmental crime and restrictive measures. By now, corporate liability is a cornerstone of the Union's broader enforcement architecture in that regard.[29]

Recently, Zazzaro described this development of the concept in EU law over the past 25 years, outlining the growing range of initiatives aimed at establishing corporate liability for criminal conduct in EU law.[30] Interestingly, Zazzaro's description shows the increase in initiatives and incentives to implement corporate liability in relation to criminal acts for the benefit of the corporate,[31] but still mainly without stipulating corporate *criminal* liability,[32] let alone the conditions for such liability more particularly. Further, the initiatives still centre around corporate liability based on attribution of certain individuals' acts.[33]

Some noteworthy relevant recent directives, namely the proposal on an EU Directive on combatting corrupting (Article 16),[34] the new EU Directive on the protection of the environment through criminal law (Article 6),[35] the EU Directive on the definition of criminal offences and penalties for the violation

[29] Federica Zazzaro, 'Corporate Criminal Liability in EU Directives: An Overview of the EU Discipline' (2025) *New Journal of European Criminal Law* 3 (first published online 17 June 2025).

[30] ibid.

[31] ibid, 3–7.

[32] ibid 8.

[33] The extensive study by Fiorella (n 21) provides an overview of various attribution criteria for corporate liability *ex crimine* (in summary at 5–8). A follow-up study underlines the importance of more sophisticated attribution criteria in that field: Antonio Fiorella, *Corporate Criminal Liability and Compliance Programs, Volume II, Towards a Common Model in the European Union* (Jovene Editore, 2012). In short, see also the overview article by Nicola Selvaggi, 'Ex Crimine Liability of Legal Persons in EU Legislation. An Overview of Substantive Criminal Law' (2014) 4 *European Criminal Law Review* 46.

[34] Proposal for a Directive of the European Parliament and of the Council on combating corruption, replacing Council Framework Decision 2003/568/JHA and the Convention on the fight against corruption involving officials of the European Communities or officials of Member States of the European Union and amending Directive (EU) 2017/1371 of the European Parliament and of the Council, COM/2023/234 final. Further, see Matilda Bellingeri and Federico Luppi, *Combating Corruption in EU Legislation. An Analysis of Some Aspects of the Commission Proposal for the EU Anti-Corruption Directive* (2023) 18 *Eucrim* 281 for some interesting remarks in relation to the concept of corporate criminal liability in this regard, some in line with the remarks in this chapter. On 2 December 2025, EU Parliament and Council negotiators reached a provisional agreement on the EU's first ever directive harmonising criminal laws to fight corruption, strengthening efforts to prevent, prosecute and punish offences across the EU: 'Agreement reached on the first EU-wide criminal law rules against corruption' Press release (2 December 2025).

[35] Directive (EU) 2024/1203 of the European Parliament and of the Council of 11 April 2024 on the protection of the environment through criminal law and replacing Directives 2008/99/EC and 2009/123/EC, [2024] OJ L2024/1203.

of Union restrictive measures (Article 6)[36] and the new EU Directive on AML (Article 53)[37] indeed stipulate on the point of the liability of corporations in these areas (worded (virtually) identically) as follows:

> 1. Member States shall take the necessary measures to ensure that legal persons can be held liable for any of the criminal offences referred to in Articles 7 to 14 committed for the benefit of those legal persons by any natural person, acting either individually or as part of an organ of the legal person, and having a leading position within the legal person, based on one or more of the following:
>
> (a) power of representation of the legal person;
> (b) the authority to take decisions on behalf of the legal person; or
> (c) the authority to exercise control within the legal person.
>
> 2. Member States shall take the necessary measures to ensure that legal persons can be held liable where the lack of supervision or control by a person referred to in section 1 has made possible the commission, including by any of the persons under his authority, of any of the criminal offences referred to in Articles 7 to 14 for the benefit of that legal person.[38]

As to the concept of corporate culpability, Zazzaro points out that the attribution of individual wrongdoing in EU legislation at present is still the principal base: 'always depends on a predicate offence committed by an individual'.[39]

However, the notion that the concept of corporate liability may (or indeed should) be grounded in the specific characteristics and structure of the legal entity itself, rather than solely in the actions of identifiable individuals, is nonetheless introduced and recognised too.[40] There is an increasing awareness, so it seems, that in order to tackle the difficulties of effectively holding corporate entities liable, a concept of corporate liability that is more closely aligned with the specific nature and structural characteristics of legal entities would be helpful indeed.[41]

[36] Directive (EU) 2024/1226 of the European Parliament and of the Council of 24 April 2024 on the definition of criminal offences and penalties for the violation of Union restrictive measures and amending Directive (EU) 2018/1673, [2024] OJ L2024/1226.

[37] Directive (EU) 2024/1640 of the European Parliament and of the Council of 31 May 2024 on the mechanisms to be put in place by Member States for the prevention of the use of the financial system for the purposes of money laundering or terrorist financing, amending Directive(EU) 2019/1937, and amending and repealing Directive (EU) 2015/849, [2024] OJ L2024/1640.

[38] This quote regards Art 16 of the proposed Directive on combatting corruption.

[39] Zazzaro (n 29) 6–7.

[40] ibid 14–16.

[41] ibid, 10; Fiorella, Volumes I (n 21) and II (n 33) described a similar line of thinking in 2012; the same goes for Selvaggi (n 33) in 2014. More recently, Stefănoaia (n 21) pleaded the same, including in relation to prosecutorial strategies and sanctioning policies (16, 18), while underlining that effectiveness is still far from a given (18–20). See nn 13 and 15.

11.5 DRIVERS FOR EFFECTIVENESS, SECURITY, AND A RIGHTS-BASED APPROACH

To date, the debates on liability of corporations *ex crimine* under EU law may have overlooked issues such as the absence of common standards for corporate criminal liability in the EU; the differences in the various concepts across the EU as a result thereof, or at least not being eliminated thereby, and the impact of those differences throughout the EU and within the EU market; together with the importance of a clear direction and qualification of such concept (focusing on the entities' own circumstances and merits, and qualifying as *criminal* indeed) for the EU and EU market. These aspects deserve more thorough consideration. Öberg already identifies three principal drivers for law and policy-making in the sensitive area of EU criminal law: ensuring the 'effectiveness' of EU policies; 'security' for EU citizens; and a 'rights-based approach' to EU criminal policy.[42]

This contribution neither attempts to provide a comprehensive set of arguments in favour of the harmonisation of standards for corporate criminal liability under EU law, nor proposes any definitive outline of what an EU-wide concept of corporate criminal liability must entail. Instead, the aim of this contribution is, more modestly, to establish that constituent conditions for corporate criminal liability are directly relevant for all three drivers, and to warn that the continuance of divergence of standards for corporate criminal liability throughout the EU Member States and the absence of any clear common understanding of that concept, the direction thereof and the qualification as such, may have unintended and unwanted implications on the same.

- *Effective corporate criminal liability tailored to corporate context and reality; also enabling and supporting proportionate, effective and dissuasive sanctioning*

Common standards for corporate liability, corporate criminal liability in particular, tailored to the reality of how corporations function in today's world, would support introducing more effective enforcement concepts than those widespread traditional concepts of corporate liability, responsibility and accountability that are solely predicated on individuals' actions, while it would also allow for hampering differences in various models throughout the EU to fade away.[43]

In Zazarro's words, referring to the EU principles and goals, such standards could, if tailored effectively, even automatically and explicitly 'emphasise the pivotal role that organizational and compliance-related factors play at the supranational level' while making progress in 'a liability model that recognizes

[42] Jacob Öberg, 'Normative Justifications of EU Criminal Law: European Public Goods and Transnational Interests' (2021) 27 *European Law Journal* 408, 411–12.

[43] Zazzaro (n 29) 9 and 14–16 ff; Fiorella, Volumes I (n 21) and II (n 33), described a similar line of thinking in 2012; the same goes for Selvaggi (n 33) in 2014. See also nn 13 and 15.

a company's capacity to act and re-organise the commission of an offence to prevent further offences and remedy the consequences.'[44]

The same would obviously go for the even more effectively establishing and supporting of the paramount EU principle of proportionate, effective and dissuasive sanctioning;[45] while this requirement might not require criminal liability per se,[46] at least standardisation of effective conditions for corporate liability *ex crimine* will no doubt contribute to the proportionate, effective and dissuasive enforcement of and sanctioning under EU law.[47]

- *Protecting and safeguarding fundamental rights, security and free movement rights*

In addition to this primarily instrumental legal perspective, protection of fundamental rights, including security, enjoyed by legal entities, also requires attention from an EU perspective.[48] Namely, if the concept of corporate criminal liability is not defined sufficiently equally within the EU and EU Member States, various additional concerns in that respect and related to the EU more specifically, pop up. If, for example, the various approaches in the EU Member States could still result in multiple, repeated investigations and prosecutions or other scenarios in different EU Member States, not recognising parallel or earlier investigations and prosecutions within the EU, solely for the reason of not recognising the actual approach and concept of corporate criminal liability applied, this could materially result in unacceptable risk of double jeopardy and its consequences, and unacceptable legal uncertainty.[49]

This potentially undermines free movement rights within the internal market too. Variations in the substantive and procedural bases for attributing liability

[44] Zazzaro (n 29) 3.

[45] See C-68/88, *Commission v Greece* EU:C:1989:339 for the originating ruling of this EU concept and principle.

[46] Zazzaro (n 29) 8.

[47] ibid, 7, 9 and 15–19; Fiorella, Volume I (n 21) and II (n 33), described a similar line of thinking in 2012; the same goes for Selvaggi (n 33) in 2014 and Stefanoaia (n 21) more recently, while underlining that effectiveness is still far from a given and therefore wholeheartedly pleading for further EU standardisation and refining of mechanisms to determine and establish corporate criminal liability *ex crimine* (20). See also nn 13 and 15.

[48] Fiorella, Volume I (n 21) also refers to that topic, but calls more implicitly for respecting the principle of 'personalism' (see eg 1–2, 631); the same goes for Selvaggi (n 33) 55–58. Far more explicit in that respect is Vincenzo Mongillo, 'The Nature of Corporate Liability for Criminal Offences: Theoretical Models and EU Member State Laws' in Fiorella, Volume II (n 33) 104–20, referring to various substantive and procedural rights that need safeguarding. See also n 12.

[49] See, for example and in short, the prosecution of ENI and Shell and some of their employees in Milan, which resulted in an irrevocable acquittal of all defendants, and the successive attempt by NGOs to reinitiate criminal prosecution of Shell and some other employees in The Netherlands The Appeal Court in The Netherlands decided that the criminal prosecution could not be restarted due to *ne bis in idem* (double jeopardy) but only after a long and intensive legal battle about the scope of the protection of said principle in a case with formal-legal differences in approaching and assessing facts and suspects in the corporate context in relation to alleged criminal acts: NL:GHDHA:2025:410, Gerechtshof Den Haag, K22/220530. NB both authors of this chapter were involved in those proceedings. Further, Mongillo (n 47) 120, for example, underlines the importance of safeguarding the principle of *ne bis in idem*, without too much further ado, but apparently not recognising or underestimating actual hinderances and difficulties as described herein.

to legal entities, leading to inconsistent or unpredictable enforcement outcomes, create barriers to free movement; corporations are presently subjected to varying and on the whole often unpredictable criminal and enforcement risks, depending on the jurisdiction enforcing laws and regulations, weakening the principle of legal certainty. Bellingeri and Luppi, for example, warn of unequal treatment and inefficiencies if the goal of standardisation is not achieved.[50]

Against this background – even more so, the authors underline – the qualification of a standardised concept for corporate liability as *criminal* liability is paramount, because this would explicitly and logically result in protection and safeguarding of relevant fundamental rights.[51] The authors therefore beg to differ with Zazzaro's argument that 'the crux of the issue lies not in the classification of liability of legal entities'.[52]

- *Interim findings*

In summary, an effective and realistic approach to the criminal liability of legal entities is needed to safeguard the rule of law and fundamental rights of corporations, by introducing a concept of corporate criminal liability that squares with it the legal concept of legal entities and corporations. While the EU framework does currently develop with this goal, it does so without explicitly acknowledging the key starting points or the importance of that direction and the qualification of such liability as *criminal*. Therefore, standardisation measures referring to these starting points, including in relation to the various promising but still less sophisticated approaches within the EU Member States, would support the drivers of effectiveness, security, and a rights-based approach.

11.6 CONCLUSION AND PLEA: WHAT SHOULD A STANDARDISED MODEL OF CORPORATE CRIMINAL LIABILITY IN THE EU ENTAIL?

On that basis, the authors advocate for a standardised concept of corporate *criminal* liability implementing an effective and realistic way to approach legal

[50] Bellingeri and Luppi (n 34) 6–7; their plea is related to the fight against corruption and mainly relates to revitalising and streamlining corruption offences, but the same would go for the concept of corporate criminal liability in general in various areas of corporate crime.

[51] Mongillo (n 47) 98–104 differs drastically and explicitly denies the necessity or value of a standardisation of the nature of the liability concept, nonetheless describing and underlining the importance of respecting the rule of law. However, he does not explain how to sufficiently and effectively safeguard and incorporate this in the instrumental approach he apparently favours. Therefore, see nn 12–16. Selvaggi (n 33) considers whether EU instruments referring to Art 83 TFEU automatically qualify as 'criminal', but ultimately calls this 'drastic'. He endorses a 'smoother interpretation' with a primarily instrumental focus. The authors believe eg de Maglie (n 15) would support their argument from an opposite and additional perspective, given that she underlines the importance and value of the 'criminal stigma' in modern society: 'the most advanced legal theory has shown that criminal law performs a positive symbolic function. ... Policy now requires that criminal law directly reshape society's moral code, rather than simply indirectly influencing it. This is why even the most sophisticated non-criminal models are inadequate to control corporate crime.' (562).

[52] Zazzaro (n 29) 10.

entities participating in society and the market, safeguarding a fair position and their fundamental rights.

In that respect, the authors strive for a concept that is not (primarily) based on individuals' liability, first of all because such a system is not sufficiently effective (neither reactively[53] nor proactively). To quote Zazzaro once again:

> From a forward-looking perspective, a framework of 'effective, dissuasive and proportionate' penalties, which integrates the genuine involvement of the corporate entity in offences by acknowledging a psychological or moral element, incentivises legal entities to implement oversight mechanisms and adopt preventative measures to deter the commission of crimes. The operational and procedural conduct of the company takes precedence, focusing on the execution and application of suitable preventative measures and the notion of organizational culpability. In this context, the fault attributed to the company lies in its failure to prevent its members from violating the law. Consequently, liability is predicated on the lack of a risk-based, structured framework. Indeed, in terms of proportionality, it seems reasonable to curtail the penalization of legal entities, if necessary, by considering the presence of 'structural negligence' attributable to the responsible organisation'[54]

That point is certainly not completely new. The Committee of Ministers of the Council of Europe, for example, advised already as early as in 1988–90:

> The increase in economic crime has accentuated the problem of bringing to justice those responsible for committing offences in connection with economic activities. A large number of these offences are committed in the course of activities pursued by enterprises. The often complex management structure of enterprises frequently makes it difficult, if not impossible, to identify the persons who are truly responsible for the commission of offences. Even where it is possible to identify an officer of an enterprise as the actual author of an offence, it may not be possible to prove directly that higher management is implicated in the offence. Furthermore, each offence may be the result of separate decisions, acts and omissions by different persons, albeit corresponding to a general ethos, generated by management, in the enterprise. In such cases, it may well be impossible to hold any one person liable, and even if this is possible, true responsibility may be more diffused.[55]

[53] In this respect, by way of example, see also the description by Zazzaro (n 29) 7 of one of the EU's telling developments: 'where the Commission has shifted its focus from an individualistic approach to corporate liability to more personal corporate liability. This shift reflects the recognition that corporate liability should not be contingent upon the final conviction of an individual, as such reliance may undermine the capacity to administer effective, proportionate and dissuasive sanctions against legal entities. Consequently, this indicates that the European legislator has taken a definitive stance in acknowledging the independent culpability of legal persons, distinct from that of natural persons.'

[54] Zazzaro (n 29) 15–16.

[55] Council of Europe, Liability of enterprises for offences Recommendation, No. R (88) 18 adopted by the Committee of Ministers of the Council of Europe on 20 October 1988 and explanatory memorandum, 10.

However, the focus of the Committee of Ministers was mainly on effectively incentivising the legal entities and less on fairness and protection of the rule of law:

> [A] sanction imposed on an individual person may, in such cases, be neither deterrent enough to prevent the enterprise from committing further offences, nor induce the management or members of the enterprise to reorganise its supervisory structure. To overcome these difficulties, legislators in many European countries have sought to render the enterprise itself criminally liable.[56]

The authors argue that the raison d'etre of their plea and proposal is the fairness of approaching legal entities on their own merits effectively, while automatically also protecting and safeguarding their fundamental rights.

An appreciated side-effect is the protection, to a certain extent, of individuals from within corporate settings. Namely, the individuals in the Committee's example and those in the current society under substantial political and societal exposure risks and pressure to hold them liable run the risk of being held liable (as the Committee describes) without 'true responsibility' just being part of 'separate decisions, acts and omissions by different persons' in challenging circumstances, like 'general ethos, generated by management, in the enterprise' outside their span of control. Such just to be able to address the entity and its alleged involvement in criminal acts, which would not be necessary with the concept the authors advocate for; when the corporate is being approached on its own merits and own actions in relation to criminal acts, this would also protect individuals within that corporate entity against unreasonable liabilities and responsibilities. Automatically, such approach could also protect them from becoming subject to a 'treasure hunt' that views individuals' liability as an end in itself due to the far-too-easy but currently often-heard call for individual responsibility in relation to corporate crimes.[57]

The authors are convinced that establishing and implementing a concept of corporate criminal liability as proposed in this chapter, whereby individuals are fairly protected, would enable and even improve existing EU initiatives to establish and implement effective corporate liability. The possibility to also hold individuals liable is reserved, namely when they were actually involved and are liable under conditions tailored to their own positions, separate to the possible liability of the corporation.

[56] ibid.

[57] See n 17. In this respect, see also Alix and Sutton (n 25) 5–6. The report also underscores the necessity of protecting individuals within corporations, especially where their behaviour is a precondition for corporate criminal liability: 'This reform was prompted by the need to protect individuals ... from disproportionate criminal liability for mere inadvertence. ... This higher threshold serves as a filter to avoid punishing minor errors when causality is remote or diffuse.' Further, the report, rightfully, underlines the need to differentiate between the interests of the legal entities and the individuals, which also favours distinguished approaches, 24.

It is beyond the scope of this chapter to develop an extensive, effective concept of corporate criminal liability, but it has argued for an approach to the concept of liability of legal entities, that have an existence of their own, on their own merits instead of approaching them just as legally non-existent (*societas delinquere non potest*) or as a sole extension of the individuals in higher or representing positions acting on its behalf (the 'directing mind' of the corporate entity). The Dutch model, as outlined in this chapter, though not yet fully developed, provides a useful foundation for further exploration and conceptual development in this regard, offering flexibility and conceptual neutrality which would accommodate an approach that genuinely engages with the legal entity.[58]

[58] See also nn 13 and 15, and 39–40.

12

Sanctioning the Facilitation of Irregular Migration: The Kinsa *Light at the End of the Overcriminalisation Tunnel*

ERMIONI XANTHOPOULOU

12.1 INTRODUCTION

The employment of criminal sanctions in EU migration and asylum law has been a long-standing interest of scholars.[1] It is usually studied as an example of 'crimmigration', a pattern referring to the convergence of crime control and immigration policies by means of using criminal law in the field of immigration to control mobility.[2] In particular, the Facilitators Package,[3] consisting of the EU Facilitation Directive establishing minimum rules for the definition of the facilitation offences and the Framework Decision on the strengthening of the penal legal framework, has been the subject of intense academic and civil society debate.[4] Key criticism contends that it has introduced an ambiguous

[1] Valsamis Mitsilegas, *The Criminalisation of Migration in Europe, Challenges for Human Rights and the Rule of Law* (Springer, 2015); Constanza Di Francesco Maesa, '(In)Effectiveness of Criminal Sanctions as regards Irregular Immigrants' (2018) 8 *European Criminal Law Review* 5.

[2] Gian Luigi Gatta, Valsamis Mitsilegas and Stefano Zirulia (eds), *Controlling Immigration Through Criminal Law. European and Comparative Perspectives on 'Crimmigration'* (Hart Publishing, 2021).

[3] Council Directive 2002/90/EC of 28 November 2002 defining the facilitation of unauthorised entry, transit and residence [2002] OJ L 328/17 (thereafter, Facilitation Directive) and Council Framework Decision 2002/946/JHA of 28 November 2002 on the strengthening of the penal framework to prevent the facilitation of unauthorised entry, transit and residence [2002] OJ L328/1 ('Facilitation Framework Decision').

[4] Eamon Aloyo and Eugenio Cusumano, 'Morally Evaluating Human Smuggling: The Case of Migration to Europe' (2021) 24 *Critical Review of International Social and Political Philosophy* 133; Violeta Moreno-Lax and Efthymios Papastavridis (eds), *Boat Refugees' and Migrants at Sea: A Comprehensive Approach* (Brill, 2016).

scope leading to overcriminalisation and a breach of fundamental rights and harming civil society.[5]

In November 2023, the European Commission proposed new legislation to reform the existing law.[6] The timeline of reform proposals has partially coincided with the litigation in the *Kinsa* case that challenged the legality and proportionality of the legal framework.[7] Both the *Kinsa* litigation and the proposed reform intensified scholarly interest in the topic. While we know what the issues of the current law are, the impact of the proposed reforms and of the ruling in *Kinsa* remain to be assessed, which is the gap that this chapter intends to fill. So, the aim of this chapter is to evaluate the *Kinsa* ruling and assess the efficacy of the proposed reform. It asks to what extent the proposed reform addresses existing issues of overcriminalisation considering international legal standards, fundamental rights, criminal law principles and EU constitutional law. The comprehension of normative choices made by the legislators would be incomplete without taking stock of the widespread climate of anti-immigration, populist rhetoric in policymaking at national and EU level. For this reason, the chapter also borrows from 'law in context' to illuminate the assessment of the debate as influenced by the social context.[8]

The chapter first outlines the current legal framework on countering the facilitation of unauthorised migration and the key criticism, which is also well presented in *Kinsa*; second, it examines the proposed reform and the persisting issues under the reform when evaluating it against international and EU legal standards on fundamental rights safeguards, principles of criminal law and EU constitutional law; third, it showcases the challenges faced by the ongoing, at the time of writing, legislative process situating the debate within the laborious inter-institutional process.

[5] Valsamis Mitsilegas, 'The Normative Foundations of the Criminalisation of Human Smuggling. Exploring the Fault Lines between European and International Law' (2019) 10 *New Journal of European Criminal Law* 68, 78; Sergio Carrera, Valsamis Mitsilegas, et al, *Policing Humanitarianism. EU Policies Against Human Smuggling and their Impact on Civil Society* (Hart, 2019); Sergio Carrera et al, 'Fit for purpose? The Facilitation Directive and the Criminalisation of Humanitarian Assistance to Irregular Migrants' (European Parliament, Policy Department for Citizens' Rights and Constitutional Affairs, 2016); Violeta Moreno-Lax, 'Towards a Thousand Little Morias: the EU (Non-)Rescue Scheme - Criminalising Solidarity, Structuralising Defection' in Daniel Thym (ed), *Reforming the Common European asylum system* (Nomos, 2022); Stefano Zirulia, 'Les Enfants de la Clarée: Why the Facilitators Package is Incompatible with the Charter of Fundamental Rights' (Border Criminologies, 2 September 2024).

[6] European Commission, 'Proposal for a Directive of the European Parliament and of the Council laying down minimum rules to prevent and counter the facilitation of unauthorised entry, transit and stay in the Union, and replacing Council Directive 2002/90/EC and Council Framework Decision 2002/946 JHA', COM(2023) 755 final ('Facilitation Directive Proposal') and European Commission, 'Proposal for a Regulation of the European Parliament and of the Council on enhancing police cooperation in relation to the prevention, detection and investigation of migrant smuggling and trafficking in human beings, and on enhancing Europol's support to preventing and combating such crimes and amending Regulation (EU) 2016/794', COM(2023) 754 final ('Europol Regulation Proposal').

[7] Case C-460/23 *Kinsa v OB Criminal proceedings brought by Procura della Repubblica presso il Tribunale di Bologna* [2025] EU:C:2025:392.

[8] Philip Selznick, '"Law in Context" Revisited' (2003) 30 *Journal of Law and Society* 177.

12.2 SANCTIONING SMUGGLING: CURRENT SITUATION

The current framework on counter-smuggling dates back to the pre-Lisbon third pillar and is governed by the Facilitators Package.[9] It is composed of a Directive that defines the crime of facilitation of irregular entry, transit and residence, which is accompanied by a Framework Decision on the strengthening of the penal framework to prevent the facilitation of unauthorised entry, transit and residence. According to the Preamble of the Directive, the common goal of these measures is to provide tools to more effectively address unauthorised immigration,[10] an aim that is broader than only countering criminal activities pertaining to exploitative migrant smuggling.

The conduct of facilitation of unauthorised entry, transit and residence is defined by the Directive and confirmed by the Framework Decision as a criminal offence attracting penalties.[11] The definition of such conduct in Article 1(1) of the Directive states:

> Each Member State shall adopt appropriate sanctions on:
>
> (a) any person who intentionally assists a person who is not a national of a Member State to enter, or transit across, the territory of a Member State in breach of the laws of the State concerned on the entry or transit of aliens;
>
> (b) any person who, for financial gain, intentionally assists a person who is not a national of a Member State to reside within the territory of a Member State in breach of the laws of the State concerned on the residence of aliens.

Therefore, the *mens rea* of the first offence requires intention and the *actus reus* includes the elements of: a) assistance; b) provided to a third country national to enter, or transit across, the territory of a Member State; and c) in breach of the laws. The second offence concerns facilitation of residence and includes the additional element of the person engaging in the conduct 'for financial gain'.

The compatibility of this provision which essentially criminalises the facilitation of irregular immigration with the EU Charter of Fundamental Rights ('the Charter') has been put in question before the Court of Justice of the European Union (CJEU) as it effectively allows the prosecution of anyone providing assistance even when the motif is not exploitative and could as well be of a humanitarian nature.[12] As discussed in the next section, the scope of criminalisation is ambiguous. Under Article 1(1a) of the Directive, intentionally assisting the unauthorised entry of a foreigner through any means, for any purpose, with or without a financial or other material benefit, is sufficient for criminalisation under EU law. The requirement of a financial gain is only necessary for the crime

[9] Facilitation Directive (n 3); Facilitation Framework Decision (n 3).
[10] Facilitation Directive (n 3), Recital 1.
[11] ibid Art 1(1)(a) combined with Art 1(1) of the Facilitation Framework Decision (n 3).
[12] *Kinsa* (n 7).

of facilitation of irregular residence as defined by Article 1(2) of the Facilitation Directive.[13] So, while the offence is a very serious one, the scope of criminalisation is broad enough to include *all* acts of facilitation.

The wide scope of criminalisation as delineated by the Directive has effectively resulted in the criminalisation of humanitarian acts of rescue. This is because Member States are free to decide, at implementation level, whether and how to introduce justifications for humanitarian acts facilitating unauthorised migration. As a result, secondary EU law is criticised for allowing the criminalisation of humanitarian acts of rescue due to its ambiguous scope. The law in its current form does not exempt actors that facilitate the smuggling of non-nationals for charitable or altruistic reasons from the scope of the offence. Under the Directive that defines the conduct of infringements, subsequently confirmed as criminal by the Framework Decision, there is no distinction between exploitative action with financial motives and action engaged for humanitarian or solidarity reasons, whether by civil society organisations, individual volunteers, or family members assisting each other.

While no mandatory exemption for humanitarian action is included in the legally binding operative part of the Directive, Article 3 of the Directive calls on Member States to 'take the measures necessary to ensure that the infringements referred to in Articles 1 and 2 are subject to effective, proportionate and dissuasive sanctions'. The broad scope of definition, coupled with the criminalisation requirement of the Framework Decision, results in a far-reaching scope of criminalisation capturing non profitable conducts with dubious connection to a harm element. For example, Italian law,[14] implementing the Facilitators Package, prohibits any act aimed at facilitating entry including facilitation that is not carried out for profit, which may even result in prosecuting parents as smugglers when accompanying their children while crossing the border. Such broad scope is contrary to the UN Smuggling Protocol, the main international law instrument governing the fight against smuggling which includes an exception to criminalisation with regard to acts of humanitarian assistance.[15] It frames the offence of smuggling strictly within the context of organised crime accompanied with receiving financial or other material benefit.[16] This strict framing, the humanitarian exception and the requirement of obtaining a financial or material benefit is not present in the Directive. Instead, there is an optional clause for Member States not to criminalise facilitation acts for rescue purposes.[17]

[13] Facilitation Directive (n 3), Art 1(1)(b).

[14] Consolidated Act of Provisions Concerning Immigration and the Condition of Foreigners (Testo unico sull'immigrazione, Legislative Decree No 286 of 25 July 1998, Italy) Art 1.

[15] UN General Assembly, 'Protocol against the Smuggling of Migrants by Land, Sea and Air: Supplementing the United Nations Convention against Transnational Organized Crime, (2000) UN Doc A/RES/55/25, Art 6(1) ('UN Smuggling Protocol'); Mitsilegas (n 5) 78.

[16] UN Smuggling Protocol (n 15), Art 6(1).

[17] Facilitation Directive (n 3), Art 1(2).

Indeed, the Facilitation Directive allows Member States to include an exemption[18] in their national implementing laws, without, however, obliging them to include such an exemption.[19] Very few states have implemented the optional clause, which explains the rise in prosecutions of civil society organisations offering rescue at sea.[20] The lack of a mandatory provision and instead an invitation for Member States to act at their discretion arguably constitutes a limited attempt to comply with international law. The provision falls short of international law *requiring* Member States to provide for a humanitarian exemption. Still, the existence of this option in the operative part of the Directive indicates that the restriction of fundamental rights in question is not necessary for the fulfilment of migration control or border protection goals. At the same time, Article 83 of the Treaty on the Functioning of the European Union (TFEU) grants powers to approximate criminal laws by establishing *minimum* and *not maximum* rules concerning the definition of criminal offences, and the EU legislator has no power under the Treaties to decriminalise. Therefore, there is a broader constitutional limitation possibly preventing the introduction of a mandatory exemption that would act as a maximum rule and limit for Member States when transposing the Directive.

12.3 THE TURNING POINT OF *KINSA* LITIGATION

At a time when criminalisation of solidarity has been on the rise[21] and while proposals for reform[22] had not, at that point, materialised, the litigation in *Kinsa* constitutes an important judicial development bringing well-reported fundamental rights concerns into the judicial arena. Responding to a request for a preliminary reference lodged by the Bologna court in Italy, the CJEU held, in a ground-breaking and much-expected ruling, delivered on 3 June 2025, that the conduct of a person bringing third-country national minors under their care into the territory of a Member State without authorisation does not fall within the scope of Article 1(1)(a) of the Facilitation Directive, regarding the crime of facilitating unauthorised entry. According to the ruling, this provision must be read under the light of Articles 7, 24, and 52(1) of the Charter to preclude national legislation criminalising as facilitation of entry such conduct of a parent.[23] The following section delves into the case, specifically showcasing the harmful effect

[18] ibid, Art 1(2).
[19] ibid.
[20] Carrera et al (n 5) 36–42.
[21] Council of Europe Commissioner for Human Rights, 'Protecting the Defenders Ending Repression of Human Rights Defenders Assisting Refugees, Asylum Seekers and Migrants in Europe' (Recommendation, CommHR (2024)11), https://rm.coe.int/recommendation-protecting-the-defenders-ending-repression-of-human-rig/1680ae9b1c.
[22] Carrera et al (n 5).
[23] '[T]hose articles preclude national legislation criminalising such conduct' *Kinsa* (n 7), para 73.

of ambiguity, before exploring the proposed reforms that are still, at the time of writing, being deliberated by the legislators. Indeed, the European Commission tabled a reform proposal soon after the preliminary question was lodged.[24] Therefore, the ruling can influence the ongoing legislative deliberations.[25]

12.3.1 The Facts

The case concerns the prosecution of a Congolese woman (OB) for the facilitation of the unauthorised entry of her minor daughter and niece. On 28 August 2019, OB was arrested at Bologna airport after attempting to pass through border controls with false documents for herself, her minor daughter and minor niece. Proceedings were brought against her for the offence of facilitating the unauthorised entry of third-country nationals,[26] in conjunction with the offence of holding false identity documents.[27] The arrest was pursuant to Italian law that prohibits any act aimed at facilitating the entry of an undocumented foreigner implementing the Facilitation Directive.[28] OB stated that she had fled her country of origin to escape the death threats imposed upon her and her family by her former partner, and that she exercises care over both her daughter and her niece, whose mother had died.

The referring court asked the CJEU to determine whether the Facilitators Package, as well as the Italian legislation implementing it,[29] are compatible with the principle of proportionality set out in Article 52(1) of the Charter, read in conjunction with the right to personal liberty and the right to property referred to in Articles 6 and 17, as well as the rights to life and physical integrity referred to in Articles 2 and 3, the right to asylum referred to in Article 18, and respect for family life referred to in Article 7. The applicant criticised the EU legislator for disregarding the principle of legality of criminal offences and penalties, enshrined in Article 49(1) of the Charter, in its requirements relating to the clarity and foreseeability of criminal law.[30] The referring judge argued that the criminalisation of humanitarian activities in Italian legislation implementing the Facilitators Package fails to respect the principle of proportionality.

[24] *Kinsa* (n 7).

[25] Valsamis Mitsilegas, 'Reforming EU Criminal Law on the Facilitation of Unauthorised Entry: The New Commission Proposal in the Light of the Kinshasa Litigation' (2024) 15 *New Journal of European Criminal Law* 3.

[26] Consolidated Act of Provisions concerning Immigration and the Condition of Foreigners (Testo unico sull'immigrazione, Legislative Decree No 286 of 25 July 1998, Italy) Art 1.

[27] *Codice Penale* (Italian Criminal Code), Art 497-bis.

[28] Facilitators Package (n 3), Art 1(1) a.

[29] Art 12 of the Consolidated Law on Immigration, Legislative Decree No 286 of 25 July 1998 (n 26).

[30] *Kinsa* (n 7).

12.3.2 Opinion of AG de la Tour

On 18 June 2024, the Court completed its hearing on the *Kinsa* preliminary question, and, on 7 November 2024, Advocate General de la Tour issued his opinion.[31] He opined that the Facilitation Directive complies with the principle of legality in Article 49(1) of the Charter considering that the Directive is being implemented by Member States. In this respect, he deemed the Directive to be sufficiently clear for the purpose that it serves, as it is Member States when transposing it that should ensure that the domestic law, which actually creates criminal liability, is compliant with the principles of legality in criminal law and proportionality.

Although it is true that the Directive itself does not create criminal liability, it does set the scope within which Member States can create criminal liability in their respective criminal transposing legislation by establishing minimum rules. EU criminal law is bound to adhere to principles enshrined in the Charter, so it is disappointing that the Opinion does not capture this as an opportunity to urge for legal certainty.

The Court has often highlighted in its case law the significance, of the principle of legality of criminal offences and penalties in its requirements relating to the foreseeability, precision and non-retroactivity of the applicable criminal law.[32] Besides, a two-stage, EU and national, legality check must serve as an additional guarantee.[33] For example, in *Intertanko and Others*, not only did the Court not deny the application of the principle of legality of criminal offences and penalties to Directives, but it also held that the principle is additionally binding on national law. Yet, the opinion does not come completely as a surprise as it aligns with a previous restrictive approach of the CJEU on the principle of legality reminding that the test is ought to be performed at national stage.[34] The opinion prioritises criminal justice interests vis-a-vis a strict compliance of legal certainty in line with earlier case law.[35]

[31] Case C460/23, *Kinsa v OB Criminal proceedings brought by Procura della Repubblica presso il Tribunale di Bologna* [2024] EU:C:2024:941, Opinion of AG Collins ('Opinion in *Kinsa*').

[32] Case C42/17, *MAS and MB* [2017] EU:C:2017:936, paras 51–56 citing the following cases: Case C-500/10, *Belvedere Costruzioni* [2012] EU:C:2012:186, para 23; Case C-331/88, *Fedesa and Others* [1990] EU:C:1990:391, para 42; Case C-60/02, *X* [2004] EU:C:2004:10, para 63; Case C-303/05, *Advocaten voor de Wereld* [2007] EU:C:2007:261, para 49; Case C-72/15, *Rosneft* [2017] EU:C:2017:236, para 162.

[33] Maria Kaiafa-Gbandi, 'Approximation of Substantive Criminal Law Provisions in the EU and Fundamental Principles of Criminal Law' in Francesca Galli and Anne Weyembergh (eds), *Approximation of Substantive Criminal Law in the EU – The Way Forward* (Éditions de l'Université de Bruxelles, 2013).

[34] Case C303/05, *Advocaten voor de Wereld v Leden van de Ministerraad* [2007] EU:C:2007:261. Here, the Court held that the abolition of double criminality in the Framework Decision on the European Arrest Warrant and the Surrender Procedures is in line with both the principle of legality in criminal law and the principle of non-discrimination.

[35] Case C-105/03, *Criminal proceedings against Maria Pupino* [2005] ECR I-05285, EU:C:2005:386; For a comprehensive and systematic review of the principle of legality in EU criminal law, see Christina Peristeridou, *The Principle of Legality in European Criminal Law* (Intersentia, 2015)

However, the double yardstick of legality check at both levels is useful as long as it applied as a guarantee rather than as an opportunity for escaping the check at either level. The opinion, in this regard, fully entrusting the legality check to Member States, does not make full use of the two-stage legality check. Indeed, a Directive only sets minimum rules and does allow a space for manoeuvre for Member States, but they also need to ensure that legal certainty will not be compromised, at least as far as this minimum degree of definition is concerned.

AG de la Tour, moreover, opined that the criminalisation of facilitating unauthorised immigration is not contrary to the principle of proportionality of criminal offences and penalties enshrined in Article 49(3) of the Charter, considering the risks that smuggled persons are exposed to even by acts that might appear to be performed in the name of solidarity, which makes it necessary to adopt a broad scope of criminalisation.[36] AG de la Tour suggests that expansive criminalisation is compensated by a balancing act that national courts and authorities are expected to exercise when considering whether a person is acting out of humanity, necessity, or motivated by criminal intent to gain financial or material benefit.[37]

According to settled case law, Member States must exercise their powers in compliance with EU law and its general principles that prescribe that 'the severity of a penalty must correspond to the seriousness of the infringement concerned', ie cardinal proportionality,[38] in line with Article 52(1) of the Charter and the principle of proportionality of penalties in Article 49(3) of the Charter.[39] Member States' latitude is thus limited by the prohibition on providing for inappropriate and disproportionate penalties.[40] In fact, 'the fact that those provisions [of the Directive] must be transposed is not such as to call into question the unconditional nature of the requirement relating to the appropriate and proportionate nature of penalties'.[41] The Opinion does not engage with the proportionality of criminalisation itself as prompted by the request but rather with the proportionality of sanction leaving the preliminary question unanswered.

who raises 'questions, inconsistencies and lacunae' in the fragments of legality as developing in EU criminal law.

[36] Opinion in *Kinsa* (n 31), paras 76–96.

[37] ibid, para 90.

[38] Peter Asp, *The Substantive Criminal Law Competence of the EU: Towards an Area of Freedom, Security & Justice* (Jure, 2013) 199.

[39] Case C-544/19, *Ecotex Bulgaria LTD v Teritorialna direktsia na Natsionalnata agentsia za prihodite* [2021] EU:C:2021:100, para 97; Case C40/21, *TAC v Agenţia Naţională de Integritate* [2023] ECLI:EU:C:2023:367, paras 33–34.

[40] Opinion in *Kinsa* (n 31) para 94.

[41] ibid, para 93; Case C–205/20, *Bezirkshauptmannschaft Hartberg-Fürstenfeld* [2022] EU:C:2022:168, para 26.

12.3.3 CJEU Ruling

The Court, in its turn, rephrased the question to limit the analysis around the specific circumstances of the individuals concerned. Departing from the approach of both the referring judge and the AG, the ruling engaged with the question of whether the national criminalisation in question is proportionate, in the specific circumstances at least of this case and found that the scope of the law must not include the conduct in question. So, it did recognise that criminalising such conduct would disproportionally interfere with the rights to family life and the right of the child, thereby violating the principle of proportionality under Article 52(1) of the Charter and excluded these cases from its scope, avoiding a broader conflict within EU law. The ruling also highlighted that such measures countering migrant-smuggling must not breach the right to asylum,[42] which was relevant considering the mother's subsequent asylum application and the principle of non-penalisation of international refugee law.[43] The Court additionally held that the mother must not be prosecuted for attempting an unauthorised entry as the principle of non-penalisation affords putative refugees protection from prosecution.

The ruling, while not squarely addressing the broader issue of criminalising solidarity, is 'a candle in the dark',[44] as it calls for the interpretation of the current but also of the reform Directive to be aligned with fundamental rights. Member States cannot rely on the Directive's minimum-harmonisation character to justify additional criminalisation that will not comply with the Charter, since *Kinsa* confirms that the Charter constrains national measures implementing EU law. The ruling is arguably encouraging for national courts to pose more requests for preliminary references to further clarify the interpretation of the Directive. This focus on the prospective check of proportionality, despite being limited on the specific circumstances of the case, is significant, as it can have broad implications for the compliance check of criminalisation beyond the confines of this case.[45] Indeed, the chosen approach that is distinct from the opinion's approach focusing on retrospective cardinal proportionality, at the time that a reform is deliberated, might appear as a call for the legislator and the national prosecutors and courts to be more careful of prospective proportionality of criminalisation. This is quite a significant prompt considering the ongoing reform deliberation, which is discussed next.

[42] Art 18 of the Charter.

[43] Art 31 Refugee Convention.

[44] Steve Peers, 'A Candle in the Dark: the CJEU Rules against Criminalising Parents for Smuggling their Children' EU Law Analysis (2025), https://eulawanalysis.blogspot.com/2025/06/a-candle-in-dark-cjeu-rules-against.html.

[45] Stefano Zirulia, 'The Legacy of Kinsa: Using Proportionality to Limit the Criminalisation of Solidarity' Verfassungsblog (26 June 2025), https://verfassungsblog.de/kinsa-judgment-proportionality.

12.4 PROPOSED REFORM, PERSISTING ISSUES AND THE WAY FORWARD FOR COUNTER-SMUGGLING LAW

Until 2023 the Commission had only adopted non-binding guidelines for the implementation of the Facilitation Package.[46] However, this changed shortly after the *Kinsa* litigation started. On 28 November 2023, four months after the submission of the *Kinsa* reference, the European Commission presented a package of legislative proposals to reform the EU legal framework on migrant smuggling. The package consists of a proposal for a revised Facilitation Directive,[47] and a proposal for a regulation to enhance police cooperation and strengthen Europol's role in the fight against migrant smuggling and human trafficking.[48]

At a policy level, the Commission had also adopted a renewed EU action plan against migrant smuggling for the period 2021–25,[49] following up on an earlier EU action plan against migrant smuggling,[50] which was adopted in May 2015. Considering these political proclamations, the adoption of a proposal on 28 November 2023 does not come as a surprise. What is interesting, though, is that the Commission acted straight after the *Kinsa* preliminary question was lodged in July 2023. The proposed amendments to a number of provisions, focused primarily on criminal offences (Articles 3 and 4), penalties for natural persons (Article 6), liability of and sanctions for legal persons (Articles 7 and 8), jurisdiction (Article 12), prevention (Article 13), investigation (Article 16) and data collection (Article 17).

The proposal continues to criminalise the facilitation of irregular migration but there are also some welcome changes. The necessity for change is finally acknowledged and this, on its own, is a shift in the Commission's stance.[51] The Preamble to the proposed Directive specifically acknowledges the need for precise and detailed definition of the offence. What is also welcome is the presence of an express *actus reus* constituent element that there must be a financial/material benefit, aligning the offence with the UN Smuggling Protocol.[52] The Directive also introduces several aggravated offences (eg offences committed as part of an organised criminal group, causing serious harm or endangering life or health, or causing death). The expansion in the proposed Directive of the jurisdiction of Member States to cases in which the facilitation of unauthorised entry

[46] European Commission, 'Communication from the Commission, Commission Guidance on the implementation of EU rules on definition and prevention of the facilitation of unauthorised entry, transit and residence' [2020] OJ C323/1.

[47] Facilitation Directive Proposal (n 6).

[48] Europol Regulation Proposal (n 6).

[49] European Commission, 'EU Action Plan against Migrant Smuggling (2015 - 2020)' COM (2015) 285 final; European Commission, 'A Renewed EU Action Plan against Migrant Smuggling (2021–2025)' COM(2021) 591 final.

[50] European Commission COM(2015) 285 final (n 49).

[51] Facilitation Directive Proposal (n 6) Preamble, Recital 6.

[52] Arts 3(a) and 6(1) UN Smuggling Protocol (n 15).

into the EU fails and third-country nationals lose their lives is also welcome. The Preamble also emphasises that the Directive does not seek to criminalise third-country nationals for the fact of being smuggled, for helping family members, for providing humanitarian aid or for meeting basic human needs, when such assistance is given in accordance with the law.[53]

However, there are several shortcomings within the proposal. The targeted substitute impact assessment drafted by Moreno-Lax notes the misalignment of the proposal with both EU and international legal obligations.[54] Most importantly, the assessment highlights 'definitional issues, the lack of sufficient human rights safeguards, and the absence of a clear distinction between facilitation offences and the legitimate provision of services and humanitarian assistance'. These issues are directly linked to key legal principles of criminalisation such as legality, legal certainty, proportionality and *ultima ratio*.

12.4.1 International Legal Standards and Fundamental Rights Safeguards

First of all, the broad concept of facilitation of irregular migration adopted by the proposal by way of facilitating entry, transit or residence does not align with the specific terms of the universal definition as provided by the UN Smuggling Protocol that specifically refers to 'the procurement' of 'illegal entry' that is 'committed intentionally' and 'in order to obtain' a financial or other material benefit[55] and as part of an 'organised criminal group'.[56] The twofold objective of the UN Smuggling Protocol is to 'prevent and combat the smuggling of migrants, as well as to promote cooperation among States Parties to that end', and to do so 'while protecting the rights of smuggled migrants'.[57] The EU legislator must address this inconsistency and take an approach that targets acts of organised crime of which migrants themselves are victims.

Moreover, the financial gain requirement is now present only in some respect, thus retaining a leeway for Member States to criminalise acts that are not conducted for the purpose of gaining a financial benefit, such as where acts of facilitation are highly likely to cause serious harm to a person even though conducted without financial or material benefit,[58] or in cases of 'public instigation' of third-country nationals, for instance through the internet, to enter, transit across or stay irregularly in the EU.[59] It is worth noting that Article 31 of the 1951 Geneva Convention affords migrants who are also asylum-seekers

[53] Facilitation Directive Proposal (n 6), Preamble, Recital 7.

[54] European Parliament, 'Commission Proposal for a Revised Facilitation Directive: Targeted Substitute Impact Assessment' (EPRS Publications Office, 2025).

[55] UN Palermo Protocol (n 15) Arts 3(a) and 6(1).

[56] ibid, Art 4.

[57] ibid, Art 2.

[58] Facilitation Directive Proposal (n 6), Art 3(1)(b).

[59] ibid, Art 3(2).

immunity against penalisation for their irregular entry, recognising the difficulty they might have to obtain documentation and make their way through a legal route.[60] The text of the proposed legislation as presented by the Commission does not seem to recognise such basic principles of international refugee law including in the asylum *acquis*.

In addition, the proposal as it stands does not align with the international law of the sea and the duty to rescue,[61] which is important for the maritime context of anti-smuggling laws. According to Article 98 of the UN Convention on the Law of the Sea (UNCLOS), ratified by the EU and all Member States,[62] 'every State' is obliged to require all ships flying its flag 'to render assistance to any person found at sea in danger of being lost' and 'to proceed to the rescue of persons in distress'. The scope of application benefits 'any person' including migrants.[63] Search and Rescue (SAR) obligations must be considered by the EU and its Member States when formulating the anti-smuggling legal framework, so it does not clash with obligations of shipmasters arising under the duty to rescue.

Furthermore, the humanitarian exemption has equally not been included in the body of the law, as a binding provision, except for in a preambular non-binding recital. As a result, there is no distinction between facilitation offences and the provision of humanitarian assistance, and subsequently no protection of the latter that can fall within the scope of criminalisation. Besides, as discussed above with regard to the proposal's misalignment with the UN Smuggling Protocol, the requirement of a financial gain or other material benefit as part of the crime of facilitation vanishes in some undefined cases.[64] As noted by the Advocate General in the Opinion in *Kinsa*, facilitation offences are 'defined objectively' and 'irrespective of [the] person's motives' without a distinction between exploitative and humanitarian motifs, which opens the Pandora box of policing civil society.[65]

Recital 7 is arguably not sufficient as a safeguard against authorities poised to prosecute humanitarian assistance, and in the current climate of populism and anti-immigration politics an unambiguous and clear legal provision with a mandatory and binding effect is necessary. The inclusion of a mandatory

[60] John Trajer, Gillian Kane, Marta Minetti and Sarah Craig, 'Input for the Report on the Implementation of the Non-Punishment Principle' [2021] QUB Human Rights Centre, https://pureadmin.qub.ac.uk/ws/portalfiles/portal/231110346/Queen_s_University_Belfast_Human_Rights_Centre_HTRN_Submission.UNSRT.pdf.

[61] The UN Convention on the Law of the Sea (UNCLOS) [1982] 1833 UNTS 3; International Convention on Maritime Search and Rescue, [1979] 1405 UNTS 119 ('SAR Convention'); International Convention for the Safety of Life at Sea, [1974] 1184 UNTS 278 ('SOLAS Convention').

[62] The Council of the European Union, 'Council Decision of 23 March 1998 concerning the conclusion by the European Community of the United Nations Convention of 10 December 1982 on the Law of the Sea and the Agreement of 28 July 1994 relating to the implementation of Part XI thereof: (98/392/EC)' [1998] OJ L179/1.

[63] SAR Convention (n 61) annex, para 2.1.10.

[64] Where there is a possibility of causing 'serious harm' (Art 3(1)(b)) or in cases of 'public instigation' (Art 3(2)) See Facilitation Directive Proposal (n 6).

[65] Opinion in *Kinsa* (n 31) paras 40, 46.

humanitarian exception, as currently proposed by the European Parliament,[66] excluding acts of solidarity is also advocated for by the UN Special Rapporteur on Human Rights Defenders.[67] Indeed, although the Preamble in Recital 7 highlights that there is no intention to over-criminalise or indeed 'criminalise third-country nationals for the fact of being smuggled, for helping family members, for providing humanitarian aid or for meeting basic human needs, when such assistance is given in accordance with the law', this is merely a preambular proclamation and effectively non-binding for states. The Preamble could positively inform a reinterpretation of the law, but with the current climate of policing civil society and anti-migration sentiments across Europe, this is not a sufficient safeguard.

12.4.2 Criminal Law Principles

Having assessed the proposed legislation considering several international legal safeguards, this section turns to key principles of criminal law. In addition to the noted departure from international legal standards, the proposed law does not sit well with the principle of legality in criminal law that requires for criminal law to be well defined. The terms 'serious harm' and 'public instigation' should be defined or removed, as otherwise they could be used to criminalise human rights defenders. This is a Trojan horse to maintain ambiguity leading to implementation discrepancies. Not surprisingly, *lex certa* is offered as the justification for proposed amendments on three separate occasions by the Committee on Civil Liberties, Justice and Home Affairs (LIBE) in its draft report delivered on 26 March 2025.[68] The ambiguity might also expand the mandate of the European Police Office (Europol), as the package includes a proposal for a regulation to enhance police cooperation and strengthen Europol's role in the fight against migrant smuggling and human trafficking.[69]

The conformity of measures with the principle of proportionality should also be assessed.[70] Proportionality is a general principle of EU law that criminal

[66] European Parliament Committee on Civil Liberties, Justice and Home Affairs, 'Amendments 111–586: Draft Report on the proposal for a directive laying down minimum rules to prevent and counter the facilitation of unauthorised entry, transit and stay in the Union and replacing Council Directive 2002/90/EC and Council Framework Decision 2002/946 JHA' (30 April 2025) PE773.119v01-00.

[67] UN Special Rapporteur on Human Rights Defenders, *Position Paper: on the EU Commission's proposed Directive to update the EU legal framework on people smuggling* (February 2024).

[68] European Parliament Committee on Civil Liberties, Justice and Home Affairs, 'Draft Report 2023/0439(COD) on the proposal for a directive of the European Parliament and of the Council Laying down minimum rules to prevent and counter the facilitation of unauthorised entry, transit and stay in the Union, and replacing Council Directive 2002/90/EC and Council Framework Decision 2002/946 JHA (26 March 2025) COM(2023) 0755 – C9-0430/2023 – 2023/0439(COD).

[69] As defined in the UN Smuggling Protocol (n 15).

[70] Ermioni Xanthopoulou, *Fundamental Rights and Mutual Trust in the Area of Freedom, Security and Justice: A Role for Proportionality?* (Hart, 2020) ch 3.

sanctions must respect.[71] The proportionality of a sanction or a penalty must be assessed by reference to the importance of its objective. The sanction must not go beyond what is necessary to achieve its aim. Proportionality is rooted in the constitutional traditions of Member States, enshrined in the Charter and recognised by the CJEU.[72] In this respect, criminalisation of smuggling must not go beyond what is necessary for the law to achieve, which reflects prospective proportionality with regards to criminalisation itself.

One wonders whether the employment of criminal law only serves objectives of criminal law. The legal basis used, Article 83(2) TFEU, refers to the effective implementation of a Union policy in an area which has been subject to harmonisation measures, rather than Article 83(1) TFEU that would refer to addressing major security threats including organised crime, which would be more suitable under the UN Smuggling Protocol. Thus, the justification of the employment of criminal law is linked to the effectiveness of a Union policy. It appears that criminal law is here instrumentalised to achieve migration control objectives. Still, the effectiveness of using criminal sanctions in this respect has been challenged.[73] Essentiality can also be put into question, as criminal sanctions are not always essential to ensure the effective implementation of EU law, with non-criminal sanctions being more appropriate where empirical relevant proof justifying criminalisation as effective is missing.[74] In fact, the Commission asserted that the Package 'has not significantly contributed to reducing irregular migration' and that it has had 'little deterrent effect'.[75] In the absence of an evaluation report ordered by the Commission, the essentiality question remains open.

Proportionality is also significant for the offence's penalty range. In the realm of penology, sentencing theories underpin the choice of a form of sanctions over another and the definition of their intensity. Deterrence theories would see harsh penalties as dissuading potential offenders from committing a certain act while emphasising the importance of the public interest in relation to what is harmed. Proportionality would be relevant to demarcate the sanction in question so that it is just and proportionate to the cause of harm. In particular, there are several dimensions of proportionality when considering penalties and, of course,

[71] Takis Tridimas, 'Wreaking the Wrongs: Balancing Rights and the Public Interest the EU Way' (2023) 29 *Columbia Journal of European Law*85.

[72] Charter of Fundamental Rights of the European Union [2012] OJ C326/391, Art 49; CJEU, Case C-42/17 *Criminal proceedings against MAS and MB* EU:C:2017:936; CJEU, Case C-534/16 *Finančné riaditeľstvo Slovenskej republiky v BB construct sro* EU:C:2017:820; CJEU, Case C-218/15 *Gianpaolo Paoletti and Others v Procura della Repubblica* EU:C:2016:748.

[73] Constanza Di Francesco Maesa, '(In)Effectiveness of Criminal Sanctions as Regards Irregular Immigrants' (2018) 8 *European Criminal Law Review* 5.

[74] Jacob Öberg, 'Do We Really Need Criminal Sanctions for the Enforcement of EU Law?' (2014) 5 *New Journal of European Criminal Law* 370, 376.

[75] European Commission, Commission Staff Working Document, 'REFIT Evaluation of the EU legal framework against facilitation of unauthorised entry, transit and residence: the Facilitators Package (Directive 2002/90/EC and Framework Decision 2002/946/JHA)' SWD(2017) 117 final, 18–19.

distinctive functions of proportionality in distinct contexts.[76] Öberg conceptualises proportionality that is relevant to criminal sanctions in EU law, ie the retrospective version as enshrined in Article 49 of the Charter that requires that 'the severity of penalties must not be disproportionate to the criminal offence'. Indeed, a proportionality check could serve as a guardrail for preventing the imposition of excessive penalties.

The penalty scheme of the proposal[77] appears to be exceedingly harsh. The Commission asserts that the Directive 'ensure[s] the proportionality of the criminal penalties' and is 'in line with the principle of proportionality of criminal penalties as enshrined in Article 49(3) of the Charter'.[78] However, measures such as the 'permanent' disqualification and closure of premises, 'withdrawal of permits or authorisations' to conduct activities, the confiscation of vehicles (including rescue vessels) are a few examples of disproportionate measures. This would not have been the case if the law offered certainty in terms of its definitional scope and merely targeted exploitative and abusive criminal organisation networks of smugglers. Instead, when the vague scope of the law leads to targeting non-governmental organisations (NGOs), family members, and migrants facilitating their own unauthorised entry, often for the purpose of seeking international protection, the penalties appear to be harsh.[79]

The Advocate General's opinion in *Kinsa* has for the first time recognised that the Facilitation Package criminalises solidarity, which is an example of disproportionality.[80] The CJEU has ruled that 'the principle of proportionality requires that measures adopted by European Union institutions do not exceed the limits of what is appropriate and necessary in order to attain the objectives legitimately pursued by the legislation in question' and that 'when there is a choice between several appropriate measures recourse must be had to the least onerous'.[81] The obligation to impose effective, proportionate and dissuasive penalties is well settled in the CJEU case law[82] and requires that resort to coercive powers must be confined within the limits set by the principle of proportionality.[83] Besides, an additional dimension of proportionality is that the sanction imposed must be

[76] Jacob Öberg, 'Conceptualising Proportionality and Criminal Sanctions in EU Law: Three Different Visions' in Lorenzo Grossio, Stefano Montaldo and Valsamis Mitsilegas (eds), *Proportionality of Criminal Penalties in EU Law* (Hart, 2025); Susan Easton, and Christine Piper, *Sentencing and Punishment*, 5th edn (Oxford University Press, 2023).

[77] Facilitation Directive (n 3) Arts 6 and 8.

[78] Facilitation Directive Proposal (n 6) explanatory memorandum, 8.

[79] European Parliament (n 54).

[80] '[T]he EU legislature did indeed intend to define a general infringement, covering all actions intended to facilitate unauthorised entry into the territory of a Member State, including where such acts are committed disinterestedly, out of altruism, compassion or solidarity, for humanitarian reasons or because of the existence of family ties': Opinion in *Kinsa* (n 31) para 46.

[81] Case C-283/11, *Sky Österreich GmbH v Österreichischer Rundfunk* EU:C:2013:28, parz 50.

[82] Case C-68/88, *Commission of the European Communities v Hellenic Republic* EU:C:1989:339.

[83] Grossio et al (n 76).

commensurate to the gravity of the offence as prescribed by the Charter[84] and the Court's case law.[85]

In the same spirit, there is no justification of criminalisation as *ultima ratio* meaning that criminal law is the right avenue of regulation as compared to administrative law, for example. This seems to be a typical example of 'crimmigration'[86] where criminal law is used to foster objectives of immigration and border control. The lack of an impact assessment ordered by the European Commission does not inspire confidence in the justifications provided. Equally, the proposal does not focus at all on protecting the rights of people on the move, while ensuring safe pathways as proposed by the Committee on Migration, International Protection and Economic Co-operation (PACE), in recent deliberations regarding the adoption of a new Council of Europe instrument that takes a much-needed dual approach to tackling migrant smuggling, that both focuses on international co-operation to ensure safe and legal migration pathways while also cracking down on cross-border criminal groups.[87]

12.4.3 EU Constitutional Challenges and *Kinsa*

A key issue at the heart of the debate pertains to EU constitutional law and a broader constraint regarding the limits of EU law vis-a-vis national law. In principle, a Directive cannot require Member States to decriminalise or not to criminalise, and this presents a broader constitutional challenge for EU criminal law. In the absence of a clear legal basis under the TFEU to legitimise decriminalisation, it is not clear whether a Directive can require Member States not to render acts illegal under their domestic criminal law. Such absence highlights a broader structural constitutional difficulty when challenging the nature of the humanitarian exemption as non-mandatory. Article 83 TFEU only provides for an approximated floor rather than a ceiling. This allows Member States some room for manoeuvre and offers a constitutional exegesis of the drafting of the Directive without a mandatory exemption that might be seen as encroaching upon Member States' competence on shaping their degree of criminalisation to the extent not shaped by EU minimum rules under Article 83.[88]

[84] Art 49(4) Charter.

[85] eg Case C-743/24, *Alchaster II EU:C:2025:230*.

[86] Juliet P Stumpf, 'The Process is the Punishment in Crimmigration Law' in Katja Franko Aas and Mary Bosworth (eds), *The Borders of Punishment: Migration, Citizenship, and Social Exclusion* (Oxford University Press, 2013) 58–75.

[87] Lord Simon Russel, *Setting out New Ways to Tackle Migrant Smuggling, Proposes a Council of Europe Instrument* (PACE committee report, 2024).

[88] Konstantinos Zoumpoulakis, 'Approximation of Criminal Sanctions in the European Union: A Wild Goose Chase?' (2022) 13 *New Journal of European Criminal Law* 333, 335.

Nevertheless, as Member States have signed and ratified the UN Smuggling Protocol, they are obliged to exempt humanitarian acts of rescue or compassionate acts of accompanying a family member that have no element of profiteering. Considering that the EU has also signed the UN Smuggling Protocol and that the Charter is a binding instrument enshrining an array of relevant rights, as analysed above, a secondary EU legislation, even when not requiring Member States to decriminalise, must be interpreted in a way that aligns with the Charter and international law. An article stating such mandatory obligations in clear terms would be preferable to the current optional exemption as it would at least provide clearer guidance to national judiciary, if domestic national legislators choose to ignore their states' obligations to uphold the UN Smuggling Protocol. The Directive might not itself be able to oblige Member States to decriminalise or criminalise less, but it can set clearly the framework by which both EU and Member States are bound to respect as an interpretative guide.

Besides, the decriminalisation potential of EU law is now well recognised.[89] The CJEU had early confirmed that EU law can place limits on the application of national criminal law, where the latter disproportionately interfered with the effective exercise of rights to free movement.[90] In *El-Dridi*,[91] the Court even confirmed this limiting potential of EU law for national criminalisation of immigration offences, this time to ensure the effectiveness of the EU Returns Directive, an instrument of immigration enforcement. The decriminalisation effect of the rulings in *Cassati and El-Dridi* is linked to effectiveness, and by analogy the effectiveness of Charter rights could be invoked before national courts.[92]

In a similar vein, the ruling of *Kinsa* presented an opportunity for the Court to set limits on disproportionality and potentially expand the decriminalisation potential of EU law. *Kinsa* has revealed a potential effect of decriminalisation through a judicial refining of the interpretation of secondary EU law provisions. The message of *Kinsa* ruling was clear in that 'those articles preclude national legislation criminalising such conduct'.[93] Indeed, the Court held in *Kinsa* that when transposing Article 1(1)(a) of Directive 2002/90, Member States may not establish, in national law, rules that would go beyond the scope of the general offence of facilitating unauthorised entry in breach of Articles 7 and 24 and Article 52(1) of the Charter.[94] Therefore, any new legislation must not ignore this.

[89] Valsamis Mitsilegas, 'From Overcriminalisation to Decriminalisation. The Many Faces of Effectiveness in European Criminal Law' (2014) 5 *New Journal of European Criminal Law* 415.

[90] Case 203/ 80, *Casati* [1981] EU:C:1981:261, para 27.

[91] Case C- 61/11 PPU, *El- Dridi* [2011] EU:C:2011:268.

[92] Valsamis Mitsilegas, 'Reforming the "Facilitators' Package" through the Kinsa litigation: Legality, Effectiveness and taking International Law into account' (2024) 3 *Eurojus* 155, 159.

[93] *Kinsa* (n 7) para 73.

[94] ibid, para 71.

12.4.4 A Laborious Legislative Process

At the time of writing, a new law is not yet adopted and deliberations are ongoing. Several reasoned opinions were issued by Member States' national parliaments such as by the Netherlands Senate, Czech Chamber of Deputies, Italian Chamber of Deputies, Czech Senate, Romanian Chamber of Deputies and the Spanish Parliament.[95] The Working Party on Judicial Cooperation in Criminal Matters (COPEN) examined the proposal under the Spanish, Belgian and Hungarian Presidency and, on 29 November 2024, the Council adopted its own position.[96]

In its turn, the Council's proposed version simplifies the main criminal offence by removing the provision about causing serious harm as well as the 'public instigation' offence. The offence is then defined as assistance to illegal entry or stay, with a financial benefit element. However, the Council version maintains the absence of a humanitarian exemption and clearly reserves the discretion of Member States to criminalise solidarity acts, which is justified in the Preamble in the name of 'interests of enhancing the effectiveness of the fight against migrant smugglers. Indeed, the Council version emphasises the role of the Directive in setting minimum rules of criminalisation.[97]

As far as the European Parliament is concerned, LIBE has the lead responsibility. On 23 January 2024, the Commission presented the proposal to the LIBE committee members, who received it with reservations that point to several shortcomings. No impact assessment was completed for either proposal which sparked criticisms, in response to which, the Commission produced an analytical staff working document for each of the proposals in spring 2024[98] and a

[95] Czech Chamber of Deputies, 'Contribution on COM(2023) 755' (21 February 2024) Procedure 2023/0439(COD); Spanish Parliament, 'Contribution on COM(2023) 755' (18 March 2024) Procedure 2023/0439(COD); Czech Senate, 'Contribution on COM(2023)755' (18 March 2024) Procedure 2023/0439(COD); Netherlands Senate, 'Contribution on COM(18 March 2024) 755' (2024) Procedure 2023/0439(COD); Italian Chamber of Deputies, 'Contribution on COM(2023) 755' (27 March 2024) Procedure 2023/0439(COD); Romanian Chamber of Deputies, 'Contribution on COM(2023) 755' (15 May 2024) Procedure 2023/0439(COD); Netherlands Senate, 'Contribution on COM(2023)0755', (24 January 2025) Procedure 2023/0439(COD).

[96] Council of the European Union, 'Proposal for a Directive of the European Parliament and of the Council laying down minimum rules to prevent and counter the facilitation of unauthorised entry, transit and stay in the Union, and replacing Council Directive 2002/90/EC and Council Framework Decision 2002/946 JHA' [2024] ST-15916/1/24.

[97] ibid, Preamble, Recital 6a. 'This Directive is an instrument of minimum harmonisation. As a consequence, Member States are free to adopt or maintain legislation providing for a broader incrimination than what is set out in this Directive, in the interests of enhancing the effectiveness of the fight against migrant smugglers.'

[98] European Commission, 'Analytical document accompanying the document Proposal for a Regulation on enhancing police cooperation in relation to the prevention, detection and investigation of migrant smuggling and trafficking in human beings, and on enhancing Europol's support to preventing and combating such crimes and amending Regulation (EU) 2016/794', SWD(2024) 94 final; European Commission, 'Analytical supporting document accompanying the proposal for a Directive laying down minimum rules to prevent and counter the facilitation of unauthorised entry,

supporting study on the implementation of the existing Package.[99] In March 2025, the European Parliamentary Research Service (EPRS) published a targeted substitute impact assessment, written by Professor Dr Violeta Moreno-Lax, in the absence of one delivered by the Commission.[100] This document is prepared for, and addressed to, the members and staff of the European Parliament as background material to assist them in their parliamentary work.

A draft report was issued on 26 March 2025 that welcomes the intention to modernise the law and align it with the UN Smuggling Protocol and includes several amendments to the proposed legislation,[101] with the aim of addressing persisting criticism. The Rapporteur welcomed the introduction of the financial or material gain to the definition of the criminal offence but noted the absence of an exemption for humanitarian assistance and in this respect proposed amendments. For example, Amendment 32 expressly includes the addition of a subparagraph in Article 3 that stipulates that 'The provision of "humanitarian assistance" shall not constitute a criminal offence.' The justification for this addition directly relies on the principle of legal certainty and the requirement of legality in criminal law. When 'establishing a criminal offence, it is necessary to allow an individual to ascertain whether their actions lead to criminal liability or not'.[102] Amendment 33 also adds a provision stating that 'Third country nationals shall not become liable under this Article for the sole fact of having been the object of the conduct set out in paragraph 1' which aims to protect smuggled migrants. Most of the proposed amendments of the European Parliament reflect the targeted substitute impact assessment that elaborately analyses persisting issues which, if left unaddressed, would risk the law's compliance with both international legal standards and criminal law principles. Parliament's thorough report is welcome and much needed under a pan-European climate of populism and deterrence permeating asylum and immigration law.[103]

---

transit and stay in the Union, and replacing Council Directive 2002/90/EC and Council Framework Decision 2002/946 JHA, SWD(2024) 134 ('Analytical supporting document').

[99] European Commission: Directorate-General for Migration and Home Affairs, Law and Policy Consulting and Milieu, Study supporting the implementation of the facilitators package: final report (Publications Office of the European Union. 2024) ('Milieu Study').

[100] European Parliament, 'Commission proposal for a revised Facilitation Directive: Targeted substitute impact assessment' (EPRS Publications Office, 2025).

[101] European Parliament Committee on Civil Liberties, Justice and Home Affairs, 'DRAFT REPORT 2023/0439(COD) on the proposal for a directive of the European Parliament and of the Council Laying down minimum rules to prevent and counter the facilitation of unauthorised entry, transit and stay in the Union, and replacing Council Directive 2002/90/EC and Council Framework Decision 2002/946 JHA (26 March 2025) COM(2023) 0755 – C9-0430/2023 – 2023/0439(COD).

[102] ibid, 26.

[103] Marta Minetti, 'The Facilitators Package, Penal Populism and the Rule of Law: Lessons from Italy' (2020) 11 (3) *New Journal of European Criminal Law* 335; Vladislava Stoyanova and Stijn Smet (eds), *Migrants' Rights, Populism and Legal Resilience in Europe* (Cambridge University Press, 2022) 118–38.

12.5 CONCLUSION: CRIMINALISING SOLIDARITY IN A POPULIST CONTEXT

The Facilitators' Package, both in its current and proposed reformed version, is an example of 'crimmigration', a term referring to the use of criminal law in the field of immigration. Criminal law is instrumentalised to control mobility and leads to policing civil society offering humanitarian assistance.[104] 'Crimmigration' is associated with the climate of populism whose shadow hangs over politics and policymaking. Borrowing from the methodological approach entitled 'law in context' would be a useful approach here to evaluate the social pressures that shape law-making.[105] Under this methodological lens, law is a product of society and is not autonomous from social tendencies. In the current widespread climate of populism in Europe, anti-immigration voices have infiltrated policymaking.

Criminalisation of solidarity is arguably connected to a populist turn in immigration law[106] and the policy of deterrence.[107] These are realised by a plethora of measures ranging from the elimination of safe and legal routes, the externalisation of immigration control, pushbacks and pullbacks to the prosecution, intimidation and weakening of civil society.[108] While a counter-smuggling law is designated to tackle migrant smugglers exploiting and abusing vulnerable people on the move, it has systematically been used to police and disempower civil society. Indeed, the prosecution of humanitarian acts of rescue appears to be on the rise.[109] There is an alarming increase of prosecution of NGOs that offer humanitarian assistance to irregular migrants including refugees who need rescue after crossing borders.[110] In 2023 alone, at least 117 individuals faced criminal or administrative proceedings for acting in solidarity with migrants[111] while in 2022 at least 102 individuals faced criminal or administrative proceedings for

[104] Stumpf (n 86); Valsamis Mitsilegas, 'The Criminalisation of Migration in the Law of the European Union. Challenging the Preventive Paradigm' in Gian Luigi Gatta, Valsamis Mitsilegas and Stefano Zirulia (eds), *Controlling Immigration Through Criminal Law. European and Comparative Perspectives on 'Crimmigration'* (Hart, 2021).

[105] Selznick (n 8) 177.

[106] Mohammad Nayyeri, 'Populism, Backlash Morality and Immigrants' (2025) 21 *International Journal of Law and Context* 58; Minetti (n 103).

[107] Matilde Rosina, *The Criminalisation of Irregular Migration in Europe: Globalisation, Deterrence, and Vicious Cycles* (Springer, 2022).

[108] Ermioni Xanthopoulou, 'Mapping EU Externalisation Devices through a Critical Eye' (2024) 26 *European Journal of Migration and Law* 108.

[109] Council of Europe Commissioner for Human Rights, 'Protecting the Defenders Ending repression of human rights defenders assisting refugees, asylum seekers and migrants in Europe' (Recommendation, CommHR(2024)11), www.ecoi.net/en/file/local/2106504/CommHR%282024%2911_Recommendation+on+Migration+HRD_EN.pdf.

[110] Carrera et al (n 5).

[111] Platform for International Cooperation on Undocumented Migrants, 'Cases of Criminalisation of Migration and Solidarity in the EU in 2023' (PICUM Briefing, 2024).

acts of solidarity with migrants.[112] The prosecution is widespread, ranging from acts of rescuing migrants at sea and photographing coastguard vessels to driving migrants by car or assisting them during a train ride, and even providing food and water.[113]

The recent proposal tabled by the European Commission for a new instrument to regulate the facilitation of unauthorised migration would require Member States to criminalise the facilitation of irregular entry only when it is carried out for profit or when conducted in a way that endangers human life. However, the proposal is still missing an explicit clause to exempt humanitarian assistance from criminal liability. On the contrary, the Parliament and civil society propose the clear introduction of a humanitarian exception due to persisting concerns about overcriminalisation, legality and proportionality. A major challenge is that the EU Treaties do not provide for a legal basis for decriminalisation. Instead, Article 83 TFEU provides the EU legislator power only for establishing minimum rules concerning the definition of the offence rather than maximum rules. Therefore, from an EU constitutional perspective, it transpires that a Directive itself cannot require Member States not to criminalise beyond the point of the Directive. Yet, both the EU and Member States are bound by their obligation to respect international law, and particularly the UN Smuggling Protocol, which specifically requires signatory parties not to criminalise humanitarian acts. So, unless a solution is found to bypass the constitutional constraints of Article 83 TFEU, signing the Treaty would risk being devoid of substantive effect.

The chapter contends that a reformed Directive must contain a provision that will clearly refer to these international law obligations not to criminalise humanitarian or compassionate acts of facilitation, to serve at least as an interpretative guide for national legislators and judicial authorities. On a positive note, the Court's ruling in *Kinsa* serves as a shinning beacon in the dark times of populism, as it confirms that the Charter may be relied on for a rights-oriented interpretation of the new Directive. Article 52(1) in tandem with *Kinsa* could be invoked before trying courts to challenge the prosecution of a conduct that is merely of humanitarian nature. At times of populist penal agenda, where criminal law is used as a tool of migration deterrence, the principle of proportionality and the CJEU case law can serve as a guardrail to prevent excessive criminalisation.

[112] Platform for International Cooperation on Undocumented Migrants, 'More than 100 People Criminalised for Acting in Solidarity with Migrants in the EU in 2022' (PICUM Briefing, 2023).

[113] ibid, 5.

Part IV

Administrative Dimension of EU Sanctions

13

The Relationship between Financial Sanctions and the Prevention of Money Laundering

LOUISE DAMKJÆR CHRISTENSEN

13.1 INTRODUCTION

What comes to mind first, when thinking about sanctions in relation to money laundering, is perhaps the penalty imposed on someone found guilty of committing money laundering. In the EU legal order, though, this is not a possibility, as the competence to adopt and enforce such regulations rests with the individual Member State. Instead, the EU has adopted extensive and increasingly complex regulation on the prevention of money laundering: so-called anti-money laundering (AML) legislation. These regulatory frameworks include the option to impose a penalty, in the form of a monetary sanction, upon, among other subjects, a financial institution.[1]

Why then, if we have an extensive regulatory framework, do we need financial sanctions? AML legislation places complex and cost-expensive requirements on financial institutions to prevent money laundering.[2] The question therefore becomes, first, why financial institutions? And second, why add monetary

[1] Regulation (EU) No 575/2013 of the European Parliament and of the Council of 26 June 2013 on prudential requirements for credit institutions and investment firms and amending Regulation (EU) No 648/2012 [2013] OJ L176/1, Art 4(1)(26) defines a financial institution as being 'an undertaking other than an institution (which encompasses credit institutions and investment firms) the principal activity of which is to acquire holdings or to pursue one or more of the activities listed in points 2 to 12 and point 15 of Annex I to Directive 2013/36/EU, including a financial holding company, a mixed financial holding company, a payment institution within the meaning of Directive 2007/64 /EC of the European Parliament and of the Council of 13 November 2007 on payment services in the internal market (23), and an asset management company, but excluding insurance holding companies and mixed-activity insurance holding companies as defined in point (g) of Article 212(1) of Directive 2009/138/E'. In this contribution, credit institutions and other financial institutions are treated collectively under the term 'financial institutions', which are the core subject of this chapter.

[2] Kalle Johannes Rose, 'The Problem of Regulating the Easy Way Out – EU Money Laundering Regulation' (2019) 22 *Journal of Money Laundering Control* 666 also notes that financial institutions, in particular, are targeted by regulation to prevent money laundering.

penalty sanctions onto the already extensive costs financial institutions must invest to comply with regulations?[3] To answer these questions, it is necessary to interrogate the origin of money laundering in financial institutions and examine their ability to prevent it. Furthermore, it is necessary to consider whether regulatory frameworks can be effectively enforced without any measures which create incentives for the subjects to comply. As such, this can be framed as the relationship between financial sanctions and the prevention of money laundering. This topic has not received much attention in legal scholarship, as most contributions focus on the measures used to prevent money laundering, and hence, not the reason why these obligations are placed on financial institutions.[4]

This contribution explores why financial institutions are the target of financial sanctions when the objective is to prevent money laundering. This includes an examination of the relationship between the activity of money laundering and the business model of financial institutions. The chapter also considers the monetary size of the sanctions in comparison to the costs of compliance and supervision. The focus will be on financial institutions, as these have been the focus of regulatory measures since the inception of the AML regulatory regime.[5] Section 13.2 will present the notion of sanctions in AML legislation in the EU, spanning from the first Directive to the most recent AML package introducing the sixth Anti-Money Laundering Directive (AMLD6)[6] and the Anti-Money Laundering and Terrorist Financing Regulation (AMLR).[7,8] This section also provides a legal definition of the term 'money laundering'. Then, section 13.3 examines why financial institutions are the focus of AML legislation. It will be explained how money laundering can be framed as an externality of financial markets, making financial institutions key in its prevention. The section also looks at sanctions as an incentive which the legislator can use to control

[3] Fourthline, 'How much do banks spend on compliance? A look at 2025 trends' (11 July 2025), www.fourthline.com/blog/how-much-do-banks-spend-on-compliance provides an overview of compliance costs across selected European countries.

[4] Michael Levi, 'Money for Crime and Money from Crime: Financing Crime and Laundering Crime Proceeds' (2015) 21 *European Journal on Criminal Policy and Research* 275, 285 briefly connects money laundering to insufficient back-office monitoring in banks; Christopher Wilkes, 'A Case for Reforming the Anti-Money Laundering Regulatory Regime: How Financial Institutions' Criminal Reporting Duties Have Created an Unfunded Private Police Force' (2020) 95 *Indiana Law Journal* 649 notes that financial institutions carry a heavy burden in the AML fight but without any funding from the government; Kalle Rose, 'Regulating the Externality of Money Laundering - Halfway there' (2019) No 19-12 CBS Law Research Paper Series talks about money laundering as an externality.

[5] Directive 91/308/EEC, the first AML package, primarily subjected financial institutions. Other professions were only subject to it if a Member State extended the provisions to it via Art 12.

[6] Directive (EU) 2024/1640 of the European Parliament and of the Council of 31 May 2024 on the mechanisms to be put in place by Member States for the prevention of the use of the financial system for the purposes of money laundering or terrorist financing, amending Directive(EU) 2019/1937, and amending and repealing Directive (EU) 2015/849 [2024] OJ L2024/1640.

[7] Regulation (EU) 2024/1624 of the European Parliament and of the Council of 31 May 2024 on the prevention of the use of the financial system for the purposes of money laundering or terrorist financing [2024] OJ L2024/1624.

[8] Although AMLD6 and AMLR do not yet apply, they have been adopted and entered into force. Therefore, the text of the legislative acts are settled and will be applied by 10 July 2027.

the behaviour of financial institutions. Section 13.4 will consider the incentive strategy in comparison to the associated costs of complying with the extensive regulatory framework and consider whether the EU is essentially outsourcing the costs of preventing money laundering to financial institutions. Finally, section 13.5 will conclude on the findings of this chapter.

13.2 SANCTIONS IN EU ANTI-MONEY LAUNDERING LEGISLATION

Money laundering and terrorist financing[9] have been global problems for many years. In the 1990s and early 2000s, a substantial number of legislative measures were adopted in the EU to combat this substantial externality of the financial sector.[10] With each AML package, new measures were either introduced, or existing measures were expanded on and intensified. Among these were the introduction of Know-Your-Customer (KYC) procedures, politically exposed persons (PEP), financial intelligence units (FUI), and of particular relevance for this contribution, sanctions for non-compliance, ie, monetary penalties in the form of fines.[11] The target of the AML packages is a variety of branches but most prominent are the financial institutions. In the following sub-sections, first, a legal definition of 'money laundering' will be presented, then, the development of sanctions in AML legislation will be examined.

13.2.1 Defining 'Money Laundering' in EU Legislation

Before diving further into monetary sanctions in EU AML legislation, it is necessary to define what the letter of the law considers as 'money laundering'. When defining what 'money laundering' is, Article 2(1)(1) AMLR refers to Article 3(1)(1) and (5) of Directive (EU) 2018/1673.[12] Here, the following conduct, when committed intentionally, is considered a money laundering offence:[13]

(a) the conversion or transfer of property, knowing that such property is derived from criminal activity, for the purpose of concealing or disguising

[9] This contribution will refer only to 'money laundering' for readability.

[10] The first, Directive 91/308/EEC, was adopted in 1991; the second, Directive 2001/97/EC in 2001, and by 2005 the third, Directive 2005/60/EC, had been adopted.

[11] Maria Bergström, 'The Global AML Regime and the EU AML Directives: Prevention and Control' in Colin King, Clive Walker and Jimmy Gurulé (eds), *The Palgrave Handbook of Criminal and Terrorism Financing Law* (Springer International Publishing, 2018) 39 also describes this development as the introduction of the risk-based approach.

[12] Directive (EU) 2018/1673 of the European Parliament and of the Council of 23 October 2018 on combating money laundering by criminal law [2018] OJ L284.

[13] On this Directive and its potential in the prevention of money laundering also see Stanisław Tosza, 'Enforcement of International Sanctions as the Third Pillar of the Anti-money Laundering Framework. An Unannounced Effect of the AML Reform and the Sanctions Directive' (2024) 15 *New Journal of European Criminal Law* 336.

the illicit origin of the property or of assisting any person who is involved in the commission of such an activity to evade the legal consequences of that person's action,

(b) the concealment or disguise of the true nature, source, locations, disposition, movement, rights with respect to, or ownership of, property, knowing that such property is derived from criminal activity,

(c) the acquisition, possession, or use of property, knowing at the time of receipt, that such property was derived from criminal activity.

The provision mirrors the three stages of money laundering: placement, layering, and integration.[14] In the first stage, as letter a) describes, the 'dirty money' is converted or transferred into the financial system, for example cash being converted to casino chips or placed in smaller amounts on different bank accounts. Then, to conceal or disguise that the money is of an illicit origin, they can, for example, be moved through complex financial transactions, invested into stocks, property, or crypto-assets. The 'dirty money' now appears as legitimate assets which can be transferred or converted back to funds on a bank account.

So-called 'self-laundering' must also be considered a criminal offence. 'Self-laundering' concerns cases where the money launderer, performing the conduct above in a) and b), is also the perpetrator of the predicate criminal offence. For example, if the person committing fraud themselves afterwards launders the money, this would be self-laundering. This activity, on top of the predicate offence, must be punishable as a criminal activity.[15]

The definition of 'money laundering' in AMLR Article 2(1)(1) includes aiding and abetting, inciting, and attempting to commit money laundering, whether the activities generated the property to be laundered was carried out in a Member State or in a third country.

To summarise, 'money laundering' is committed when proceeds of a crime are converted or transferred with the purpose of concealing or disguising its illicit origin. If this is successful, the proceeds can be reinvested as they now appear 'clean' instead of 'dirty'.[16]

[14] Stefan D Cassella, 'Toward a New Model of Money Laundering: Is the "Placement, Layering, Integration" Model Obsolete?' (2018) 21 *Journal of Money Laundering Control* 494; Levi (n 4); Jan van Koningsveld, 'Money Laundering – You Don't See It, until You See It: Rethinking the Stages of Money Laundering Process to Make Enforcement More Effective' in Birgitte Unger and Daan van der Linde (eds), *Research Handbook on Money Laundering* (Edward Elgar, 2013) 435.

[15] This distinction between perpetrator and a third party performing the money laundering was treated in Case C-790/19, *LG and MH (self-laundering)* EU:C:2021:661, where the ECJ found that Art 1(3)(a) AMLD4 does not preclude the perpetrator from being punished for self-laundering. Nonetheless, Directive 2018/1673 contains a specific paragraph on this to ensure that self-laundering is considered illegal and punishable in Member States, see paras 71, 72, and 86 of the judgment.

[16] Which, as suggested in Donato Masciandaro, Elöd Takáts and Brigitte Unger, *Black Finance: The Economics of Money Laundering* (Edward Elgar Publishing, 2007) ix is also the purpose of money laundering.

13.2.2 The Development of Financial Sanctions in EU AML Legislation

A key measure in the prevention of money laundering has come to be the sanctions that can be placed on financial institutions for non-compliance.[17] The first adoption of sanctions in the EU legal order to combat money laundering was introduced in Directive 2005/60/EC (AMLD3).[18] Article 39 AMLD3 placed an obligation on Member States to ensure that entities that were covered by, but not complying with, the national provisions adopted pursuant to the Directive, could be held liable through effective, proportionate, and dissuasive penalties.[19] Since this first introduction of financial sanctions, which was rather vague and simple, the possibilities in terms of sanctions have expanded considerably in the EU.[20] The most recent example is the adoption of AMLD6[21] which takes a more comprehensive and complex approach to sanctioning infringements and non-compliance.[22]

First, AMLD6 places an obligation on Member States similar to that of Article 39 AMLD3, though Article 37(6)(b) AMLD6 states that the national competent authority must have adequate powers to perform their tasks, including the power to apply appropriate and proportionate administrative measures in case of breaches, which includes imposition of pecuniary sanctions. Article 53 AMLD6 further exemplifies the powers that must be placed with the national competent authority to ensure that obliged entities can be held liable for breaches of AMLR and the Transfer of Funds Regulation[23] in accordance with the provisions of section 4 AMLD6.

Next, AMLD6 presents two forms of financial sanctions for cases of non-compliance. The first is the pecuniary sanction in Article 55 (see below). The

[17] It should be noted that the national competent authorities also have the option to apply general competences such as withdrawing the institution's licence, fit and proper, rules, prudential requirements, etc.

[18] Directive 2005/60/EC of the European Parliament and of the Council of 26 October 2005 on the prevention of the use of the financial system for the purpose of money laundering and terrorist financing [2005] OJ L309.

[19] Case 68/88, *Commission v Greece (Greek Maize)* EU:C:1989:339 established the principle that Member States must impose effective, proportionate and dissuasive penalties for infringements of EU law where EU legislation does not specifically provide for a penalty for an infringement. Here, AMLD3 Art 39 implements the same principle directly into EU legislation.

[20] Oldrich Bures, 'The New EU Authority for Anti-Money Laundering and Countering the Financing of Terrorism: A Paradigm Shift in EU Efforts to Combat Terrorist Financing?' (2025) *Studies in Conflict & Terrorism* 1 also provides an overview of the evolution of measures in EU AML legislation.

[21] Although the penalty provisions are not applicable, the Directive has been adopted. The penalties are therefore relevant to include here.

[22] For a more general introduction to the new reform of EU AML legislation see Andrea Minto, 'Banks' Internal Governance Obligations Vis-à-vis Money Laundering Risks Emerging from the New Technology-enabled Means to Transfer Funds or Value ("crypto assets")' (2024) 27 *Journal of Money Laundering Control* 43, 47.

[23] Regulation (EU) 2023/1113 of the European Parliament and of the Council of 31 May 2023 on information accompanying transfers of funds and certain crypto-assets and amending Directive (EU) 2015/849 [2023] OJ L150.

second is a periodic penalty payment in Article 57, with the purpose of ensuring compliance with administrative measures issued in accordance with Article 56 which relates to breaches of the entity's anti-money laundering obligations.[24]

The pecuniary sanctions provided in Article 55 AMLD6 are more complex than that of Article 57. The provision relates to serious, repeated, or systematic breaches of the AMLR, specifically the provisions on internal policies, procedures, and controls of obliged entities, customer due diligence, reporting obligations, and record retention.[25] The provision is applicable whether the breaches were committed intentionally or negligently. For non-financial institutions, the sanctions must amount to at least EUR 1 million,[26] but for financial institutions, a legal person will be sanctioned with at least EUR 10 million,[27] and for at natural person at least EUR 5 million.[28]

For the legal person – for example, a credit institution having failed to perform sufficient customer due diligence – the fine will be at least EUR 10 million, but if 10 per cent of the company's annual turnover is higher than this amount, the higher amount will be the pecuniary sanction's size. For example, this would mean that the German credit institution Deutsche Bank, which had an annual turnover of EUR 30.1 billion in 2024,[29] the pecuniary sanction, for a breach covered by Article 55, would be around EUR 3 billion, as this amount is higher than EUR 10 million. This should also be seen in reference to the bank's profit before taxes, which in 2024 was approximately EUR 5 billion.[30] Despite the seemingly enormous amount of EUR 3 billion as the sanction, Article 55(4) also allows Member States to empower national competent authorities to impose pecuniary sanctions which exceeds the amounts provided in paragraphs 2 and 3.

While the size of pecuniary sanctions so far has been ever growing, the last paragraph of Article 55 places an obligation on the Member States to ensure that the sanction does not result in the bankruptcy of the breaching entity. The provision states that when determining the amount of the pecuniary sanction, the ability of the obliged entity to pay the sanction must be considered. The entity's ability to comply with prudential regulation, such as the capital requirements of the Capital Requirements Regulation (CRR),[31] must also be considered when setting the amount of the pecuniary sanction. This constitutes a balance of objectives between prevention of money laundering on the one side, and financial stability on the other. A similar balance has been found between prevention

[24] Specifically, see Art 56(1).

[25] The pecuniary sanctions must also be able to be imposed where obliged entities have not complied with administrative measures issued in accordance with Art 56 or for breaches that are not serious, repeated, or systematic.

[26] Art 55(2).

[27] Art 55(3)(a).

[28] Art 55(3)(b).

[29] Deutsche Bank, Annual Report 2024, https://investor-relations.db.com/files/documents/other-presentations-and-events/2024/Annual-Report-2024.pdf.

[30] ibid.

[31] Regulation (EU) No 575/2013.

of money laundering and financial inclusion with regards to the right to open a basic payment account which can only be denied if opening the account would result in an infringement of AML regulations.[32]

The movement from rather simple sanctions in AMLD3 to the more complex system provided in AMLD6 shows how the EU has intensified its approach in preventing money laundering over the years. This can be interpreted as the legislator's heightened sensitivity to money laundering activities as this would explain the increasing stringent regulation.[33] The choice to adopt a regulation, the AMLR, alongside the AMLD6 is also in harmony with the Single Rulebook approach, which is characteristic of financial regulation.[34] But this does not explain why, in particular, financial institutions are targets of financial sanctions when aiming to prevent money laundering. To explain this, it is necessary to have a further look into the financial institution's role in modern money laundering.

13.3 FINANCIAL INSTITUTIONS AS THE TARGET OF AML LEGISLATION

While the complexity of AML legislation has continuously increased, the primary target has remained the same from the AMLD1 through to the AMLD6 and AMLR: financial institutions.[35] To understand why financial institutions are so essential in the prevention of money laundering, it is necessary to examine, first, how these institutions enable money laundering, and, second, why they possess one of the most effective measures in the fight against money laundering activities.

13.3.1 Money Laundering as an Externality

The title of this section can be understood in two different ways. The first is the notion of money laundering as an activity. It is undisputable that negative externalities are connected to the activity of money laundering.[36] The second is perceiving banking and payment services – not to forget other financial services – as creating the negative externality that constitute the activity of

[32] Directive 2014/92/EU of the European Parliament and of the Council of 23 July 2014 on the comparability of fees related to payment accounts, payment account switching and access to payment accounts with basic features [2014] OJ L257, Art 16(4)

[33] Donato Masciandaro, 'Money Laundering: the Economics of Regulation' (1999) 7 *European Journal of Law and Economics* 225, 226.

[34] The single rulebook can be accessed at www.eba.europa.eu/single-rulebook.

[35] However, the subjected group of sectors that are covered has expanded with the development of directives.

[36] Imen Khelil, Hichem Khlif and Imen Achek, 'The Economic Consequences of Money Laundering: A Review of Empirical Literature' (2023) 27 *Journal of Money Laundering Control* 901.

laundering money. Needless to say, the financial system does not intend for this activity to be enabled; it is simply an unintentional result of their business.[37]

In section 13.2.1 the legal definition of 'money laundering' was presented and compared to the process of money laundering, which the definition in fact mirrors. The financial institution can be used for placement of money on a payment account, then the 'dirty money' can be split into smaller amounts and transferred to other accounts before being transferred back to the person committing money laundering.[38] In such an example, the core function or business of banking and payment services is being exploited to commit money laundering.[39]

Financial services, such as banking and payment services, unintentionally create this opportunity for criminals to exploit them to launder assets obtained illegally. In theory, when a business, or in this case a whole sector, creates a negative externality, government can intervene in different ways.[40] These include subsidising, taxation, and regulation.[41] As the instrument used to prevent money laundering here is regulation, only that instrument will be considered in the following.

As the externality is created because it is an element which the business does not naturally consider when designing their product, government intervention can take the form of legislation which either makes up for the externality, or which forces the business to address, or internalise, the externality to avoid harm on others.[42] When the business can reduce the probability of money laundering activities taking place through their services, at a cost to that business, then regulation enforcing a sanction upon businesses not implementing effective measures towards preventing money laundering can be effective.

Regulation places monetary sanctions on financial institutions when they do not contribute effectively towards internalising the externality that consists of money laundering through their financial services. The financial institutions become subjects of such regulation because they create the externality and are therefore best suited to preventing it by internalising the costs, placing the bill at the individual financial institution instead of society in general.

[37] This is also in the very definition of an externality; see Howell E Jackson, 'Analytical Methods for Lawyers' (2003) 53 *Journal of Legal Education* 321, 336.

[38] Or to the person having hired another to commit money laundering. Levi (n 4) 284 reflects on how money laundering is executed.

[39] Peter Yeoh, 'Banks' Vulnerabilities to Money Laundering Activities' (2020) 23 *Journal of Money Laundering Control* 122 examines how banks' business model makes them vulnerable to money laundering activities.

[40] 'Government' can be understood as different actors including, and in no way excluding, national governments, the EU, and any other authority; see Julian Le Grand, 'The Theory of Government Failure' (1991) 21 British Journal of Political Science 423, 431

[41] John Armour and others, *Principles of Financial Regulation* (Oxford University Press, 2016) 70; Tyler Cowen (ed), *The Theory of Market Failure - A Critical Examination* (George Mason University Press 1988) 209; Louise Damkjær Christensen, *EU Payment Services: Regulation and Innovation* (Oxford University Press, 2025) 29.

[42] Robert Cooter and Ariel Porat, 'Does Risk to Oneself Increase the Care Owed to Others? Law and Economics in Conflict' (2000) 29 *The Journal of Legal Studies* 19.

13.3.2 Sanctions as Incentives

In anti-money laundering legislation, the timing of sanctions has been moved compared to regular criminal sanctions. Where criminal law sanctions the money launderer when money laundering has been committed or attempted, the financial sanctions are applied if the financial institution has 'left open' a possibility for a money launderer to launder money. This way, the system attempts to prevent money laundering from happening by applying financial sanctions upon financial institutions before the crime has been committed.

To understand how sanctions can work as incentives for financial institutions to prevent money laundering, it is necessary to look further into the process of money laundering. Particularly in these modern times, the financial system is essential in the process of money laundering. Setting up an account, placing money on the account, making transfers between accounts, etc, are all relevant steps when laundering money. Therefore, legislation has countered this behaviour with a systematic approach to ensuring that financial institutions are not utilised for illicit purposes. This starts with KYC procedures at the point of requesting an account and continues with, among other things, mandatory reports to flag suspicious activity.[43]

The sanctions for not complying with regulatory safeguards is a means to an end. By placing financial sanctions upon financial institutions if they do not comply with the rules, the institutions are incentivised to implement and comply with all relevant regulations. As such, they are internalising the externality their business creates. For this to work, the sanction needs to be greater than the cost of implementing and adhering to the rules.[44] As illustrated in section 13.2.2, the financial sanctions are rather hefty. This is necessary to create sufficient incentive, as the costs of implementing preventive measures are also high, and the sanction symbolises the price of non-compliance, making it efficient to comply to regulation when compliance costs are less than the size of the sanction.[45]

However, it is not only the financial institutions that experiences a rise in costs when regulation becomes more stringent and expansive. For the criminal, there are costs attached to laundering money too. The more effective AML legislation is, the more expensive it will be for the criminal to perform money laundering.[46] There exists an inverse relationship between the amount of money laundering activities and the effectiveness of AML regulation.[47] It is therefore

[43] This can also be read from the requirements in the AMLR, for example Art 19 on the application of customer due diligence or identification and verification requirements in Art 22.

[44] A Mitchell Polinsky and Steven Shavell, 'The Optimal Use of Fines and Imprisonment' (1984) 24 *Journal of Public Economics* 89.

[45] Robert Cooter, 'Prices and Sanctions' (1984) 84 *Columbia Law Review* 1523, 1525; Steven Shavell, 'The Optimal Structure of Law Enforcement' (1993) 36 *Journal of Law and Economics* 255.

[46] Masciandaro (n 33) 227.

[47] ibid, 239; Levi (n 4) 280 also notes that the more difficult it is to launder money, the more criminals rely on reinvestment of prior illicit profits to grow their illicit business, essentially lowering the amount of money being laundered but not the amount of crime in general.

important that the financial system implement effective mechanisms to prevent money laundering, making it more costly for criminals to perform money laundering activities. If the costs of money laundering are greater than the potential creation of wealth, and the risk of detection and sentencing are considerable,[48] it will deter criminals further.

As the financial institutions' services create the externality of money laundering, and there exists an inverse relationship between the amount of money laundering activities and the effectiveness of AML regulation, it is necessary to install effective prevention mechanisms through the financial institutions. The use of sanctions to enforce AML regulation upon financial institutions creates an incentive for them to comply and prevent money laundering.

13.4 Outsourcing the Costs of Prevention

Regulation comes at a cost. There are costs associated with government drafting and adopting regulation. Implementing and continuously monitoring compliance costs a good deal of resources for both government and the subjected businesses.[49] Prosecuting criminals for money laundering activities, sentencing them, and having them incarcerated is also expensive for the government.[50] Therefore, there is a compelling rationale for creating regulation which can prevent money laundering activities.[51]

The regulator – here the EU –could increase AML regulation and make for more stringent rules, though this would not be without costs. Regulation is not costless; in fact, the more regulation that is adopted, the more costly it becomes for the subjected sector to implement and continuously comply with the regulations. It is therefore necessary to find a balance between preventing money laundering and an optimal amount of regulation, which is one that can minimise the social costs of regulation.[52]

Enforcing a complex regime of anti-money laundering requirements on financial institutions makes for an incentive to invest funds into preventing money laundering. How these costs are allocated between national competent authorities supervising financial institutions and the financial institutions'

[48] On the deterrence of the criminal actor, see Steven Shavell, 'Criminal Law and the Optimal Use of Nonmonetary Sanctions as a Deterrent' (1985) 85 *Columbia Law Review* 1232; Gary S Becker, 'Crime and Punishment: An Economic Approach' (1968) 76 *Journal of Political Economy* 169.

[49] As shown in the previous section, regulation also makes it more expensive for criminals to launder money. As we are not concerned with making crime cheaper, this will not be explored further.

[50] Richard A Posner, 'Optimal Sentences for White-Collar Criminals' (1980) 17 *American Criminal Law Review* 409 also argues that a sufficiently large fine is equally effective as a deterrent than imprisonment, but the fine is cheaper to administer and therefore socially preferable.

[51] Shavell (n 45) neatly delineates when we should let private actors be gatekeepers, ie have them prevent the undesired activity, here money laundering.

[52] Masciandaro (n 33) 231; Shavell (n 45) 266.

costs invested in preventing money laundering makes for an uneven distribution of costs.

In Denmark, the Government's costs directly related to supervising financial institutions in general amounted to DKK 230,800,000 in 2024,[53,54] which includes the specific supervision on AML requirements.[55] The Danish credit institutions, on the other hand, reached costs of DKK 3.4 billion[56] as early as 2019, which only covered yearly AML compliance.[57]

Within the EU, the comparison numbers for the sector are even greater. The compliance costs for financial institutions are in the billions. In 2023, German financial institutions spent USD 32.5 billion, while the equivalent figure was USD 25.3 billion in France, and USD 12 billion in the Netherlands.[58]

On top of the compliance costs, which financial institutions are forced to invest, comes the pecuniary sanctions which supervisory authorities can impose on them in cases on non-compliance, ie, even in cases where no harm has yet been done. The pecuniary sanctions are an essential element in preventing money laundering, as they, because of their economic size, function as an incentive for financial institutions to ensure regulatory compliance.[59]

A regulatory framework with measures to prevent money laundering is, in itself, insufficient as a mechanism. Enforcement of the rules laid out in legislation becomes difficult if there are no means to enforce compliance upon the subject. Therefore, the EU's AML framework sets out minimum sanctions for non-compliance. To be efficient, these monetary sanctions must be of a size that makes it desirable for the subjects to undertake the costs of compliance to avoid being sanctioned.[60]

The national competent authorities bear enforcement costs. Specifically for the AML prevention, these constitute of supervisory visits to check compliance with regulations, as well as sanctioning non-compliance. The latter can be divided into two categories. The first is non-compliance discovered during a supervisory visit; the second is non-compliance discovered because of the uncovering of a money laundering scandal.

During an inspection of the AML compliance in Jyske Bank A/S in Denmark, the Danish Financial Supervisory Authority found that the bank

[53] Finanstilsynet, 'Årsrapport 2024' (18 March 2025) 0, www.finanstilsynet.dk/Media/638781440807195312/Finanstilsynets%20rsrapport_2024.pdf.

[54] Exchange rate as of 16 October 2025, EUR 1 = DKK 7.47; so this amounts to EUR 30,910,802.43.

[55] Note that in Denmark the appropriation to the Financial Supervisory Authority is based on an indirect tax on the subjected financial institutions. The total amount for 2024 was DKK 508 million.

[56] Using the exchange rate in n 54, this amounts to EUR 455,153,949.

[57] Finans Danmark, 'Antallet af hvidvask og complianceansatte i bankerne eksploderer' (17 November 2019), https://finansdanmark.dk/nyheder/2019/november/antallet-af-hvidvask-og-complianceansatte-i-bankerne-eksploderer.

[58] Fourthline, 'How much do banks spend on compliance? A look at 2025 trends' (11 July 2025), www.fourthline.com/blog/how-much-do-banks-spend-on-compliance.

[59] Shavell (n 45) 259; Cooter (n 45) 1529.

[60] Cooter (n 45) 1529; Shavell (n 45) 261; Polinsky and Shavell (n 44) 96.

was non-compliant. This resulted in a monetary fine of DKK 23,961,500.[61] In cases where the money laundering scandal came before the sanction, one of the most recited cases in recent times is the Estonia branch of Danske Bank. The most prominent monetary sanction, which was imposed on Danske Bank for the severe breach of AML regulations, was a $2 billion settlement with the US Department of Justice, the US Securities and Exchange Commission and the Danish Special Crime Unit.[62] Following this settlement, the bank could also disclose that it had in the period 2018–22 invested EUR 1.6 billion in maintaining and improving its overall financial crime risk management framework and was keen to continue investing in this area.[63]

Considering the enormous amounts financial institutions spend on compliance to prevent financial crime, including AML measures, compared to the moderate amount spend by government to enforce AML regulations, it is fair to conclude that the prevention of money laundering has, to a large extent, been outsourced to financial institutions. These institutions are being charged double: first, the compliance costs, which they are forced to invest to avoid sanctions; and then, in the case of any non-compliance, a considerable monetary sanction.

13.5 Conclusions

The aim of this contribution was to explore why financial institutions are the target of AML legislation and the hefty monetary sanctions which that regulation authorises. The most recently adopted legislation, the AMLR and AMLD6, warrants fines that can amount to at least 10 per cent of the company's annual turnover if the financial institution does not comply with regulations. Such grand monetary sanctions were found to be necessary to make AML legislation enforceable upon market actors.[64] Yet, this does not answer the initial concern, why financial institutions?

This question was answered in section 13.3, where money laundering as an externality was examined. The business of financial institutions, such as banking and payment services, unintentionally creates a negative externality: money laundering activities. Through the way financial services are structured, it becomes possible to utilise the system to perform money laundering activities.

[61] Finanstilsynet, 'Bøde vedtaget for overtrædelse af Hvidvaskloven' (16 December 2024), www.finanstilsynet.dk/tilsyn/inspektion-og-afgoerelser/2024/dec/boede-vedtaget-for-overtraedelse-af-hvidvaskloven_161224; Using the exchange rate in n 54, this amounts to EUR 3,207,697.46.

[62] Dansk Bank, 'Danske Bank reaches coordinated resolutions with the US and Danish authorities regarding the Estonia matter' Company announcement no 18/2022 of 13 December 2022, https://danskebank.com/news-and-insights/news-archive/company-announcements/2022/ca13122022b. Exchange rate as of 31 October 2025, EUR 1 = USD 1.16; so this amounts to EUR 1,730,680,000.

[63] ibid.

[64] Polinsky and Shavell (n 44) also notes that the more wealthy the receiver of a fine is, the bigger the fine needs to be to sufficiently deter.

This brings a cost to society in general. The government has therefore chosen to adopt regulation to persuade financial institutions to internalise the externality their businesses create, essentially making them gatekeepers.

The regulation brings considerable costs for financial institutions as they must implement and continuously monitor and maintain their AML prevention mechanisms. As such, the costs of AML prevention have been outsourced to the businesses that, unintentionally, enables money laundering activities. To ensure that financial institutions take sufficient precaution, hence securing effective money laundering prevention, the government has authorised that financial institutions, when not taking sufficient precaution, can be subject to monetary sanctions. As these sanctions are considerable when comparing to the costs of compliance, as examined in sections 13.2.2 and 13.4, they create sufficient incentive for financial institutions to comply.

In essence, the relationship between financial sanctions and the prevention of money laundering can be denoted to function as an incentive for financial institutions to take sufficient precautions and internalise the externality their business creates. This makes financial institutions gatekeepers, tasked with keeping money launderers out of the financial system. From a government perspective, this is a cost-effective solution, and considering the financial institutions' role in enabling money laundering, it cannot be considered an unfair burden to place on them.

Index

www.ingramcontent.com/pod-product-compliance
Ingram Content Group UK Ltd.
Pitfield, Milton Keynes, MK11 3LW, UK
UKHW022205220926
475873UK00003B/56

9 781509 987443